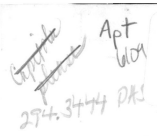

"I see *Awakening the Buddha Within* as a beautiful
flower blooming on a beautiful tree that is
wholeheartedly committed to true inquiry and
practice. Lama Surya Das uses the appropriate
language that can communicate the wisdom
and experience of Buddhism to the people
of his times and environments. To me this
is a great achievement and I feel deeply grateful
for it. I wish Lama Surya Das a great deal
of happiness in living and sharing the
Buddha Dharma in the West."

—THICH NHAT HANH
PLUM VILLAGE, APRIL, 1997

# Eight Steps to Enlightenment

*Tibetan Wisdom for the*

*Western World*

BROADWAY BOOKS

*New York*

# AWAKENING

# THE

# BUDDHA

# WITHIN

*Lama Surya Das*

BROADWAY

Broadway Books titles may be purchased for business or promotional use or for special sales. For information, please write to: Special Markets Department, Bantam Doubleday Dell Publishing Group, Inc., 1540 Broadway, New York, NY 10036.

BROADWAY BOOKS and its logo, a letter B bisected on the diagonal, are trademarks of Broadway Books, a division of Bantam Doubleday Dell Publishing Group, Inc.

*Library of Congress Cataloging-in-Publication Data*
Das, Surya.
Awakening the Buddha within : eight steps to enlightenment : Tibetan wisdom for the Western world / by Lama Surya Das.
p. cm.
Includes bibliographical references and index.
ISBN 0-553-06695-1
1. Eight-Fold Path. 2. Spiritual life—Buddhism. I. Title.
804320.D37 1997
294.3'444—DC21 97-8346 CIP

FIRST EDITION

*Designed by Dana Leigh Treglia*

97 98 99 00 10 9 8 7 6 5 4 3 2 1

*Dedicated to*

*my parents,*

*Joyce and*

*Harold Miller*

# CONTENTS

# WISDOM TRAINING:
*Seeing Things As They Are* 95

## STEP ONE: RIGHT VIEW
*The Wisdom of Clear Vision* 97

## STEP TWO: RIGHT INTENTIONS
*Plumbing Your Wise Buddha-Nature* 130

# ETHICS TRAINING:
*Living a Sacred Life* 167

## STEP THREE: RIGHT SPEECH
*Speaking the Truth* 171

## STEP FOUR: RIGHT ACTION
*The Art of Living* 197

## STEP FIVE: RIGHT LIVELIHOOD
*Work Is Love Made Visible* 230

# MEDITATION TRAINING:
*Awareness, Attention, and Focus* 259

## STEP SIX: RIGHT EFFORT
*A Passion for Enlightenment* 265

## STEP SEVEN: RIGHT MINDFULNESS
*Keeping Your Eyes Open* 296

## STEP EIGHT: RIGHT CONCENTRATION
*The Joy of Meditation* 334

# ACKNOWLEDGMENTS

I wish to gratefully acknowledge the inspiration and guidance of my gracious late Buddhist teachers Kalu Rinpoche, Gyalwa Karmapa, Dilgo Khyentse Rinpoche, Dudjom Rinpoche, Tulku Urgyen Rinpoche; my living mentors, the Dalai Lama, Nyoshul Khenpo Rinpoche, and Tulku Pema Wangyal; and all the many others who so lovingly shared their wisdom.

Also, many thanks to my spiritual friends, colleagues, and companions along the Way; and to the people who helped hands-on with this book—Dan Goleman, Anandi Friend, Paul Crafts, John Miller, Suil, Roger Walsh, Sylvia Boorstein, Julia Coopersmith, Bob Hildebrand, Lewis Richmond, Josh Baran, Mitch Kapor, Sharon Salzberg, Jack Kornfield, Stephen Batchelor, Kate Wheeler, Amy Elizabeth Fox, Gary Cohen, Mirabai Bush, Lucy Duggan, David Berman, Martha Ley, Florence Tambone, John Bush, Rebecca Holland, Michele Tempesta, and my publisher at Broadway Books, Bill Shinker, as well as my editor Janet Goldstein, and literary agents Eileen Cope and Barbara Lowenstein.

May joy, blessings, and peace be theirs.

# PREFACE

Many people have asked me in recent years to explain Buddhism from the ground up, and to speak about what timeless Tibetan wisdom has to contribute to us today. People want to know about the spiritual path and practical steps to enlightenment from an American perspective as well as how to meditate and find peace of mind.

Today there is a genuine need for an essential, Western Buddhism: pragmatic, effective, and experiential, rather than theoretical or doctrinal. We are drawn to spirituality that is simple, direct, and demystified—a sane, nonsectarian, integrated path to wisdom, personal transformation, and enlightenment for modern men and women actively engaged with life.

This book is one response.

In the Himalayas, I found a veritable treasury of living, vibrant Dharma, a gold mine of truth and delight. The lessons of enlightenment offer profound insights and a liberating, life-enhancing, healing message: good for the home, family, the inner life, relationships, workplace, for conscious death and dying, and even the afterlife.

Buddhism originally reached the Western world mainly through books and translations, starting approximately two hundred years ago. May this book further open a gateway to the time-

less treasure that is our deep spiritual inheritance. May it be helpful. May it advance virtue and be a source of hope, strength, and
blessings in our turbulent times.

Homage to the natural Buddha within you.

May all realize it.

SURYA DAS
*Cambridge, Massachusetts, 1997*

# PART ONE

## *Discovering Ancient*

## *Wisdom in a*

## *Modern World*

*The religion of the future will be a cosmic religion. It should transcend personal God and avoid dogma and theology. Covering both the natural and the spiritual, it should be based on a religious sense arising from the experience of all things natural and spiritual as a meaningful unity. Buddhism answers this description. . . . If there is any religion that could cope with modern scientific needs it would be Buddhism.*

—ALBERT EINSTEIN

*The coming of Buddhism to the West may well prove to be the most important event of the Twentieth Century.*

—ARNOLD TOYNBEE, HISTORIAN

# WE ARE ALL BUDDHAS

*May all beings everywhere, with whom we are inseparably interconnected, be fulfilled, awakened, and free. May there be peace in this world and throughout the entire universe, and may we all together complete the spiritual journey.*

## 1971 Kopan, Nepal

It is morning in the lush Kathmandu Valley. I am in a small, clay, mud-floored hut at the top of Kopan Hill, surrounded by gleaming snow-covered Himalayan mountaintops. The rising sun has started to evaporate the mist covering the rice paddies below. At the bottom of the hill I can see three barefoot young Nepalese villagers filling water jugs from a spring. Soon one of them will put a jug on his head and carry it up the hill and leave it outside my hut.

I am alone for a week on my first solitary meditation retreat. As I watch the sun rise and set each day, I meditate, watching my breath and looking within. Later in the day, following the ancient oral teaching traditions, a Tibetan lama will come to guide me.

———

There is a joke about spiritual seekers and travelers—men and women like me: Margie Smith, a pleasant-looking woman who gave birth to her children in the 1950s (think June Cleaver or Harriet Nelson), approaches a travel agent.

"I must get to the Himalayas for my vacation," Mrs. Smith says. "I've got to talk to a guru."

"The Himalayas, Mrs. Smith! Are you sure?" the travel agent asks. "It's a long trip, different language, funny food, smelly oxcarts. How about London, or Florida? Florida is lovely this time of year."

Mrs. Smith is adamant. She must go to the Himalayas to talk to a guru. So Mrs. Smith, wearing her best blue suit and her black pumps with the sensible heels, heads East, taking a plane, a train, a bus, and, yes, an oxcart, until she finally arrives at a far-off Buddhist monastery in Nepal. There an old lama in maroon and saffron robes tells her that the guru she seeks is meditating in a cave at the top of the mountain and cannot be disturbed. But Mrs. Smith came a long way and she is a determined woman who won't be put off.

Finally the lama relents. "All right," he says, "if you must, you must. But there are some ground rules. You can't stay long, and when you speak to the guru, you can say no more than ten words. He lives there alone, in silence and meditation."

Mrs. Smith agrees; and with the help of a few lamas, monks, and Sherpa porters, she starts trudging up the mountain. It's a long hard climb, but she doesn't give up. With an enormous effort of will and energy, she reaches the top—and the cave in which the guru is meditating. Her mission accomplished, Mrs. Smith stands at the entrance, and in a loud clear voice, she says what she came to say:

"Sheldon. . . . Enough is enough! It's your mother. Come home already."

———

My name was Jeffrey Miller. But it could have been Sheldon. There was a Sheldon living on the next block in the suburban Long Island town where I was brought up and Bar Mitzvahed. My parents were long-time members of a synagogue; we were a middle-class Jewish family. I was always a regular guy, a three-letter high school jock. I grew up wanting to be a ballplayer. I had friends, good grades, and an intact suburban family. What was I doing meditating and chanting Buddhist mantras and prayers on a mountaintop in the Himalayas? Today, my own mother, Joyce Miller, jokingly refers to me as "my son, the lama," or even more amusingly as "The Deli Lama."

## FOLLOWING THE OVERLAND ROUTE

Like many young people, I first discovered the ancient wisdom traditions as a college student. In my case I was a student at SUNY, Buffalo, when I attended a Zen retreat in Rochester, New York, in the late 1960s. You know the adage about the turbulent sixties: If you can remember them, you weren't really there. In many ways I was very representative of my generation. I went to San Francisco for be-ins, discovered encounter groups and the hot springs at Esalen, marched on Washington, got teargassed at an anti-war demonstration near the Pentagon, and was rained on at the Woodstock Festival in 1969.

The war, student politics, and the peace movement created a special level of intensity. In 1970, my best friend Barry's nineteen-year-old girlfriend, Allison Krause, was killed at Kent State when, incredibly, fellow Americans who were National Guardsmen from our heartland shot and killed four students. I was deeply and personally affected. As always, death, the great teacher, presented an opportunity for a wide range of penetrating and life-changing lessons. There was also a peculiar coincidence at Kent State that touched my life: One of the other students who was killed was, like me, named Jeffrey Miller, and he too came from Long Island. Friends and acquaintances who heard the news bulletin knew that

I sometimes visited friends at Kent State; they became convinced that I was dead. In my parents' home and my student apartment, the phones began ringing nonstop.

Allison's funeral was a blur of emotions, so much sadness and so much grief. For months it seemed as though thoughts of Allison's life and sudden violent death trivialized everything else. I was nineteen years old, and I had been brought face to face with death for the first time.

Only a few weekends earlier, Allison and Barry had come to visit me; I had been sleeping on the couch because they were sleeping in my bedroom. We had all been in the same kitchen, pouring milk out of the same cardboard container while we talked about our shared plans. Allison, like Barry, was an artist; I loved to write. We talked about traveling and the things we could do together. Allison and Barry were in love and wanted to get engaged; I had advised them against it, saying they had plenty of time. Teenage death was the last thing on my mind.

In this period following Kent State, I also couldn't help thinking more about the Jeffrey Miller who was gunned down on his own college campus. The tragic photograph of his body lying in a pool of blood with an anguished young woman crying over him was everywhere. It could have been me. If I were to believe my ringing phone, it was me. This swift never-to-be-forgotten lesson in the fleeting nature of this life accelerated the ways in which my direction was changing.

During this painful time, my original life goals seemed more and more misguided and out of touch. I had spent the summer of 1969 working in a Manhattan law firm. Listening to the young Fifth Avenue lawyers complain had convinced me that I was not cut out to be one of the Gray Flannel fifties men, vying ceaselessly for a better berth on the *Titanic*. I knew that I wanted to learn more, not earn more. I had also begun to be disillusioned with radical politics and angry rhetoric. The concept of fighting for peace seemed a contradiction in terms. Kent State helped me realize that more than anything else I wanted to gentle myself and find a nonviolent way to contribute to a more harmonious and sane world.

The day after I graduated from college—alone with only the company of the Eternal Companion who I was still seeking—I started on my search by boarding a plane for London, where I had friends who were staying at a Sufi center. In my money belt was five hundred dollars saved from summer jobs and graduation presents, which I planned to stretch as far as possible. Within a short time, I crossed the channel to France. Writing poetry and hitchhiking, I started to make my way across Europe. In those days I had one main mantra, "Teach me what you know, whatever you call it."

Looking for "wisdom" and answers to questions I hadn't even framed, I was on my way to the Greek Islands to meet a wise man I had heard about in college. He was an elderly goatherd named Theos. When I arrived at the small island of Simi, I found Theos as promised. I stayed with him for a few days, but he spoke no English, and I spoke no Greek. His words of wisdom, if there were any, were wasted on me. Trying to conserve money, I slept on beaches, I slept in pensiones, I slept in Theos' goat shed.

Without realizing it, I found myself traveling through Turkey, Afghanistan, Iran, and Pakistan on the old overland route through the Khyber Pass and on to India. The farthest reach on this route was Kathmandu. To this day I don't consciously know what drew me to Nepal, except that I was following my heart, and it was pulling me East.

As I traveled, I began to hear more and more about wise Tibetan lamas who, after the Chinese invasion of their remote country, had fled across the borders into India and Nepal. Rumor said that the closer you got to Tibet, the more likely you were to find one of these genuine sages. There was also talk that one of these learned lamas had a monastery on a hilltop in the Kathmandu Valley and that he had learned a little English and was willing to teach Westerners. That's why in the summer of 1971 I boarded a Kathmandu public bus packed with people and chickens—squawking room only—and headed out of town to meet my first Tibetan lama, Lama Thubten Yeshe. But first I would have to wade my way through the rice paddies and climb Kopan Hill.

# WHAT IS REAL, WHAT IS LIFE, WHAT IS TRUTH?

When I first met Lama Yeshe, I had a thousand and one questions about the meaning of life in general and my life in particular. I was twenty, and my questions were often more subtle than I was. What is the meaning of life? What is my purpose? Where did we all come from? Is there a God? Where is He, She, It? Is God with me? Is God nature? Is God the entire mountain and everything that lives and grows on it? Could I learn to live in a sacred manner? Lama Yeshe's eyes would twinkle with amusement at the cosmic absurdity of some of my questioning. Sometimes he would laugh and say, "You too much, boy." The first time we met, I remember that he asked me what I was looking for, and I had to honestly admit that I didn't exactly know. He said, "Let's see if we can't find out together." *Together* was a magical word.

The next day I went back to Kathmandu to my funky hotel; collected my backpack, sleeping bag, and passport; reclimbed Kopan Hill and moved in. As I settled in at Lama Yeshe's, I discovered that several other Westerners were already there. There was no fuss, no requirements, no membership dues. Lama Yeshe was still young, in his mid-thirties. Two Tibetan lamas were living at Kopan there on the side of the towering Shiva Puri Mountain, along with a few Westerners in what used to be an old British villa.

It was a wonderful place. The air was thin and the sun was hot; there was no electricity, road, phone, or distractions. We had two latrines, side by side—one called Sam, the other called Sara. I was starting to learn Tibetan; we were all building houses and huts for the new students who kept coming. Once a day Lama Yeshe would personally teach me for an hour or two.

Lama Thubten Yeshe, a true bridge builder, was eager to learn more English. I gave him English lessons, and another Westerner taught him about psychology and Freud. Lama Yeshe was like a mother hen to everyone, deeply concerned with our spiritual life, but also aware of our physical well-being. One of the things that most drew me to Lama Yeshe was that he seemed genuinely happy, and he laughed a lot. I like to think that he still does, even though he has since died. Not only was he an erudite teacher, he was also a wonderful living example of the compassionate wisdom he taught.

At the time, there was nowhere else I would rather have been. It felt as if we were on top of the world with all the promise and possibility open to us. The lamas, who had time and only a few students, were unchanged and uncorrupted by modern civilization. The students, like myself, were mostly young, unformed, and open to the beneficent influence of spiritual teachings. It seemed a match made in heaven.

Here, among a community of seekers living on Kopan Hill, my questions and search for purpose no longer seemed strange, weird, or out of place. Suddenly I discovered that it wasn't just me who wanted to find a deeper sense of meaning. My questions were the universal questions asked by generations of seekers—scientists seeking truth, mystics looking for a direct experience of the divine, the pious seeking God. Buddhist, Jewish, Hindu, Christian, Muslim—it didn't matter—there was a whole world and an entire lineage of seekers, of whom I was a part. I *belonged*.

At Kopan I discovered that a trail through the spiritual universe had already been blazed. I learned that there was already a map, explicit directions, and guideposts, and there were ways to measure progress. As I began to learn about the compassionate wisdom of Tibetan Buddhism, I saw that others had been to the mountaintop and they were able to help us get there too. Here, I no longer felt alienated or separate. There was a sense of kinship. I was on the way home.

## ADDRESSING THE BIG QUESTIONS

"How," Lama Yeshe asked, "can you help others if you cannot help yourself? Liberate yourself, and you liberate the world." Lama Yeshe told us there was nothing that he had and knew that we could not have and know. He said, "Open your heart and awaken your mind, and you'll be there."

Almost thirty years ago in Nepal, Lama Yeshe addressed my big questions—questions about life, death, self, illusion, reality, love, and transformation. Now I find myself addressing the same issues and hearing the same questions almost daily from a new generation of seekers and in many forms. The questions come in private meetings as well as large workshops, by letters, phone calls, and now by e-mail, through my "Ask the Lama" column on my home page on the World Wide Web. It's old wine in new recyclable bottles, the same circus with different performers, an ancient tradition with extraordinarily relevant modern applications.

The spiritual life has always been a search for meaning and a search for answers to the two existential questions: "Who am I?" and "Why am I?" A search for truth, personal authenticity and reality, a search for "what is," a search for purpose; these are the foundations of the spiritual way. Men and women who are ready to deepen or formally embark on a spiritual journey are typically standing at some kind of an emotional crossroads. Often they are grieving over some loss or disappointment—separation from or death of a loved one, a personal crisis, health problems, or an overriding sense that something is wrong or missing. Sometimes they are simply looking for a way to better love the world.

In a very real sense all of our day-to-day problems can be linked to spiritual issues and understanding. For example, I frequently speak to men and women who complain that even though they have painstakingly followed Life's Little Operating Manual, they feel as though they are coming up empty-handed. Superficially, it may seem as though they are having work problems or relationship problems or health problems, but scratch the surface and there are deeper unresolved questions. Some of these people seem to have so much—family, career, education. Everything seems to be going their way, yet they are often dissatisfied.

At the beginning of *The Divine Comedy*, Dante, who was just turning thirty-five, wrote, "Midway upon the journey of our life, I found myself in a dark wood where the right way was lost. Ah! How hard a thing it is to tell what this wild and rough and difficult wood was. . . ." It was the year 1300 when Dante acknowledged being confused and lost in a dark wood. Yet here on the cusp of the twenty-first century, I can easily relate to these feelings, and in all probability you can too.

Too often life's paths seem paradoxical and confusing. Even in the brightest daylight, the atmosphere is murky; the guideposts are barely visible; and the arrows and directional signals, when and if we find them, seem to be pointing every which way. Don't we sometimes have regrets about heading off in the wrong direction? Staying too long even when we knew we were misguided—why do we do the things we do?

Often when we think about our lives and our experiences, we feel certain that in some cosmic way it must be making sense, but sometimes it seems there are too many problems and too much chaos for us to ever get a handle on life. We don't know why this is so, but on some level we know that we are responsible for our own destiny. When we first hear about karma, the possibility of re-birth, and the ineluctable laws of cause and effect, these teachings not only make sense, they are reassuring.

For Tibetan Buddhists, because karma affects everything, there are no chance occurrences. It is no accident, for example, that you are picking up this book. As you read this sentence, all of your past actions, your present thoughts, as well as your intentions for the fu-ture have brought you to this specific intersection of your life where you have opened a book talking about a timeless way of life that was first introduced in Asia some 2,500 years ago.

Those of us who embark on spiritual paths are motivated in different ways. Some of us want to know the unknowable; others want to know themselves; still others want to know everything. Some people want transformation; others want miracles. Many want to alleviate suffering, help others, and leave the world a bet-ter place. Most of us are seeking love and fulfillment in one way or another. Everyone wants inner peace, acceptance, satisfaction, and happiness. We all want genuine remedies to feelings of despair, alienation, and hopelessness. Don't we all want to find spiritual nourishment and healing, renewal and a greater sense of meaning?

Don't we all hope to meet God, with his/her myriad faces? Gandhi once said, "I claim to be a passionate seeker after truth, which is but another name for God." As we all search for truth or God, don't we pray that we will find our way, our purpose? Don't we hope to find our true selves, all we are and can be? Too often, however, our search for truth or meaning lacks focus or di-rection.

Like many others, for example, you may have looked for meaning in relationships that failed you, or you may be frustrated by a career that isn't delivering the rewards you expected. It could be that you're disturbed by shaky values and rampant materialism. You can't help asking yourself if this is all there is. Is this really my life? Is this what I will be when I grow up—which is now? Is there nothing more? When does my real life begin? Is there no greater connection, no deeper purpose and sense of truly belonging? Why does life so often feel barren and lonely, and why is there so much fear, doubt, and anxiety in my heart?

Perhaps you sometimes feel a homesickness, a sadness, and a sense that something is terribly wrong. You might experience this as a yearning for something that is lost, something that seems so familiar and yet so distant. You might feel hungry and needy and aware that nothing has been able to fully satisfy you—at least not for very long. It's like drinking salt water while floating adrift on the great ocean; it's a drink that can't possibly alleviate your thirst.

*Rejoice!* You are living the core issues grappled with by every consciously alive human being. This is no small thing—this is the "Big Time," the Great Way walked by all those who have awakened to freedom, peace, and enlightenment. You're in the heavyweight division, wrestling with the multidimensional angels of life. You want to see them, you want to understand them, and—like Jacob—you want to be blessed by them.

Men and women on such a path traditionally have been known as "seekers." As you read this, are you aware of your journey, and do you understand what you are seeking? Are you ready to find it? It is probable that as a seeker, you've always engaged in a fair amount of self-examination and self-inquiry. You may already have a spiritual practice or religious faith and are looking for additional guidance to help you go further and deeper. Searching for more meaning has always been considered an admirable human quality. The French writer André Gide once wrote, "Believe those who are seeking truth. Doubt those who find it."

People are often drawn to Tibetan Buddhism for more esoteric reasons. They may have heard or read wonderful stories about amazing saints and yogis, men and women who have mastered body, mind, breath, and energy, as well as retained the memory of past lives. Seekers, curious about the unknown, might want to know more about levitation, conscious dying, lucid dreaming, astral travel, rainbow bodies, and clairvoyance. However, that's finally not what it's all about. The Buddha did perform certain miracles, but he always instructed his disciples not to demonstrate miraculous powers except to inspire faith in the skeptical. Lamas say the same thing. The magical, mysterious, and occult are special effects that can be produced, but it's not the whole story. The miracle of Buddhism is a miracle of love, not levitation. The goal of Buddhism is enlightenment, not astral travel. The goal is the path, the way of enlightened living.

## ON THE PATH TO ENLIGHTENMENT

The basic, most fundamental characteristic of Buddhism is the promise of enlightenment. Starting with the example of the Buddha, its teachings contain 2,500 years of wisdom about how ordinary human beings can become enlightened—as enlightened as the Buddha himself. These teachings offer explanations about the nature of enlightenment, describe different degrees, depths, and experiences of enlightenment, as well as provide detailed instructions on how to reach this exalted spiritual state. In fact, the Buddhist path can be called a well-laid-out road map to enlightenment and spiritual rebirth.

The concept of spiritual rebirth is not unique to Buddhism. All Christians know the story of Saul being "reborn" on the road to Damascus when self-realization turned Saul from a bigoted persecutor to a saintly soul named Paul. Of course not everyone can experience spiritual rebirth or self-transformation in a flash of light as Paul did. In Buddhism, for example, there are many different perspectives on enlightenment. Some think it happens suddenly; others believe it only comes about through a gradual process of deepening awareness.

When people ask me about enlightenment I almost always answer by saying that it's not what we think it is. Enlightenment is a mysterious process, not unlike God, truth, or love. No one definition is large enough to encompass it. Each experience is unique—

as we are each unique. Enlightenment—whether you call it spiritual awakening, liberation, illumination, or satori—means profound inner transformation and self-realization. In fact, there are different degrees and depths of enlightenment experience, stretching from an initial momentary glimpse of reality all the way to the fullest actualization of Buddhahood, the fullest form of enlightenment.

Having said that, I think it's important to understand that spiritual rebirth in Buddhism is not a mystical encounter with God. Enlightenment is not about becoming divine. Instead, it's about becoming more fully human. In examining the archetypical experience of the Buddha, we see that his enlightenment represents a direct realization of the nature of reality—how things are and how things work. Enlightenment is the end of ignorance. When we talk about walking the path to enlightenment, we are talking about walking a compassionate path of enlightened living. The Zen master Dogen said, "To be enlightened is to be one with all things."

Today I am firm in my conviction that enlightenment is a real possibility for each and every one of us. However, when I first discovered Buddhism, I wondered whether it was possible for anyone or if it was just a myth. Then I personally encountered some wise masters who seemed to embody it, as well as others who had committed their lives to trying to achieve it. In Tibet, it sometimes seems as though every grandmother, monk, nun, beggar, yak herder, farmer, or healer has an enlightenment story. Tibetans tell stories of monasteries as well as remarkable provinces in which all the inhabitants became enlightened through spiritual practice. A beautiful Tibetan prayer wishes that we may all together reach enlightenment—that we may all find the Buddha within and awaken to who and what we really are.

## AWAKENING THE BUDDHA WITHIN

Not that long ago, while I was leading a weekend retreat in Texas at a church there, a local Montessori school invited me to come and talk to their students. There were about seventy-five children between the ages of seven and eleven, and I wondered exactly what I was going to do. From the moment the kids started trickling in the door, they came right up, climbed on my lap and all over me and started asking questions. I had a brass bowl-shaped gong with me, and at the end, we did the Gong Meditation: Follow the sound of the gong, see where it goes, and "just be there" for a moment or two with the sound.

The next day one of the women in the retreat came up to me at lunch to tell me that her eight-year-old son Ryan had come home and told her that something very unusual had happened that day at school. "A monk from Tibet, New York, came," Ryan reported excitedly.

Ryan said that the monk—me—taught them about God and Buddha and the Gong Meditation. When his mother asked what that was, he said, "Well, he told us to watch where the sound went and to listen carefully. I didn't know you could watch a sound and listen at the same time. It was very interesting. He said that if you followed where the sound went, that you might get closer to God and Buddha. And I did that."

His mother said, "Yes, and . . . ?"

The boy said, "Well, when I watched and listened to where the sound went, I didn't get closer to God. I *was* God."

What a delight, I thought to myself. "From the mouth of babes," as the scripture says.

When I had finished the Gong Meditation, which only takes about thirty seconds, I asked, "So where did the sound go?" And every hand went up. I said, "Sshhh, don't say." I couldn't believe it. Some kids even had both hands raised! How much we adults have forgotten.

I was very touched by their youthful experience of just sensing. They didn't even question their belief, "What is God?" "What is Buddha?" or "Who am I to say I am God, who am I to know these things?" No such self-editing takes place at that age. Just "Oh yeah, God, I am that."

Whether you say "The kingdom of God is within" as Jesus did (in Luke 17:21) or that we all have innate Buddha nature as Tibetans do, in the end, doesn't it come down to the same thing: *We are all lit up from within as if from a sacred source.* Even a child can experience it. Amazing!

In other words, don't seek externally for fulfillment; rather turn the searchlight inward. "Hey, what are you gawking at? Don't you see, it's all about you!" the twentieth-century Zen master Sawaki Roshi once said. It's a fact: You're not going to find truth outside yourself. Not through lovers or mates, not with friends, not with family, and certainly not via material success. The only place you are going to be able to find your truth is in your genuine spiritual center. Truth is found by living truly—in your own authentic way.

Wouldn't it be sweet to come home and find the Buddha there, simply and utterly at peace, desireless with a hearty warmth and genuine nobility of spirit? Wouldn't it be satisfying to be like that, to be in touch with your own authentic being? That's why an Indian master, when asked what advice he had for Westerners seeking enlightenment, said, "Stay where you are." A statement that is simple, yet profound. Be wherever you are; be whoever you are. When *you* genuinely become *you,* a Buddha realizes Buddhahood. You become a Buddha by actualizing your own original innate nature. This nature is primordially pure. This is your true nature, your natural mind. This innate Buddha-nature doesn't need to achieve enlightenment because it is always already perfect, from the beginningless beginning. We only have to awaken to it. There is nothing more to seek or look for.

## INNATE AWARENESS IS
## THE NATURAL STATE

The wonderful wisdom of the deepest secret teachings of Tibet tell us this: *Each of us can (and ultimately must) become enlightened.* All we have to do is search inward and discover our own innate perfection. Everything we seek is there. *The Dzogchen masters of Tibet say we are all Buddhas.* Not Buddhists, *Buddhas.* I emphasize this because once after a lecture, a woman approached me and said, "But Surya, I'm not a Buddhist; I'm a Roman Catholic. Why do you say we are all Buddhists?" I would like to be more clear about this. Even if you are not a Buddhist, and have no intention of becoming a Buddhist, you are still capable of being a living Buddha. For Buddhism is less a theology or a religion than a promise that certain meditative practices and mind trainings can effectively show us how to awaken our Buddha-nature and liberate us from suffering and confusion.

Buddhism says yes, change is possible. It tells us that no matter what our background, each of us is the creator of his or her own destiny. It tells us that our thoughts, our words, and our deeds create the experience that is our future. It tells us that everything has its own place, everything is sacred, and everything is interconnected, and it introduces a system of integrating all experiences into the path toward realizing innate perfection. Science has made great progress in harnessing and understanding matter. Buddhism, on the other hand, is a profound philosophy that, over the centuries, has developed a systematic method of shaping and developing the heart and mind. a method of awakening the Buddha within.

The problem is that most of us are sleeping Buddhas. To reach enlightenment, our only task is to awaken to who and what we really *are*—and in so doing to become fully awake and conscious in the most profound sense of the word. "When I am enlightened, all are enlightened," Buddha said. Help yourself and you help the entire world.

In Pali, the original language of the Buddha scriptures, the word *Buddha* literally means *awake.* "Awaken from what?" one might ask. Awaken from the dreams of delusion, confusion, and suffering; awake to all that you are and all you can be. Awake to reality, to truth, to things just as they are.

# TODAY, RIGHT NOW

*The seeker who sets out upon the way shines
bright over the world.*

—FROM THE DHAMMAPADA
(SAYINGS OF THE BUDDHA)

If you were able to go inward right now and waken your sleeping
Buddha, what would you find? Tibetan Buddhism says that at the
heart of you, me, every single person, and all other creatures great
and small, is an inner radiance that reflects our essential nature,
which is always utterly positive. Tibetans refer to this inner light as
pure radiance or innate luminosity; in fact, they call it *ground luminosity* because it is the "bottom line." There is nothing after this,
and nothing before this. This luminosity is birthless and deathless.
It is a luminescent emptiness, called "clear light," and it is endowed
with the heart of unconditional compassion and love.

Whatever your past or present religious beliefs, you will probably recognize that Tibetans are not alone in associating luminosity
with enlightenment or an incandescent spiritual presence. In
Christian churches and Jewish synagogues as well as Buddhist temples, people light candles that symbolize spiritual luminosity. Saints
and other figures are universally represented by shimmering halos
of light, surrounded by nimbuses and auras. Some people can even
see them in reality. The tradition in Judaism, the religion of my
childhood, is for the women in the household to light candles at
sundown on Friday night. Why? To invite the light and spirit of
God into the temple of the home for the Sabbath.

Think about all the millions of men and women who have
bowed their heads in prayer while lighting candles. Do any of us
really think that the Buddha, or any other penultimate image of
the absolute, needs a candle to see or to stay warm? Lighting a candle is just a symbolic, ritualized way of offering light in the darkness. The candle symbolizes the inner light and luminous wisdom
that can guide each of us through the darkness of ignorance and
confusion. The candle's shining flame is an outer reminder of inner luminosity and clarity—the living spiritual flame burning
within the temple of our heart and soul.

The timeless wisdom of Tibet assures us that when you are able to hear the Buddha's wisdom, when you are willing to ponder his insightful lessons, and when you are genuinely committed to practicing these lessons by doing your best to lead an impeccable life, you can actualize this ground luminosity. You will reach the heart of awakening; you will know where you have been, and you will see where you are going. Your own inner light and truth—the clear light by which we see and are seen—will guide you. This is total awareness; this is perfect enlightenment. Enlightenment means an end to directionless wandering through the dreamlike passageways of life and death. It means that you have found your own home Buddha. How does the Buddha feel? Completely comfortable, at peace, and at ease in every situation and every circumstance with a sense of true inner freedom, independent of both outer circumstances and internal emotions.

Waking up your inner Buddha and staying awake requires extraordinary self-knowledge and presence of mind. It means paying close attention to how you think and how you act, and it means making an ongoing commitment to searching inward for answers. *Inward*. Deeper. Beneath the surface of things, not just inside yourself.

As Westerners, this isn't how we have been conditioned to think. We keep looking outside for answers. We look for lovers, friends, parents, authorities, and even children to answer needs that they can't possibly fulfill. We have fantasies about career, romance, friendship, and intimacy. We are so full of fantasies about the past and the future. Often we don't want to let go of these fantasies because we fear that doing so means giving up on life. But that's not how it works. In truth, unrealistic expectations tarnish our appreciation of life and weigh down the buoyancy of the present moment.

Don't we all tend to think mainly in terms of the gratification of our desires and securing our place in the world? Haven't we all been conditioned to place primary emphasis on persona, or how we appear? Our common languages abound with phrases about projecting a good image. The emphasis is on how you appear to yourself as well as how you appear to others—in order to get what you want. Don't we all seek security, safety, and reassurance?

We're often told, "Don't just stand there, do something!" And we do. We do many somethings. When we are involved in unsatisfying relationships, we believe that our solutions will be found in different relationships; when we have jobs that make us angry and resentful, we believe that new jobs will give us what we want; when we're unhappy with our surroundings, we believe we can resolve our unhappiness by changing locales. Then when our problems refuse to go away, we complain that we're stuck and look for ways to get moving.

We take this kind of logic even further when we reduce life to an ongoing competition. Trained and conditioned to believe that life is about achievement, about winning, losing, and self-assertion, we put much of our energy into momentary solutions. It's no wonder so many of us feel alienated, alone, exhausted, cynical, and disheartened.

Buddhism turns these attitudes about winning and achieving upside down and inside out. Buddhist emphasis is not on new ways to conquer outer space, cyberspace—or, for that matter, Manhattan Island. The wisdom traditions tell us that we can afford to slow down, take a breather, and turn inward. To master ourselves is to arrive home at the center of being—the universal mandala. What we seek, we already *are*. "Everything is available in the natural state," as a lama of old once said. So why should we look anywhere else?

Before we go any further, I want to make it clear that I don't want anyone reading this to get hardening of the heartwaves in the name of Buddhism. Let's not use Buddhism to become quietists, or puritanical holier-than-thou fundamentalists. While sitting in meditation, let's not become stiff, rigid, or stuck in any fixed position, like an inert Buddha statue. The spontaneous fullness that is known as Buddha-nature is always open and flowing. It is not static; it is ecstatic. It is not frozen didactic, and it is not fixed. The Buddha within you isn't going to look exactly like the Buddha inside me, or inside any of your friends and family. Buddhahood—enlightenment—has myriad faces, all equally marvelous. Just take a look around.

Taking an inward path is not about cultism or blind faith. It is about genuine leadership, embodying and enacting truth's highest principles—not mere sheeplike followership. Conforming is not the deepest teaching of the spiritual traditions. The deepest teachings are about radiant awareness and the inherently joyful freedom of being. It's not just about maintaining a quiet mind. If all you want is a quiet mind, there is a huge pharmaceutical industry that would be happy to serve that need.

The path to enlightenment and awakening is the opposite of squelching and containing yourself or trying to keep up a nice, efficient, stainless-steel persona—very shiny but also very hard and cold. There is no substitute for living a juicy genuine life of Buddha activity. The Buddha is bubbling, happy, and sad. Waking up the Buddha is about letting go of your fixed persona and becoming awake, liberated, and *aware.*

Starting on a spiritual path means leaving the superficial currents and getting into the deeper waters of real sanity. We're not just swimming against the stream here; we're actually plumbing the deeper waters of being in order to reconnect with our own innate nature. Where do we start? After he arrived in India in 1959, an old lama was asked, "How did you manage to escape from Tibet and cross the high and snowy Himalayas by foot?" He answered, "One step at a time."

The path, as always, begins beneath your feet with the first step you take. Where do you stand right now? This is where we begin.

*Breathe.*

*Breathe again.*

*Smile.*

*Relax.*

*Arrive*

*Where you are.*

*Be natural.*

*Open to effortlessness,*

*To being*

*Rather than doing.*

*Drop everything.*

*Let go.*

*Enjoy for a moment*

*This marvelous joy of meditation.*

# A TIBETAN PROPHECY

*When the iron bird flies, and horses run on wheels, the Tibetan people will be scattered like ants across the World, and the Dharma will come to the land of red-faced people.*

—PADMA SAMBHAVA, EIGHTH-
CENTURY INDIAN GURU AND
FOUNDER OF THE FIRST TIBETAN
MONASTERY

Tibet has always been renowned for its arcane knowledge and esoteric secrets. Therefore it should hardly come as a surprise that Padma Sambhava, the Indian guru who introduced Buddhism to Tibet, left behind a prophecy not only about the Tibetan people and the spread of Buddhism, but also about the future of transportation.

Anyone interested in Tibetan Buddhism quickly discovers the importance of Padma Sambhava in Tibetan history. Revered by the Tibetan people as being fully enlightened, Padma Sambhava is often referred to as Guru Rinpoche (Precious Guru) or the Second Buddha. It was sometime around A.D. 763 when Padma Sambhava founded the first Buddhist monastery in Tibet at Samyé, yet his life and work had a direct impact on the West. That's because Padma Sambhava is credited with imparting and preserving many of the core teachings that first attracted Westerners to Tibetan Buddhism. Practical as well as visionary, Padma Sambhava foresaw that there would be an attempt by an early Tibetan ruler to suppress Buddhism. He therefore instructed his disciples to conceal sacred writings and ritual implements in the many rocks and caves in the mountains and countryside of Tibet. Tradition holds that there were more than a hundred such texts, known as terma, the Tibetan word for treasure.

Padma Sambhava told his disciples that although it was essential for these terma to be well hidden from any immediate threat of destruction, they would be revealed again when the world was ready to hear the truth contained therein, "for the benefit of future generations," as he said. Centuries later, teachers whom Tibetans formally recognized as reincarnations of Padma Sambhava's original twenty-five disciples began to discover these hidden treasures. This is not just ancient myth. Several of the lamas who unearthed these terma—including my teachers Dudjom Rinpoche, Kangyur Rinpoche, and Dilgo Khyentse Rinpoche—were able to transmit the precious teachings to Westerners.

Padma Sambhava introduced the practice of reciting the *Bardo Thodol,* known to Westerners as *The Tibetan Book of the Dead,* as a guide for conscious dying. The *Bardo Thodol* describes the death experience and the stages (bardos) through which one passes on the way to rebirth. The *Bardo Thodol* is among Padma Sambhava's hidden treasures—rediscovered in the fourteenth century.

The *Bardo Thodol* was first published in English in 1927 as *The Tibetan Book of the Dead* by W. Y. Evans-Wentz. It introduced concepts such as karma, the bardo, the inner clear light, reincarnation, and rebirth. This provided Westerners with their first real exposure to a revolutionary new way of thinking about life, as well as shedding new light on the death experience. Carl Jung, who wrote an introduction to *The Tibetan Book of the Dead,* said, "For years, ever since it was first published, the *Bardo Thodol* has been my constant companion, and to it I owe not only many stimulating ideas and discoveries, but also many fundamental insights." The steady interest generated by the English publication of *The Tibetan Book of the Dead* showed that many Westerners wanted to hear more about the secrets of Tibetan Buddhism.

## DHARMA HEARTLAND

*In all my future lives,*
*May I never fall under the influence of evil*
  *companions;*
*May I never harm even a single hair of any*
  *living being;*
*May I never be deprived of the sublime light*
  *of Dharma.*

— TRADITIONAL TIBETAN PRAYER

In Tibet it's considered a privilege to be born in a country where the Dharma is taught. The Dharma is the most abundant gift of wisdom and like all true gifts, it benefits both the giver and the receiver. The word Dharma is frequently used as a synonym for Buddha Dharma, the teachings of the compassionate enlightened Buddha, the founder of Buddhism who lived in the fifth century B.C. in northern India.

Dharma is a Sanskrit word with a complex meaning. It can be translated as teaching, truth, doctrine, religion, spirituality, or reality. Its literal meaning is "that which supports or upholds." Dharma is thus often likened to truth itself—the ground we stand on—as well as the spiritual way, or the path that can be trusted to support, uphold, and embrace us all. Another, lesser-known meaning of Dharma is "that which remedies, alleviates, heals, and restores." On the very deepest level, the truths embodied in Dharma teachings heal what ails us. Wherever truth or Dharma is taught, the possibility for enlightenment exists. Buddha called places where the Dharma is taught "central lands." Most Westerners now live in central lands—places where this sublime light, the gift of the

Dharma, is available to all. Here in the West, you can find references to the Dharma everywhere, even on the Internet:

"What did the Dalai Lama say to the New York hot dog vendor?"

"Make me *one* with everything."

I first found this joke on America Online. The Dharma on the Internet is an example of the surge in interest in Buddhism in the West. As Westerners become more interested in developing their spiritual lives, Buddhism's ideas are becoming a part of everyday experience. On a popular sitcom, a character tells the audience, "In my next life, it's going to be very different," reflecting the fact that few average Americans have not at one time or another, if only half-jokingly, made a reference to their past or some future life.

To date, approximately fifteen Western children have been sought out and recognized as lama reincarnations—known as tulkus. Lama Thubten Yeshe, for example, was reincarnated in Spain. Recently one of the most unusual reincarnate recognitions took place when a revered senior Tibetan lama visiting in this country recognized a thirty-eight-year-old Christian woman from Maryland as the reincarnation of a Tibetan teacher.

If we leave our skepticism aside for a moment, the next question is why are so many reincarnate lamas reportedly choosing to be born in the United States? Of course, there are no simple answers. It might be our commitment to maintaining a democratic country and a home for religious freedom. Or perhaps there's another answer: As Padma Sambhava predicted so long ago, Tibetans are now scattered around the world, especially in North America—"the land of the red-faced people" of the ancient prophecy, and they have brought their teachings with them. Perhaps as a nation, the United States needs the wisdom of these spiritually accomplished reincarnations, and we are now, for the first time, open to hearing their lessons.

# TIBETAN WISDOM ARRIVES
# IN THE WEST

Until the Chinese invasion in 1950, Tibet was primarily thought of as Shangri-La, a magical land of ancient wisdom and inaccessible beauty in which foreigners were rarely allowed to travel. One of the first bestselling paperbacks in the world, James Hilton's 1933 adventure novel *Lost Horizon,* was about a monastery in Tibet. Shrouded in myth, two miles high, and protected by the snow-capped Himalayas, Tibet's capital city, Lhasa, the home of the Dalai Lama, was often called "The Forbidden City." Isolated and cloistered, Tibet had not changed for many centuries, and modernization and technological progress were strongly resisted. It had never gone through an age of reason or scientific development.

There is an understandable tendency to romanticize the Tibet that existed before China's violent takeover. However, it's a mistake to think that Tibet was a Shangri-La where everyone was enlightened, happy, and a nonviolent vegetarian. Although Tibet probably enjoyed the most sophisticated spiritual technology and understanding of the "inner" sciences, we can't pretend that it was a perfect society. It had a long way to go in bringing into the everyday world what it had seemed to master in a spiritual world. In fact when we examine it closely through rational humanistic eyes, we can't help seeing that it was a medieval theocracy which democracy, literacy, and modern medical advances had yet to reach. What is essential for us today is to extract gold from that Himalayan ore—to find the unchangeable essence of wisdom teachings in the rocky mountainsides of Asian culture, theology, and anachronistic cosmology.

Before China's takeover, a devoted spiritual life and monastic vocation was considered the profession of choice. One-third of Tibet's male population inhabited the thousands of monasteries scattered across the land; well-populated nunneries were also widespread. Until recently, the only wheels in general use in Tibet were prayer wheels, which, along with the beaded rosaries known as malas, were constantly in hand, transforming all activities and one's entire life into an ongoing prayer.

Around 1920, the current Dalai Lama's predecessor (the pre-scient Thirteenth Dalai Lama) had issued ominous predictions about the Chinese government's plan to conquer Tibet and sup-press the practice of Buddhism. But Tibetans, more committed to preserving the status quo than to evolving to modern times, ig-nored these warnings. When the United Nations was formed after World War II, Tibet chose not to join and paid dearly for that backward-looking choice.

In 1950 when China entered Tibet, some of the lamas, monks, and laypeople had the foresight to leave the country; fortunately a few were able to carry with them some ancient sacred objects and writings. Most Tibetans, however, remained. Although the young Dalai Lama feared the worst, for nine long years he remained in Lhasa, trying vainly to come to some peaceful agreement with the Chinese government.

Then, in 1959, the tension and insecurity under which native Tibetans had been living took its toll, and a revolt began in the east-ern province of Kham and spread to Lhasa. The Dalai Lama was alerted when the Chinese Communist government invited him to attend a theatrical performance and insisted that he leave his body-guard and attendants at home. Worried about their leader's safety, thousands of Tibetans surrounded his palace. When fighting broke out, the Dalai Lama, dressed as a peasant, slipped out of the palace under the cover of darkness and started the difficult and dangerous three-week trek by horseback and foot across the mountains out of Tibet and to political asylum in India. Without knowing that the Dalai Lama had departed, the Chinese Army shelled his palace the day after he left, and thousands of unarmed Tibetan civilians died.

As the Chinese moved quickly to take over the monasteries and stamp out the practice of Buddhism, many other lamas and monks also made the arduous flight from their homeland. Close to a hun-dred thousand Tibetans were able to leave before the Chinese closed the borders, but many who started the trip disappeared in the Himalayan wilderness and were never heard from again. For those left behind, life has been cruel and harsh. Nuns, monks, and lamas, as well as laypeople, have been tortured and murdered. Amnesty International has estimated that as many as 1.2 million

Tibetans have been killed by the Chinese Army, and many Tibetans still remain in prison camps northeast of Tibet. Of the countless centuries-old monasteries that once adorned the barren Himalayan plateau, only two dozen remain, which the Chinese have left standing mainly for show.

The lamas and monks who escaped needed new homes. Many, like the Dalai Lama, who now makes his home in Dharamsala in India, settled in neighboring regions and countries—India, Nepal, Sikkim, Ladakh, and Bhutan. Others traveled farther afield, ending up in France, Switzerland, Great Britain, and the United States. These teachers also remembered the Buddha's instructions to his first sixty enlightened disciples to continue to spread his teachings: "Go forth, oh monks, for the good of the many, for the happiness of the many, out of compassion for the world."

## EAST GOES WEST / WEST GOES EAST

*Buddhism has transformed every culture it has entered, and Buddhism has been transformed by its entry into that culture.*

—A R N O L D   T O Y N B E E

With the Chinese invasion of Tibet, it was as if a dam had burst: Suddenly Tibetan wisdom began to flow freely down from the roof of the world and to the West. Nuns, monks, lamas, and teachers who had never left their cloistered monasteries and hermitage retreats were confronted with a new world—filled with men and women eager to learn the Dharma. Tibetan teachers say that if it's possible for any good to have come from the Chinese invasion, that good has been found in the dissemination of the teachings to so many new students.

Lama Yeshe may have been the first lama in Nepal to teach Westerners, but he was far from the last. By 1971, the lamas in exile had realized that the only way for the Buddhism they cherished to survive was to pass it on. These Tibetan masters remembered very well Padma Sambhava's prophecy; several, in fact, were even recognized reincarnations of his disciples. And there to fulfill the prophecy came Westerners looking for guidance and eager to develop their own spiritual lives and transplant the flowering tree of enlightenment to their own countries.

————

When I arrived in Kathmandu in 1971, it was still a virginal valley essentially unchanged by tourism and almost as remote as Tibet. For centuries, if you were "on the road," Kathmandu was the link between Europe and the mystical East; it was a destination for explorers, hippies, mountain climbers trying to conquer Everest, as well as seekers trying to climb the spiritual mountain and conquer their inner selves. Until the 1950s when the first car arrived, the Himalayan trade routes following nature's mountain passes may have converged in Kathmandu, but there were no adequate roads. The first automobiles were carried—in pieces—over the mountains by porters. Like Tibet, Nepal—known as the Land of the Gods—was awash in its own magical mystic traditions. The yeti, the mythological abominable snowman, was an officially protected species until the 1950s, and even today expeditions continue to hunt for them in a region where history and myth remain almost inextricably entwined.

In 1971, there was one Tibetan Buddhist monastery in Kathmandu Valley; now eighty or more dot the countryside. Back then, in Lama Yeshe's monastery there were two lamas—Lama Yeshe and Lama Zopa—and only five students. It was very easy to immerse yourself in Buddhism; it was very easy to be a disciple—to live and work intensively with a lama. We lived as they lived: up at dawn, bed after dusk because there was no electricity. Morning, noon, and night they were absorbed in meditative practices, and we were too. I remember Lama Yeshe's concern that Lama Zopa was so involved in his meditation practice that he would neglect eating or sleeping.

With all the study, work, and self-discipline, it was still easy to have a good time with these delightful lamas. They were so filled with joy and devotion that it was contagious. Tibetans assume, for example, that everyone is able to sit and meditate without moving for hours, and to have visions of Buddhas and strikingly memorable lucid dreams, so the lamas showed us how, and we were able to do it too. Amazing! Whatever weaknesses may have existed beneath the surface of the feudal Tibetan hierarchy, we were far from having to deal with them during those halcyon days.

We all ate lentil soup ladled out of tin buckets and vegetarian food from leaf plates while we worked at building monasteries and living quarters for the steady stream of new students who were beginning to arrive. All the while, we meditated, we prayed, we chanted, we discussed and debated, and we celebrated Buddhist festivals. Occasionally we went on pilgrimages to sacred sites such as Padma Sambhava's main meditation cave where rainbows appeared as we approached the site. Lama Yeshe began to teach us the Graduated Path to Enlightenment known in Tibetan as the Lam-rim. These are the step-by-step stages that have been taught time and time again to seekers and are part and parcel of what I teach now.

When I left New York in May of 1971, my original plans were to stay in Asia until August, then return home to participate in the Breadloaf Writer's Conference in Vermont, and enter graduate school in the fall. I had no idea that Asia was soon to become my permanent residence, but that's what happened. There in the Indian subcontinent, I felt as though I had stumbled into a gold mine of wisdom and a spiritual sanctuary. I felt increasingly at home in the Himalayas, whatever the physical difficulties. It was a true homecoming. My teachers explained this feeling by talking about past lives and my "Buddhist blood." Who knows?

With the Tibetan masters, I began to have some personal experience of another, transcendent, reality. The lamas who taught me personified and exemplified a deep wisdom and acceptance that was unlike anything I had ever known in my own cultural upbringing. With teachings and by example, they showed me how to develop spiritually. Where I grew up, the best and the brightest were extremely competitive; they went to med school, law school, Madison Avenue or Wall Street. In the Buddhist Himalayas, the best and the brightest chose monastic life. On these mountaintops, the monasteries were the living centers of energy and erudition. I felt totally safe in that spiritual refuge.

For me the choice was obvious. I put grad school on hold, and Buddhism became my priority. Unfortunately, Indian government regulations didn't exactly coincide with my intentions. An American couldn't stay anywhere in India or Nepal indefinitely because of problems with visas and weather, even if economics were not an issue. Therefore, in the winter most Westerners like myself left the mountains, traveled south, crossed borders, and by hook or by crook got new visas, new passports, or even, in some cases, new identities.

In the winter of 1971–1972, my teacher Lama Yeshe made a pilgrimage to Bodh Gaya, the village in the desert of northern India where the Buddha reached enlightenment while sitting under the bodhi tree. Taking a bus, a train and, yes, an oxcart too, I followed him. In Bodh Gaya that winter, I was lucky enough to be able to participate in several ten-day silent Vipassana (insight) meditation retreats led by S. N. Goenka and A. Munindra at the Burmese Monastery and Meditation Center.

These days provided a wonderful opportunity for us Westerners to train in meditation. We didn't think about it then, but the bridge that would help the Dharma cross from East to West was being constructed right before our eyes and under our noses. I met many Westerners there who today teach Dharma all over the world. Many of them remain among my closest friends and colleagues, men and women like Joseph Goldstein, Sharon Salzberg, Dan Goleman, Christopher Titmuss, Fred Von Allmen, Tsultrim Allione, Christina Feldman, Stephen Batchelor, and Ram Dass.

I returned to Nepal to study further with Lama Yeshe in March 1972, but I was running out of money. I mined another month or two of sustenance out of my backpack by pulling out my jean jacket and selling it in the Freak Street Bazaar in Kathmandu to someone who wanted to look like an American. Finally, by late summer I knew I had to go home. Not only did I have to attend a family wedding, I was also totally broke.

But before I left Nepal, since I was traveling near Dharamsala, Lama Yeshe asked me to bring with me hundreds of sticks of incense as a gift to the Dalai Lama. Carrying all this incense wrapped in black plastic along with a letter of introduction, along the way I fell asleep in the luggage rack in the third-class compartment of an overnight train through India. When I woke up seven hours later I discovered that the railway car had been unhooked, and I was in the wrong city. A group of men were pointing at my incense bundle and whispering that I must be with the CIA, carrying collapsible equipment and radio antennae. How our minds can speculate. As I got off the train, I found myself at the head of the Ganges in Haridwar with a gathering of Hindu holy men celebrating a huge Hindu festival.

When I finally arrived two days later for my appointment with the Dalai Lama, he shook my hand in the most friendly manner and sat me down on a couch in his simple motel-like villa and we talked. His Holiness—as he is called—struck me as the kindest, most humble and egoless person I had ever met. This is the effect he has on just about everyone. He turned out to be very interested in my Jewish background because he thought the Tibetans, who were now without a homeland, could learn a great deal from the Jewish experience of survival in exile; he was very impressed by the ability of the Jewish people to maintain religious and cultural traditions for centuries without a country or homeland.

The Dalai Lama seemed genuinely enthusiastic about the foreigners who had recently come to Buddhism; he said he thought Americans and other Westerners had an affinity for Buddhism because they didn't believe anything until it was proven. The Buddha, he reminded me, told people not to follow anything blindly, for Buddhism is not based on belief so much as rational experiment. If, like a scientist, you replicated the Buddha's experiment, you should get the same good results—enlightenment.

His Holiness said that he very much respected the new students who were spending so much time in spiritual practice—particularly since he felt that his time to practice and study was limited because of the plight of Tibetans and his diplomatic role as head of the Tibetan government-in-exile. As I left, I felt both moved and empowered. The Dalai Lama made me, a Jewish guy from Long Island, feel as though I could be as Buddhist, and even as enlightened, as anyone else. That meeting helped me decide to return to Nepal indefinitely in order to deepen my study of Buddhism in the authentic, traditional, Tibetan way at my teacher's hilltop monastery.

Upon my return to the States, I discovered that another Tibetan lama, Chogyam Trungpa Rinpoche, had arrived in this country and was beginning to teach. A brilliant, high-ranking lama with a complex personality, Trungpa Rinpoche had led a large group of his followers out of Tibet while he was still a teenager. But then his path took a unique turn. Instead of staying in Nepal or India, Trungpa traveled to the British Isles and enrolled, with a scholarship, at Oxford. After graduation, he started the first Tibetan monastery in the West in Scotland. Ultimately he decided, in light of Padma Sambhava's prophecy, that North America would be his Buddha Field, his field of enlightening activity.

In the late fall of 1972, I traveled west to Colorado and onward to Wyoming to hear Trungpa Rinpoche give his first "Crazy Wisdom" seminar at Jackson Hole. Unlike most of the other lamas I had met, Trungpa was not a monk, at least not any longer. He had disrobed years earlier after a serious auto accident in Scotland. In fact he was married to an Englishwoman, and had a young family. Trungpa, who consistently taught that everything in life can be incorporated into one's spiritual path, didn't just sit on a mountaintop and meditate. He definitely knew how to enjoy himself, perhaps sometimes even to excess. Buddhists, at least in Boulder, were having more fun—but it would not last for long. The shadows of excessive abandon were beginning to gather beneath the surface even then.

Chogyam Trungpa was a Buddhist pioneer in the West. Although many have criticized him for his sometimes outrageous behavior and heavy drinking, no one can question his brilliance and his real achievements. He founded an accredited Buddhist university, the first in the West—Naropa Institute in Boulder. He taught thousands of students, and he wrote and published over a dozen books before his death at the age of forty-eight. Wearing Western suits and ties, he was a new kind of spiritual master—outrageous, iconoclastic, provocative, ironic, and artistic, as well as learned and traditionally trained.

As the summer of 1973 approached, I wanted to return to Nepal. To solve the immediate problem of money, I sold my possessions—typewriter, guitar, car (a 1968 orange Mercury convertible), and vacuum cleaner. It seems amazing now, but that was enough money to allow me to return to India and to stay indefinitely.

*Some questionable Buddhist humor:*
"Did you hear the one about the Buddhist vacuum cleaner?"
"It comes with no attachments."

I was young, enthusiastic, carefree, and without wordly attachments. My original plan had been to go back to Kathmandu and Lama Yeshe for more instruction. But in the States that year I heard that Kalu Rinpoche, a greatly revered elderly Tibetan lama, had made a visit to the West in 1971 and, although he spoke no English, was willing to teach Westerners.

## SONADA MONASTERY

*"Make of yourself a light,"*
*I used to hear*
*from Buddha's long-lost lips*
*each day as I woke before dawn*
*in this mountain hermitage.*
*The five-peaked jeweled mountain*
*Kanchenjunga*
*towers over the Darjeeling horizon*
*as I start a fire for tea*
*and prepare my morning prayers.*

—DIARY ENTRY, 1973

Kalu Rinpoche was a legendary figure. After walking out of Tibet in 1959, Kalu Rinpoche, along with several other lamas, ended up in the town of Sonada, near the old British hill station of Darjeeling, in an old run-down monastery right above the train tracks. Kalu Rinpoche and the other lamas in his monastery were not jet-set gurus. They were hunkered down to stay in their Himalayan hills. There was a splendid view of the eternally snow-covered Kanchenjunga, the third highest mountain in the world, but the monastery was without electricity, phones, or hot water.

The only way to get there was by Jeep over a difficult single-lane road or by the old narrow-gauge train. The train, which had been left behind by the British, looked like a toy as it traveled ten miles an hour on the down slope, through the tea plantations, and into the foothills of the Himalayas. It was so slow we were able to jump on and off without waiting for it to stop.

We foreign Dharma fanatics took the train often because we needed special Darjeeling police permits to be in that restricted border zone, a flashpoint close to China, Nepal, Sikkim, Bhutan, and India. These permits required extra machinations on top of the ordinary visa hassles because the local police feared we gentle pilgrims might be spies, underground "commies," or worse. During the yearly monsoon season, landslides typically blocked every way in to and out of the mountains for as much as a month. Sometimes the hillside washed out, and the train tracks were left hanging in the air. Traveling on that train helped us avoid the prying eyes of the visa police.

Kalu Rinpoche was a wizened old Himalayan yogi. When he was twenty-five, after a three-year retreat in his guru's Palpung Monastery in the eastern Tibetan province of Kham, he began a solitary retreat in desolate Tibetan mountains and wilderness caves. He stayed in retreat for more than twelve years. He would have continued to live in this way, but his aged teacher, Tai Situ Rinpoche, sent for him, saying it was time for him to return to the Palpung Monastery and teach.

When I met Kalu Rinpoche, his face was lined like a road map, and he seemed ageless and timeless; another teacher of mine who knew Kalu Rinpoche when he was much younger said that he had always looked that way. Isn't the Old Lama always the Old Lama? Kalu Rinpoche, his face full of compassion and his heart full of love, would bless even the smallest insects and animals as he walked. And he was always surrounded by the monks and nuns training under his supervision.

When Kalu Rinpoche came for a second visit to the U.S. late in 1976, I was one of his drivers and hosts. While he was teaching in Boston, we decided that he might like to see Boston Harbor, a historic place for American beginnings. In the aquarium located at the harbor, there is an enormous three-story-high tank filled with a vast number of fish, turtles, and other marine life. Lama Kalu spent most of the afternoon gently tapping on the tank with his forefinger to get the attention of the fish. Then one by one as each fish swam past, he would look into its eyes saying, "Om Mani Pedmé Hung," the mantra of great compassion, blessing each fish and speeding it on toward higher rebirth. It was another first on the freedom trail for Boston Harbor.

In Darjeeling, each morning Kalu Rinpoche blessed a box of sand, then spread it around on the hillside with the prayer "May any living creature who comes into contact with even a single grain of this sand be blessed, protected, and eventually enlightened." Among Tibetan lamas, of course, this is not unusual. Lama Kalu's best friend was a Dzogchen master named Chatral Rinpoche. At the new and full moon each month, Chatral Rinpoche would go from his Ghoom Monastery down to the Darjeeling or Siliguri market where they sold live fish. He would buy as many fish as he could; then he and several monks would carry them away in buckets, bless them, and set them free in local lakes and rivers. In Tibet, of course, it is taught that animals are also sentient beings and, like humans, evolve through lifetime after lifetime. They too are endowed with Buddha-nature and the potential for enlightenment. Therefore the Buddha preached nonharming of any living creature and absolute reverence for all forms of life.

It was in Darjeeling that I came to know well my first tulku, or young reincarnated lama: He was a ten-year-old grand lama, Drukchen Rinpoche, the head of a large sect. His white-bearded guru, Thuksay Rinpoche, asked me if I would serve as the boy's English tutor because they wanted him to be fully prepared for the future as an effective teacher. This child and his family provided me with many real insights into Tibetan life. For example, one day the young tulku turned to me and said, "You know, as I get older, I'm beginning to lose my memory of my past lives. It's as if my awakened mind is becoming obscured by the events of this lifetime." At that time I felt less than sure about rebirth, but was beginning to reflect more deeply about it as a real possibility. I did not think my unique young student was lying as he talked about his experience and memories. There was no reason for him to lie to me.

For me Darjeeling was a magical place, a Buddha Field where

the greatest exemplars of Buddha's teachings—the living lamas, authentic spiritual masters—were in monasteries lined up in the mountains along the ridge road that snaked through the lush tea estates. Since those golden years of the early seventies, I've been back many times. I was fortunate to be able to be at the Sonada Monastery during Kalu Rinpoche's last days when he died in 1989, and also four years later when his reincarnated tulku was enthroned. Several of my dear old teachers and Dharma sisters and brothers still live in those blessed, decrepit, but spiritually thriving monasteries today.

Kalu Rinpoche was one of my root gurus, and his monastery was my primary home for five years in the early and mid-1970s. I once asked another dear teacher in Darjeeling, Tulku Pema, how one decided which lama was your root guru or primary teacher—especially if, like me and many of my friends, you had studied and practiced under the guidance of many. He told me that one's root guru is the one to whom you are the most grateful. Kalu Rinpoche taught me so much at an early age and I owe him the deepest debt of gratitude for his wisdom, his patience, and his love. I feel as though he is always with me, and I often see him in dreams.

A month after we first met, Kalu Rinpoche asked me what kind of meditation I was doing. I told him that I was following my breath, concentrating on breathing. "What," he asked, "are you going to concentrate on when you stop breathing?" That woke me to the level of master I was talking to. Kalu Rinpoche was a truly transcendent man who lived, breathed, and exuded Dharma. That is the meaning of "lama." Literally in Tibetan it means heavy or weighty: A lama is a teacher who embodies the weighty Dharma. Kalu Rinpoche was a true spiritual heavyweight.

Following Tibetan tradition, most of Kalu Rinpoche's teachings were orally transmitted, along with esoteric initiations, spontaneous songs of enlightenment, and delightful teaching tales. Monks and lamas typically committed vast quantities of scripture and prayers to memory and passed them on that way, often embedded in stories and parables. In order to receive full transmission of the Buddhist tradition, Tibetan lamas are still required to receive oral transmission of Buddhist scriptures and teachings from a qualified lama in the oral lineage; this is called lhung, or oral authorization. As astonishing as it may seem, I was told that there have been several lamas with such miraculous powers of memory that they have been able to repeat by rote the entire Buddhist canon, over one hundred volumes of scriptures.

Much of the most profound guidance and instruction in Tibet have been done orally, intimately passed from master to disciple, on a one-to-one basis. These teachings were privately held, going from generation to generation, creating a lineage of "ear whispered" sacred instructions. This is often called the secret teachings of Tibet, known as the pith instructions, the boiled down distilled essence of all the teachings—centuries of wisdom. What this means is that there is an unbroken chain of teaching, a living flame of truth and realization handed down personally from the Buddha until today.

In Tibet it is said that your spiritual teacher is more important to you than the Buddha. This is because although you can't easily meet the Buddha, you meet him in your guru who is supposed to be the living personification of enlightenment. They say your guru is even more important than your parents because while your parents raise you in one lifetime, your guru takes you through all your lives and brings you up in the most profound way. Tibetans cultivate respect and gratitude to their teachers as they would to the Buddha in order to develop inspiration and devotion, receive blessings, and progress spiritually.

At Kalu Rinpoche's monastery, I met another lama who I always feel is with me. The Sixteenth Gyalwa Karmapa, who was the head of the large, very meditation-oriented Kagyu School, came to our Sonada Monastery to give teachings and a long series of initiations in the fall of 1973. The Karmapas are the longest continuous tulku line in Tibet, stretching back eight hundred years; the Sixteenth Karmapa, known as a living Buddha, was considered by many to be the greatest lama of his time. He was also one of the first lamas to understand the significance of the Chinese government's intentions and had traveled from Tibet to establish a monastery in Sikkim well before 1959.

During special ritual ceremonies, the Karmapa often wore a jeweled black crown which the Emperor of China had made for the Fifth Karmapa centuries ago. The Karmapa performs this Black Crown Ceremony in order to activate people's innate enlightenment potential. It is said that everyone who sees this crown is assured of enlightenment—if not now, later.

In Tibetan Buddhism, there are ceremonies known as initiations or empowerments in which spiritual power is transmitted through the teacher to the student. This is a lineage transmission by which the guru empowers the disciple to practice certain esoteric meditations. Because the Karmapa was extraordinarily spiritually accomplished, amazing things happened when he gave empowerments. In front of him, disciples, myself included, would have experiences including visions, spiritual dreams of the Buddha and deities, heart chakra openings, energy eruptions, and satori (awakening) experiences. Not only was the Karmapa spiritually realized, he was powerful, compassionate, loving, buoyantly joyful, and clairvoyant. He was also a lot of fun.

Amused that I was Jewish *and* Buddhist, he would tease me by twisting my ear and saying, "Jewish, Jewish . . . very good!" "Very good" was one of the few English phrases he knew. One day at his monastery, a large group of Westerners were streaming through his room, and he blessed each of them by touching the top of their heads with his hands and saying "Very good!" as they bowed down before him. Khandro-La, the highly accomplished wife of Jamyang Khyentse Rinpoche, happened to be visiting, and saw through his language skills. "Wow, you spoke to each of them personally in their own language. You are truly omniscient!" she teased the august Master Karmapa, who was generally considered all-knowing.

When I stayed at the Karmapa's monastery in Sikkim, it seemed that his light was on all night long. His attendants told me that the Karmapa only needed two or three hours of sleep a night because his mind was unclouded by the darkness of ignorance. I would see him walking around the courtyard in informal garb at three or four in the morning with his mala in hand, chanting mantras and beaming. Occasionally I tagged along. He was always very kind to me.

In one of my first meetings with the Karmapa, without thinking about the propriety of the question, I asked him, "What does it mean when people say you are a living Buddha?" His translator became so flustered that he could barely repeat the question. The Karmapa locked his eyes with mine and said, "It means that I have fully realized for myself what you also are."

The Karmapa was deeply committed to spreading the Dharma in the West. During his final illness, he was in the United States. For part of the time, we cared for him in the monastery we had built for him in Woodstock, New York; he finally died in a hospital near Chicago in 1981. His many Asian disciples in the East wanted him to return home to Sikkim, his main monastery in exile, but he chose to die in America. This was a part of the tremendous transmission and blessings that his school and its teachings have contributed to the growth of the Dharma in the West.

I was blessed with many gracious and wise teachers who generously shared their spiritual legacy with us. Tibetan lamas like Venerable Kalu Rinpoche, Dilgo Khyentse Rinpoche, Dudjom Rinpoche, Kangyur Rinpoche, and Tulku Urgyen generously taught me the Dharma. In opening the great highway to enlightenment for me, they emphatically showed me that it is open to *anyone*. In fact, probably the most essential thing they taught me is that the Dharma is waiting for anyone who wants to start on the path to awakening. We each only have to find a Dharma gate that suits us as individuals.

Whether you are male or female, Westerner or Easterner, young or old, it doesn't matter; there are an infinite number of Dharma gates, and they are easy to find. Rick Fields, the first American historian of Buddhism, wrote a poem called *The Mantra of the Goddess and the Buddha.* In it he writes:

> *Be your breath, Ah*
> *Smile, Hey*
> *And relax, Ho*
> *And remember this, You can't miss.*

## FINDING YOUR OWN TRUTH, YOUR OWN DHARMA GATE

You don't have to be a card-carrying Buddhist to long for spiritual insight and guidance. My Indian guru, Neem Karoli Baba, always admonished us to learn from everyone. No one has a corner on the market of truth. "All one" was his favorite maxim. He encouraged me to serve and apprentice myself to all sages, seekers, and saints, no matter what their denomination or belief system, for it is the heart of the matter that counts—the living spirit, not just the letter, of the law.

The traditional elder, Kalu Rinpoche, once told me that he didn't believe that a seeker who had ties to Christianity or any other faith had to convert to Buddhism in order to practice Dharma. The truth, after all, belongs to anyone who cherishes it, lives it, loves it, and is committed to it.

Some 2,500 years ago, the Buddha left his wife, his infant son, his home, his family, his extraordinary royal wealth, and his safe, secure, and luxurious life. When the Buddha put on a mendicant's patched ochre robe and began the life of an ascetic monk, he renounced a great deal. Dancing girls and succulent food served on golden plates, not to mention love, human attachments, and the power and prestige that came with his role as a crown prince. As a young man, the prince was known as Siddhartha Gautama; as an adult, he would be called Shakyamuni, the Sage of the Shakya Clan, or Lord Buddha, the Blessed One.

Before the Buddha's birth, seers told his father, the king who was head of the Shakya clan, that the child who was about to be born would either be a very powerful king or a fully enlightened one. According to their prediction, the Buddha could go one of two ways; it was one or the other. No easy choice. At the age of twenty-nine, the Buddha chose the life of a wandering monk because he wanted to understand suffering and the end of suffering; he wanted to know more about life and death, and he wanted to detoxify, to purify his body, mind, and heart from delusion and destructive emotions. In short, he wanted to know truth and find inner peace and freedom.

The Buddha renounced a great deal in the name of truth. Yet in some ways it was a much less complicated process for him to make his decision than it would be for a man or woman living today. The average young parent, for example, couldn't contemplate leaving a child as the Buddha did to begin a spiritual path. Unlike the youthful Buddha, few men or women today would have the assurance that all the child's financial and wordly needs would be satisfied. In traditional Buddhism, there used to be only one way to walk a sacred or holy path. That way involved decisive detachment from the world. We have a mental picture of ascetic monks, carrying their alms bowls, walking or meditating along dusty Himalayan pathways. Can you imagine someone doing that in America or in Europe today for any length of time?

Jack Kornfield, a spiritual teacher and author who returned from Thailand in the mid-1970s as an ordained monk, started out by begging in New York City for his sole daily meal, lunch, as he had been trained in Thailand to do daily. Jack, who has a doctorate in psychology, was very determined, spiritually aware, and committed. However the Thai embassy turned out to be his only benefactor, and he soon decided to return to lay life as a Dharma teacher. He has since become a leading spokesman for Buddhism, an extremely popular meditation teacher and author, as well as husband and parent. He exemplifies the well-trained, deeply rooted modern Buddhist, working in this world, but not totally of it.

## WHAT HAS THE POWER TO TRULY TRANSFORM US?

That seems to be the question for our time. Often raising the right questions—your own real, deep-down, burning questions—may actually be more important than having the right answer, should there even be one. I'm a firm believer in authentic tradition and the wisdom of the ancient experience. Many have walked this sacred path. However it's not the only way. The haiku poet, Basho, said, "I do not seek to follow in the footsteps of the men of old; I seek what they sought." Each of us must find our own way, at our own speed, and in our own place.

The joy of the Dharma is that it can accommodate an infinite number of forms and styles. In fact, in Asia this has always been recognized; thus there are numerous schools of Buddhism, each of which in turn allows for different levels of personal involvement and commitment, depending on whether you are a monk, nun, teacher, or lay person. The three different schools with which we are most familiar in the West today are Zen Buddhism, Theravadin Buddhism (sometimes called Vipassana), and Tibetan Buddhism. Today we call these the Three Great Traditions.

My own training is as a Tibetan lama. My lineage is called the Rimé, or nonsectarian practicing lineage of Tibet. Most of the teachers we see in the West come from that lineage. My personal teachers came from all four of the major schools of Tibetan Buddhism (Nyingma, Sakya, Kagyu, and Gelug) so a nonsectarian approach resonates with my life experience as well as my understanding of contemporary Dharma. My root gurus were mainly Nyingma-Kagyu; that's where my greatest devotion lies. My particular spiritual heritage is Dzogchen, often called the consummate practice or secret teachings of Tibet. Some masters have called Dzogchen self-secret, meaning that the truth may be hidden, but it is always there for those ready to perceive it. About the truth of Dzogchen it has been said:

> *It's too close so we overlook it.*
> *It seems too good to be true so we can't believe it.*
> *It's too profound so we can't fathom it.*
> *It's not outside ourselves so we can't obtain it anew.*

## DZOGCHEN, THE NATURAL GREAT PERFECTION

*One instant of total awareness is one instant*
*of perfect freedom and enlightenment.*

—THE WISDOM DEITY, MANJUSRI

One ongoing controversy in Buddhism revolves around how long it takes to become enlightened. Some schools feel that enlightenment is a gradual process that takes place over many lifetimes. Dzogchen is a tradition that believes one can become enlightened within one lifetime—even within a decade. The direct path of Dzogchen was first practiced and taught in Tibet by Padma Sambhava 1,300 years ago although it is actually much older than that.

The earliest Indian Dzogchen master, Garab Dorje, who lived two centuries before Jesus Christ, wrote about Dzogchen, saying, "Don't follow past thoughts, don't anticipate the future, and don't follow illusory thoughts that arise in the present; but turning within, observe your own true nature and maintain awareness of your natural mind, just as it is, beyond the conceptual limitations of past, present, and future."

Dzogchen is a naked awareness practice; it doesn't depend on cultural forms or unfamiliar deities. In fact, nowness—awareness— is the true Buddha, as my own lamas said. Dzogchen's unique message is that, by nature, we are all Buddhas for whom enlightenment is possible within this lifetime. In the light of our speeded-up world, many believe that Dzogchen is the teaching for our time.

Contemporary Tibetan teacher Sogyal Rinpoche points out that Dzogchen is particularly meaningful for spiritual living as well as conscious dying. In *The Tibetan Book of Living and Dying,* he says:

> No one can die fearlessly and in complete security until they have truly realized the nature of mind. For only this realization, deep- ened over years of sustained practice, can keep the mind stable during the molten chaos of the process of death. Of all the ways I know of helping people to realize the nature of mind, that of the practice of Dzogchen, the most ancient and direct stream of wis- dom within the teachings of Buddhism, and the source of the bardo teachings themselves, is the clearest, most effective, and most relevant to the environment and needs of today.

Dzogchen, known as the Natural Great Perfection, cuts to the heart of the matter and provides a view from above—an overarch- ing perspective that includes all the many ways of practice while climbing the spiritual mountain. This formless truth of the view can be adapted to fit anyone, anywhere, in any circumstance or sit- uation; it can enhance, facilitate, and be integrated into any formal practice. That's why it's so well-suited for our pluralistic multicul- tural era.

My own life experience has many times shown me the neces- sity of keeping in mind the bigger picture and adapting to chang- ing times and places. In my own life, I've had to resolve the conflict between the marvelous simplicity of classical monastic life and the delicious diversity of having to dance with life day to day. Men and women living today always seem to be passing modern versions of Scylla and Charybdis, caught between the dentist and the therapist, the mate and the boss, the taxman and the personal trainer. Open-mindedness and flexibility is extraordinarily helpful.

# STARTING ON THE SPIRITUAL PATH RIGHT HERE

Like it or not, every day we face the bustling world with its confusion and chaos along with its joys and possibilities. Few people are able to spend endless hours in meditation, and I doubt if there are many livable wilderness caves where one can withdraw for a solitary retreat. Even the Dalai Lama often says that he doesn't have sufficient time for quiet meditation and reflection. Yet he has found peace amidst it all. How can we do the same? How can we transform ourselves; how can we awaken the Buddha within?

Today it seems to me that we have little choice but to assimilate all we experience into our spiritual lives; it is all grist for the mill, manure on fertile fields of spiritual flowers. The sacred and the mundane are inseparable. Your life is your path. Your disappointments are part of your path; your joys are your path; your dry cleaning, and your dry cleaner are on your path; ditto your credit card payments. It's not helpful to wait until you have more time for meditation or contemplation, because it may never happen. Cultivating spirituality and awareness has to become a full-time vocation, and for most of us this has to take place within the context of a secular life here in the Western Hemisphere.

For you, the seeker, what matters is how you attend to the present moment. This includes motivation, intention, aspiration, desire, hope, and expectation. This is not just about what you do but *how* you do it. The present moment is where the rubber actually meets the road. Your traction on the path, spiritually speaking, depends on how you apply your heart and soul.

What then is most truly transformative? Is it merely a matter of changing one's clothes or hairstyle, or joining up with some group that hopes its message will change the world? Could it be simply a matter of receiving the ultimate mantra or initiation; learning to perform the proper rite or ritual; finding out how to meditate; doing yoga, praying, breathing, chanting, having cosmic sex; going to the Himalayas, Jerusalem, Mecca, Machu Picchu, Mount Kailash, Mount Shasta; or meeting the right guru? I don't think so.

Or is it not most transformative, most earthshaking, to pierce the veils of self-deception and illusion, and crack the eggshell of ignorance, to most intimately encounter oneself? Through honest self-inquiry and no-holds-barred meditative introspection over a sustained period of time, one can take apart and deconstruct the hut that ego built, thus entering the mansion of authentic being. This may seem challenging, but it is actually easier than you think.

Like many of my friends and colleagues during the sixties and seventies, initially I encountered some serious difficulties with the Asian traditions and with the lamas, roshis, swamis, and masters of all sorts who are its principal exponents. As attractive as the teachings and some of the leaders immediately seemed, and actually *are*, there remained formidable cultural, linguistic, and psychological barriers to overcome in order to train in and develop a genuine spiritual practice in any Eastern practice-path or discipline.

The Tibetan lamas knew, and we Westerners eventually learned, that our practice had to reflect integrated lives and our own Western traditions. Kabir, the fifteenth-century Indian poet and saint, once sang, "I do not wish to dye my clothes saffron, the color of a holy order; I want to dye my heart with divine love."

One need not travel to distant lands, seek exotic mystical experiences, master esoteric mantras and treatises, or cultivate extraordinary states of mind in order to experience a radical change of heart and inner transformation. Spiritually speaking, everything that one wants, aspires to, and needs is ever-present, accessible here and now—for those with eyes to see. It's the old adage all over again: You don't need to see different things, but rather to see things *differently.*

I have been fortunate enough to be able to visit most of the great temples of man, study in India and Tibet, and circle the globe several times in search of what I was looking for. Now I say what others have said: that one has seen nothing until one has come face to face with oneself. Then each and every moment hosts the ultimate miracle, wherever we are. Truth and love are in the palms of our hands. For when we are illumined, the whole universe is illumined. Let's lighten up.

Intrinsic awareness is the common denominator of all sentient beings. Conscious living, contemplative self-awareness, is the means to becoming all that we are. Awareness is curative. Knowing ourselves and learning to let go is the method, the most skillful means. Spirituality is a matter of self-discovery, rather than of becoming something else. True transformation is like the legendary alchemical transmutation, in which the base metal of our limited, finite selves is, as if by magic, transformed into the spiritual gold of our transcendent original nature.

Throughout the ages, those who have heard truth's insistent call have believed in the transformative power of spiritual illumination, combined with the illuminating power of altruistic compassionate action. The same question persists: How can there be peace in the world if we, its inhabitants, are not at peace with ourselves? As long as there is a separation—between "us" and "them," self and other, "me" as separate and distinct from "you"—conflict remains, and self-transformation is a mere pipe dream. If we don't love ourselves, how can we love the earth?

Self-transformation implies self-transcendence. Therefore, inner transformation is a spiritual affair of cosmic significance, including all, animate and inanimate, everywhere. Authentic self-transformation is definitely not for oneself alone. It is for all beings—for aren't we all inseparably interconnected? Whatever befalls us, befalls one and all; harm a single strand of the web of life, and the entire web is harmed. In Africa, the Xhosa tribe has a saying which is worth remembering: "I am because we are."

# Building a Spiritual Life from Scratch

Recently I've been going through some old notebooks, looking at some of the things that I wrote down at Lama Yeshe's monastery. In one notebook, I found a "To Do" list called "Daily Necessities." If you reflect upon some of these practices and bring a few into your life every day, you will be transformed.

The living Buddha, the Sixteenth Karmapa, said, "If you have one hundred percent dedication and confidence in Dharma teachings, every living situation can be part of spiritual practice. You can be living the practice instead of just doing it."

## DAILY NECESSITIES

### Tips and Pointers for Building
### a Spiritual Life from Scratch

*Pray*

*Meditate*

*Be aware / Stay awake*

*Bow*

*Practice yoga*

*Feel*

*Chant and sing*

*Breathe and smile*

*Relax / Enjoy / Laugh / Play*

*Create / Envision*

*Let go / Forgive / Accept*

*Walk / Exercise / Move*

*Work / Serve / Contribute*

*Listen / Learn / Inquire*

*Consider / Reflect*

*Cultivate oneself / Enhance competencies*

*Cultivate contentment*

*Cultivate flexibility*

*Cultivate friendship and collaboration*

*Open up / Expand / Include*

*Lighten up*

*Dream*

*Celebrate and appreciate*

*Give thanks*

*Evolve*

*Love*

*Share / Give / Receive*

*Walk softly / Live gently*

*Expand / Radiate / Dissolve*

*Simplify*

*Surrender / Trust*

*Be born anew*

# DECONSTRUCTING THE

# HOUSE THAT EGO BUILT

*A hero ventures forth from the world of common day into a region of supernatural wonder; fabulous forces are there encountered and a decisive victory is won: The hero comes back from this mysterious adventure with the power to bestow boons on his fellow man.*

—JOSEPH CAMPBELL

It's 6:30 on a Friday evening in the early spring, and Scott, who recently celebrated his thirty-third birthday, is about to leave work. Scott had a difficult week filled with long hours and hair-raising stress. Scott, who is single, is now preparing to go out with some male friends to unwind and share war stories about the week that was. They plan to go to a Japanese restaurant for sushi and sake. As always, Scott and his friends will spend much of their time talking about career goals. All of them will complain about not making enough money; at least one will brag about a recent business coup. They will also compare notes on personal relationships. Afterward, the men will stop by a club in the hope of meeting some women.

Scott and his friends do the same thing almost every week. On one level, they think of it as networking; on another it's male camaraderie. Tonight at about 2:00 A.M., Scott follows his typical pattern, and starts to head home, alone, a little bit drunk, worrying about whether he is going to have a headache in the morning and if he has spent too much money. He will probably also feel a little bit depressed, a little bit lonely, and he'll have an overriding sense that the night was a waste of time—in fact, that much of what he does is a waste of time. Scott would like to change. But how? And in what direction?

It's as it always is, week in and week out. But this night, although he is thinking his usual thoughts, something amazing happens: As Scott walks down the dimly lit street searching for his car, he taps the sensor button on his key chain and waits for the flashing lights to lead him to his vehicle. But instead of seeing car lights, he hears the sound of low chanting and immediately becomes aware of an unusual sight. A yellow-robed man is sitting, in the lotus position, under the one visible streetlight, meditating and chanting. It's the Buddha. What is the Enlightened One doing here, and what is the wisdom that he can impart to Scott? What might the Buddha say to help Scott start to change and transform?

We actually have a fairly good idea about what the Buddha would say to Scott because once, during the Buddha's lifetime, he was called upon to address a very similar situation. In this case, the Buddha was in the forest, sitting in meditation, when a band of villagers came upon him. The distraught group consisted of some married couples and one wealthy bachelor.

It seems that the night before, the bachelor had invited his favorite courtesan to spend the night, and while he was sleeping, this woman had found money hidden under his bed, and she took it and fled. When the man woke and discovered what had happened, he rounded up some friends and neighbors, and they all set off in pursuit. That's how this group stumbled upon the Buddha. Excited by meeting the Enlightened One, the bachelor told the Buddha the whole story and sought to hear the Buddha's wisdom. The sage Buddha asked a rhetorical question:

"Instead of wandering around in this dangerous jungle seeking a woman and some money, wouldn't it be far better to seek your true self?"

When Gautama, the Buddha, asked this question 2,500 years ago, the bachelor, completely struck by the Buddha's peaceful shining countenance, recognized that his hedonistic life lacked purpose and meaning. His spiritual life seemed to him less profound than a wading pool. Immediately he began to take steps that would transform his life. Ultimately he did what men who wanted a spiritual life did in India those many centuries ago: He joined a monastery.

In all probability, today, the Buddha would ask Scott the same question as the one he asked the wealthy bachelor:

"Instead of wandering around in this dangerous concrete jungle seeking a woman and money, wouldn't it be far better to seek your true self?"

Doesn't that question have as much meaning now as it did back then? And Scott would probably answer, "What do you mean?" Scott's question would be a valid one, because Scott might not have a clue as to where or how to start such a quest. Scott would want to know, "How do I seek my true self? Where do I go?"

"How do I start?" Isn't that always the major issue for most seekers, particularly here in the Western Hemisphere? It can feel very frustrating and lonely trying to initiate and develop a spiritual path in the context of a busy contemporary life. Learned teachers, lamas, or gurus are not always readily available; spiritual role models and mentors are hard to come by; and as appealing as the notion of checking oneself into a monastery filled with other men and women on similar spiritual quests may often seem, for most people such a choice simply isn't a viable option. So how do you start? It may be reassuring to know that the first steps today are the same as they were 2,500 years ago.

## TAKING THE FIRST STEP

*Acknowledge that enlightenment is a real possibility.*

The Buddha was an actual historical person. Although he is among the leaders of the world's great religions, he did not claim that he was, in any way, divine or otherworldly. Buddhism teaches that the Buddha was born a man, not a god. Because of his inquiry into the nature of reality, of self and the world, he achieved enlightenment. This enlightenment did not come about through the intervention of outside, mystical, or otherworldly forces. The Buddha Way is the way of clear-seeing rationality; it is the way of reality; it is the way of critical examination and sustained inquiry into the nature of life. The Buddha himself taught that blind faith and devotion alone do not lead to freedom and enlightenment, useful as they might be at a certain stage.

When the Buddha was living in his palace, he was a good person, kind to his wife, family, and servants. The potential for enlightenment may have been present for all to see, but it was the arduous inner work the Buddha did on himself after he left the palace that led to his perfect enlightenment.

The Buddha was born a human being not so very different from you or me. Through his own efforts, he was able to reach perfect awareness and self-knowledge; through his own efforts, he was able to know all things knowable. The implications of this are extraordinary: *If the Buddha could achieve enlightenment, then we can all achieve enlightenment.* If the Buddha could know the truth of things as they are, then we—you and me—can know the truth of things as they are. "What? Me?" you ask. Yes, *you!* Never forget the revolutionary gospel, the good news, of Buddhism: Each of us is fully endowed with luminous Buddha-nature, the potential for awakened enlightenment.

Tibetans firmly believe that there have been and still are many enlightened beings who walk among us. In fact, there are yogis living anonymously everywhere without calling attention to themselves. Spiritual giants are universally accepted as heros in Tibet where the names that are remembered aren't those of sports figures, politicians, or movie stars. Ask any Tibetan about Milarepa, the eleventh-century cave-dwelling yogi-sage. As Tibet's most beloved poet, Milarepa gained enlightenment in a single life-time, and every child has heard his spontaneous songs of joyous wisdom.

Just as a child in the West grows up believing that it's possible to become president or an actor or sports figure, children in Tibet grow up believing in the possibility of enlightenment. The secret wisdom of Tibet pronounces that any one of us is capable of pu-rifying our negativities and obscurations, perfecting our under-standing, and practicing universal compassion. Actualize your Buddha-nature, your innate perfection, and you too will achieve enlightenment.

## MAKE A COMMITMENT TO AWAKENING

The Buddha cannot, and *would not,* force you to walk the way of truth and liberation. The Buddha cannot, and *would not,* force you to walk the path of compassion and self-purification. The Buddha cannot, and *would not,* force you to follow the liberating heart-opening lessons of the Dharma. Buddhism teaches that no one else controls your destiny. It's all in your hands—the Buddha in the palm of your hands. The potential for self-perfection is yours right now. Innate Buddha-nature expresses itself through human nature. Make a commitment to awakening and enlightenment, and the Dharma gate and the path to enlightenment will open for you, just as it has opened for countless others. In Buddhism, when you make a commitment to awakening, it is known as "taking refuge" or "go-ing for refuge."

## GOING FOR REFUGE

In Tibetan Buddhism, one of the first things a new Dharma stu-dent does is to make a commitment to wakefulness by taking part in a rite known as the *Refuge Ceremony.* Taking refuge imples find-ing a reliable spiritual sanctuary, a place to safely rest your heart and mind. The Refuge Ceremony and the recitation of the Refuge Prayer formalizes one's commitment to the *Buddha,* the *Dharma,* and the *Sangha* or spiritual community. The Buddha, Dharma, and

Sangha are known as the Three Jewels of Buddhism, or the triple-faceted gem.

### THE REFUGE PRAYER

*I go for refuge in the Buddha, the enlightened teacher; I commit
    myself to enlightenment;*
*I go for refuge in the Dharma, the spiritual teachings; I commit
    myself to the truth as it is.*
*I go for refuge in the Sangha, the spiritual community; I commit
    myself to living the enlightened life.*

In Tibetan Buddhism, when you take refuge with a teacher or lama for the first time, you are given a new Dharma name, symbolizing spiritual rebirth, as your teacher cuts a small lock of your hair. The hair is a reminder that when the Buddha left his palace to became a monk and give up the life he had known, he exchanged his regal clothes for his charioteer's humble garments, cut off his elegant princely hair with a sword, and walked alone and unencumbered into the forest and onto the path toward enlightenment.

I first made a formal commitment to Buddhism by taking part in a Refuge Ceremony with Kalu Rinpoche in his Sonada Monastery in Darjeeling in 1972. At that time, he clipped a tiny piece of my hair and gave me my Dharma name. Kalu Rinpoche guided many, many people through the Refuge Ceremony. He gave us all names beginning with Karma as part of the Karmapa's Kagyu lineage. The refuge name he gave me is Karma Dondrub Chopel (which means Accomplishing and Spreading the Highest Dharma Purpose). He said that would be the name that he, my guru, would call me when he would guide me through the bardo, or after-death experience, and beckon me toward the light. Our spiritual bond was one extending beyond death.

I was very fortunate: It was a privilege to make such a connection with an enlightened elder who was deeply embedded in sacred spiritual tradition. The ceremony took place in Darjeeling, a Himalayan province, with a lama who was wearing traditional Buddhist robes, and it represented an important decision on my part. But you can make the same kind of decision on your own without such a ceremony; even today in the Western Hemisphere, you can forge a connection that is no less authentic. In fact, we must do it here because here is where we are. And if truth, reality, and wisdom are not here, they are nowhere!

Think about the way the Buddha must have felt when he turned away from his family and his worldly possessions and began on the path to liberation. When the Buddha cut his hair, there were no lamas in burgundy robes and no monks in saffron and ochre. The Buddha made his decision without a formal ceremony, and you can too. Like the Buddha, you do this with a sincere commitment to take refuge in the way of truth. As you travel your spiritual path, there will be many times when you will want to seek refuge. You do this by reaffirming your commitment to awakening every day in everything you do, and by remembering the Refuge Prayer and what it symbolizes.

## "I GO FOR REFUGE IN THE BUDDHA"

What does it mean when you repeat the venerable ancient affirmation "I take refuge in the Buddha"? Does that mean that all you have to do is build an altar and bow down to a statue purchased in an antique store? Of course not. All representations of the Buddha, whether they are on an altar or carried around as radiant images in your heart, have a much deeper meaning. Going to the Buddha for refuge means that you are seeking awakening, Buddha-nature, Buddha-mind, Buddhahood. You are seeking an enlightened mind and spiritual realization. That alone provides shelter, sanctuary, a reliable place where you can come home.

Going for refuge in the Buddha is seeking refuge in the natural wisdom of innate awareness itself. When you say, "I take refuge in Buddha, the enlightened teacher," this is not just about bowing down to an idol, and it's not about subscribing to a dogma. The Buddha never presented himself as a savior; rather he is a role model, a teacher. He always said, "I point the way to enlightenment; it is up to each of us to travel along it."

The Buddha never said he would save you; in Buddhism, you

save yourself. Taking refuge in the Buddha is making a firm commitment to know the truth, to know how things really are. It's making a strong commitment to saving your present and your future. Total awareness, pure wakefulness, is the Buddha within, the innate purity of your own heart-mind. That natural authenticity is the ultimate refuge. That's the inner truth, the inner teacher, the absolute guru—not just to know and experience reality with the rational, logical computer brain, but to know with the intuitive heart. That's something you can really rely on: finding truth within your own experience.

## "I GO FOR REFUGE IN THE DHARMA"

> *Until you reach the path,*
> *you wander in the world*
> *with the precious Buddha*
> *Completely wrapped up inside*
> *As in a bundle of rags*
> *. . . you have this precious Buddha. Unwrap*
> *it, quickly!*

— FROM THE SUTRA OF THE
HOLY BUDDHA

To seek refuge in the Dharma is to commit oneself to seeking refuge in a way of life that reflects truth. The Buddha was remarkable because during his lifetime he didn't turn away from reality. He didn't flinch from truth just as it is. The Buddha-mind, which knows all things exactly as they are, sees reality and knows the truth. Joyfully live the truth, and you will embody the Dharma. This is the highway to enlightenment.

The Dharma is descriptive, not presciptive. It doesn't tell us how we should be; it does reveal how things actually *are*. According to this enlightened perspective, there are three primary reasons for dissatisfaction and unhappiness. These three reasons are called the *Three Poisons* or *Three Fires*. These afflictive states of mind are sometimes referred to as negative or conflicting emotions, also known in Sanskrit as kleshas—unhealthy emotions.

## POISON ONE: IGNORANCE OF THE TRUTH

It's difficult for me to say that you and I are ignorant without sounding dogmatic and repressive, like an old-fashioned fire-and-brimstone preacher. In Buddhism the concept of ignorance refers to the age-old problem of delusion and confusion. Until we reach enlightenment, we are all at least a little bit ignorant of the truth or out of touch with reality. We don't perceive the truth of how things actually are directly, without distortion or illusion. Instead, we insist on seeing things as we would like them to be. We tell ourselves stories, and we live in our fantasies.

## POISON TWO: ATTACHMENT

Who or what are you most attached to? Is it a person? Is it some object? Is it an attitude or a behavior pattern? Are you attached to some repetitive or even compulsive habit or way of doing things? Are you attached to money? Are you attached to status? How about ambition? Often our attachments take over our lives. It is as if we are possessed by our possessions. We want success so much that we give up real lives; we want beautiful things so much that we only see the imperfections in what we have; we become so attached to others that we try to control or own them; we become so attached to something or somebody that we become totally dependent and forget who we are.

The Dharma also teaches us that there are two poisonous subsets of attachment: *pride* and *jealousy*. We are so "attached" to our possessions and accomplishments that they become a source of pride. This pride causes us to define ourselves by our attachments. Who am I? "I am the president of the company"; "I am a Ph.D.."; "I am the doctor's wife"; "I am the best basketball player on the block." Pride plays a large role in maintaining a rigid persona; it fixes us in place, entangling and entrapping us, deadening the living flow of authenticity and spirit.

Jealousy, like pride, is one of the components of a dualistic world view. "She has something more or different than I have. I want that something." Or, "He is trying to take something away from me. I won't let it happen." Hanging on to pride and jealousy are manifestations of ego clinging. Purifying oneself of pride and jealousy is essential in loosening and diminishing our ego-centered and incorrect view of reality and in bringing harmony and reconciliation into our lives.

Our attachments often define our compulsions. Men and women who attend Alcoholics Anonymous meetings, trying to overcome an attachment or addiction to a substance, frequently hear and use the phrase "Let go, and let God." A traditional Buddhist might prefer the phrase "Let go, and let Buddha." Words are secondary; it's the same principle. Don't get confused: When we talk about "attachment" as an uncontrolled "poison" or "fire," we are not referring to genuine acceptance and love, which is unselfish and not codependent.

## POISON THREE: AVERSION

Aversion is another word for dislike. John's girlfriend left him for a close friend; he really *dislikes* them both. Dick's landlord keeps raising his rent; Dick really *dislikes* greedy people. Most frequently we form aversions, or dislikes, in response to frustrated attachments. Meryl feels anxious and insecure when she is alone; she *hates* feeling that way. We don't like it when we don't get what we want; we don't like unpleasant experiences. When dislike is reinforced, it often escalates to anger, hate, and enmity.

The Three Poisons usually work together to create pain in this fashion: Because we are *ignorant* of the truth, we think we can be made happy by fulfilling our *attachments* to a specific person, place, thing, feeling. Inevitably we are disappointed, and then *aversion*, dislike, or even hatred rears its ugly head.

This tragic cycle plays itself out in myriad ways, from the mundane to the cataclysmic. When you go to the supermarket attached to the notion that you will buy a pound of ripe peaches, and the only peaches you can find are green, and you become visibly annoyed, you are allowing the three poisons to perpetuate negative cycles in your life. Simple lovers' quarrels or escalated physical confrontations reflect this cycle, as do border disputes and gunfire between nations.

I think it helps to add another ingredient, or "poison," to this frustrating group of kleshas: *resistance* to change. As every psychologist (and physicist) knows, we all have a tendency to resist change, particularly in those areas where we most need transformation. Freud was very articulate in pointing out that a resistance to changing for the better is one of the defining characteristics of neurosis. The fact is that we all tend to hang on to our negative habits and frozen behavior patterns. We keep retracing our steps; we keep walking the same circular patterns. We don't climb out of our ruts, our comfort zones, however dissatisfying they really feel.

## THE DHARMA AS AN AGENT OF CHANGE

Buddhist philosophy tells us that there is a way to take charge, change direction, and peel away ignorance so that we can see with total clarity. The Dharma's ancient, timeless message for you, the seeker, is that there is a tried-and-true method for refining your mind, heightening your awareness, and transcending your dependence on outer circumstances.

In Tibet it is taught that the Dharma has two elements, the Dharma of Transmission or classical teachings and the Dharma of Realization or direct experience.

### The Dharma of Transmission

The primary doctrine of Buddhism is found in the actual words and teachings of the Buddha collected in the scriptures, known as sutras. Sutra, a Sanskrit word, was originally defined as "thread" or "string." When inspiring phrases or words were put together, as the Buddha did, they were likened to a garland of flowers or rosary woven together by a common thread.

Soon after the Buddha's death, five hundred of the Buddha's enlightened disciples assembled the First Buddhist Council in order to recall the Buddha's words and corroborate them with each other. One of Buddha's principal disciples, Ananda, a cousin as well as his constant attendant, had been present for all of the Buddha's teachings. At the council, Ananda and other monks well known for their amazing memory recited by heart all of the Buddha's sermons. People who read the sermons of the Buddha for the first time often wonder why they begin with the phrase "Thus have I heard." Tradition tells us that this is how Ananda began each of his recitations. The other enlightened disciples, many of whom had also been present for the Buddha's teachings, also remembered what the Buddha had said; they made their slight corrections and gave their approval to the recitations. Once these recitations had received the approval of the council of five hundred senior disciples, they were regarded as sutras, the genuine words of the Buddha. Thus this fresh and living oral transmission has been passed down to us today, through an unbroken lineage from master to disciple, like an inheritance.

Many people ask whether there is a Buddhist "bible" or canon of Buddhist scriptures. For reference, here is a summary of the core teachings: Along with the sutras, the Buddha left behind numerous monastic vows and disciplines (known as the Vinaya) and treatises (known as the Abhidharma) that explain Buddhist psychology. These three collections of Shakyamuni Buddha's teachings—Sutra, Vinaya, and Abhidharma—comprise the original Buddhist canon, known as the Tripitaka, which is translated as Three Baskets or collections. These are the original teachings of the historical Buddha, found in the Pali language in their earliest form.

Also included in the Dharma of Transmission are various essential works, texts, and commentaries by subsequent generations of Buddhist masters. Considered part of this are the later sutras and tantras, as well as the Mahayana sutras in Sanskrit. Also included are the esoteric, more mystical tantras, or non-dual treatises, taught by Buddha appearing in the guise of various meditational deities, in order to express the higher, non-dual Vajrayana teachings to beings of higher capacity. Thus came about all the eighty-four thousand teachings of the Buddha, subsumed in the Three Vehicles (or Yanas)—Theravada, Mahayana, and Vajrayana. These three cycles of teachings are often known as the Three Turnings of the Dharma Wheel. These are the Three Great Buddhist Traditions, which have come to us today in the West principally through the emergent modern meditation practices of Vipassana, Zen, and Dzogchen-Mahamudra.

The First Turning or Cycle of the Dharma Wheel (known as the Traditional Way of the Elders, called Theravada, and inaccurately sometimes referred to as Hinayana) includes the Four Noble Truths, the Eight-Fold Path, the Three Marks or Characteristics of Existence (impermanence, not-self, and suffering), and interdependent co-origination (how everything comes about through cause and effect). This often is described as the Way of individual liberation, purification, and highly positive behavior. It is known as the Arhant's (or saint's) Way. This Theravadin Way stresses insight, purification, morality, restraint, nonharming, renunciation, and simplicity. Ancient scriptures say that on this path one will reach liberation within seven lifetimes after the initial enlightenment experience.

The Second Turning or Cycle of the Dharma Wheel (known as the Mahayana) emphasizes sunyata, which means infinite emptiness and radiant openness. This is the heroic Bodhisattva's way of universal enlightenment; this path emphasizes the union of wisdom and compassion and unselfish attitudes. The Mahayana stresses compassion the wisdom of emptiness, openness, altruism, and fearless courage. This path can culminate in full enlightenment within a few lifetimes.

The Third Turning or Cycle of the Dharma Wheel (known as the Vajrayana) emphasizes innate Buddha-nature—spontaneous, fertile, and luminous. It elucidates non-dual tantra, unveiling the utter inseparability of nirvana and samsara, the sacred and the mundane, or heaven and earth. The Vajrayana stresses transformation, energy, empowerment, and dynamic skillful means. In this path, enlightenment has often been attained within a single lifetime.

These three approaches correspond to the Three Vehicles or major Buddhist approaches. Historically the Southern schools in Ceylon, Burma, Thailand, Laos, and Cambodia stressed the classical Hinayana and Theravada; the Northern schools in Nepal, Sikkim, Tibet, Mongolia, Korea, China, and Japan emphasized the Mahayana and Tantric Vajrayana.

According to my own teachers and the Rimé lineage (nonsectarian practice lineage) of Tibet, a secret Fourth Turning or Cycle of the Dharma Wheel is taught. This is the consummate and ultimate Buddhist teaching known in Tibetan as Dzogchen. Considered the most direct non-dual approach to awakening the Buddha within, Dzogchen stresses non-duality, ecstatic spontaneity, and the natural great perfection of things just as they are. Dzogchen masters teach that one can achieve enlightenment in this very lifetime, even in as few as three or seven years through assiduous practice.

An important thing to remember about the words of the Buddha are that these are the teachings of a living person who reached enlightenment and who, out of his kindness and compassion, shared what he knew with others. He was a visionary pathfinder, a pioneer, a wise teacher who pointed out a new way. It has been said that the Buddha was so sensitive and aware that he was able to understand the vast differences among diverse groups of people and beings. Legend tells us that when the Buddha taught the Dharma, all listeners heard exactly what they individually needed to hear, each in his or her own language.

Here today in the West that sacred Dharma Wheel is still in motion, a current of truth in motion. These truths resonate with seekers today just as they did centuries ago. The new turning of the Dharma Wheel is now your turn. You can bring forth your own truth, your Dharma, your own true vocation, in your own way. In fact, it is incumbent upon each of us to do so.

## The Dharma of Realization

Just as important as the words of the Buddha are the ways we each realize these teachings for ourselves. Tibetan masters say that we are exceedingly fortunate because our human existence makes it possible for us to develop a genuine Dharma practice. They also teach that everything that happens in life is part of your path. Thus every moment is an opportunity for awakening; every single experience you have can be assimilated into your spiritual life.

Keep that in mind, and, for just a moment, think about everything that happened to you today. Waiting in line for the bus, getting stuck in the wrong lane, hearing a great piece of music on the radio, spilling coffee on your shirt, picking up your child after school and sharing a bag of popcorn, taking the dog for a walk, going on a date, making dinner. How did you feel during each second, minute, hour of your day? What did you say? What did you do? This is your life and, if skillfully integrated, it can also be part of your path.

Developing wisdom, clarity, basic sanity, and compassion in your life expresses the Dharma of realization. This is your daily work; this is how you make your life sacred. Living the Dharma has always been a challenge for monks and nuns in Asia, and it continues to be a challenge for spiritual seekers in the West today. The relentlessly eternal questions and issues remain with us. How to balance our outer and inner lives; how to take our best intentions and direct them to others; how to maintain a full-time commitment within the context of a complicated world; how to balance compassion with wisdom; how to know the difference between selfless compassion and dualistic pity, between clinging and commitment, between love and attachment, between restraint and fear.

Tibetan lamas like Kalu Rinpoche and the Dalai Lama, who have thoroughly mingled their lives with spirit, seem to be able to embody the Dharma full-time. Through studying with them, I began to see how it is possible to live in such a way. Most of us have a difficult time bringing the Dharma into our lives and mingling it with everything we do. Yet it is doable.

A woman I know named Elise recently had an experience that resonates with many seekers. Elise, a thirty-eight-year-old single mother and lawyer, attended a weekend meditation retreat. When she returned, she felt absolutely transformed. The retreat was so inspiring that Elise vowed to herself that she was going to be a different person: she was going to keep everything in perspective and not get lost in petty office politics and her own ambition; she was going to stop being a demanding perfectionist with others; and she was going to be more patient with her children. These were her new resolutions.

Elise came back from the country retreat center on Sunday night, but by the time her Monday midmorning coffee break rolled around, despite all her good intentions, her mood had fallen apart. On the weekend, the energy of everyone around her had seemed uplifting, accepting, and healing. It was wonderful. Back at her job, however, nothing felt wonderful. It didn't even feel okay. Instead, everything felt frantic, negative, competitive, and disturbing. To compound Elise's Monday morning blues, she found herself obsessing about an attractive fellow meditator with whom she'd had minimal contact. She couldn't stop thinking about whether she should have made her feelings known and couldn't stop fantasizing about ways to find this person again. While shedding a lot of mental and emotional baggage, she had unwittingly picked up some more. To sum it all up, soon Elise could not help wondering whether the weekend was a total loss.

I certainly understand the way Elise feels; probably we all do. This is a common experience: We come away from meditation or a particularly enriching spiritual experience, or even a vacation, convinced that we have been forever altered; then within hours we are once again unconsciously caught up in some unsatisfying habitual reaction or neurotic tendency. What Elise could realize, what we all could realize, is that this is simply part of the process. What Elise gained from her weekend is a deeper awareness of how she loses touch with her own inner reality and obscures her inner sunlight. Now she has to work at changing herself little by little, until her awareness grows deeper and deeper.

Elise's problem with priorities, her impatience with her children, and her tendency to form obssessive attachments are all part of her path; Elise's task is to bring the wisdom of the Dharma into her life to help her deal with all these issues. If spiritual teachings and practices don't help us with these matters, what good are they?

Mingling the Dharma with your life means trying to make choices and decisions that are more enlightened and that stem from a commitment to awakening from illusion's dreams. The Dharma of your own internal realization is where you find inner refuge—refuge in learning the truth, expressing that truth, integrating that truth into your own being. When you are authentically and totally yourself, you embody Dharma. This is the inner triple jewel. Living the Dharma means being true to yourself.

Daily meditation is the simplest means by which we stay on the essential path of awakening. In this way we can gradually and thoroughly begin to mingle the Dharma with every activity. This is done through paying attention, through practicing mindfulness rather than mindlessness, through consciously cultivating presence of mind rather than absentmindedness. This is known as awareness practice, raising your consciousness, or living a mindful life.

In one of his sermons, the Buddha spoke to Ananda, saying,

"Oh Ananda, be lamps unto yourselves. Be refuges to yourselves. Hold fast to the Dharma as a lamp. Hold fast to the Dharma as a refuge. Look not for refuge to any one besides yourselves. . . . And whosoever, Ananda . . . shall be a refuge unto themselves . . . it is they, among the seekers, who shall reach the very topmost height."

Following a balanced, moderate path that is honest, straightforward, and impeccable is living the Dharma. Learning to live without excessive confusion, anger, clinging, vacillation, or greed—that's Dharma. Basic sanity means being in tune with things as they are—this is Dharma. Following a Dharma path means making your first priority your spiritual life and developing a warm, kind, and loving heart, along with a sense of empathy and friendliness. This includes developing integrity and character, not just seeking short-lived highs or mystical experiences. Truth is about getting free, not getting high.

## "I GO FOR REFUGE IN THE SANGHA"

There is a Tibetan saying "Only the snow lions among us can go into solitude in the wilderness and achieve enlightenment alone." Most of us depend upon being part of a sangha. The word Sangha is translated as "virtuous community." It represents the spiritual community, our fellow seekers, kindred spirits, and soulful friends we rely on and trust. Historically, it referred to the ordained, monastic community of monks and nuns.

Spiritual energy is healing energy; when any group gathers with a dedication to something greater than one's finite, individual self, the accumulated energy is almost palpable. When Jesus said, "Where two or more are gathered in my name, there shall I be also," he was affirming the miraculous spiritual power, the delightful synergy, of *sangha*. When we dedicate ourselves to a cause larger or longer-lasting than our own mortal selves, we edge in the direction of immortality.

In the seventies and eighties I found living in monastic brotherhood edifying and inspirational for my own inner development. Now, as a Dharma teacher, the society of my peers is vital in keeping my priorities straight. My Dharma friends and colleagues often

provide a sharp cutting edge of insight as clear and trustworthy a
mirror of the truth as is provided by any elder or spiritual master.
And the mirror of the Western sangha today has an additional
virtue: It's free of the cultural differences, underlying assumptions,
authoritarianism, and hierarchies that a Westerner often experiences among Buddhists in traditionally patriarchal Asian societies.
Of course, with any group or community, one has to be alert to
the dark side or shadow side represented by insularity, conforming,
herd instinct, and group-think. I think the Sangha always has to
work to keep its collective and individual energies pure, sane,
warm, and full of heart.

In an immediate sense, the Sangha also represents the people to
whom you are close or intimately connected—in short, the people you live and hang out with. These friends, colleagues, partners,
relatives often help create the situations that make up your path.
Buddhists recognize that the quality of spiritual practice is greatly
influenced by one's associates. A main reason why monks and nuns
separated themselves from the world was to avoid worldly people
and distracting influences. I remember my parents telling me that
if I hung out with the wrong kids, I would get into trouble. Some
things never change. Tibetans regularly pray that they won't fall in
with the "wrong crowd" of misguided companions and that they
won't be reborn among evil companions in hinterlands far from
the ennobling Dharma.

In a larger sense, sangha refers to a great deal more than a particular group of people who wear yellow, orange, or red robes
while they chant or meditate in the same room. Yes, the men and
women with whom you meditate and pray are members of your
sangha, but so are the people with whom you share office space,
and the birds who sing outside your window in the morning. The
Sangha signifies cooperation, collaboration, inclusiveness, and
interbeing—being connected with others. This includes the entire
community of all beings, seen and unseen, human and otherwise—
the entire boundless circle. Taking refuge in the Sangha represents
our commitment to living harmoniously with others and working
to bring all sentient beings further along on the path to enlightenment.

The Sangha represents the positive energy and support we all need. Sangha friends can help you get through the hard patches of your path, when you feel discouraged and depleted. Sangha can teach you a lot, and group sangha practice can wear down many of your rough edges.

## TAKING REFUGE IN A MORE ESOTERIC SENSE

In Tibetan Buddhism, taking refuge in the Buddha, the Dharma, and the Sangha is also reflected in other ways. For example, the teacher, or lama, is the human embodiment or manifestation of the Buddha; therefore we go for refuge and sanctuary in the spiritual experience and wisdom of our teacher. The representative of the Dharma is your own personal practice, and the internal energies and experience practice evokes. In Tibet, these energies are also personified as archetypical representations of mystical forces and energies including meditation deities, Dharma protectors and guardians who can lead you along the way. The energy you receive from spiritual experiences is an esoteric example of going for refuge to your inner, secret, internal sangha.

## THE ULTIMATE REFUGE

Knowing truth is Buddha; expressing truth is Dharma; embodying truth and living truly is Sangha. In Buddhism, there is a rather unique word that translates as "suchness." It means vital, living truth itself, here and now, right before our very eyes—the "isness" of things exactly as they are. Arrive at that place that is free of craving, a totally open luminous expanse where nothing is wanting, and there you will experience the meaning of the Dzogchen teaching that says, "Leave everything as it is and rest your weary mind." The Buddha once said, "There is nirvanic peace in things left just as they are." That is the innermost secret refuge. If you can reach this place within yourself, then you don't have to do or undo anything. That's the ultimate refuge, the ultimate practice of letting go—the art of allowing things to be as they are. That is coming home in a spiritual sense. My late teacher Khyentse Rinpoche taught:

> *Leave everything as it is in fundamental simplicity,*
> *and clarity will arise by itself.*
> *Only by doing nothing will you do all there is to be done . . .*

The secret wisdom of Dzogchen teaches us that whatever we are looking for, *it* is always right here. *We are usually elsewhere.* That's the problem.

## REFUGE IS NOT FOR ONESELF ALONE

Throughout the ages there have been many Buddhas. Our Buddha, Shakyamuni, born in what is now western Nepal 2,500 years ago, is said to be the fourth of the thousand Buddhas of this Golden Aeon. In Tibet it is taught that all these Buddhas exist in blissful celestial Buddha Fields, which are created by emanations of Buddha-wisdom. What is unique about Buddha Shakyamuni is his vow to help those in *our* present age, in our world, on this earth.

Taking refuge in the Buddha, the Dharma, and the Sangha is not only the way to enlightenment; it is also the way to let the Buddha's vow for universal enlightenment work itself out through *you*. Surrender to that vow and enter onto the great highway of awakening, plunging into the timeless current of all those beings on the path to Buddhahood.

Mahayana, the principal form of Buddhism practiced in Tibet, is sometimes referred to as The Great Vehicle. Mahayana is known as the most compassionate, altruistic, selfless way to enlightenment. The Great Vehicle can be likened to Noah's ark, a noble ship that delivers all beings across the raging oceans of continued suffering to the so-called other shore of nirvana. Let go, open your heart, unfold your spiritual sails, open your angelic wings, and soar on the wind. Enjoy the infinite.

## Mingling Dharma with Your Daily Life

When I lived in my teacher's monastery in Nepal, the most traditional lamas had thick, handwritten books of power words or phrases known as mantras. These books included a mantralike benediction for every single activity. There was a mantra for walking through a door or eating a meal, just as there was a mantra for using the toilet. These mantras were significantly more than mere words or empty rituals performed mechanically by rote. They were used to bring a practice of mindfulness, meditation, and gratitude into everything that was done. Many Western families grow up with a tradition of saying grace before meals. In Buddhism, a moment of mindfulness is like a "grace"; these moments can consecrate every activity, waking each of us up to the sacredness of what we do, as we do it. In this way, we recognize everything we do as a spiritual activity.

Here are some ways that we can cultivate mindful awareness and bring meditation, calm, and clarity into our daily activities:

◉ Breathe and smile. Relax. Take a moment to let go, and just be. Enjoy it.

◉ Do standing meditation, while waiting in line for a movie or bus or train. Just stand there, breathe, and awaken.

◉ Whenever you sit down or stand up, stop and appreciate a moment of change, of freedom.

◉ Whenever you cross a threshold, go through a doorway, or enter a room, see it as entering a temple and do so reverently.

◉ Walk barefoot in the grass or on a thick carpet and feel fully each sensation with your toes and soles.

◎ Walk on the edge of a beach, where the water meets the sand, with your eyes closed, feeling your way along, totally vigilant and attentive.

◎ Walk slowly upon crunchy snow or autumn leaves, attending to the crackle of each step.

◎ Sing, chant, or pray till you totally forget and lose yourself; then stop and drop into a moment of inexpressible *isness,* completely beyond concepts, stories, and strategies.

◎ Experience simple, repetitive work like sewing, embroidering, or even washing dishes as meditation in action, focusing totally on the moment in hand and nothing else.

◎ Try doing manual labor in a sacred manner, just doing what you are doing as if it is the ultimate divine service, for it is.

◎ When eating, chew each mouthful fifty or one hundred times, getting the most out of the food as well as being further nourished by the richness of each moment.

◎ Try chewing one single raisin for several minutes and experiencing everything you can about it.

◎ Before speaking, notice what motivates your words.

◎ Set a beeper on your watch or alarm clock to ring every hour on the hour, reminding you to wake up and appreciate the miracle of every moment. Call yourself by name and say, "Wake up!"

◎ Recognize the Buddha-light shining in everyone and everything and treat others accordingly.

◎ Enjoy the indescribable joy and peace of meditation.

# PART TWO

## Walking the Eight-Fold Path to Enlightenment—The Heroic Journey

How joyful to look upon the Awakened
and to keep company with the wise.

Follow then the shining ones,
the wise, the awakened, the loving,
for they know how to work and forbear.

But if you cannot find
friend or master to go with you,
travel on alone—
like a king who has given away his kingdom,
like an elephant in the forest.
—From the Dhammapada
(Sayings of the Buddha)

# THE FOUR NOBLE TRUTHS

## *The Facts of Life from a*

## *Buddhist Perspective*

*How wonderful!*
*How wonderful!*
*All things are*
*perfect*
*exactly as they*
*are!*

—THE BUDDHA

When the Buddha realized perfect enlightenment, the veils of illusion fell from his eyes. Free of the snares of desire, he had finally achieved lasting happiness. His wisdom-eye fully opened, the truth of "what is" became evident. He said he perceived and remembered hundreds of his past lives; he knew and understood the intricate and precise laws of karma and rebirth; and he recognized the workings of ignorance, attachment, and desire. The awakened Buddha finally realized why life often seems so troubling.

Imagine for a moment that you suddenly knew everything that could be known about all things seen and unseen—the true and ultimate secret of life. What would you do if the gossamer curtain that stands between you and complete understanding was pulled back? Some even say the Buddha attained omniscience through his enlightenment experience. For a moment, try to imagine what the Buddha must have felt when the clouds obscuring his vision suddenly parted, and the ever-present shining sun of reality broke through.

For the first few weeks after the Buddha's great awakening, he continued to meditate at the bodhi tree, reflecting upon what he had realized. He wasn't immediately sure what to do with this unique remarkable truth, this Dharma that was now one with his being; he hadn't yet decided whether to teach or remain silent. Initially he thought he might not find others who would be able to perceive and understand what he taught. Then he recalled five mendicants, seekers who had been his companions. Remembering that their eyes had been only thinly veiled by delusion's dust, he determined to find them. He would share what he knew, and they would inevitably benefit from it.

The Buddha then traveled northwest toward the town now known as Benares. Crossing the Ganges, he walked for several days until he arrived at the Deer Park in Sarnath. There he met the five mendicants who would become his first disciples. To them he gave his first Dharma talk explaining the Four Noble Truths, the facts of life from an enlightened perspective. We are told that the Buddha's message was so transformative that they became enlightened on the spot.

## THE FOUR NOBLE TRUTHS

The Four Noble Truths are the core of the Buddhist Dharma. Yet they are probably the most misunderstood of the Buddha's teachings. On the face of it, the Four Noble Truths have a clear and simple message: *It is the nature of life that all beings will face difficulties; through enlightened living one can transcend these difficulties, ultimately becoming fulfilled, liberated, and free.*

*The First Noble Truth:* Life is difficult.

*The Second Noble Truth:* Life is difficult because of attachment, because we crave satisfaction in ways that are inherently dissatisfying.

*The Third Noble Truth:* The possibility of liberation from difficulties exists for everyone.

*The Fourth Noble Truth:* The way to realize this liberation and enlightenment is by leading a compassionate life of virtue, wisdom, and meditation. These three spiritual trainings comprise the teachings of the Eight-Fold Path to Enlightenment.

The above is a brief summary. Now let's unpack the Four Noble Truths in a more thorough way.

## FACT OF LIFE #1

*The First Noble Truth* is known as the truth of dukkha. Etymologically speaking, the literal meanings of dukkha are "hard to bear," "dissatisfactory," "off the mark," "frustrating," and "hollow." The word dukkha, however, is frequently translated as suffering. This concept, the so-called "bad news" of Buddhism, has led some people to misconstrue Buddhism as pessimistic and life-denying. Yet Buddha's primary message, the "good news" of Dharma, is that there is a way to be free of suffering. The message of the Dharma is inherently optimistic; it contains the promise, the real possibility, of spiritual rebirth and the end of suffering—the deathless spiritual enlightenment known as nirvana.

Buddha Dharma *does not* teach that everything is suffering. What Buddhism does say is that life, by its nature, is difficult, flawed, and imperfect. For most of us, this fact of life hardly merits a news flash. Who among us has a perfect life? Of course we would like it to be delightful and wonderful all the time. But it's not going to happen. That's the nature of life, and that's the First Noble Truth. From a Buddhist point of view, this is not a judgment of life's joys or sorrows; this is a simple, down-to-earth, matter-of-fact description. The fact is that we will all experience ups and downs no matter who we are. That's part of the roller-coaster ride. Buddhism is neither pessimistic nor optimistic; it is realistic.

For a moment, let's stop and think about the First Noble Truth, the truth of dukkha from the Buddha's point of view. As a child and young adult, he was protected from the facts of life—the facts of illness, death, unhappiness, and poverty. In his father's palace, totally sheltered from reality, he was taught that his riches, his beauty, his physical prowess, and his power would protect him from any hardship.

On a visceral level, the Buddha must have always realized that the world was filled with suffering no matter how much his father tried to shield him from reality. It's interesting to note that the Buddha's mother died within weeks of giving birth, and Buddha must have had questions about what had happened to her, but those questions were never answered. Modern psychologists might even say that the Buddha was raised to be in denial. We all know that denial is the psychological defense system we use to protect ourselves when the truth seems too painful to bear. As he matured, the Buddha didn't want that kind of insulation from reality. He recognized that no matter how many possessions or how much power he had, ultimately he would not be able to avoid life's inherent problems. No one can.

Like all of us, the Buddha was challenged by his own attachment to worldly values. An essential part of his path to freedom was to put those values in perspective and recognize any residual clinging he might have to worldly pleasures. He had to break through the obscurations of delusion—his own denial—and see the reality of conditioned existence, known as samsara, with all its inherent shortcomings. For all of us, this is an essential part of the path to enlightenment: Awaken your innate, inner Buddha; break through the denial systems in your life; see through the veils of illusion; recognize who and what you truly are; and know the truth of things exactly as they are.

The Buddha broke down life's problems into three separate categories of dukkha, or difficulties.

## 1. Ordinary, Everyday Difficulties or Dukkha

You don't always get what you think you want, and that makes most people feel unhappy at least some of the time. If you are born, you are eventually bound to experience both physical and emotional pain. Birth, aging, illness, loss, grieving, as well as disappointments happen to every single one of us. This isn't all bad. We can learn a great deal from the problems, both large and small, that we experience. Everyday problems teach us to have a realistic attitude. They teach us that life is what life is: flawed, yet with tremendous potential for joy and fulfillment. Everything is workable. Until we fully learn this lesson, we are burned time and again by our unrealistic expectations.

One of the Buddha's most famous sermons is known as the Fire Sermon. In it, he said that we are all afire with uncontrolled passions that consume and dominate our lives. Because of these passions, we are like children in burning houses. We don't have the maturity or the self-mastery to recognize our situation and swiftly douse those fires. We must grow up and learn how to be mature and liberated adults, who understand the nature of reality. Balloons break, love affairs carry no guarantees, and everyone has to visit the dentist. Everything in life is at least a little bit broken or unreliable and tenuous.

My father's greatest wish for me was that I would become what is known in Yiddish as a "mensch" or *real* person. By that he meant that he wanted me to be a mature adult, a human being, not otherworldly and divine; he wanted me to be fully present and accounted for, here in this world, a contributing member of society, a decent citizen and a righteous man. Maturity brings understanding, discernment, character, responsibility, moderation, and balance.

## 2. Difficulties or Dukkha Caused by Changing Circumstances

My favorite season is autumn; my favorite time of the day is sunset. These are beautiful times—poignant and ever so fleeting. Isn't that true of many of life's loveliest moments? Of course, there are times in all our lives when we feel totally overjoyed by the wonder of being alive. Think about your own life: Perhaps you spent last night listening to a great piece of music; perhaps you had a terrific conversation with your best friends while sharing a splendid meal in comfortable surroundings; perhaps you just celebrated the promotion you wanted; perhaps you experienced a spiritual epiphany. These are moments of genuine happiness. The difficulty, or dukkha, that we all face is that these moments don't last: The music ends, your friends get a divorce, the new job you thought you wanted turns into a stress-producing headache, moments of cosmic love and bliss are fleeting. Thus we frequently end up feeling nostalgia, disappointment, and loss. Nothing good lasts forever; even the best moments of life are laced with a bittersweet quality. This is known as the dukkha of changing circumstances.

## 3. Difficulties or Dukkha Caused by the Flawed Nature of Conditioned Existence

When we look inside—when we wonder who and what we are and what's going on, when we ask who is experiencing our experience—what do we find, if anything? Who am I? What am I? Where is the experiencer? Is it in my head? My brain? My heart? My legs? My body? My mind? What do we find? What are we really?

The Buddha said that as individuals, we are composed of nothing but the Five Skandhas. The word skandha is difficult to translate with precision. It means heap, aggregate, or conglomeration of individuality. It means that we are all congeries, complex collections and combinations; we are ever-changing, not the eternal, independently existing individuals we often think we are.

The Five Skandhas (or components of individuality) are:

### 1. Form
Are you tall, short, medium? Ectomorph? Endomorph? This is your form, your corporeal body. Form includes all matter or materiality: the physical elements of earth (solidity); water (fluidity); fire (heat); air (movement); and space (cavities)—all of which comprise our human being.

### 2. Feelings or sensations
Westerners learned in school that there are five senses—sight (eye), sound (ear), smell (nose), taste (tongue), and touch (skin). To this group mentalistic Buddhists add another sensory organ, and that is

"mind." We "see" a sunset; we "hear" a bell; we "smell" a lilac; we "taste" a lemon; we "touch" a cat. These five physical senses help us experience much of the physical world. But there is the world of ideas and thoughts; this world cannot be seen, heard, smelled, tasted, or touched. To cope with this world we use the faculties, or senses, of the mind and of thought. We "know" how to drive; we "know" how to speak a foreign language. Thus the faculties of mind are our sixth sense.

### 3. Perceptions
Perception combines feelings and sensations with recognition and judgments. What looks good to you? What tastes good to you? What kind of music do you like? Have your tastes in music changed as you've matured? How about your taste in people? Do you perceive people differently now than you did when you were younger? What are your personal likes and dislikes?

### 4. Intentionality or will
Are you basically a person of good will, which means that you have good intentions? What do you wish or intend for yourself? Your children? Your friends? What motivates or moves you? What are your intentions? Why do you do what you do? This skandha includes all volitional activities. As the Buddha pointed out, your intentions create your karma. Your will and intentions direct your mind, which controls the way you think, speak, and act. Your intentions establish the priorities in your life. Your past intentions condition or perpetuate your present intentions, habits, and propensities. This is where karma is created.

### 5. Consciousness
A dog walks into the room, and you become conscious of it. A loud radio blares on the street, and the sound stimulates your ear consciousness. The Buddha, who was very precise in his psychological analysis and definitions, taught that there is visual (eye) consciousness, auditory (ear) consciousness, olfactory (nose) consciousness, gustatory (taste) consciousness, tactile (body) consciousness, and mental consciousness. In short, one is conscious of each of the six senses; this consciousness, which you presently think of as yours, is comprised of six different basic facets.

Now what, you may ask, do the Five Skandhas have to do with the First Noble Truth? Buddha Dharma, which directs our attention to the real possibility of living something deeper and ultimately more satisfying, outlines the Five Skandhas as a way to point out the tenuous and unreliable nature of the shifting conditional reality we know as life.

Our bodies have limited shelf lives; they are impermanent and changeable. This is not religious dogma; this is just how it is. Being ephemeral, our bodies are ultimately dissatisfying. Who can get lasting fulfillment from a mere body, from sensual experiences? Even the most exquisite body experiences are fleeting and ephemeral, leaving us thirsting for more.

Our feelings are certainly ephemeral; so are our perceptions. Ditto our intentions. States of consciousness change all the time. In fact, we are all works in progress; like it or not, we are never the same. Remember the Greek philosopher, Heraclitus, who said, "You can't step into the same river twice." Each of us is like a river, whose waters are forever changing. Westerners often use "mind" as a primary definition for the self. "I think, therefore I am." But Buddhism points out that you are not what you think; like the weather, what you think is unpredictable and subject to change. Because of this the untrained mind is also essentially unreliable. Your thoughts and feelings lack permanence. This is a fact of conditioned, conventional existence. Moreover, who and what are you when you are not thinking, or in the brief moment in between thoughts? Do we intermittently cease to exist?

On the other hand, your innate, ineffable Buddha-nature is not impermanent; it is not subject to change. This inner light is unbound, untrammelled, and immaculate. It can be relied on; it can be depended upon. It is perfect, inherently wise and warm, free and complete from the beginningless beginning. Actualizing that luminous, formless, and intangible core is what awakening is all about.

## FACT OF LIFE #2

*The Second Noble Truth* tells us that there is a cause for life's difficulties (or dukkha) and that cause is craving. The Pali word is tanha, and it suggests a state of incessant, never-ending thirst—a craving that won't quit. Because all of us consistently desire, hunger, and thirst for various experiences and different things, we continue to suffer. It's not that we have to get rid of the things we desire. The objects are not the problem. It is our attachment and our identification with what we crave that causes suffering. Tilopa, a wandering tenth-century yogi, sang, "It is not the outer objects that entangle us. It is the inner clinging that entangles us."

People who misinterpret the Buddha's teachings often worry that if they rid themselves of craving, they will no longer be able to love or live with passion. Quite the opposite is true. We will still have our healthy desires, but now they won't be contaminated and misdirected by insatiable craving. The Buddha never taught that we shouldn't feel love. In fact, he preached universal love and compassion. One entire sutra spoken by Buddha teaches how we can learn to love, to cultivate loving-kindness, empathy, and inclusiveness. What the Buddha taught is that we shouldn't try to own each other, nor should we become so identified or attached to anything (person, thought, feeling, career, goal, or material object) that we lose sight of reality—of the relativism and changing nature of all that is.

To understand why the Dharma teaches that the insatiable thirst and clinging of craving causes life's problems, you have to be very clear about what Craving and Clinging with capital Cs do. Have you ever heard someone say, "I wanted it/him/her so badly I was out of my mind," or "I would do anything to get [fill in the blank]"? The issue with craving is that it grabs control of your mind and your life. It takes over. In its most intense form, it is like being possessed by a demon.

How many hours of your day do you spend on a treadmill of activity trying to get what you think you want? At what point do all those endless hours spell out obsession? How much of your mind and time is spent fantasizing about the things you desire? It's all too easy to use up most of the hours in our lives being obsessed with romance, career, money, unrequited or turbulent love, hobbies, sex, or pleasure. Like a muddy cloud, craving obscures your unfettered, radiant spiritual nature.

In this culture who can resist an almost mindless thirst for sensual pleasures, wealth, or power? There are so many billboards, so many advertisements, and so many shopping malls grabbing our attention. Don't you often feel buffeted by the gusts of "coming attractions" clamoring for your attention? Catalogues arrive in the mail daily. How can we learn to look at them without craving the Adirondack chairs, the outdoor equipment, the overstuffed sofas with removable slipcovers, the perfect winter jackets worn by the equally perfect models, or even the models themselves? What can we do with our craving in a world in which we are all encouraged to lead fantasy lives in which we are always investing in the uncertain future, waiting and hoping to be picked up and carried off by a savior on a white horse, in a red convertible, or even in a friendly spaceship.

There is a one-word antidote to thirst or craving: *wisdom*. The wisdom of freedom from craving. The secret teachings of Tibet tell us that we can rediscover our innate wisdom, awareness, and inner joy through spiritual practices, including meditation, self-inquiry, prayer, and the cultivation of our naturally warm, tender, loving heart. Wisdom is the means to transcend craving and transform a treadmill existence into a lovely inspiring garden walk. This is true freedom.

Speaking to his disciples, the Buddha said, "Whoever in this world overcomes this craving so hard to transcend will find that suffering falls away like drops of water falling from a flower."

## FACT OF LIFE #3

*The Third Noble Truth* is that nirvana exists, and that it can exist for you. Nirvana is inconceivable inner peace, the cessation of craving and clinging. It is the end of suffering. Nirvana is liberation, everlasting freedom, fulfillment, and enlightenment itself.

Where is nirvana? If it's not right here, it is nowhere. So how do we experience it? Jesus Christ taught that the kingdom of heaven is within, and always available to everyone. The Tibetan masters teach that nirvana is ever present, just on the other side of our knot of clinging. According to the Tibetan teachings of Dzogchen, we can actually experience nirvana in a moment. It's not something that we have to build up or fabricate; it's available through spiritual breakthrough. These are the "Aha!" experiences that can be precipitated by simply letting go, by relinquishing craving, attachment, greed, and delusion, by waking up even for a moment from the dream of our semiconscious lives.

The word nirvana etymologically means extinction of thirst and the annihilation of suffering. Buddhist masters teach that within each of us there is always a fire. Sometimes this fire is quietly smoldering; other times it is raging out of control. This fire is caused by the friction of duality rubbing against itself, like two sticks. This friction is generated by me (as subject) wanting other (as object) and the interaction between the two. This ever-present friction that irritates us blazes up into the fires of suffering. When we realize emptiness and perfect oneness with all, the fires of duality go out. When even the embers themselves are cool, when conflicting emotions are no longer burning us—this is nirvana, the end of dissatisfaction and suffering. This is liberation; this is bliss; this is true freedom.

The freedom from craving spoken of by the Buddha is an inconceivable inner peace, a sense of at-one-ness and completion. Yet many people are terrified by this concept because they associate craving with passion. "What!" they say, "no passion? No passion equals no life! No passion means I might as well be dead!" This is a nihilistic, or extreme, version of what freedom from craving means. The mind that is free of craving is much more abundant and fruitful than such superficial notions might suggest.

All freedom from craving really means is peace and contentment. When you are momentarily satisfied, don't you feel even more aliveness and enlivenment? Fearing desirelessness is akin to running from lasting happiness. The lasting happiness the Buddha speaks of does not mean having no personality or passion. Desirelessness means lacking nothing. Consider this possibility with all its implications for your life and behavior.

The point is that you are much more than your cravings and desires. Enlightened people have preferences. I don't know if you know any people who you believe are enlightened. I have known a few, and they all have their own likes and dislikes, their own individual, personal style. This tells us that enlightenment, freedom,

Buddha-nature, lives and expresses itself through each personality. Each of us is different, thank God, not uniformly bland like some kind of fake dessert topping.

When they are visiting in this country, enlightened lamas still prefer their Tibetan noodles over pizza. But they don't get upset about not being able to attain their preferred food. They are not invested or identified with their desires. Spiritual masters are able to be in the world, but not of it. They are sometimes likened to graceful, snow-colored swans who travel the lakes of this world without making waves.

## In the World, but Not of It

One of the principal Buddhist images is the lotus, which grows up through the water and raises its face to the shining sun; it is in the mud, but not of it. The Buddha is most often imaged sitting on a lotus. In fact, the sitting position with legs crossed and the soles of the feet upturned on the thighs is called the lotus posture. The lotus symbolizes purity, development, and transcendence; the fully blossomed lotus represents our fully unfolded innate Buddha-nature.

Achieving freedom from craving and being in the world, yet not quite *of* it, is up to us; achieving liberation, lasting happiness, and freedom is up to us. We are the fire starters; we are the troublemakers; our clouded vision and limited understanding creates the duality of subject and object, grasper and grasped. That's why the Dzogchen meditation instruction of resting at ease in the natural state is so relevant. When there is nothing wanting, there is nothing working against anything. There is no grasping at anything; there is no grasper and nothing being grasped. There are no karmic sticks rubbing together igniting these fiery conflicting passions; there is no clinging to sights or sounds or smells or tastes or touches. There is just the unimpeded, spontaneous, free experiencing of things just as they are, moment after miraculous moment. This is the natural great perfection.

As Buddha said, "In seeing, there is just seeing; no seer and nothing seen. In hearing, there is just hearing; no hearer and nothing heard." This suggests *Thoughts Without a Thinker,* as Buddhist psychologist Mark Epstein called his book on psychotherapy and Dharma. Buddha said that in hearing there is just hearing; no one hearing and nothing heard. Can we be that empty, open, vividly present, and transparently clear? The answer is that we choose not to be. The concept of thoughts without a thinker is too scary—particularly when you are the thinker, and they are your thoughts. Letting go of the dualistic perspective takes a valiant heart—the courage of a spiritual warrior intent on transcendence and total integration.

Once, when Allen Ginsberg was in Colorado to do a one-month solitary meditation retreat, he told his lama, Trungpa Rinpoche, that he was going to bring little notepads that he would keep by his meditation cushion so he could write down the beautiful haiku that would flash into his mind after many hours of meditation. The lama said, "Can I see your pads and pens?" When Ginsberg displayed the tools of his literary trade, the lama snatched them away, saying that the reason to go on retreat and meditate is to *stop* collecting and holding on to all those transient thought bubbles. He exhorted Ginsberg simply to be aware of the ongoing process of transparent awareness itself, rather than getting caught up in collecting the flotsam and jetsam of the mind and continuously rearranging its contents in the display cases of artistic ambition.

Ginsberg loved to tell this story, because he was still—like all of us—so attached to displaying beautiful thought bubbles. The more we meditate, the more good ideas we seem to get, don't we? We can't wait to get back home and tell somebody, write about them, paint them, bottle them, and market them. Samsara cologne, nirvana books and tapes, enlightenment records, greeting cards, and calendars. Guru Beer! (Yes, there is such a brand, made in India.)

Nirvana, the end of all our troubles, the extinction of this fire of craving, is just on the other side of each moment of craving, of hanging on. That's where the great "letting go" comes in and must take place. Then ultimate peace is right there; total fulfillment, wholeness, the end of all craving, luminous and profound; simple not complicated; unfathomable, bottomless, yet inexhaustibly rich. Not like those little thought bubbles we are always trying to collect so that at least we have something to show for ourselves—a whole pile of little thought bubbles on a pad, big deal! Is that all we shall have at the sunset of our lives, a big, frothy pile of foam?

Of course we love poetry, and we love everything that is sparkling, original, and fresh. Still, all that is stale compared to simply experiencing the absolutely startling, poetic freshness of the present moment without having to write down, collect, preserve, or fabricate *anything*. Then every moment bespeaks truth.

According to the Buddha himself, nirvana is simply the relinquishment of craving, of clinging, of attachment. Yet this is not a small thing. The more our spiritual practice, our meditation, and our daily activity is congruent with desirelessness and nonattachment—the less inflexible, demanding, selfish, and greedy we are—the more nirvana starts to creep in, almost insidiously. Even if nirvana is right here, *we* are often elsewhere!

Nirvana is always trying to seep through the small chinks in our ego's armor. You can widen these openings by relinquishing some of the defenses and barricades of your persona, your holding on, your repetitive, addictive, habitual behavior—in short, your psychological conditioning. When we really do "let go" and get used to letting go, that inner conflict, that irritation, that friction heat of dukkha actually does die down, and we can experience more and more of the inner peace that nirvana epitomizes. We become less dependent, less demanding, less complicated, less scattered and alienated, less speedy, needy, and greedy. We become more healed, whole, happy, healthy, and wise. We feel totally renewed.

## FACT OF LIFE #4

*The Fourth Noble Truth* tells us that there is a tried-and-true path that leads us away from the dissatisfaction of conditioned existence and toward the end of craving known as nirvana. This path is known as the Noble Eight-Fold Path to Enlightenment, and it reflects the Buddha's specific instructions on how to purify one's heart and mind by living an impeccable and enlightened life. This is about living the Dharma day to day through everything you do. We Westerners often just grab hold of one meditation technique from the entire Dharma teaching; then we may wonder why our lives haven't changed as promised. Of course it helps to train our minds by meditating every morning, but it helps a lot more if we try to round out our lives by assimilating all of the various elements of the Dharma. Following this path is the way of the spiritual hero.

## CHALLENGES, HANG-UPS, AND HINDRANCES ON THE EIGHT-FOLD PATH

*The one who has conquered himself is a far greater hero than he who has defeated a thousand times a thousand men.*

—FROM THE DHAMMAPADA
(SAYINGS OF THE BUDDHA)

The Buddha taught that the spiritual seeker could expect to be confronted with some classic hindrances on his way. As you walk the inner path of awakening, recognize that it is most definitely a heroic and mythic journey. Like all heroic journeys, yours will be filled with awe-inspiring mysteries, fearful difficulties, and outstanding adventures. But you must be prepared to meet and overcome obstacles; you must be prepared for roadblocks; you must be prepared to go places that at first seem frightening and incomprehensible. You must be prepared to make sacrifices, and yes, of course you must be prepared to change. Just as a caterpillar must shed its familiar cocoon in order to become a butterfly and fly, we must be willing to change and shed the cocoon or hard armor of self-centered egotism.

As compelling as the inner journey is, it can be difficult because it brings you face to face with reality; it brings you face to face with who and what you really are. Trying to embody the Dharma and live truly must have its perilous moments because there will always be challenges to meet, leaps and stretches to be made, and obstacles to overcome.

A spiritual journey inevitably includes low valleys as well as high mountains, dense forests as well as seemingly barren deserts, plateaus, and plains. This is the landscape and territory of your own being. It is all-revealing and it all needs exploration. Everything you experience along the way can be a way of helping you awaken the Buddha within.

As you journey, obstacles will attempt to get in your way—for you are in your own way. Recognize the ways that difficulties and challenges are born from your own hang-ups, obscurations, fears, and karma. Whether the path on which you find yourself is momentarily steep or level; rough, smooth, or slippery; turbulent or calm, you will prove to be your own greatest asset, as well as your greatest stumbling block. How will you help yourself, and how will you hinder yourself? Which habits and patterns will you let go of easily, and which will have the tenacity of superglue? Are we desperate enough to really undergo total change and transformation?

The Buddha's teachings were initially directed to disciples and serious students, and his instructions were specifically addressed to those living, or preparing to live, the monastic life of simplicity and renunciation. The stumbling blocks or hindrances that these ancient seekers confronted sometimes took a different form than the challenges we meet today. Nonetheless the underlying themes are exactly the same. *Then, and now, the hindrances, or challenges, all have the power to distort the seeker's view of reality.*

How do you know that you are confronting a classic "hindrance" on your spiritual path? Just ask yourself: Am I losing my sense of balance, my sense of priorities, and my sense of what's really important? Am I being carried away by temporary reactions, by destructive emotions? That's what challenges do; they obstruct your insight and prevent you from seeing things as they really are. They stand between you and the calm clear awareness of the enlightened mind. The Buddha listed five primary hindrances or challenges:

- craving

- ill will

- sloth and torpor (spiritual laziness)

- restlessness

- doubt

The Buddha personally confronted each of these challenges; he had firsthand experience of how these challenges confuse the spiritual seeker. Like the Buddha, at one time or another, you can expect to confront all of these on the spiritual path. As we learn more about the Eight-Fold Path, we will also be examining some of the ways these challenges will present themselves.

Buddha himself recognized that each of us will be facing different situations; we each have our own karma to work with. The all-knowing Buddha, who understood that each of us has to walk our own spiritual path to enlightenment, said, "Each one has to practice and strive for himself, the Perfect Ones have only pointed the way."

## MAINTAINING THE BALANCE BETWEEN COMPASSION AND WISDOM

The Eight-Fold Path is also known as the Middle Path or Middle Way. To understand the significance of this, let's once again remember the historical Buddha. During his lifetime, spiritual seekers and yogis typically chose a path of extreme asceticism, including self-mortification. This was in marked contrast to those who tried to find happiness solely through the worldly search for sensual or material pleasure.

The Buddha knew firsthand both ways of life. Like many of us, the man we know as Buddha initially experienced life as a series of extremes: extreme attitudes toward money, pleasure, and entitlement; extreme emotional needs and desires; and extreme physical and spiritual conditions. Despite his luxurious surroundings, the

Buddha was dissatisfied, bored, and somewhat depressed living in his palace. H. G. Wells once wrote of the Buddha that his "was the unhappiness of a fine mind that needs employment." Perhaps we can identify with that ourselves.

When the Buddha first left his palace and donned a mendicant's tattered yellow robe, he became an ascetic wandering holy man, determined to reach enlightenment as quickly as possible for the benefit of the world. For six years, he led a life of the most rigorous austerity. While he was meditating day and night, it is said that for several weeks he ate only a single grain of rice every day, becoming starved and emaciated. Yet despite all his efforts, he felt that the goal of enlightenment was eluding him.

What the Buddha finally realized after reaching the verge of death from starvation is that the man or woman who is seeking truth first has to move away from the extremes of either self-indulgent passion or self-inflicted mortification in order to find the path that is moderation's Middle Way. The Buddha saw that a perfectly realized spiritual life is not a carnival ride of exhilarating ups and terror-inspiring lows.

The Buddha's lesson for all of us is that happiness and/or nirvana cannot be found in a life mainly devoted to caring for sensual gratification (more money, sex, vacations, status, pride, or any other materialistic variation on the theme of more). But surprisingly enough, the Buddha also taught us that a life devoted to self-denial, self-deprecation, or self-blame and guilt is equally foolish and misdirected. Attachment is still attachment, even if that attachment takes the inverted form of self-denial and self-loathing.

The Middle Way is the way of balance, sanity, inner strength, purity and restraint, steadfastness, and moderation. The Middle Way points the seeker in the direction of an impeccable *and* integrated life. To remain whole, as well as to become whole, requires a complete inward arc, or full circle, rather than just a linear achievement-oriented race to grace. With these eight-step Middle Way instructions, Buddhism shows us that in life, each of us is capable of developing qualities of the heart in equal measure with qualities of the head: compassion with wisdom; love with truth. We need to awaken the mind as well as open the heart to let reality in, to let others in, to realize for ourselves the natural great perfection that is our birthright—the Buddha's legacy for us today.

# THE EIGHT-FOLD PATH, ONE STEP AT A TIME

*Best among paths is the Eight-Fold Path.*

—THE BUDDHA

The eight steps to enlightenment on the Noble Eight-Fold Path are as follows:

WISDOM TRAINING

Step 1. Right View

Step 2. Right Intentions

ETHICS TRAINING

Step 3. Right Speech

Step 4. Right Action

Step 5. Right Livelihood

MEDITATION TRAINING

Step 6. Right Effort

Step 7. Right Mindfulness

Step 8. Right Concentration

Although these are listed in numerical order, the Buddha's intent was that they were to be thought of as a circle, or an eight-spoked wheel with interconnected links directed at helping you develop the three essential values of Buddhism: wisdom, ethics, meditative awareness.

Wisdom, ethics, and meditative awareness are known as the Three Higher or Enlightenment Trainings. Inseparable, they support each other, like a tripod or three facets of a single, luminous jewel. Waking your inner Buddha depends upon actualizing these qualities in your life.

# WISDOM

# TRAINING

## *Seeing Things As*

## *They Are*

*In order to swim one takes off all one's clothes—in order to aspire to the truth one must undress in a far more inward sense, divest oneself of all one's inward clothes, of thoughts, conceptions, selfishness, etc., before one is sufficiently naked.*
—SÖREN KIERKEGAARD

Right View and Right Intentions are the two steps on the Eight-Fold Path that focus on wisdom. The Sanskrit word for wisdom is prajna, which reminds us to see the truth by cultivating enlightened awareness and self-knowledge.

Outwardly, we find wisdom functioning in life very practically as sagacity and even as uncommon common sense. Wise people are usually discerning about many things, not just about one narrow, specialized field. Rather, they are wise in the ways of this world and, perhaps, "other worlds" as well. People who are wise seem to be able to deal with life—and the reality of death.

Inwardly, wisdom shows up as sanity, centeredness, and equanimity. Men and women who are wise seem fulfilled and radiate a sense of inner peace—at home with self and others. With wisdom comes joy, warmth, kindness, connectedness, integrity, and love. We can all cultivate this; we can all plumb the deep inner well and heal ourselves.

Innately, another form of wisdom—gnosis, transcendence, and wise unselfishness—is within us all. The ultimate form of wisdom is not something we do; it is our true nature and being. It isn't just information or intellectual learning. Wisdom may sound like knowledge, but it is more like our luminous pure authentic inner being. Can we tune into that? Can we trust that? That awareness is transcendental wisdom. We may or may not have a formal religious or spiritual affiliation. Most religious groups have only been around a few thousand years. But *being* itself—that mystical sacrament, that mysterious and sacred space, or infinite expanse of spirit—has been around much longer. Primordial being is what we call it in the Dzogchen tradition. Authentic primordial being is Pure Presence, or Rigpa. Buddha-mind. Dharmakaya, the invisible body of truth. This is true wisdom.

Right View or Authentic Vision comes first on the Dharma path of wisdom and enlightenment, because your worldview determines the direction your life will take. Right Intentions, the second step, helps us direct our sights to that goal.

# RIGHT VIEW

## *The Wisdom of Clear Vision*

The Radiant Buddha said:
Regard this fleeting world like this:
Like stars fading and vanishing at dawn,
like bubbles on a fast moving stream,
like morning dewdrops evaporating on blades
    of grass,
like a candle flickering in a strong wind,
echos, mirages, and phantoms, hallucinations,
and like a dream.

—THE EIGHT SIMILES OF ILLUSION,
    FROM THE PRAJNA PARAMITA
        SUTRAS

Many Buddhist teachers, including myself, often chant these eight similes of illusion, particularly at the beginning or end of certain meditation sessions. I love these poetic similes and find them useful as a meditative reflection in the form of a series of striking images that can be contemplated daily.

In his many teachings, the Buddha was very clear about his view of the world, which he liked to call "this *saha* world." Saha is a Sanskrit word meaning impossible to grasp, or insubstantial. It's sometimes translated as this floating world, this vaporous or dew-drop world. Literally saha means "rosebush-like"—beautifully replete with flowers, but thorny to those who choose to try to grab it too tightly. This presents another vivid view of samsara, or conditioned existence.

Right View is the reliable touchstone that reminds us to look at the world without any delusions or distortions about reality, or ourselves; to see roses where there are roses, thorns where there are thorns. Right View emphasizes the development of wisdom or prajna, which at its essence means knowing what is, knowing how things work, and knowing oneself and others.

Long before psychologists were talking about "reality testing," "delusional systems," or "denial," Buddha Dharma was exhorting spiritual seekers to know and understand themselves; it was telling them to look at the world realistically and see the truth of exactly what is taking place in the here and now at any given moment in time. When we open our wisdom eyes, we don't necessarily get to choose what we see. It's just what *is*. This can be challenging, yet when we move away from fantasy and see how things actually are, we are freed from illusion and can begin to live more fully in accord with reality.

## GETTING REAL, BECOMING CLUED IN

Can you see the world as it really is; are you ready to see yourself as you really are? We're on the cutting edge of the new millennium, and we have new terms to describe human behavior that the Buddha first talked about centuries ago. "Clueless" is a workable, colorful word that on some level can be applied to most of us, for at least part of our lives. "Without a clue," "out of it," "in a fog," "not in touch with the real world," "can't see the forest for the trees," "controlled by fantasies," "spaced out." We could go on at some length, but all these words and terms reach the same conclusions.

Aren't we all somewhat unrealistic and even fantasy driven? Don't we all spend too much time in foggy mental states? Don't we mess up our lives because we don't process reality as it's objectively taking place? We tell ourselves stories about our lives; we tell ourselves what we want to hear, and in so doing we create and perpetuate fantasies. This first step on the Noble Eight-Fold Path tells seekers to wipe the dust from their eyes, open their inner wisdom eyes, and discover clear vision. It tells us all that the time has come to "get real." Or at least as real as we get in this saha world.

Right View brings us in touch with some of the most important concepts in Buddhist philosophy. How do you perceive life, death, impermanence, suffering, dissatisfaction, and cause and effect? Do we really believe, and know, that we reap what we sow, or do we regard that as just another cliché? In the West, we are typically conditioned to push these serious matters aside, telling ourselves that we will deal with them later. Buddhism says deal with them now, and you will transform your life.

## THE DYSFUNCTIONAL MYTHS
## WE LIVE BY

Self-knowledge is in our own higher self-interest. Wisdom works for us. During his lifetime, the Buddha was asked a great many questions by his followers and others. Some of these dealt with large matters such as the origin of the universe; where we come from and where we are going; and what happens beyond death. But many other questions examined the specific issues of daily reality and everyday life. People faced the same kinds of issues we face now, but with different window dressing. In the time of the Buddha, men and women were arguing, gossiping, judging others, losing their perspective, overreacting, sexualizing their experiences, chasing after greener pastures, obsessing about nonessentials, feeling lonely, and creating too many pipe dreams. Nothing has fundamentally altered.

How many of us, for example, are still convinced, mature as we may be, that if our mate would only change, or if we could only meet the perfect person, everything would be fine? These are the dysfunctional myths and illusions that drive our lives in very dissatisfying directions. How many of you remember the song from the musical *Fiddler on the Roof*—"If I were a rich man . . ." What's your big "if"? The big "if" that leads you away from wisdom and reality?

The development of wisdom is greatly facilitated by seeing our little hypocrisies and large illusions and learning to be more forthright and honest with ourselves and others. Wisdom is seeing the true nature of things—exactly as described in the Four Noble Truths, or the Four Facts of Life according to enlightened vision. Wisdom is higher consciousness, wakefulness, and awareness. Wisdom is self-knowledge: Wisdom is truth manifested as clarity of vision. Wisdom sees that light and dark are inseparable and that shadows are also light.

## SAMSARA: THE CYCLE OF CONDITIONED EXISTENCE

Conditioned existence—that's a technical way of describing this flawed world. When we talk about people trying to fully embody a spiritual practice, we tend to speak in very lofty terms, but on a day-to-day level, many of us are trying to resolve gritty, here-and-now issues. As much as we may like to think of our concerns as primarily spiritual and having higher meaning and value, in fact we are also coping with the physical and psychological issues of this life, this world, and the times in which we live. Consider the following examples:

◎ Robert, who wants to connect with others in a more meaningful and satisfying way, feels that his lonely neediness has contributed to the several intense attachments he has formed to rejective women. He wants to be done with such unsatisfying patterns.

◎ Jennifer needs to do something about her anxiety. The smallest upset and she feels overwhelmed; her heart starts racing as she begins preparing for disaster. She wants to calm down.

◉ Debra is overly attached to her family and dependent on their approval; even as an adult, she is terrified of being alone. In search of herself, Debra has consulted sages and savants as well as crystals, psychic channels, and Tarot.

◉ Steven doesn't know to handle his fatigue and generalized sense of anger. Like many others Steven has taken a good look at the ladder of his own success and found that it is leaning against the wrong wall.

Conditioned existence, as these people experience it, often means living a life of superficial habits and compulsions. To some extent, that's how most of us live. Controlled by our psychological patterns (our internal conditioning), we are hostages to unconscious drives, needs, and impulses. We stay in jobs we hate; we repetitively choose relationships that are hurtful. We don't know how to break habits that are self-defeating; we don't know how to change patterns that are misguided; we don't know how to find better, more creatively satisfying ways of being. That's unconscious behavior and that's conditioned existence.

Whether your unconscious behavior finds its source in something that occurred in your childhood, as Freud thought, or in something that happened lifetimes ago, as a Buddhist belief in rebirth suggests, the end result is the same. What you are doing isn't working. Dissatisfied is dissatisfied. Unconscious is unconscious. Is there really a distinction between psychological or spiritual distress? Psychology and Buddhism are two different traditions with a shared truth: As long as you stay unconscious, asleep at the switch of your own life, true happiness will prove elusive.

The Buddha gave conditioned existence a name: samsara. Samsara is the Sanskrit word that describes the wheel of suffering that we perpetuate by doing the same thing time and time again. The literal definition of samsara is "perpetual wandering." In Western terms, samsara describes deeply entrenched conditioning and beings (all of us) who are looking for fulfillment and satisfaction in all the wrong places. More often than not, even though we are avidly seeking happiness, we are creating a certain amount of misery in the process.

Becoming enlightened means an end to samsara. It means spiritual renewal, returning to our own original, naturally clear and whole minds and hearts. We travel the spiritual path in order to gain freedom from compulsion, and from unfulfilling, frozen patterns of behavior, and to rediscover our authentic lives.

# DIAMONDLIKE VISION

"Develop a mind that clings to nothing" is a meditative maxim that comes from the Diamond Sutra, one of the wisdom scriptures of Mahayana Buddhism. The original Sanskrit name for this sutra refers to the diamond that can cut anything but cannot itself be cut. In this case, the word "diamond" refers to the keen discriminating edge of penetrating wisdom.

A large part of clear vision and diamondlike wisdom is seeing everything exactly as it is with all its magical but ephemeral beauty. The wise mind understands the limits in hanging on to that which is transient and dreamlike. The awakened mind is free flowing, natural, and well rounded. It's like Teflon—nothing sticks. On the other hand, the unawakened, ordinary mind is rigid, limited, and sticky like flypaper; the ordinary mind has corners and sharp jagged edges on which ideas get caught, hanging us up. Dualistic thinking is like Velcro; it takes two to tangle. Unitary vision is more like a crystal through which all forms of light can pass unimpeded.

In life this is played out when we find it difficult to shake off our thoughts or worries, as well as unable to get off our fixed positions and entrenched opinions. Even insignificant emotional memories don't roll off; instead they get attached and stuck; sometimes they fester and rot in place. The unawakened mind tries to grasp and hold on to emotions and things, which by their very nature are fleeting; it's like trying to grasp water between your hands.

If we understand that the cause of suffering and dissatisfaction is attachment, then it's obvious that the remedy is simply letting go. This is an absolutely essential ingredient in the Buddhist recipe for wisdom and enlightenment. Why are we afraid to let go and let the natural mind just be as it is, radiant, free, and aware? Why do we hold on to the past and resist the fresh current of nowness? Neurotic behavior is sometimes defined as a frozen pattern. It's very therapeutic to thaw our frozen patterns and develop spontaneity and awareness of "what is" and the joy of the present moment. *If you cling to nothing, you can handle anything.* This is wisdom. Try to grasp this, but lightly.

Let your mind flow, free from attachment to your belongings, ideas, agendas, schedule, passions—your very self identity, and develop the wisdom, self-detachment, and equanimity that realizes that all things are essentially equal. Each of us is unique, but we are not especially special; we are all interconnected notes in the same cosmic symphony. We may be differently shaped clay pots, but we are all made from the same mortal clay. Develop a god's eye view and appreciate the wisdom of clear vision.

## DEATH AS AN OPPORTUNITY FOR GROWTH

*If I had my life over again I should form the habit of nightly composing myself to thoughts of death. I would practice, as it were, the remembrance of death. There is no other practice which so intensifies life. Death, when it approaches, ought not to take one by surprise. It should be part of the full expectancy of life. Without an ever-present sense of death life is insipid. You might as well live on the whites of eggs.*

— MURIEL SPARK

We're all going to die one day. But who among us really believes it? It's such an obvious fact; why do we pretend it's never going to happen to us? Buddha called death and impermanence the most important teaching. He said, "Just as the elephant's footprint is the biggest footprint on the jungle floor, death is the greatest teacher . . . Yama Raja—the Lord of Death—is my teacher.

Death drove me to seek the deathless, to seek liberation from the bonds of birth and death."

Think about that: the Buddha said death—not some human teacher—was his primary guru. He said we should all keep the reality of death in the forefront of our consciousness so we can better prioritize our daily activities and thus better direct our attention to that which is most significant and meaningful. People sometimes find Buddhism pessimistic, saying there is too much talk about death. It's essential to understand that Buddhists don't contemplate death because they are morbid or depressed; they focus on death, mortality, and human frailty as a means of better understanding and appreciating life. After all, the Buddha lived and taught tirelessly for forty-five years after his enlightenment, enjoying his full term of life as a vibrant spiritual teacher in the society of his times.

About death, we say in the West, "Nobody returns to tell the tale." However, the reincarnated Tibetan lamas think otherwise. When I was twenty-one, my teacher Kalu Rinpoche told me that I should always prepare myself for the moment of death. That wasn't what I wanted to hear. I thought, this is just old monk's talk. What's he saying? I'm a young person! I'm like Zorba, the Buddha! I want to live; I don't want to think about death.

I wanted to "follow my bliss" as Joseph Campbell said. That was my way of thinking then, but my kind, patient, and elderly Rinpoche helped me realize that illness, pain, and death are inevitable. This teaching helped me be more present in my life now. When we are able to prioritize our activities in the light of the tenuousness of life and the indisputable certainty of death, we are freed from a lot of procrastination, vacillation, and attachment. This has helped me stop building sandcastles that are just washed away with the changing tides of time. It helped me stop investing in fool's gold and impelled me to seek deeper riches. Everything is impermanent and washes away. This is a hard lesson to learn and accept. We are surrounded by death even if our gaze is averted.

Donna, a single mother I know, has two boys, Joseph and Fred, ages six and eight. Donna and her boys say grace every night before dinner. A few years ago, Donna's sister died suddenly. When they said their nightly grace, Donna, Joey, and Freddie added a little prayer for Aunt Pattie. Then Daisy, the family dog, died; they added a prayer for Daisy. Then a friend's dog, Paddington, also died so they added a prayer for him. Then a playmate's father died, so they added a prayer for him. Freddie and Joey became quite worried: If this kept on throughout their lives, with all the people they would have to pray for they would never get around to eating.

The point is that everybody dies. Kalu Rinpoche himself died; the Buddha died; kings, queens, doctors, scientists, artists, and the greatest and richest people in the world have died. We all die. Everything that is compounded or fabricated dies. All those who come together are separated; everything that is built falls apart. It's a fact of life.

When Kalu Rinpoche breathed out his last breath in 1989, although he was clinically dead, he sat up for two days meditating with his eyes open and a rosy complexion. He was in what Tibetans call Clear Light Meditation. Instead of wandering through the intermediate stages after death, known in Tibet as the bardo—he was resting in inner luminosity. This is what is known as Dharmakaya, absolute reality, the true nature of the heart-mind. Then, after two days in the undifferentiated light of pure being, or Rigpa, Kalu Rinpoche finally slumped over and was gone.

Tibetan Buddhism tells us that the clear light of Rigpa—innate awareness, spontaneous wakefulness—dawns momentarily for everyone at the moment of death. *Anybody* who is sufficiently aware can merge consciously with this transcendent pure light at that crucial moment of transition. Herbert Guenther, one of the foremost Buddhist scholars of our time, defines Rigpa as ecstatic presence or ecstatic radiance. Think about this a little bit: ecstatic, not static. *Rigpa,* innate awareness, is ecstatic radiance. I think this is a very important thought. I'm quoting a respected scholar because I don't want readers to think that I'm cobbling together some outlandish New Age Dharma here. The natural mind is intrinsically beautiful, buoyant, free, and tranquil. This is our pure original being, which existed before we saw ourself as a self, before we perceived others, and before we started to think others were the source of our pleasure and our suffering.

According to the Tibetan Tantras, there are four great moments for recognizing this dawning clear light of Rigpa: death, falling asleep, orgasm, and, believe it or not, sneezing. What's the common denominator of all these experiences? Releasing and letting go in the natural state. Masters like Kalu Rinpoche train their whole lives in this type of mystical meditation so they will maintain awareness at the moment of death and dissolve into or return to that inner spiritual light.

Who can doubt that an awareness of death is the greatest teacher for learning to live? We see this all the time with people who have serious illnesses, accidents, or other traumatic experiences. I know a beautiful woman named Maria who says that she learned how to live when she was being wheeled into the operating room for cancer surgery. At that moment everything changed, because she started rearranging her priorities rather than taking life for granted. She learned to find joy in everything she did and every interpersonal contact.

For most of us, there is no greater fear than the fear of death. It's difficult to believe that an easy acceptance of the possibility of death can help put joy in the life you are living, but it can—and will. The Sufis say, "Die before you die, and you shall never die." What they mean is ego death. If you are able to let go of ego then you will not be afraid because you will no longer feel incomplete; you will not cling to the material world and conditioned existence, or samsara. The ego can be likened to samsara's aorta.

If there is no ego, there is no one afraid of dying; there is absolute completeness and oneness. Death is a transformation, a passage, a transitional stage on the journey, but the ego sets up this finite little territory that it's afraid to lose. Why be afraid? Why assume that each of us began at birth and will end at death? We might find the possibility of rebirth surprising, but it's really no more surprising than being born at all. What a marvel to be alive at all, and who can explain it rationally, really?

Of course, everyone is probably at least a little bit nervous around death. The Buddha died at the age of eighty, lying under a tree, on his right side, very peacefully, but the monks around him were all wailing. The fact is that no one wants to die, not even Tibetan lamas. One Japanese Zen master died saying, "I don't want to die." And when his students pressed him again for some last words of wisdom, he repeated, "I *really* don't want to die." That was his truth in that moment, and he didn't hesitate to express it.

I was at my teacher Tulku Urgyen Rinpoche's monastery in Nepal when his wife, Ma-yum Kunsang Dechen, died. Ma-yum had suffered from pancreatic cancer for several months without complaint. Shortly before her death, when she was asked to write a eulogy about her life, she said, "Now that my time to die has come, I have no attachments whatsoever. When I was young I was afraid of death; for that reason I practiced the Dharma diligently for my whole life. Now I am at the very brink of death. I am happy to die, fearless without regrets. The moment this trap of my old material body falls apart, I will fly off like a bird, escaping its snare." She passed away in meditation sitting up.

All Tibetan monks, nuns, and lamas learn how to meditate as they are dying. Kalu Rinpoche taught me how to meditate at the time of death, how to breathe out with a great exhalation—as if soaring up and out through a skylight—and dissolve all the four elements into mind and the mind into infinite space. This is hard to do without training throughout one's lifetime. Kalu Rinpoche seemed able to do that. I was at his Darjeeling monastery when he died. It was sad, the end of an era, yet his death was a powerful learning experience. It brought home to me, once again, that as incredible as it may seem, these Dharma teachings are actually true. During his life, Kalu Rinpoche taught that it was all about conscious living, self-transcendence, and relinquishing control. Stay awake, and stop grasping for things that can't be grasped. That's also a good lesson for this brief bardo or transition called our life. We can afford to just authentically be, without proving or doing anything. This is the wisdom of allowing.

The Tibetans love life. In fact, few people have as much reverence for life as Tibetan Buddhists, who advocate compassion and nonviolence toward all living creatures. Tibetan teachings stress how important it is to understand that we need the same kind of wisdom to prepare for death as we do to prepare for life. This isn't just about nirvana and enlightenment; this is about living sanely and gracefully, living impeccably without regrets, without leaving behind any unfinished mess. When it's time to die, no one exclaims, "I wish I had spent more time in the office." We must set priorities in our lives with the understanding that death is a reality.

Tibetan tradition says that we must all live up to death. This means living up to the truth of death; it also means living until the very moment we die, without deadening ourselves by sleepwalking through our days. What does it profit us to kill time just to get by while we wait for the weekend or the next summer vacation and consequently overlook the miracle of the present moment? Tibetan teachings say that an inner clear light dawns at the moment of death, and if we are not present and aware, we will miss the moment. But the clear light actually dawns every moment, and if we're not careful, we miss it all the time. Life is a miracle to be celebrated, not something to be escaped from or avoided. We are all going to die, aren't we? But are we each going to truly *live*?

Tibetan masters teach what the mystic European monks in the Middle Ages called *ars moriendi,* or the "art of dying." There is an ancient European work from that period called *Book of the Craft of Dying* that says:

> Learn to die and you shall live,
> for there shall be none who learn to truly live
> who have not learned to die.

It says in the Dzogchen teachings that whether our nature descends into samsara or ascends into nirvana, it is not ruined in samsara, and it is not improved in nirvana. It is beyond both. According to the tantric teachings, samsara and nirvana are inseparable. Inseparable. Nirvana is not just the distant other shore—it's right here. Of course, we are usually sort of elsewhere and not fully present, but, as in some prize drawings, you must be present to win.

# KARMA

Karma means that you don't get away with anything; we all reap exactly what we sow. People sometimes think of karma as destiny, but in fact, the word actually translates as action and reaction. In the Buddhist view, there are no accidents. In very simple terms, the traditional Buddhist Law of Dependent Origination means that every cause has an effect, and every effect has a cause.

There's a country song I sometimes hear on the radio that reminds us how cause and effect typically sets up a chain of events. In it, if I remember correctly, because she has a fight with her boyfriend, a woman calls her sister, who comes over, leaving her husband at home alone. Bored, he goes to the store, leaving his pickup with the keys in the ignition; the pickup is then stolen by some teenagers and driven into an electrical transformer, leaving the whole town dark. You get the point: cause and effect.

"Where does our karma come from?" you ask. Each of us is a composite of different experiences, a whirling, changing congeries of conflicting forces and habits. Some of these experiences are within our memory banks; some are in our body; some are like knots, kinks, blocks, and twists in our energy. Some of these experiences happened last week; according to Buddhist belief, some may have happened a hundred or more years ago. Each of these experiences has impacted us and left a karmic imprint which conditions us with an equally conditioned reaction or response in kind.

Something happens to you. You respond with an action, a word, or a thought. This action leaves an imprint in your mind (or, to be more technically precise, in your stream-of-being) that creates further karma. When you become accustomed to behaving a certain way, or being treated and reacting in a certain way, you become conditioned to it. This conditioning is part of your karma. It reminds me of the feeling we all know so well of being stuck in a rut that just keeps getting deeper from the spinning wheels. The more we deepen that rut through use, the harder it becomes to break free of it.

New karma is being made all the time. When one acts with a positive motivation, goodness is furthered. When one acts out of negative motivation, negativity is furthered. We can recondition ourselves to act with wisdom. The important thing to understand here is that you are not a victim. You are your own master. "As you sow, so shall you reap."

Maybe yesterday when you were making lunch, the phone rang

just as you were putting a jar of pickles into the refrigerator. In your haste, you weren't attentive, forgot to be mindful, and didn't put the top back on correctly. Today when you take the pickle jar out of the refrigerator, you pick it up by the top and it all spills on the floor—pickles, pickle juice, and the glass container, which breaks into many jagged pieces. That's simply karmic cause and effect. There is no one else to blame. This is the bad news, but also the good news, all in one. If you pick up the remains of the pickles mindfully and carefully, you won't get cut. But, if you're not careful, you will need Band-Aids. You may even need stitches.

The law of karma spells out very meticulously that everything has its implications; every thought, word, and deed has an effect. Everything, absolutely everything, we think, say, or do makes a difference. Wrap your mind around that thought. Karma implies conditioning and repetition. This is a joyous liberating message because every moment we are presented with the possibility of changing the future. We change, and our future changes too. This is the truth. This is karma. We are responsible; the lever of our own destiny remains in our hands.

# REBIRTH:
# IT'S NOT OVER TILL IT'S OVER

The Buddha did not introduce the notion of reincarnation. Rebirth is a timeless belief that comes from the ancient wisdom traditions of this world. It's found in both Hinduism and Taoism, which predate Buddhism, as well as in the ancient mystic teachings of Christianity and Judaism. Before the Buddha's enlightenment, the concept as it was understood in India was that there was an eternal soul, called the atman, which came into being to fulfill its spiritual lessons, to evolve toward liberation and illumination. A pre-Buddhist prayer from the mystical scriptures of Hinduism, known as the Upanishads, says, "Lead me from darkness to the light, lead me from ignorance to knowledge, lead me from bondage to freedom, lead me from death to immortality." Hinduism taught that this eternal soul would continue to be reborn again and again in order to complete its spiritual growth.

The Buddha, however, said he had looked throughout the entire universe through the wisdom of clear vision and didn't find any fixed, eternal atman or soul. The Buddha took an agnostic position on the existence of a creator or God. When asked whether he was a god or a man, Buddha replied, simply, "I am awake." During his lifetime, there were actually fourteen questions that the Buddha did not answer because he said speculation about these questions was not conducive to nirvanic peace, freedom, and the end of suffering, which was his sole message. Buddhism today is best thought of as an ethical psychological philosophy or nontheistic spiritual practice, needing neither dogma nor belief to be practiced and accomplished.

When asked, "Does God exist or not?" Buddha remained silent. "Does the universe have a beginning or an end?" Again, the Buddha remained silent. He did not feel that speculating about such questions greatly facilitates our progress toward freedom and peace.

Samsara is without beginning but it has an end in enlightenment and deliverance. We can also say that samsara has a beginning in ignorance, but no end. Buddhist logic likes to play both sides of a question against the middle, to point out the relativism of our assertions.

According to the Buddha, each of us is endowed with perfect Buddha-nature, which has the full potential for everlasting peace and nirvanic happiness. In this promise we find the rich soulfulness of Buddhist spirituality. Until each of us is able to purify and transform our obscurations, defilements, and delusions, this inner sun is as if obscured by the clouds of duality and illusion.

The Buddha taught that everything is ephemeral, interdependent, and in process—subject to karma and conditioning. He taught that at death the ordinary, unevolved, conditioned consciousness is like a dead leaf blown about by the autumn wind, while the consciousness of a realized liberated saint—who is master of himself, master of awareness, and master of karma—is like an unswerving bullet shooting through the wind, directed at fulfilling his evolution. This is the same as it is in life: Some people seem to have a clear purpose and direction; others are blown about by every passing breeze.

In Buddhism there is a tradition of storytelling to make a point. One such well-known teaching tale is about a Buddhist master who lived "once upon a time." According to legend, not only was this master very learned and devoted, but he had also been blessed by visions and had developed selfless loving-kindness and unconditional compassion.

The Buddhist was involved in a public religious debate with a non-Buddhist teacher. The latter stated that he did not believe there was any firm evidence to support the rebirth doctrine, which therefore brought into question the entire teaching regarding karmic cause and effect. "If there is no proof of former lifetimes," the non-Buddhist teacher asked, "how can we believe in future incarnations?" He then promised the Buddhist master: "Prove conclusively that reincarnation actually exists, and I and all my students will convert to the Buddha's way."

The Buddhist thought about this. Then he said, "I will die and intentionally be reborn in a manner that demonstrates that rebirth is possible, taking the king as my witness. Then you shall have your proof."

Shortly after that, the Buddhist died. But before doing so, he placed a vermillion mark on his forehead, and he put a pearl in his mouth. As he had requested, the king and his counselors placed his corpse in a sealed copper coffin.

Because he had completely mastered the illusion of birth and death, the Buddhist master was immediately reborn, as he intended, as the son of a learned person in that region. Many auspicious signs and omens attended the infant's birth; among them were a vermillion mark on the baby's brow and a pearl in his mouth. These marvels were, of course, brought to the attention of the royal advisors who, in turn, informed the king.

Then the king summoned the non-Buddhist teacher and other witnesses, and ordered the sealed casket opened. The pearl was gone, as was the vermillion mark. Finally convinced, the non-Buddhist led his followers into the Buddhist path.

The Buddha himself said that he recollected countless rebirths. Mahayana teachings emphasize that he recalled five hundred pre-

vious lives as an awakening being evolving on the way to full enlightenment. The sutras tell us how we can all develop mental
powers such as clairvoyance and recall of past lives when we are
able to achieve very deep meditative levels. Today many believe
that we can learn to recall past lives through a variety of means:
deep meditation, lucid dreaming, dream yoga practices, and hyp-
notic regression are just a few.

All traditional Buddhist teachers believe in rebirth. The more
classical Tibetan texts and teachers stress that to be considered a
Buddhist you must: take refuge in the Three Jewels (Buddha,
Dharma, Sangha); seek liberation from suffering (samsara); and believe in karma and rebirth. They say it is meaningless to seek liberation if you don't accept karma and its implication of continuity.

Many current Western teachers including myself agree that traditional belief in rebirth is not necessary to be a genuine Buddhist,
and that an agnostic position on rebirth teachings is fine until one
discovers certainty within oneself. I personally feel the most important criteria or characteristic of Buddhist spirituality is a sincere
commitment to the possibility of spiritual awakening and enlightenment, combined with an open heart, an inquiring mind, and
daily awareness practice based on ethics, meditation, and wisdom.

## DIFFERENT KINDS OF REBIRTH

There are actually four different ways of interpreting rebirth:

1. Life to life, in sequential and linear time (For example, I die and
I am reborn.)

2. Intentional rebirth, in linear time (Masters and reincarnate
lamas like the Dalai Lama vow intentionally to keep coming back
to fulfill their mission to liberate all beings till the end of samsara
or suffering.)

3. Spiritual rebirth (Total renewal and personal transformation in
this very life.)

4. Moment-to-moment rebirth, in the timeless present—the eternal now (This moment, impulse, or thought arises and passes away.)

## Every Moment, There Is a New You

I would like to remind you that science tells us that almost every cell in your body changes every seven years. You don't have the same body you did ten or twelve years ago; none of us do. You are not exactly the same person you were yesterday; none of us are. Do you remember your dreams from last night, and how intensely involved you were with what you experienced in them? What happened to that person—the dreamer—those feelings, those dreams? What happened to the person you were a month ago or a year ago, or ten years ago?

I vaguely remember how I was twenty or more years ago. I remember my "past lives" as a high school jock, as a kid in Long Island, New York, and as a college student in Buffalo during the sixties. People always ask questions about who or what they were in a past life. Some people even go to "regression therapists" for hypnosis to see if they can remember. The fact is that if you want to know what you were like in a past life, just scrutinize how you are right now.

If you're not comfortable with the traditional Buddhist concept of rebirth—if you think it's just somebody else's dogma—why not consider it this way: In this life you're reborn every moment. Every single second is a rebirth, a time when we re-create ourselves and our self-concepts. Who knows about after we die, but look at your experience now. It's like the movie *Groundhog Day*. Every day you wake up; it's the exact same day, and you can recreate it according to your interpretations. Or you can continue to relive the same daily drama—as Yogi Berra said, "Déjà vu, all over again." Can you change? Where will you go, what will you do? Will it be different?

We are all drawn to the familiar; when something or someone resonates familiarity, our conditioning responds to what modern psychologists describe as a return to the patterns of your family of origin. However, you can break the pattern; you can change the next moment; you can do something different, something enlightened; something creative, imaginative, and fresh; something compassionate and wise. That's how you get off your karmic gerbil wheel and transform your existence. That's rebirth in the immediate here and now. Tibetans believe that spiritual rebirth now is the best preparation for the rebirth that occurs after death.

Milarepa, Tibet's best known yogi and poet, lived almost a thousand years ago. He practiced meditation and yoga in solitude in desolate Himalayan caves. His devotion was so great that he has continued to serve as an inspiration for generations of spiritual practitioners. Milarepa was once a vengeful sorcerer, responsible for several deaths. Fearful for his future, Milarepa determined to change his karma. And he succeeded. In the "One Hundred Thousand Songs of Milarepa," he sang:

> *The fear of death and infernal rebirths due to my evil actions has led*
> *me to practice in solitude in the snowcapped mountains.*
> *On the uncertainty of life's duration and the moment of death I*
> *have deeply meditated.*
> *Thus I have reached the deathless, unshakable citadel of realization*
> *of the absolute essence.*
> *My fear and doubts have vanished like mist into the distance, never*
> *to disturb me again.*
> *I will die content and free from regrets.*
> *This is the fruit of Dharma practice.*

Milarepa was spiritually reborn on those Himalayan peaks, and in so doing he changed his karma. He changed so much that he reached perfect enlightenment—*in a single lifetime.*

Each of us can do the same thing. The wilderness of Tibet is no more or less desolate than the wilderness of corporate America with its materialistic, consumer culture. Who doesn't sometimes feel alienated and lost in the jungle of doubt, meaninglessness, and despair as life goes by, seemingly slipping through our fingers?

# THE DHARMA'S VIEW OF SELF

*Having a wonderful time; wish I was here.*

The earth is not the center of the universe! Grasping the truth of that statement was an amazing achievement for mankind. When Copernicus first presented his revolutionary theory that the earth revolved around the sun rather than vice versa, people thought he was mad. In fact, when Galileo used a telescope to prove Copernican heliocentric theory, he was considered a heretic for challenging the prevalent religious beliefs with his scientific views; Galileo was tried and ordered to recant his views. Faced with torture, he recanted and was placed under house arrest, where he remained for the last eight years of his life. On Galileo's deathbed, his last words reportedly were, "No matter what they say, the earth revolves around the sun."

People simply couldn't accept a scientific truth. The earth not the center? How could that be? How could our planet on which we walk not be the place of primary importance? We accept Copernicus' truth, but even now, it's difficult to fathom its full significance. Let's be honest here: For most of us, it's also sometimes difficult to accept any view of the universe in which each of us, as individuals, are not the centers of our *own* universe. Some solipsism lives in each of us, doesn't it?

It's very seductive to believe, "*I* am the center of all *I* see." After all, that's how we start out as infants: seeing ourselves as the center around which everything revolves. Some of us may have had childhoods in which almost nobody ever seriously challenged that point of view. Small wonder that it's so difficult for Westerners to grasp the Buddhist concept of non-self, egolessness, or anatta. At first glance it seems so foreign, so different, and so confusing, but much of the difficulty rests in how to accurately translate Sanskrit and Pali words and phrases.

The Dharma's view of the self is as evolved and radical as Copernicus' view of the universe: The self, as we know it, doesn't really exist. The key phrase is *"as we know it."* The self is simply not what we think it is. Once someone asked me what I had learned in all my years of Buddhist practice, and I spontaneously answered, "I'm not who I think I am." We are often so identified with who we think we are that it not only determines how we live, but it limits how we can be. Our thoughts and concepts obscure reality, circumscribing us and our world.

If you had to quickly answer the question, "Who are you? What are you?" what would you answer? Do you, for example, identify with your body? Would you answer, "I'm young, old, middle-aged?" Are you identified with your sex? Would you answer, "I'm a man or a woman?" Would you say your nationality, your species, your religious affiliation? Are you identified with your physical characteristics? Tall, short, brunet, dark-skinned, light-skinned? Do you identify with physical assets such as athletic ability, or do you identify with your physical conditioning? Healthy or unhealthy, overweight or underweight? How about political beliefs? How about your job description? Do you think of yourself as a doctor, lawyer, cabinetmaker? How about your thoughts? Do you consider yourself a peaceful person or an angry person? Quick witted or a dim lightbulb? Or perhaps you identify with your personal history. You may say, "I'm somebody who has a rotten relationship history," or "I'm the victim of a tormented childhood/bad luck with the opposite sex/unfortunate employment." When you meet someone at a party, how do you introduce yourself: by occupation, perhaps? When asked, do you say something like, "I am an accountant" or "I'm a feminist"?

As we begin to meditate and delve more deeply into the subtle issues of the spirit, our self-concepts become very revealing. We begin to recognize the stories we tell ourselves for what they are: reflections of the fantasy self we construct, and keep constructing, moment after moment. We start to see how this projected fantasy self, in turn, conditions and creates what we experience. Each of us becomes a self-fulfilling prophecy, the proverbial accident waiting to happen. When we look around at the people we meet, it sometimes seems easy to see this process at work; it's much more difficult to recognize how it is operating in our own lives.

With others, we often see how their self-concepts and self-imposed limitations help shape and determine their future. We can, for example, go to a party with David who complains that he never meets a woman with whom he could settle down; then watch as he quickly becomes smitten with a woman who has just joined the Peace Corps and is heading for Bulgaria. In his life, longing and love are seemingly synonymous. Elusive women attract him, obviously, but why? Or we watch as Uncle George who defines himself as a conservative alienates his children with his rigidly reactionary attitudes. We watch as Dora, who acknowledges her many image issues, creates more financial anxiety by purchasing yet another expensive antique. Why can't we see more clearly how self-concepts control our lives? The question is: Who or what is determining our self-concepts? Where do these patterns come from; how do they emerge and function; how can we find better ways to handle our karmic conditioning?

Maybe you've read some Buddhist books, so you know about the teaching of anatta, egolessness, or "no-self." The concept of anatta is at the heart of the Buddha's teachings on the Five Skandhas or aggregates of individuality, as discussed. According to this teaching, we are each comprised of form, feelings, perceptions, intentionality, and consciousness—all of which change moment to moment. Behind these Five Skandhas, there is no abiding, independently existing permanent self—or soul—to be found. There is no fixed, eternal *I,* or ego. Everything changes according to the laws of cause and effect. All is in flux or flow.

This is the teaching that we sometimes joke about, saying, "The lights are on, but nobody's home." It's a good joke as well as a meaningful example of enlightened humor. The animating light within is on, but nobody in particular is home. Let's go deeper. Who is thinking that witty remark? Some days we feel bright, but in actuality we might find that we don't know very much. Yet not knowing can be quite liberating. Not knowing is a good balance to our usual judgmental surety. It is better to know nothing than to know what isn't so. How about an open-ended approach, a little not knowing and mystery, leaving some room for wonder and to experience what lies beyond the rational mind?

# SELF AS PROCESS

Anatta, or no-self, means that each of us is a process rather than a fixed, independent, eternal self, or concrete entity. One of the meanings given for anatta is "no governor." It's like in *The Wizard of Oz* when we discover that there is no great overlord behind the screen, just more facets beneath each multifaceted surface. Everything we think about things is merely conceptual imputation. We impute absolute concreteness to things that are relative, and we mistake our concepts and ideas for actual reality. People from the Arctic, for example, think southern Canada is a warm southern climate; Texans think it's up north and colder. Both groups are correct, but only in a relative sense. The Lankavatara Sutra says, just to blow our conceptual minds, "Things are not what they seem to be; nor are they otherwise."

Perhaps yesterday you went for a walk. There was a pleasant breeze and the sun was shining on your face, but you were feeling a little bit glum because of some small disappointment. As you walked along, you ran into a few neighbors—the cat who lives next door, the people who live down the block. As you strolled around the corner, thinking about your disappointment, you decided to do something to cheer yourself up, so you went into a store and bought some daisies. Walking home you ran into an elderly neighbor couple, and you impulsively gave them the flowers. So many things happened on your little walk. So many moods, so many feelings, so many changes. Today you are on to other things, emotionally in a different place, and yesterday's walk seems like a dream. Yesterday, who or what was experiencing your experience? How about today? Now? So many mind-moments in even one instant. Who can analyze them all?

When you try to analyze who or what is experiencing your experience, don't just settle for a quick superficial conclusion. As the Buddha said, in describing his process-oriented view of the world, "In hearing, there is just hearing, no hearer, and nothing heard; in seeing there is just seeing, no seer and nothing seen." Like the sound of a drum, which arises from the interplay between the stick beating on drum skin held together by wood and brackets, it's all like echos and reflections. Everything is in process.

There is no sound somewhere waiting to be heard. Of course when the drum beats, we hear a sound, but sound is not a concrete entity, is it?

The Korean Zen master I studied with, Nine Mountains, used to exclaim with gusto, "What is it?" This, his main koan or Zen conundrum, was boldly calligraphed in Korean as a hanging scroll on the wall. This is an intense, heartfelt, visceral question: "What the hell is it?" That was his whole teaching. What the hell is going on? What is this? Who is this? This is a fundamental existential question, turning our exploration inward. What is this presenting itself right now?

# EVERYTHING CAN BE VIEWED
# FROM MANY ANGLES

In life we may keep looking for the right answer, but there is no right answer. Everything is relative rather than absolute. That's the answer. In meditating we strive to keep going deeper and deeper, peeling off layers of the onion until we find the center of the onion, called sunyata, the Sanskrit term for emptiness. As we keep peeling and peeling, we begin the process of unmasking our personas. First we unmask the body, then the mind. Then we go deeper and unmask the psyche, continuously letting go and unmasking all the layers. We all have so many masks it's as though every day in our life has been Halloween. When we remove the masks, we are shedding our fantasies about ourselves, others, and the world. We can see and be seen. We know and are known. We *are*.

Emptiness does not mean that you should deny yourself, abnegate yourself, or pretend that nobody's there. Simply put, this teaching is meant to help you empty yourself when you are too full of yourself. This is meant to help you look at yourself realistically and lighten up when your ego is taking itself too seriously. In this way we can dissolve our deluded view of ourselves and the universe, until we ultimately arrive at sunyata, emptiness, and the radiant, infinite openness of our original, unprocessed natural state, our genuine being. That is Buddha-nature, aware and empty of fantasy.

## EMPTINESS, OPENNESS:
## FULLY PRESENT AND ACCOUNTED FOR

The sunyata doctrine further develops the understanding of "no-self" or egolessness (anatta), providing it with a more universal application. Emptiness, voidness—sunyata—is a central concept in Mahayana Buddhism, which explains that it is not just the self that is inherently empty, but anything—and everything.

But do not become confused: *This certainly does not mean that the world and everything in it doesn't exist;* it simply means that there is nothing behind appearances. It's all surface, mere temporary appearances. It is all cause and effect. All things, by definition, are impermanent—like dreams, echos, or mirages. We know, of course, that we dream, some nights peacefully, others chaotically; we also know that these dreams are not as real as we think they are while they are taking place. They, and everything else, are empty and relative—arising because of cause and effect, or inter-dependent origination. Everything arises as if from emptiness and is resolved back into the unborn nature of emptiness. We do not need to rid ourselves of these dreams, merely to under-stand and see through them, even as they vividly manifest in our perceptions.

Different schools of Buddhism define sunyata differently. The Idealist Mind-Only School, which profoundly influenced the development of Zen Buddhism, says that everything is empty because all things are projections created by the mind. The Tibetan Middle Way School (Madhyamika) says everything is empty because everything is relative, merely an expression of various conditions temporarily coming together—like the sound of the drum. There is nothing concrete or absolutely real be-hind the sound—or behind anything else. It is all like magic, yet how marvelous!

In traditional Mahayana Middle Way philosophy, emptiness is indicated by saying what something is not, or by some form of un-dogmatic negation. Therefore sunyata comes to mean void, or devoid of concrete ultimate reality.

In the non-dual Dzogchen-Mahamudra teachings, sunyata is viewed in positive terms as the supreme reality. This is not a nihilistic black void or vacuum, not an independently existing reality. It's intangible, yet vividly dancing with sounds and colors—shimmering, fertile, and effulgent—a radiant, rainbowlike display, not unlike a cinema projection. That's why we call it the fertile womb of emptiness from which all Buddhas emerge. Sunyata, the mother of all the Buddhas, is the mother of all of us too.

Buddhism is a very hearty spiritual tradition. The essential message is that each of us has the soul or spirit of a Buddha. It just doesn't use those same words, because the word "soul" implies a fixed entity, which runs contrary to the laws of cause and effect, and the fact of impermanence. All beings have Buddha-nature. All creatures great and small.

# MEETING THE CHALLENGE OF DOUBT ON THE PATH

*Small doubt, small enlightenment; big doubt, big enlightenment.*

That's what Korean Zen master Nine Mountains always told us. He understood that doubt and perplexity play a vital role in the spiritual path. The Buddha warned seekers to be prepared to meet five primary challenges or hindrances on the spiritual path. Doubt, which is one of these five, is a likely challenge that Westerners will encounter as they ponder the Buddhist view of reality and the world. Karma, rebirth, no-self, enlightenment, innate Buddha-nature—the Dharma's perspective on all of these can seem quite questionable and foreign to someone with a Western worldview and upbringing.

The wonderful thing about doubt and healthy skepticism is that it's not just an obstacle; it's also the propellant that fuels the spiritual engine. I realize that this positive take on doubt may sound overly upbeat when you are going through the barren deserts or fearsome minefields of what Saint John of the Cross called "the dark night of the soul." I have to admit that I myself don't always feel at one with life, but more like "at two." Yet don't these fluctuating moods become increasingly transparent as we mature spiritually? Seeing through the antics of our monkeylike minds is liberating. We don't want to reinforce any form of mood addiction or mental fixation.

When you experience your own doubts—and almost everyone has doubts—you will wonder what to do and where you go with your questioning. In my own spiritual practice, I have several times struggled with doubts about what I was doing, and I would like to share some of my experiences. Doubt presented itself to me as a major challenge when I was in the middle of my second cloistered three-year retreat in the forest hermitage started for Westerners in the South of France and guided by Khyentse Rinpoche. In 1980, this was a newly built intensive meditation retreat center, and more than a dozen Westerners committed themselves to the traditional three years, three months, and three days in this monastery. Spiritual masters like Dudjom Rinpoche, Gyalwa Karmapa, and Kalu Rinpoche gave teachings, and it was the first time that Dzogchen was taught and practiced thoroughly in the West.

As exciting as the prospect of studying with these many extraordinary lamas was, three years in a cloistered monastery, spending most of one's time in solitary meditation, was a huge commitment, and I worried that I might have doubts about the validity of what I was doing. I certainly did not go into the first three years intending to stay on for another four, yet that's what happened.

During the first three-year retreat my crisis was primarily physical because I hurt my back doing strenuous Tibetan yoga jumps. I ended up lying on my back in my small, square cell for about a month looking at the ceiling with no distractions nor much modern medical attention. Once my slipped disk healed, my other problems were also physical. Each of us had been assigned a cell with a meditation box, in which, in the Tibetan tradition, we spent most of the day in solitary meditation, interspersed with several hours of daily group meditation, chanting, and prayers.

Tibetan monks in three-year retreats usually sleep sitting up in the same tiny box in which they meditate. This is part of the traditional lama-training discipline, and serves as excellent preparation for Dream Yoga, lucid dreaming, and other yogic and psychic transformations. I admit there were times when it was too much for me, and I occasionally found myself stretched out on the floor, blissfully asleep. Nonetheless, the experience of retreat life was so filled with vitality and blessings, so enriching and fulfilling that as soon as the first retreat ended, I committed myself to another three years.

About one year into this second retreat, I became overwhelmed with feelings of doubt and confusion: What, I asked myself, was I doing cut off from the world for more than half a decade? How was that helping anyone? Is this what I was born into this world for? This became a genuine spiritual crisis. I felt as though nothing was happening, and I was stuck, stagnant, and depressed. I began questioning everything. My head buzzed with obsessive thoughts, which made meditating a challenge as I kept losing focus and motivation. My Tibetan teacher pointed out how helpful this would be later when counseling someone with similar difficulties, but at the time that thought was not very comforting. He lovingly advised me to relax a little and go easier on myself, which was very helpful.

Wise lamas encouraged me to meditate on the difficulties themselves—just to be present with the difficulty, as it were, instead of trying to get over it as quickly as possible. To face the doubt rather than try to avoid or suppress it. In this process I learned something that millions of seekers had also learned before me and millions will after me: You have to go through the darkness to truly know the light. This may sound like a cliché, but it's true nonetheless. Often the greatest doubts occur just before a breakthrough. My lamas encouraged me to view doubt as a great teacher. I encourage you to do the same and to trust your inquisitive, skeptical, postmodern inquiring mind and find out for yourself the answers to all your questions. Things are not really as difficult or complicated as they sometimes seem. To remember that truth can be extraordinarily helpful in a crisis.

Because I tend to be skeptical in general, one of the things that has always appealed to me about Buddha Dharma is that there is nothing to believe and everything to discover. Yes, faith and devotion are helpful qualities to bring to a spiritual practice, but that doesn't mean blind faith. The Buddha encouraged seekers to investigate and inquire for themselves. Seekers become genuine *finders* through critical examination and personal experience. Honest investigation and inquiry are said to be the most powerful agents of transformation, or in the traditional Buddhist parlance, the main factors of enlightenment. Lifeless, inert dogma lacks the living intelligence of radiant Buddha-nature.

I remember that when I first arrived in Asia and I heard many miraculous stories about Buddha, they seemed to be just stories— mere legends and tales; I took them, like most things in this category, with a large grain of salt. For similar reasons, I also had trouble with the gospels of Jesus when I first read them. But the heart of the gospels definitely moved me. I believe that it doesn't really matter whether or not you believe that Jesus walked on water or was resurrected, he still preached to the heart of the matter. The same thing is true with Buddhist teaching tales: The point is still the point; the moral of the story is what is true about them.

Tibetan lamas like to tell stories about supernatural, magical, mystical happenings that often seem incredible. They say it's possible to reincarnate intentionally, and even emanate in more than one body at once; to experience different realms of existence; and to prolong life through longevity practices, remarkable diets, and long-life empowerments. They talk about ancient monasteries like Katok in eastern Tibet where there were so many enlightened monks that the sky itself turned yellow from their glowing robes; they speak of rainbow-light bodies and Himalayan yogis who can fly, hold their breath for days, and perform other incredible feats.

Those of you who have read Robert Heinlein's *Stranger in a Strange Land* will remember Heinlein's coined word "grok." Grok means chewing on a concept and assimilating it until it becomes one with you and your understanding rather than swallowing it whole and half-digested. It's sometimes difficult to grok concepts like rebirth and rainbow-light bodies. Although some Westerners are specifically drawn to esoteric and magical special effects, others are not. Initially I myself was not very much drawn to the super-natural. Incredible events severely tested my credulity and beliefs. I did not find extraordinary events, legends, and marvels very relevant to my personal search. It was more often the moral of the story or teaching tale that sparked my inner flame.

It's been many years since I first went to Asia, and I still don't "believe" anything, but now I do know a few things through my own experience. I know that there is much that is unseen. As I go along on the path and follow the Buddha's Own Operator's Manual, I continue to discover—much to my delight, but also much to my chagrin and surprise—that the Dharma teachings are all too true. I have come to deeply appreciate the value of traditional Buddhist teaching tales, myths, anecdotes, and parables. Like elders the world over, lamas love to regale us with colorful evocative illustrations for their spiritual teachings.

According to the Dharma, there are three different kinds of faith. The first can be described as a longing or a wish that what you hope and believe to be true really is true. The second is described as a lucid faith in which you conclude that what you believe to be true actually is true. The third kind of faith is un-shakable faith, which is total conviction. When we consider the three kinds of faith outlined in Buddhist texts, we see how one moves from blind faith and semiconscious longing to higher aspiration and self-knowledge, and finally toward unshakable inner conviction.

## Daily Meditation: Four Transforming Thoughts That Redirect the Mind

The most fundamental daily reflection or meditation in Tibetan Buddhism is known as the Four Thoughts That Turn the Mind from Samsara and Toward Nirvana and Enlightenment. It's also known as the Four Mind Changers. All Tibetan lamas, without exception, teach and practice it regularly. In the 1970s and early 1980s, Kalu Rinpoche went around the world five times teaching this *before* introducing the non-dual Dzogchen-Mahamudra teachings on naked awareness, innate wakefulness, and the natural great perfection.

In my own life, I have found this contemplative practice extremely helpful. In the seventies, I began meditating on the meaning contained in these Four Thoughts and experiencing them gradually myself. This practice really did help me loosen my preoccupation with worldly aims. My teachers told me that meditating on these Four Mind Changers would help me turn from seeking happiness from outer experiences (from others and through cheap thrills and highs) toward more lasting happiness, peace, and fulfillment, and they were right. This reflection helps loosen our preoccupation with this body, this life, and this world, opening up wider horizons and a far more unselfish, universal perspective.

In a very natural way, these meditations helped me to practice more enthusiastically, not just because I thought I should or because authority figures told me to do so, but for my own enlightened self-interest. Reflecting on the Four Mind Changers helps make ethics, honesty, altruism, and loving-kindness more possible, not just as superimposed morality but for its own obvious sake, and even as a necessity. Inner certainty and conviction always bring increased motivation and perseverance combined with a passion for truth and spiritual realization.

These four transforming thoughts are reflections or contemplations on: 1) Precious human existence; 2) Death, mortality, and impermanence; 3) The Ineluctible Law of Karma: Cause and Effect; and 4) The defects and shortcomings of samsara, which include eight kinds of problems and suffering.

## 1. Precious Human Existence
This precious human existence, this lifetime, well-endowed with leisure, qualities, and opportunities, is difficult to attain, tenuous, and easily lost, so this is the time to practice spirituality with diligence.

Shantideva, the eighth-century Mahayana Indian saint (his name translates as "The Peaceful Angel") and author of *The Way of the Bodhisattva,* wrote:

"These human leisures, opportunities, and faculties are very
  rare to obtain and easily lost;
If one squanders the chance to fulfill the aim of human life,
  How will such an opportunity arise again?"

## 2. Death, Mortality, and Impermanence

**All things are impermanent; our life breath especially is just like a bubble on a swift-moving stream. The time of our death is uncertain, and we depart alone from this world.**

All that is born, dies, even the enlightened masters, saints, sages,
  and powerful leaders;
Our longevity and hour of death are uncertain, and then we
  sally forth alone and unaccompanied;
All constructions eventually fall to ruin;
All those who are gathered together, eventually separate.
Everything passes and dissolves;
Even the mountains and the seas;
So resolve now to realize the deathless reality and undying
  peace of freedom and nirvana.
In the Lalitavistara Sutra, the Buddha says:
"The universe and its inhabitants are as ephemeral as the clouds
  in the sky;
Beings being born and dying are like a spectacular dance or
  drama show.
The duration of our lives is like a flash of lightning or a firefly's
  brief twinkle;
Everything passes like the flowing waters of a steep waterfall."

## 3. The Ineluctible Law of Karma

**The law of karma follows us like a shadow follows the body; virtue and nonvirtuous words, thoughts, and deeds procreate in kind.**

The lawful workings of cause and effect, virtue and vice, are unavoidable.

When we die we leave everything behind, except our karma and our spiritual realization.

This karmic conditioning propels us forward according to what we have set in motion through our actions, words, and deeds.

Karmic cause and effect (interdependent origination) creates everything, and by thorough understanding of karmic causation and skillful means we can become free. The Buddha said:

"If a king or householder shall die,

His wealth, family, friends, and retinue cannot follow him.

Wherever we go, wherever we remain,

The results of our actions follow us."

### 4. The Defects and Shortcomings of Samsara

**Samsara and all its contents, pleasure as well as pain, are like a public feast we are passing through on our way to the grave.**

◎ Birth is difficult, growing up is difficult, illness is difficult, aging and death are painful.

◎ Losing what we care for hurts; not getting what we want is frustrating.

◎ We feel lost and powerless, anxious and insecure by a sense of being out of control, blown about by circumstances and conditions we don't understand.

◎ Being unaware and half-asleep in our own lives is wasteful and meaningless.

◎ We are continually tormented by our fears of the unknown and ignorance and doubt about where we will go and why.

These are just a few of the myriad waves in the ocean of suffering called samsara or cyclic existence. Cross beyond this raging tide of confusion and misery to the other shore, and you'll find the joyous waters of nirvana—peace, freedom, and the everlasting happiness of perfect enlightenment.

# RIGHT INTENTIONS

## *Plumbing Your Wise Buddha-Nature*

*The thought manifests as the word;*
*The word manifests as the deed;*
*The deed develops into habit;*
*And habit hardens into character;*
*So watch the thought and its ways with care,*
*And let it spring from love*
*Born out of concern for all beings. . . .*

*As the shadow follows the body,*
*as we think, so we become.*

—FROM THE DHAMMAPADA
(SAYINGS OF THE BUDDHA)

When you look at the people you love, what do you wish for them? Do you wish them all the happiness, goodness, abundance, blessings, and well-being that they would wish for themselves? How about strangers? What do you wish for them? How about people who aren't kind to you, or those you consider downright hateful? What do you wish for them? Do you feel a natural sense of kinship with everyone you meet? Or are you so caught up with your own life that you don't have the time to think about others except when they directly impinge on you or are part of your plans?

The second step on the Noble Eight-Fold Path is traditionally known as Right Thought or Right Intentions. This step speaks about the possibility, and necessity, of using our minds and firm determination, or resolve, to free ourselves from ignorance, delusion, negativity, and selfishness. This step asks us, as seekers, to purify our attitudes and thoughts—to become totally straightforward and honest with ourselves—and, in so doing, to develop a working loving-kindness, empathy, and compassion toward all creatures. We cannot find deeper spiritual understanding without developing the faculties and qualities of the heart and mind.

## THE STORIES WE TELL OURSELVES

It's much easier to talk about universal compassion and love than it is to practice it. When personally involved with a situation that provokes insecurity, anger, resistance, or conflict, don't we all tend to focus first on our own immediate concerns? Don't we all sometimes have self-involved and absurdly wild thoughts bumping into each other—mental static ad infinitum? For example:

The scene: A large party somewhere in a resort area.

Ted (a forty-two-year-old writer) *says:* "It was really nice meeting you here; maybe we can get together for coffee back in the city." Ted *thinks:* She seems to like me. I wonder if she would like me so much if she knew that after this vacation, it's questionable whether I'm even going to be able to afford coffee.

Naomi (a thirty-six-year-old social worker) *says:* "That would really be nice; I would like that." Naomi *thinks:* He seemed to like me better before he saw me in a bathing suit. I probably should have spent more time at the gym. I wonder if he likes cats. I don't want to go out with one more man who is allergic to cats. Not after James, and all that sneezing. . . . blah, blah, blah.

We all have so many random thoughts and concerns, it can seem as though the air around our heads is filled with flak rather than just clouds, space, and light. Dharma teachers sometimes refer to the stream of consciousness of a person with an untrained mind (most of us, much of the time) as a continuous stream of delusion. This continuous stream is built up through years (or lifetimes) of deeply confused habitual and distorted thinking. We think so much, yet we truly know and understand so very little.

The dramatized encounter between Ted and Naomi points out how most of us tend to run fantasy scenarios in our heads—all the time. Ted and Naomi are basically decent, kind people, but at this moment, they are both thinking only of themselves. Ted is worried that he is not successful enough to really attract a woman. Naomi is anxious that Ted may never call her, and she remembers difficulties with an old boyfriend. As benign as Ted and Naomi's thoughts may be, they also reveal how self-absorbed we are most of the time—even when we think we're not.

Consider how self-absorption rules everyone's thoughts and intentions. When we watch the president on television talking about taxes, don't we think: *"What does this mean for me?"* We hear that a new shopping mall is going up, and we immediately think about it in terms of our interests—our property values, traffic patterns, and consumer needs. Everything is seen through the filter of our own personal concerns. The first question we often ask ourselves: Is it good or bad for me and mine? Even when we are doing something for others, don't we often expect something out of it for ourselves?

A Tibetan saying is that thoughts and concepts are delusions; awareness is wisdom. Self-absorption acts as a veil of delusion that distorts everything. Many people bring preconceived notions of themselves to everything they do, even if they don't acknowledge it to themselves. If our thoughts reflect insecurity, we don't typically think of them as self-involved. For example: "I'm not good enough" or "Nobody understands me" or "Why does this always happen to me?" or "How come the other person has all the luck?" Just because you're not thinking, "I'm the best, the most terrific, the best looking, the smartest, etcetera," doesn't mean that you're not involved with your ego. Examples of egotism can be subtle and more slippery than a wet bar of soap. Self-denial, for example, is just one more inverted form of egotism.

It's often tempting to use our thoughts to make ourselves feel okay about what we are going to do anyway, rationalizing all sorts of crookedness through self-justification. We drink the extra drink, then drive home, telling ourselves that it doesn't really matter this time, and that we won't do it again. We cut corners in business deals or cheat on taxes and rationalize away any guilty feelings. I've certainly made excuses to myself in order to do things I want to do and to be where I want to be. Haven't you? Haven't you dredged up seemingly sensible or noble-sounding reasons for questionable behavior? Haven't you told yourself it really doesn't matter, when you know very well that it does? We all have. Let's not fool ourselves. How can we learn instead to approach the world with pure intentions and an open honest awareness? We will be a lot happier and less care-worn if and when we can do so.

Can we admit it when we are being selfish, or do we pretend and hope it goes away—which of course it never does, since we constantly reinforce that habitual pattern. Can we acknowledge the costly downside to our self-absorption? Some men and women complain loudly about not being able to "connect" with others. Yet they sometimes seem so narcissistic and self-absorbed that it would be difficult for them to connect with almost anyone. Instead of seeing "the other," aren't they relating primarily to their own illusory needs and egocentric projections?

To embody the Dharma, we have to learn to let go of self-deception and be honest with ourselves as well as the rest of the world. This level of honesty requires conscientious attention, discernment, emotional intelligence, self-knowledge, and sincere internal scrutiny. Your future, your karma, your Dharma rests on the thoughts and intentions you form today. So keep your eyes peeled.

Everything depends on motivation and intention. What you tell yourself about any situation reflects where you are coming from. It all starts in your head, with what you tell yourself. Sometimes we get so caught up in our habitual storylines that we've lost track of who and what we were before the current movie or this week's sitcom flashed on the screen. A classic Buddhist question is: "Who were you and what did you look like before your parents were born?" Reflect on this for a moment. It's a mind bender, which can crack open the eggshell of ignorance. We could find our identity, who and what we are, on a deeper level than externals, appearances, and our own personality.

Right now: Stop, take a few breaths, and turn down the volume of the incessant internal dialogue in your head. To wake up, you need to fully arrive just where you are, and reknow it, as if for the first time . . . to fully "be here now," as the saying goes. Not to be high now, by rolling-your-own Dharma. Relax. Be here and now, right now. Stop. Drop everything, and let yourself arrive fully . . . here . . . where you are; this is the starting point as well as the goal. Between these two—origin and goal, the ground and the fruit— lies the path. Fully inhabit this present moment. It's worth it.

## LET BUDDHA BREATHE THROUGH YOU

Dharma purifies karma, transcends dogma, and dissolves obscurations and obstacles. One moment of genuine insight dispels aeons of ignorance and confusion. Dzogchen masters say that our minds are so suffused with ignorance and deluded thinking that we have forgotten our perfect Buddha-nature—our tender hearts richly endowed with wisdom and compassion. Children sometimes seem to be born with this kind of naturally loving attitude. I remember when I was a kid, I wanted everybody to be happy. By everybody, of course, I meant the few people in my immediate world—my parents, my siblings, and the rest of my family. When we were very little children, didn't we all often wish the very best for everyone? But then what happened? In my case, I remember how much it would upset me if something was bothering anyone in our precious little family circle. I really thought that everybody should always be smiling and content. Why not? But as time progressed, life seemed to get more complex, and that childlike simplicity was socialized out of me. In a world that often seems to place more emphasis on competition and exploitation than it does on compassion, collaboration, and mutual benefit, didn't that happen to most of us?

Can any of us honestly say that we think as much about the happiness of others as we do about our own pleasures and well-being? Don't we sometimes go even one step further, and experience downright negativity toward others? Unfortunately, in many super-charged competitive—not to mention hostile—environments, it often appears that in order for one person to succeed, someone else has to fail. And unkind thoughts and intentions be-gin to cloud, or obscure, our naturally positive attitudes.

Who among us has never felt the impulse to cheer, or at least smile, at someone else's bad fortune or fall from grace? So often it seems as though the "other guy" is the person standing between you and what you want. Have you never tried to get ahead of someone else—at school, in traffic, on the job, on a line? Who hasn't? Weren't most of us raised to be competitive, to fight to win, to be more important, to be first? My junior high football coach used to say, "Winning is not the most important thing; it is the *only* thing." By some, this competitive spirit is much admired. Get the best deal for ourselves; get the best parking space; get the best score. Treat others as natural enemies. Push, shove, do what you have to do. Get ahead. *Me First!!!* As much as we may sit in judgment on such behavior, there are times when we all have this impulse. How and when can we retool our competitive win/lose attitude into one that is win/win?

Right Intentions, the second step on the Buddha's Eight-Fold Path, tells us to turn these attitudes about winning and achieving upside down and inside out. It suggests to the spiritual seeker that it is in our own highest interest to be less selfish. When our ener-gies are taken up with thoughts of "me" or "mine," we are honor-ing neither our human dignity nor our innate Buddha-nature. The Dharma urges seekers to develop an unselfish view of the world because the reality is that we are all interconnected; our fates are intertwined. It takes an entire community to raise a Buddha.

# Visualizing Your World as a Buddha Field

A meditation instruction that really suits today's world is built on a traditional tantric transformation and self-visualization. The meditation is designed to help you transport your ordinary self and ordinary world into the dimension of Buddha-body, in a Buddha palace, in Buddha Fields; where your thoughts are Buddha's thoughts, your world is Buddha's world, and you see a Buddha in everyone you meet. As a supremely enlightened being, the Buddha had a realistic, unselfish, and compassionate view of the world. You too can participate in such a world. Try the following:

*When Sitting, sit like a Buddha. Be Buddha.*

*When Standing, stand like a Buddha. Be Buddha.*

*When Walking, walk like a Buddha. Be Buddha.*

*When Thinking, think like a Buddha. Let Buddha think*
    *through you.*

*When Breathing, breathe like a Buddha. Let Buddha breathe*
    *through you.*

*Let Buddha live through you. Be Buddha. Enjoy the natural great*
    *perfection. You are far more Buddha-like than you think.*

# SEEING THE BUDDHA IN ALL:
# THE PRACTICE OF PURE PERCEPTION

You are not the only unawakened Buddha or amnesiac saint on the block. Seeing others as Buddhas is taught in Vajrayana practices as the cultivation of pure perception or sacred outlook. Pure perception is about inner vision.

As an example, all you pet lovers might want to think about a dog that you know. The mailman may see that dog as an unholy terror; an allergic relative may see it as a dirty dust ball; a child may see it as a best friend; its owner may see it as an angelic blessing and an oasis of unconditional loyalty and win/win mutuality in his life. The Dharma teaches us that all beings have Buddha-nature, including that dog. Can you look at that dog and

perceive its Buddha-nature? Can you look in the eyes of someone you love and see Buddha-nature? Can you look at someone you fear or someone who has been unkind to you and see
Buddha-nature?

The question is how far can any of us extend ourselves toward
including one and all in our unconditional loving hearts? Can we
love and respect even those whose actions or personalities we don't
happen to like? How far can we genuinely extend ourselves to include all in our wishes, thoughts, prayers, and hearts? Can we forgive others and forgive ourselves too? Seeing the Buddha in all is
a challenge, but it's also a mirror for clearly seeing into your own
heart and soul. This sacred outlook and penetrating spiritual gaze
could prove extraordinarily revealing.

# ILL WILL:
# A CHALLENGE TO PURE PERCEPTION

Margaret and Paul have been divorced for almost a year, but they
are both still furious. Neither can leave anger behind; neither can
let go of recriminations and unhappy memories; both are still trying to "get" each other where it hurts. Some nights, lying in bed,
Margaret can't stop ruminating about the many ways she believes
Paul betrayed her; she gets so upset, she doesn't know what to do
with her resentment and even wonders about revenge. When Paul
wakes up thinking about some of the things Margaret said, he
thinks about all the things he could say that would really hurt her
amd make her sorry.

It's been centuries since the Buddha listed for his disciples the
five primary challenges they were likely to meet on a spiritual path.
Isn't it extraordinary that we are still facing the same obstacles and
hindrances? One of the primary challenges to developing impeccable intentions or bodhicitta (the awakened heart-mind) is the
hindrance of *ill will,* enmity, or negativity.

Dealing with this challenge in today's world really does require
round-the-clock diligence; so many things are potentially disturbing. The only hardware store in town charges you twice what you
think something is worth; your ex—best friend leaves town with

your VCR; little Janie's third-grade teacher is mean and punitive; some hit-and-run artist did six hundred dollars' worth of damage to your parked car before driving off. How could you not feel angry, resentful, and mean-spirited?

I think it's important to remember that there is nothing in the Dharma that tells us never to be angry. Anger is a human emotion; it doesn't automatically disappear. Also it has its own logic, its own intelligence and function. If you bottle up and swallow your anger too often, you are going to make yourself ill. Meeting the challenge of ill will is not about denying, repressing, or suppressing anger. It's about staying up to date with anger and other emotions by experiencing and releasing their energy moment by moment rather than storing them up. It's about not carrying grudges or blaming yourself, or turning your anger inward and becoming depressed and despondent. Ideally we should be able to be sensitive and aware enough not only to feel life fully but also to let it go.

Have you ever been in a situation where you felt that someone had treated you very badly, and you couldn't let it go? You continued to want some kind of resolution or vindication. Perhaps this went on for so long that you felt out of control, and instead of briefly befriending your anger and disappointment, you allowed these feelings to become uncomfortably close companions? The Dharma doesn't tell you to turn your anger inward. Buddhist wisdom encourages you to look at these situations realistically, experience freely and feelingly, stop grasping, and transform your attitude.

Right now as I look out the window, a group of deer have gathered around some corn that my neighbor has put down in the snow. Most of them are grazing peacefully, but two appear jealous and are shoving the others away while trying to get more than their share. Observe animals closely, and you realize that jealousy, ill will, and, yes, compassion, arise even among the wildest. The animal kingdom has its Mother Teresas as well as its Caligulas. Think about the dogs who help take care of the physically challenged. Animal trainers recognize that some dogs are clearly more compassionate than others. Animal behaviorists have amazing stories of compassionate dolphins, elephants, and gorillas.

In his teachings, the Buddha spoke about remembering his past lives. The scriptures say that he began his path to enlightenment during a lifetime when he was a bull in one of the infernal realms. Pulling a cart, he felt compassion for the weaker animal joined with him. When he told the demon in charge of this particular hell realm that he would pull the load alone, the demon became so enraged that he struck him on the head with his trident, killing him on the spot. Thus the Buddha, by putting another being's needs before his own, began his path to perfect enlightenment and Buddhahood. This is a lesson in Compassion 101.

On a very subtle, but no less real level, every time you see yourself on one side of the fence, with someone else on the other, you're being tripped up by the challenge of ill will. If you empathize with them—try to see through their eyes—you might miraculously find yourself on the same side. Ill will, left on its own, can easily escalate into mean-spiritedness, anger, or rage, sometimes without our even knowing that the escalation is taking place.

Working to embody a selfless, altruistic bodhicitta and walking the Mahayana Way is living the Golden Rule. When the astronauts visited the moon or traveled through space, many commented on the transformative experience of looking at the earth and seeing it as a whole, with no fences, no borders, no countries, no wars. Just a thumb-size blue orb in a black sky. Only us here together on Spaceship Earth.

## PURIFIED INTENTIONS: COMPASSION AS A WAY OF LIFE

*All the happiness there is in this world comes from thinking about others, and all the suffering comes from preoccupation with yourself.*

—SHANTIDEVA

As a child, I remember hearing adults refer to some people as having "good hearts." They were not talking about the aerobically inclined. The world over, "good heart" refers to someone who is compassionate and has a loving, caring, and generous spirit. In the

Tibetan language, compassion is translated as "nobility or greatness of heart," a phrase that includes open-hearted wisdom and discernment as well as empathy, unselfishness, and abundant kindness. The most exalted compassionate archetype in Tibet is the great-hearted Buddha of unconditional love, known as Chenresig.

Although in Tibet, the Buddha of Compassion, Chenresig, is given the male pronoun "he," the archetype is intrinsically androgynous and embraces the sacred feminine principle along with the sacred male. The name Chenresig has several meanings including the compassionate eye that sees with the heart, or one who cares for and looks after us. Chenresig is considered Tibet's national protector; Tibetans feel with all their hearts that this archetype is their special protector and embodies unconditional divine love, empathy, and tenderhearted compassion.

Typically the first Tibetan mantra that Westerners hear or learn about is Chenresig's mantra "Om Mani Pedmé Hung." This mantra literally translates as "The jewel is in the lotus." What it means is that wisdom and compassion—the jewels that we all seek—are inherently within us all, like pure seeds blossoming and unfolding within our own tender unguarded hearts. What we seek, we *are*.

"Om Mani Pedmé Hung," commonly called the six-syllable mantra, can legitimately be referred to as the national mantra of Tibet. Always on the lips of Tibetans, the six syllables create a constant background sound wherever one travels. Lay people, adults and children, holding their malas and twirling prayer wheels, mutter it while doing daily chores, while lamas, nuns, and monks chant it prayerfully as part of their meditative and contemplative practices and visualizations.

"Om Mani Pedmé Hung" is the Dalai Lama's mantra; it was Kalu Rinpoche's mantra, and Karmapa's too; for all of these great teachers are considered to be reincarnations, or embodiments on earth of the transcendent Buddha of Compassion, Chenresig (Avalokitesvara). Almost everyone who has ever spent time in the presence of masters such as these Buddha-lamas agrees that they carried their own spiritually awakened atmosphere with them, wherever they went. I have certainly felt it. I feel them and that atmosphere of blessings with me today wherever I go and can enhance such presence by chanting the mantra.

# The Six-syllable Mantra Meditation: *Om Mani Pedmé Hung*

To yourself enter into that sacred dimension of the sound of loving-kindness, you only need to stop for a moment. Right now, take a break; take a breath. Visualize the most genuinely exalted loving image of unconditional love and compassion you can imagine. It might be Buddha, Padma Sambhava, Tara, Jesus, Mary, a personal saint or archangel, or your own spiritual teacher or guide. Toward this image, cultivate thoughts of gratitude, devotion, trust, faith, and appreciation.

With that thought or image in your mind, chant *Om Mani Pedmé Hung* softly, regularly. Use this mantra of love and compassion to soften, to ease and gentle your mind, energy, and spirit. Use it to dissolve any hardness or constriction around your heart, to warm up and loosen your gut. Chant it again and again, awakening to the presence of that exalted being, that sacred reality or spiritual dimension. Sense where you are, what you are, and who you are and can be. Let everything dissolve into that purring, stream, that songlike repetitive sound of Great Compassion's mantra.

> *Om Mani Pedmé Hung . . . Om Mani Pedmé Hung . . .*
> *Om Mani Pedmé Hung*

Now think of someone you truly love—a spouse, a child, a parent, a friend, a pet, and extend unconditional love and empathy to them . . . then to a few more people. Keep reaching out with radiant, visualized light rays of your love. How far can you go? Keep going.

# LOVING-KINDNESS IS
# THE HEART OF THE DHARMA

The Buddha once described the spiritual path that leads to nirvana or perfect freedom as "the liberation of the heart and mind, which is love." Learning to love life in all its forms, and to love unconditionally is the way of Dharma. Unconditional love and compassion, as embodied by Chenresig and as taught by many Buddhist masters, is something that I personally feel strongly about. In the presence of my spiritual friends and teachers I have often experienced both unconditional love and a total acceptance of myself, just as I am. This is a very rare and precious experience I think; this sense of belonging is probably one of the main reasons why I stayed in the monastic sangha in Asia as long as I did.

My teacher's pure perception of me, just as I am, helped me to connect more completely to who I am. In the mirror of the awakened teacher's clear seeing, I could better know my higher sense and my true inner nature. I had a distorted picture of myself, and perhaps you have one of yourself. These invaluable Dharma teachings encouraged me to know that it is possible for everyone—not just a guru or monk, and not just the Buddha—but me and you too—to connect to the Buddha within. The authentic Buddha is beyond time and place, beyond gender, beyond form or nationality. You carry a Buddha with you right now, in your heart.

A great Indian master once said, "Wisdom tells me I am nothing; love tells me I am everything. Between the two, my life flows."

## CHOOSING UNIVERSAL LOVE:
## THE BODHISATTVA VOW

Traditional teachings about rebirth say that most of us are unwitting prisoners on the wheel of samsara; we keep returning because we have no choice. According to this way of thinking, there are also men and women walking among us who are here of their own

conscious volition. These men and women are known as Bodhisattvas. Bodhi means awakening; sattva means being. This is a
being who is ready for nirvana but whose compassion is so great
that he or she remains on this earth solely in order to reduce suffering and help free others. A Bodhisattva is someone with pure,
impeccable intentions—a gentle yet fearless spiritual warrior who
strives unceasingly to help everyone reach nirvanic peace and enlightenment.

A transcendent Bodhisattva has seen beyond delusion and selfishness; he or she has felt and experienced the intolerable despair,
alienation, misery, and suffering in the world. Because such a person is able to understand that we are all caught in the same existential plight, he or she seeks to alleviate the suffering of all.

In Mahayana Buddhism, one is encouraged to take what we call
the Bodhisattva Vow. Taking this vow means you understand the
world's pain, and you commit to work for the enlightenment of all.
That means *all* the people, *all* the creatures, including *all* the inhabitants of the air and sea—insects, birds, shellfish, dolphins,
whales *and* sharks, *all* the shiny little eyes in the dark forests, as well
as *all* the creepy crawly, buzzing things trying to get in and chew
on your house or on you.

The first time I heard the Bodhisattva Vow was in 1971, and I
was at Lama Thubten Yeshe's monastery in Nepal. I felt overwhelmed by the magnitude of it all. And I'm still somewhat in-
timidated by it. Lama Yeshe explained the vow very simply. He
said, "Think of what you want, and realize that all beings want
and need the same things. They are just seeking it through different ways."

If you were to take the Bodhisattva Vow, you would commit
yourself in this way:

Sentient beings are numberless: I vow to liberate them.
Delusions are inexhaustible: I vow to transcend them.
Dharma teachings are boundless: I vow to master them.
The Buddha's enlightened way is unsurpassable: I vow to embody it.

This is a four-line affirmation sangha members chant and avow
every day. To take the Bodhisattva Vow means that at least for a

moment, one can see past one's own problems and preoccupations and elevate the spiritual gaze toward universal fulfillment. The moment you affirm that great intention—to work for the good of all living creatures—whether or not you are always able to follow it as perfectly as you might wish—you are called a Bodhisattva, a child of the Buddhas.

When this epiphany occurs, all the Buddhas rejoice. The scriptures say that as soon as you make this Bodhisattva Vow to realize enlightenment and relieve universal suffering, all the Buddhas, Bodhisattvas, devas, angels, and guardians of the Dharma clap their hands and rain down celestial flowers and divine nectar. It's like you scored a touchdown or hit a home run. As poetic as that seems, I really feel that this is true in a spiritual sense. You can feel it yourself as you open a little more to the joy of spiritual awakening. It also says in the scriptures that when the Bodhisattva Vow has taken root in your heart, then everything you do is beneficial—even snoring, sleeping, and brushing your teeth. They say that when a Bodhisattva turns over in his or her sleep, beings are awakened. Even if this is mainly metaphorical, it still means that this awakening mind and aspiration for enlightenment is extraordinarily important.

# BODHICITTA: THE ENLIGHTENED MIND
## OF THE BODHISATTVA

*From among all the vast divisions of the*
  *Buddha's teachings.*
*Bodhicitta is the very quintessence.*
*Bodhicitta is the supreme protection from evil*
  *and wrongdoing.*
*Bodhicitta repels the harm of the lower*
  *realms;*
*Bodhicitta opens the supreme path of*
  *liberation. . . .*
*Don't be distracted, don't be distracted*
*Train in Bodhicitta.*
*Don't be mistaken, don't be mistaken—train*
  *in Bodhicitta.*
*Don't err, don't err—train in Bodhicitta.*

—NYOSHUL KHENPO RINPOCHE,
FROM A SPONTANEOUS
ENLIGHTENMENT SONG

Bodhicitta means the purified and fully developed heart-mind. This is the heart, the very soul, of enlightenment. Practicing bodhicitta means cultivating all one's innate enlightened qualities and following the path of awakening.

My living Dzogchen teacher Nyoshul Khenpo often points out that the primary distinction between the deluded mind and the enlightened mind is mainly a difference of narrowness and openness, being narrow-minded versus open-minded. The more constricted and narrow your attitude, the more ego-centered you are. The more open your attitude, the more conscious you are of everyone's well-being. Thus the entire path from an ordinary sentient being to Buddhahood is the gradual opening of heart and mind.

The whole Dzogchen teaching, the entire Vajrayana teaching, the Great Vehicle known as Mahayana is based on trying to live bodhicitta by becoming more enlightened and helping others in everything we do. Realizing suffering, we intuitively wish to end it everywhere. Not just in our own living room, but *everywhere*. We want to end pain, not just the pain in our own lives, but in everyone's life.

Obviously the Bodhisattva Vow is an enormous intentional undertaking. It might even seem beyond the scope of our minds to imagine—to never stop doing spiritual work until there is no more suffering left in the universe. It is a huge boundless intention. Fortunately we only have to take one step at a time. How does one start?

We start here and now by trying to purify our thoughts and our lives so that we help, not harm, others. We don't have to use fancy words like bodhicitta or Bodhisattva for that. In our own Western languages, we too can find words that work. How about unselfish, compassionate, good heart, warm heart, empathetic, virtuous, kind? If bodhicitta doesn't show up in our lives in ways and words we understand, what kind of spiritual practice are we involved in? If spiritual practice doesn't work—if the Dharma doesn't deliver as promised—what good is it?

We don't have to believe in karma, rebirth, enlightenment, or anything explicitly religious or esoteric to start striving to practice bodhicitta as a way of life. As the Dalai Lama said:

> We are visitors on this planet. We are here for ninety, a hundred years at the very most. During that period we must try to do something good, something useful with our lives. Try to be at peace with yourself and help others share that peace. If you contribute to other people's happiness, you will find the true goal, the true meaning of life.

## YOUR THOUGHTS SHAPE AND DEFINE YOUR EXPERIENCE

How do we apply impeccable intentions to the mundane, dog-eat-dog world that we often perceive around us? A real Bodhisattva has pure intentions toward everyone and everything. There is no selfishness, no neurosis, no rough edges, and no hidden agendas. This is the ideal that we strive to cultivate when we take the Bodhisattva's selfless altruistic vow. This is what we are hoping to achieve as we work on ourselves and set about purifying our intentions.

Our internal thoughts and intentions ideally could reflect a purity of heart and a sincere sense of interconnectedness with all humanity. Our lives can reflect generosity, tolerance, hope, forgiveness, honesty, and commitment. This is true whether we're thinking about the survival of the rain forest, the person in the next room, or a snail struggling across a blacktop driveway.

Sometimes it's easier to feel this high-minded purity of intention toward the world as a whole than it is toward those in your own immediate environment. Take Annie, for example. She's probably going to move within a few months, but she hasn't informed her roommate. Because she wants to leave her options open, she plans to tell her at the last moment. She knows perfectly well that this will greatly inconvenience her roommate, but she figures it's an every-roommate-for-herself situation. If questioned about her intentions, she would probably say that this is a practical matter of self-protection. It's often a trade-off: How much will it cost to do what we know is right, compared to what is the best deal we can get for ourselves? In this way we separate ourselves from others, which has a certain cost.

Consider Edward. His immediate boss is in his fifties, and company gossip says that he's about to get the ax because the board of directors seeks a more youthful leadership and image. If his boss gets replaced, Edward will probably get the job. How can Edward keep his thoughts pure and wish his boss a long, healthy, happy, well-employed life, without his own ambition and desire for economic advancement coloring his wishes? Can he cultivate bodhicitta and recognize that his boss wants and needs much the same things that he does?

Marion has a problem some people might consider peculiar. Ants! Lots of ants of all sizes parading determinedly through her living room, into her bathroom, across her kitchen. Last week Marion saw an ad for an ant killer that talked about "getting" ants outside before they get into your house. Marion would like very much to get rid of her ants. But does she want to poison the great outdoors—or the ants? Marion worries that by giving the ants a toxic substance she would also be poisoning the birds who might feast on ant carcasses. This predicament creates genuine conflict for Marion. Is there any way that Marion can maintain her concerned thoughts for the environment and all beings and still not have ants in her sugar bowl and her bedclothes? The monks and nuns in some Buddhist countries don't even go outdoors during the rainy monsoon season in order to avoid squashing bugs. Can we strive so conscientiously toward nonviolence, even in our own Western environment?

Intentions and thoughts about others obviously take place on many different levels. Nathan, for example, loves his wife and, for the most part, wants only the best for her. But they recently had a new baby, and his wife is so absorbed with the child that he often feels left out and ignored. This has made him both resentful and guilty. It was more fun when marriage meant enjoying himself with his wife. Now, it's beginning to mean something different— something that appears to be more connected to responsibility and obligation than it is to fun. Sometimes these feelings drown out his good intentions toward his wife and his new child, and he would rather be out of the house.

Nathan needs to stop and be still with himself in order to get clear about the situation. Just as when you stop stirring and shaking river water the mud settles and its innate clarity emerges. If Nathan could stop struggling and tugging irritably at the knots of his own tangled relationships, there would be more room for things to fall into place and for what really matters to him in the long run to make itself clear. But Nathan has established behavior patterns for dealing with conflict that are not always constructive. Like most of us when anxiety, panic, distress, or depression gains a good grip, Nathan responds by seeking distractions and quick fixes. Some people reach for carbohydrates, chocolate, booze, or department store credit cards; Nathan tends to rely on sex and the heady fantasies created by new romance.

Just last week, for example, when Nathan was in a client's office, he met a very attractive woman with whom he had a good conversation. He's thinking obsessively about her now, and he's thinking about calling her. This is an obvious example of a situation in which his complex, conflicting thoughts and feelings are providing the groundwork for behavior—in this case behavior that could end up creating a lot of pain. How are Nathan's feelings toward his wife and child going to be altered by his conflict? What are Nathan's intentions toward this female acquaintance? Obviously nothing is simple, not even one small set of good intentions. Right now, Nathan is having a difficult time seeing beyond his emotional and physical needs and the immediacy of his current sense of dissatisfaction. How will Nathan behave? That depends. Can he be honest with himself? Can he put another's well-being before his own? Can he be wise? Can he be loving?

# TRUTH AND LOVE, IN EVERYTHING WE DO

It is no easy task to move from an ego-centered selfish point of view toward one of openness, love, and compassion. To live a life of open-handed and open-hearted love, forgiveness, patience, and acceptance requires a great deal of inner work. And yet this is what must be undertaken, step by step, if we are to walk the spiritual path to enlightenment.

Bodhicitta, "awakened mind," is the luminous heart of the Dharma. Wisdom and compassion—truth and love—are absolutely indispensable, mutually supportive, and totally inseparable.

*If it looks like wisdom, but is unkind rather than loving, it's not wisdom.*

*If it feels like love, but it's not wise, it's not love.*

Like the two wings that together enable a bird to fly, love and wisdom are interdependent. These complementary facets of the heart-jewel of bodhicitta—clear, precise, sharp swordlike wisdom and warm, nurturing, open-hearted compassion—facilitate swift transformation on the great highway of awakening. If these qualities don't show up in our daily lives, our Dharma needs better grounding in our bodies and on this earth.

Bodhicitta is the core of spiritual development. The ultimate absolutely transcendent aspect of bodhicitta is sunyata, luminous emptiness or pure and untrammelled, radiant openness. The relative, more conventional aspect of bodhicitta is an unselfish aspiration for enlightenment, best embodied in the Bodhisattva's vow to alleviate the suffering of all beings.

# ACTUALIZING YOUR
# TENDER LOVING HEART

It is said that a long time ago, a Mahayana Buddhist master was teaching about bodhicitta in ancient India, when his words were interrupted by the barking of a dog. The loud insistent barking so annoyed one man in the crowd that he threw a rock at the dog, striking him on the left side. At that instant, the master fell to the ground and cried out in pain. Later, when his worried disciples asked what had happened, they saw that on the teacher's left side there was a large bruise. The dog's pain had so touched this teacher's noble and tender heart that it became his pain. He took it on himself. Whether or not we take teaching tales like this one literally, the moral of the story remains the same. It is said that enlightened teachers can take the suffering of others upon themselves, helping to free others from the heavy karma and the residual debt accrued through negative actions.

Like this Bodhisattva, innately we all have noble and tender hearts, but unlike him, our hearts are not always so open and available. We harden and shield our hearts with our negativity, we protect them with anger, and we conceal them with hostile emotions. We build hard shells and emotional armor to protect us from the suffering of life, but this armor ultimately keeps us so desensitized and frozen in place that we are no longer sensitive and vulnerable, no longer readily able to experience heartfelt compassion or spontaneous joy.

Buddhism consistently presents a practical path-oriented philosophy. The Dharma doesn't just teach that these are the ideals of Buddhism. It says here are the ideals, and these are the tools and techniques for cultivating and achieving these ideals. This is the true genius of the path of Buddha Dharma. It's impossible to change our hardened hearts and entrenched attitudes overnight.

Yet over time, it can definitely be done. The Dharma presents a do-it yourself method of gradually transforming the mind and opening the heart, thus turning thoughts away from narcissistic self-absorption and over-preoccupation with personal anxieties and to-ward altruistic, warm-hearted love for the universal web of being.

Perhaps the most radical teaching of the enlightened Buddha is that ordinary men and women, like you and me, can perfect their innately noble hearts by training the mind. This is something everyone can do. The special training is known as the "Seven Points of Mind-Training," Lo-jong (in Tibetan), and Mahayana mind-training.

# LO-JONG: AWAKENING THE MIND, AND OPENING THE HEART

*To understand where a man is coming from,*
*walk a few miles in his moccasins.*

—NATIVE AMERICAN SAYING

Mahayana mind-training—known as Lo-jong—is the very practi-cal enlightened technique by which we work at transforming our egotistical and selfish attitudes. Through this thorough mind-training, putting ourselves in another's shoes, we soon learn how to treat others as we would like to be treated. By developing that em-pathic, visceral feeling-experience, we actually begin to be able to act differently. Cultivating warmth, fearlessness, and acceptance of both others and ourselves, we really can become more friendly, for-giving, and happy. By changing the atmosphere in which we live, we can favorably alter our entire environment.

These profound mind-training teachings date back to the mid-eleventh century, when a Tibetan king prevailed upon the erudite Indian abbot named Atisha to come from distant India to spread the Dharma in Tibet. It is said that Atisha long contemplated the royal invitation before praying to his meditation deity, the female Buddha Green Tara, for guidance and inspiration. Noble Tara ap-peared to him in a luminous dream, telling the august master that if he went to Tibet, the longevity of the Dharma would increase, but his own life would be shortened by twelve years. At that time, Atisha was considered India's greatest spiritual master. He decided that it was more important to share the liberating Dharma than it was to prolong his mortal existence. At the age of sixty, he traveled by foot from the plains of India through the arduous Himalayan mountain passes of Nepal to the snowy roof of the world, Tibet, where he spent the last years of his life transmitting his teachings orally. He finally passed away in Tibet just as Tara had foretold.

One hundred years after Master Atisha's death, a monk named Geshe Chékawa was in his lama's room one day, and there he noticed some lines of verse that were written down on parchment. They said, "Give all the profit and gain to others, and unselfishly accept all the blame and loss." My teacher Dilgo Khyentse Rinpoche, the enlightened lama who first told me this tale, said that Geshe Chékawa was so moved by the notion of such saintly selfless compassion that the hair rose on the back of his neck and on his head. For Chékawa, finding these lines was a defining moment in his life's path, an epiphany of unspeakable clarity and truth.

Then and there, Geshe Chékawa committed himself to finding the teacher who had written such inspiring lines, but when he inquired, no one in the village knew where these lines came from. So Geshe Chékawa set out on a spiritual quest. And, as he walked, asking everyone he met, he came upon a leper who told him with authority that Atisha, the master who had written this saying, had died. Master Atisha, however, had a disciple, named Layman Drom who could be found; Geshe Chékawa, determined to learn everything he could about these wonderful teachings, trudged on.

When Geshe Chékawa finally met Atisha's disciple, he immediately asked him how important these two lines were. According to our oral teaching tradition, Geshe Chékawa was told, "Whether you believe this or not, whether you like it or not, you have to practice this teaching if you want to attain enlightenment." This statement astonished Geshe Chékawa, and yet its truth resonated in his heart. He stayed with Atisha's disciple, Layman Drom, for twelve years, apprenticing himself to the master and studying and practicing all the mind-training teachings.

At first Geshe Chékawa kept these teachings close to his chest. Then some mendicant lepers came to him, and Geshe Chékawa, who felt he owed a karmic debt of gratitude to the leper who had helped him, began to teach them. Soon rumors began to circulate that these lepers were being healed in body and spirit. People began joking that Geshe Chékawa's place seemed like an infirmary.

And another amazing thing happened. Geshe Chékawa's cynical older brother, who had been extremely skeptical and never practiced Dharma, had a change of heart. Chékawa's brother couldn't help but notice the transformation among the lepers, a transformation he sought for himself. He was too proud to request teachings, so he hid outside an open window where he too could learn about Lo-jong mind-training. Secretly he began to practice what his monk brother taught. As he did so, his recalcitrant character began to noticeably change and soften. Seeing the change in his brother astonished Geshe Chékawa. If it could work for his brother, it could work for anyone!

This inspired Geshe Chékawa to begin writing down all the Lo-jong teachings. As he continued to practice and teach, he codified, structured, and wrote down what Layman Drom had remembered and passed on of the wisdom Atisha had taught, in the form of fifty-nine wise slogans or aphorisms. This became renowned in Tibet as Atisha's "Seven Points of Mind-Training." This training has always been transmitted in the form of short pithy slogans. They are amazingly contemporary and to the point. These essential teachings form the core of the Tibetan Buddhist mind-training practice to cultivate bodhicitta, altruism, and compassion.

Geshe Chékawa was so sincerely committed to the practice of bodhicitta that as his death approached, he prayed to be reborn in the hell realms so he could take on the suffering of beings tormented by heavy negative karma. As the story goes, Chékawa had several blessed clear light dreams as he was dying, indicating that he would be reborn in Buddha Fields, but that his prayers would emanate like bright light rays as blessings even into the depths of hell. I remember Dilgo Khyentse saying, "It is rare to find spiritual masters today who have such incredible compassion." Geshe Chékawa will always be remembered in Tibet as the monk who made certain that Atisha's methods for cultivating loving-kindness would be available for us all. The Dalai Lama has often said, "My religion is loving-kindness."

## THINKING ABOUT OTHERS FIRST

What a unique concept! It's not something we are accustomed to doing. That's why we need ongoing training and practice. It's like learning to be a dancer, gymnast, or pianist: You begin with basic stretches, stances, and finger exercises. Training the mind in bodhicitta also requires diligent practice. And that's exactly what the Lo-jong training provides. Lo means mind; jong means to train, transform, refine, or soften. The image in Tibet is of the habitual, deluded mind as hardened leather being made soft and supple.

The aphorisms and slogans that make up this training are generally considered part of the arcane mystical teachings of Tibet. But as you read them, you can see that they are completely practical and filled with common sense. Cultivating and adapting these truly purified intentions are part of the innate wisdom that we all carry within us. The challenge is to gradually integrate them into your entire being—body, speech, and mind—and to live them more and more through what you do.

Just as a bad workman blames his tools, so a weak Bodhisattva is often tempted to blame difficult life circumstances for his shortcomings. These slogans have helped me keep the ideals and values of bodhicitta in mind whenever life seems to be conspiring to push or drag me off center. We all regularly confront situations that challenge our ability to feel universal love and compassion: Think traffic jams, world chaos, messy roommates, world hunger, partners who don't want to compromise, political chaos. Whether you are thinking about a cruel dictator, a demanding employer, a hyperactive child, or an obstinate mate or ex-lover, it's not always easy to live out of the heart of bodhicitta. Here are some of the slogans I have found particularly useful:

## "*Regard Everything as Though It Is a Dream*"

The original source text says, "Consider how all phenomena are like dreams, and examine the nature of unborn awareness." Things are not what they seem to be; don't be deceived by appearances. The alchemical secret embodied in Buddhism is that nothing is absolutely real; everything is ephemeral, ungovernable, and hollow. Everything is relative and depends upon the mind and its projections and interpretation. How we relate to things makes all the difference. This does not mean that everything exists solely in the mind, as some idealists would have it. It does not mean that nothing matters at all, as nihilists suggest. Nor does it mean that all things are merely projections of mind—for one might just as well then posit that the mind is a projection of all things.

What it means is that everything is impermanent, interdependent, as malleable as soft plastic. Reality is not fixed. Alter the global situation, atmosphere, or temperature, and all local events are affected. Transform any aspect or part of the universal mandala, the cosmic hologram, and all aspects are affected. Presence of mind, or innate awareness, is the pivot upon which all things turn. The genuine master of mindfulness, who stands nowhere, assumes no position or stance and fits in anywhere—he or she can move the universe. The lever of awareness is in his or her hand, and the fulcrum is nowhere else but the present moment.

Working with mind and its essential nature, rather than struggling to alter mere circumstantial conditions, reveals reality—both as it is and as it seemingly appears. Penetrating insight reveals that the responsibility for what we experience lies nowhere but within ourselves, and that the steering wheel of our own lives and evolution is in our hands. Wouldn't it be irresponsible to overlook this fact and continue uncontrollably thrashing around, trashing others as well as ourselves? Check and see: Are your hands on the steering wheel of your life, or are they holding the rearview mirror while you wonder why you are careening around in such an unintended fashion?

### *"Put the Responsibility Where It Belongs"*

This statement reflects an essential bottom-line spiritual position: By clinging to the ego and a self-centered notion of I, me, and mine, each of us sets the stage for our own difficulties. We are all interconnected and interdependent. Thinking about others represents enlightened self-interest; wrong-headed self-cherishing is the root of all our problems. Nothing else can be blamed: When you are selfish and self-involved, you too easily bring grief on yourself. You are in charge of your own karma, your own life, your own spiritual path, and your own liberation, just as I am in charge of mine.

### *"Reflect on the Kindness of Everyone You Meet"*

> *We give thanks to the many beings who helped bring us this food.*
>
> —ZEN MEALTIME PRAYER

Those of you who went to summer camp may remember the lyrics of a camp song "Be kind to your web-footed friends, for a duck may be somebody's mother." Tibetans say that not only is that duck somebody's mother, it may have been *your* mother. It might have been your father, brother, cousin, or best friend, or anyone with whom you have unfinished karma to work out. According to traditional belief, we have all been cycled and recycled through innumerable forms in an inconceivable number of lifetimes—not unlike old wine in new, recyclable bottles. Everyone has been kind and helpful to you in some past life, because everyone you meet has been a loving relative; they should be treated accordingly.

If you are uncomfortable with this traditional rebirth teaching, think of it this way: Everyone you meet, both the wise and the foolish, has something to teach you. Everyone and everything can be celebrated and appreciated, each in its own way. Everyone can learn from your kindness, and everyone deserves your kindness. This is a very important teaching in Tibetan Buddhism. It's also a commonsense approach to life: Learn from all, judge no one, be kind to all, and say thank you.

## "All Activities Should Be Done with One Intention"

Let precious bodhicitta be your organizing principle. Help, and do not harm others. Cultivate these remembrances in everything you do: be gentle, be kind, be thoughtful, be caring, be compassionate, be loving, be fair, be reasonable, be generous to everyone—including yourself.

It really is possible to love everyone—even if you don't always *like* everyone. I had to personally learn this lesson when for several years I was privileged to wear a monk's robe and have a shaved head in cloistered retreats. At first it felt to me as though I was in a no-exit, arranged marriage with an international group of strangers. But eventually one couldn't escape the fact that we all pretty much wanted and needed the same things—that we're all on the same team, the same side on the spiritual battlefield.

I've also learned that you don't always get to pick the people with whom you travel the journey. You might sometimes think you do, but don't be deceived. And the corollary of that—and this was my real lesson—is that you start to realize that you can love even the people you don't like and must love and help everybody.

## "All Teachings Are in Agreement"

The original root text translates this as "All Dharmas agree at one point." This slogan addresses the issues of ego. Whatever form of Buddhist spirituality you are studying, they are all in accord: Ego, self-cherishing, and clinging stand between you and liberation. Step out of the hut of narrow egotism for a moment and enjoy the mansion of boundless freedom and ease. Truths are many, but truth is one. There are many teachings, but only one core: the vital throbbing heart of bodhicitta. Everyone wants and needs the same things. With all the beings you encounter, try momentarily to step away from your self-centered concerns and reflect on what they too are experiencing. This practice can be very rewarding.

## *"Always Reflect on What Provokes Difficulties in Your Life"*

What attracts you? What repels you? What pushes your buttons? Does the slightest bit of criticism wipe you out? Are you easily manipulated by flattery? Do you sexualize every situation? Are you struggling against anger? Reflecting on what pushes your buttons helps you go deeper toward developing equanimity and spiritual detachment.

Take out a notebook, and starting with the Five Hindrances as outlined by the Buddha (see page 91), try to see how these hindrances try to create obstacles to your spiritual development.

## *"Don't Transfer the Bull's Load to the Cow"*

Harry Truman said, "The buck stops here." People appreciated his strength in being able to shoulder his burdens. This slogan is a reminder to all of us not to blame others or shirk responsibility. We are all carrying burdens—emotional, financial, spiritual, and physical; and we all carry psychological issues that come from individual family dynamics. The spirit of bodhicitta suggests that we not transfer our problems to others; they have their own stress, and they may well be weaker. Clean up your own room; pick up your own belongings. Don't think of yourself as a helpless victim, and don't let the tail (emotions) wag the dog (the entire being).

## *"Don't Wallow in Self-pity"*

Do you become so intensely involved with the ups and downs of your life that you sometimes feel as though your thoughts are glued to your own problems and that you are like a human yo-yo? If so, it's extremely difficult to feel love and compassion for others. But give self-preoccupation a little tug and see if you can detach from your personal ups and downs. Like taking off a Band-Aid, it only hurts for a short time. Then it feels so much better. Let some fresh air in. It could be healing.

## "Always Maintain a Joyful Mind"

Why not be cheerful? Why be miserable? Why not pretend to be happy instead? In fact, why not pretend to be happy, free, and complete instead of pretending the contrary is true? Years ago I remember reading a survey of people who considered themselves to be happy. Many of the respondents felt that they had achieved this desirable state by making the decision to be happy and content. Try making this decision and see what happens. Anyone who has ever attended a peace demonstration knows the song "Give Peace a Chance." Why not give joy a chance?

My friend Sylvia Boorstein, a Buddhist meditation teacher who is sometimes referred to as a grandmother Bodhisattva, wrote a delightful book about achieving happiness, which is titled *It's Easier Than You Think*. This kind of teaching makes my heart sing. At the same time, let's not fool ourselves. It can sometimes also be more difficult than we think. The entire tantric teaching is one of appreciating the rich tapestry and beauty of things just as they are. The good and the bad. The shadow and the light. The dark days of February, and the sunny days of May. I think of it as dancing with life, not just trying to control it or figure it out.

The spiritual masters of Tibet say that the ability to maintain inner joy and a larger perspective in the face of adversity is a sign that mind-training is taking effect and transforming our lives.

# CREATING YOUR OWN SLOGANS FOR YOUR OWN PATH

Mind-training slogans are a richly rewarding method for keeping you on the path. There is no reason why you can't find your own homegrown, native slogans. One of my favorite Western-style slogans is *Have a Nice Day, Unless You've Made Other Plans*. It sits on the wall above my desk, and I often post it on bulletin boards at meditation retreats. It certainly wasn't written by a lama of ancient times, but it still reflects the message and meaning of Dharma. I also have a lapel pin stuck to the dashboard of my car that says *Celebrate Life*. I like having it there to remind Serious Das to lighten up and find joy in whatever needs to be done. Try to mine your own life for the wisdom sayings that resonate with your heart. Your life and your path are unique; why not have a few unique slogans that have meaning to you? Reach into your heart cave and awaken the wisdom in your heart-mind.

When you come up with slogans that speak to your experience, write them down so you don't forget them. Carry a small pocket notebook for the purpose. Don't be distressed if your slogans sound like clichés. No one else has to see them. When something true has been repeated millions of times, it may sound very familiar, but it still carries truth. Think about the slogan that has been used by so many 12-Step programs—*Let Go, And Let God*. It's had meaning for a great many people; why shouldn't it have meaning for you? Perhaps you have a variation on the same theme. Several people I know tell me that when they are stressed, the homegrown slogan they pull up is *Take a Deep Breath and Count to Ten*. Dzogchen know-it-alls like to say *There Is Nothing to Do but Remain in the View*, as in "Step back for a moment, and take it all in." I see some connection here.

Why don't you see if you can access your own inner wisdom, right now? Find a slogan that reminds *you* of the heart of the Dharma. *Hi Mom!* for example, might be a phrase that calls to mind the Buddhist belief that all beings deserve your love and compassion. Whatever cheers you up deserves to be written down and put where you can see it. Enjoy yourself; exploit your own natural internal resources.

# ADVANCED ALCHEMY:
# TRANSFORMING PAIN INTO LOVE

> *The quality of mercy is not strain'd.*
> *It droppeth as the gentle rain from heaven*
> *Upon the place beneath: it is twice blest;*
> *It blesseth him that gives and him that*
> *takes . . .*

— FROM *THE MERCHANT OF VENICE* BY
WILLIAM SHAKESPEARE

*"May all the suffering of all beings come upon me, and may they have all my joy and happiness."* The first time I heard this prayer being chanted in Tibetan, it reminded me of Jesus' selfless life and words, and how far away this kind of attitude seemed from my life experience. I thought this exalted attitude was reserved for saints, certainly not for me, a Jewish guy from Long Island.

The words also scared me. Suppose I prayed along with the group, and I really did take on somebody else's suffering and became ill. In Asia? With Asian medical care? Even if I could get back to a high-tech hospital in America, the doctors might not even know what I had! Such were my fearful thoughts at my first exposure to this intense practice. It took me a bit of time to appreciate the remarkable meditation practice known as tonglen.

Tonglen—literally known as Sending-and-Taking—is an integral part of the Mahayana mind-training. Some Westerners balk at the practice of tonglen because they tend to take it too literally. They don't see it for what it is: a way of transforming the recalcitrant hardened heart into a heart softened by love and empathy. My suggestion is: Don't be afraid of it; rather, regard it initially as an advanced mind-training technique to be used as a way of increasing one's capacity for unconditional love, generosity, and openness of heart. When you are ready to undertake such selfless practice, it awaits you.

This powerful and advanced practice is not a parlor trick; it's not something you should do for kicks or to prove anything. When you replace self-concern with a concern for others, you soften your character and refine your spirituality. Tonglen is not taught with the idea that practitioners should take on diseases and become ill; it is taught as a way to open up and reverse our conditioned habits of clinging to desired circumstances and aversion to whatever is unwanted.

Tonglen—the taking on of burdens without feeling burdened— is a lesson in letting go of self-clinging and attachment, and transforming egotism into love. For centuries the learned practitioners of Tibet have used sending-and-taking as a way of freeing up, loosening up, and dissolving the barriers between self and others by transforming self-centered attitudes. For example, if you are in the middle of an acrimonious situation, don't expect tonglen to fix it on the spot, but it can help you change your point of view and, in the process, change the entire atmosphere. This actually works.

# *Tonglen Meditation:*
## *Exchanging Oneself for Others*

One is asked to approach this Sending-and-Taking meditation with an attitude of extraordinary compassion and love for all. Think about all the suffering in the world. Wouldn't it be wonderful to be able to take that pain and convert it to happiness, health, and well-being? Wouldn't it be a worthwhile thing if you could open your heart, accepting suffering and being able to transform it into love and goodness? Let's do it now.

### START BY ACCEPTING YOUR OWN BEING

Many teachers recommend that you begin the practice of sending-and-taking with yourself. To do this, you simply consider yourself as having two parts. One part is loving and compassionate; the other needs love and compassion. Envision yourself being able to send love, care, and acceptance back to your own being.

I highly recommend that you begin your sending-and-taking practice with thoughts of your own being, your life, and your journey. When trying to generate compassion for all beings, it is essential to remember that you are one of them. You have to be strong, confident, and accepting of yourself before you can begin accepting others. Use tonglen to forgive yourself for the things about which you feel guilty, inadequate, or responsible; use tonglen as a spiritual healing, and return to wholeness and wellness through this soulful healing practice. As Lao Tzu said, "When you accept yourself, the whole world accepts you."

## EXTEND YOUR LOVE AND ACCEPTANCE TO OTHERS

After you have warmed your own heart with love, extend the circle of beings for whom you feel love and compassion. Begin with those who are close to you—your parents, your family, your children, and friends. Gradually extend that circle until you are able to encompass enemies as well as friends. Finally, extend your circle of compassion until you feel that all the beings in the world are soothed and healed by the tenderness of your love.

## EXCHANGE HAPPINESS AND LOVE FOR SUFFERING AND PAIN

Begin the tonglen practice by relaxing and centering yourself. Return to yourself, come home to the present moment. To start this practice, just for a moment flash on absolute bodhicitta as you understand it. Pure presence, being itself. Gaze into the sky and become aware of emptiness. Everything is empty, like a dream. But it's not just like an empty room; it's a sparkling sunlit day, and the sun is filling all the spaces. Awaken to ultimate presence, and dissolve in the luminous emptiness of the moment. Open to the infinite boundless expanse, startling yourself into total wakefulness. Enjoy this natural great perfection, things just as they are.

## RIDE UPON THE MOVING BREATH

In the tonglen meditation, you follow your breath. Ride the in-breath; ride the out-breath. Concentrate. Follow the inhalation; follow the exhalation. Breathe in through your nose, out through your mouth. Breathe in and out, again. Accept the in-breath; let go of the out-breath. Don't be stingy; take it all in, and breathe it all out. Let it flow, let it go. Why hold back?

As you breathe, visualize that you are inhaling darkness, like smog. Hoover it up like a giant vacuum cleaner. But you're not getting stuck with this dark smog. You hold the breath for a moment, letting everything dissolve. Everything is resolved in the spacious, clear awareness of bodhicitta. Then exhale; visualize all that smog streaming out of you as shining light. You are exhaling luminosity, like sunlight and cool fresh spring breezes.

## MEDITATE ON INTERWOVEN SENDING AND RECEIVING AND BEGIN THE RECEIVING WITH YOURSELF

This is one of Atisha's slogans from the "Seven Points of Mind-training." The practice begins by inhaling your own conflicting emotions, your own negative karma, and your own difficulties. A moment of transformation. Then exhale, as you visualize all this negativity riding out as a breath stream of happiness and joy.

Continue exhaling and inhaling—riding the breath, as you begin to empathize with the problems of the world. Inhale all the darkness, disease, unhappiness. Inhale: "May all the difficulties, doubts, and fears in the world be absorbed into the empty nature of my mind." Exhale: "May all beings have all my happiness, faith, and fearlessness."

# A HEALING ATTITUDE

As we think, so we become. The tonglen meditation is done with the hope of healing one's attitude and restoring it to wholeness, as well as healing the troubles of the world. It helps train us to be genuinely present with difficult situations, and to bring more enlightened principles into daily life, without excessive reactivity. Through tonglen practice, we can change the entire atmosphere. We can loosen up and dissolve the dualism between light and dark, good and bad, positive and negative, wanted and unwanted circumstances. We take in the bad, and we give away all that is desirable. We do this as an exercise in generosity, transcendence, and nonattachment.

When you first start this practice, you may have some difficulties as you try to visualize giving away all your advantages, assets, and delights to people you dislike as well as people you care about. But over time, this will change. As you explore your inner resources, you will discover that you have an abundance, more positive resources than you can possibly imagine. Reach into the infinite spiritual richness of your innately compassionate and wise Buddha-nature.

# ETHICS
# TRAINING

## *Living a Sacred Life*

*Each thought, each action in the sunlight of awareness becomes sacred. In this light, no boundary exists between the sacred and the profane.*

—THICH NHAT HANH,
*PEACE IS EVERY STEP*

Because so many of us are first introduced to Buddhism through meditation, it's sometimes easy to forget that the Dharma actually includes Three Liberating Trainings: Wisdom, Ethics, and Meditation. The Ethics section of the Noble Eight-Fold Path includes Right Speech, Right Action, and Right Livelihood. It shows us how—through mindful attention and nonattachment— to make our daily lives sacred by practicing ethical restraint, moral- ity, and sincere virtue in all that we do. It is not enough to think wisely; we must also speak, act, work, and love wisely. This is how we integrate meditation and awareness into our daily life.

The Sanskrit word for virtue or morality is sila (pronounced sheela). This beautiful ancient word reminds us always to practice ethical conduct, and a wholesome, balanced self-discipline. Before you speak or act, stop for a moment and think about sila: Are you about to be helpful or harmful? Skillful or unskillful? Selfless or selfish? Do your words and actions accurately reflect your deeper inner intentions and sincere commitment to loving-kindness and bodhicitta? Myth has it that the fragrance of a holy person's righ- teousness wafts up even to realms of the gods and Buddhas; they, in turn, rejoice by raining down flowers and nectars upon such goodness.

Sila (virtue or ethics) is traditionally likened to a cool shade tree; under its branches, a pilgrim trekking through the hot desert sun of conflicting emotions can find relief from the fierce storms of impulsive and compulsive behavior. In your life, trust virtue, righteousness, and self-discipline to lubricate the friction of both internal and external conflicts.

On an outer level, sila means contributing to a better world by living your life in a straightforward, honest, healing, nonviolent, unselfish, and caring manner. It implies character development— straightening out whatever is bent or crooked in your behavior and yourself.

On an inner level, sila means being genuinely honest and true to yourself, free from self-deception, ill-will, selfish bias, and prej- udice.

On an innate or natural level, sila means understanding that we are all inherently virtuous and immaculate, for don't we all have purity of heart and the basic goodness of Buddha-nature at the core of our innermost authentic being?

We create our world and our karma through words and deeds as well as thoughts. As your Buddhist practice develops, you can train your mind from the outside in by acting impeccably and cul- tivating authenticity in all that you say and do. At the same time, you can work on yourself from the inside out—from your innate goodness and integral wholeness—by resting in the natural state. Let your natural morality, your intrinsic worth, virtue, innate purity, and honesty flow forth in all your interactions. This is called "coming from the heart," or living from the heart. Virtue is its own reward, as they say. That means now, not later. Goodness is a good thing. Our turbulent times call for it. Check it out. In your own life you will be surprised at how rewarding it can be.

# RIGHT SPEECH

## *Speaking the Truth*

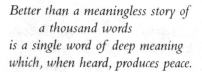

*Better than a meaningless story of
a thousand words
is a single word of deep meaning
which, when heard, produces peace.*

—FROM THE DHAMMAPADA
(SAYINGS OF THE BUDDHA)

Once the holy Hasidic master Baal Shem sent Yacov Yosef, his second-greatest pupil, an outstanding scholar and Kabbalist, to test the learning of Yechiel, a prospective son-in-law for Baal Shem's daughter, Udel. Yechiel, like the holy master, came from a simple German Jewish family.

When Yacov Yosef returned from his mission, he reported back to the Baal Shem Tov:

"Yechiel answered, 'I don't know' to everything I asked him. I wonder about this guy . . ."

The Baal Shem Tov replied, "Oh God, I'd love to have such a man as my son-in-law."

The young man told the simple truth, which is sometimes easier said than done, and the old rabbi recognized his wisdom. Words can be gifts, words can be weapons, words can be magic; words can be prayer, poetry, or song. What is traditionally known as Right Speech is the third touchstone on the Eight-Fold Path. So speak your truth. Tell it like it is. There is no reason to do otherwise.

# EVERYTHING YOU SAY CAN EXPRESS YOUR BUDDHA-NATURE

In a world of exaggerated advertising campaigns, exploitative talk shows, hate radio, and political spin doctors, Right Speech and impeccable expression may seem to be a rather tall order. Yet if we are sincere about embodying the Dharma, our words ideally will become a reflection of our desire to help others. Think kindly; speak gently and clearly. The wisdom of cause and effect, or karma, teaches us that everything matters—every breath, every syllable, every sentence. As we walk the path to enlightenment, nothing is meaningless, and it all counts. Imagine that all the thoughts and fragmented sentences that are just now swirling through your head were printed out on a giant chalkboard—like the daily menu in some restaurants. Which thoughts do you sincerely want to express? It's a choice we make—sometimes hundreds of times every day. With your words you confirm to the world, and yourself, what you think is important. Words help concretize our thoughts and concepts; they define our priorities, reify our ideas and opinions, and express our worldview and intentions. Words have power; to be specific, *your* words have power. We can use speech patterns to help us communicate with others in a more considered, conscious way, or we can be careless and create trouble with our words— trouble for ourselves as well as others.

In the context of Dharma, speech is a particularly compelling issue because to reflect upon speech is to think about self, non-self, and others. Don't most of us use speech as an expression of ego and the need to hang on to and confirm our illusory self? Don't we use speech to communicate that we exist? "I'm here," we say, confirming and marking out our territorial space. To some extent, we all habitually use words to express ego and a false self. By putting forth our views, we use speech to shore up the concrete citadel of ego and the notion of "me" and "mine." We tell ourselves and others stories about ourselves and our lives. We speak to others; we speak to ourselves. What do we say? And why do we say it?

When the Buddha talked about Right Speech or impeccable speech, what he meant was excellent speech that reflected inner wisdom, clear vision, and Buddha-nature. The instructions that come down to us from the Buddha concerning everyday speech are simple yet profound. On a mundane level, we are instructed as follows:

## SPEAK THE TRUTH, TELL NO LIES

On this point, the Buddha's advice was remarkably straightforward. He said: "If he is called to tell what he knows, he answers if he knows nothing. 'I know nothing.' And if he knows, he answers, 'I know.' If he has seen nothing, he answers: 'I have seen nothing.' And if he has seen, he answers: 'I have seen.' Thus, he never knowingly speaks a lie, neither for the sake of his own advantage, nor for the sake of another person's advantage, nor for the sake of any advantage whatsoever."

Words articulated without guile, masked ego needs, conflict, or hidden agendas—wouldn't it be wonderful to be able to speak with such clarity and simplicity, all the time? Haven't there been times in your life when you are so centered and clear that your words, like the Buddha's, ring with truth and sanity? Don't we all sometimes have these breakthrough moments, times when we are in touch with who we are and what we know? These are precious moments, minutes, or hours when each of us is able to speak his or her own truth, honestly and fearlessly. But these breakthroughs are difficult to sustain.

As a seeker, you have probably already wrestled with the problems connected to outright lying; in all likelihood, you've made an appropriate decision not to be evasive or indulge in direct false-hoods or deceitful, manipulative statements. We all agree that out-right lying is counterproductive. But as we walk further along the spiritual path, chances are we will each arrive at checkpoints where the subtleties of truth come into play. We may discover time after time that it's difficult to be clear and forthright in everything we say, and we may find ourselves compromising and shading the truth. Instead of saying what we know is true, for example, we say things that others want to hear. Or we say things that we want to hear—and believe.

When we don't want to appear weak or vulnerable, we say things that make us look strong and powerful. When we don't want others to think we are out of control, we use words to con-trol what others do. It's very easy to spot the manipulations of the spin doctors from Madison Avenue or Washington, D.C.; it's more complex when we create our own egotistical advertising cam-paigns. Yet this is what we do all the time by presenting ourselves as we would like to appear and hiding behind the stories we tell ourselves and others to get what we think we want. All this only serves to create false personas that leave us feeling incomplete and alienated from our authentic selves.

Don't you sometimes use words to distance others and protect your true feelings? Haven't you ever told people that you were feeling "fine" even when you were depressed and sad? We don't al-ways use words to communicate from our hearts and then we ex-pect others to be mind readers. Sometimes we even tell ourselves stories. "I don't eat *so* many sweets," we say to ourselves as we reach again into the bag of cookies. "I'm not really lying to Miranda," we think as we make up a plausible excuse to break an appointment. "It doesn't really matter," we reassure ourselves, even when we know it matters a great deal.

Everyone says that communication and mutual understanding is the essence of good relationships. And nowhere are the subtleties of honest speech more apparent than in our personal relationships. However, as much as we may want to express ourselves authenti-cally with words that reflect love, warmth, and openness, we don't always manage to do it. Our expectations get in the way and distort the picture; so do our desires, fears, illusions, and projections. That's why we all regularly need to stop and ask ourselves if we are moving in the direction of more honesty, or not.

I often speak to people who tell me they are unhappy because their loved ones don't seem to be listening to what they have to say. They feel invalidated and as though their opinions are being disregarded. But when these people delve a little bit deeper below the surface of their complaints, they often realize they are failing to express their feelings and wishes in a clear and direct manner. When we withhold our true feelings, protect our emotions, and construct false personas to present to the world, we become part of the problem.

Reality—seeing things just as they are—is a central issue of Buddhist practice. Pure attention, unclouded by distortion or delusion, knows things exactly as they are, in the present moment. We bring Right Speech into our relationships by trying always to be honest and forthright and by letting go of our intricate defense systems and being truthful and open about who we are and how we feel.

As part of awareness practice involving Right Speech, try listening to yourself so you can hear how you sound from a different perspective, as if being outside of yourself as an objective listener. Speaking the truth is a very present-moment activity; truth-telling begins by becoming aware of what you tell yourself. Then try listening to the way you sound to others. Do you sound tentative, confused, angry, rattled, tense? Are you using speech to manipulate feelings or emotions, yours or someone else's? Do you use speech, or even silence, as a way of hiding who you are? Are you communicating what you think you're communicating? Are you able to recognize and acknowledge reality? Are you able to speak your truth in your own authentic voice, unflinchingly and without hesitation?

## USE WORDS TO HELP, NOT HARM

Right Speech reminds us to refrain from causing trouble with speech that is hurtful or unnecessarily disruptive. Have you ever had the experience of saying something and regretting it later? Perhaps something sarcastic that you thought was funny? Of course. We all have. When I began teaching, I quickly realized that if I made what I thought was a little ironic or facetious joke, some sensitive soul might end up feeling hurt, ridiculed, exposed, or betrayed.

One of Atisha's mind-training Lo-jong Slogans is "Don't Talk About Injured Limbs." It's a good slogan to remember because what we describe as a joke may in reality be pointing out another being's defects and weaknesses—not unlike staring or pointing a finger. It can be hurtful even though we are backing into it through a joke. And yet how hard it is to walk this talk. What a temptation it sometimes is to poke fun or show how funny and clever we can be with our quick tongues and caustic wit. Hurtful words reinforce personal alienation and a dualistic view. Slander sows discord; sensitive gentle speech can bring about peace and reconciliation.

The Dharma also reminds us that a judgmental point of view will obscure our higher view and distort our direct appreciation of how things are. In the New Testament, Jesus points out that we tend to notice the small imperfection in someone else's eye while overlooking the log sticking out of our own. A Tibetan proverb says: "Don't notice the tiny flea in the other person's hair and overlook the lumbering yak on your own nose." Judgmental words and self-righteous tones fail to help any situation.

Some people seem to be particularly gifted at using words to help others. They are so constructive, positive, and empathetic that they make you feel good whenever you talk to them. "How great for you," they say. "Tell me about it; I want to hear what you have to say." You can feel their intention to give support and encouragement. These communicative geniuses seem to have a special gift—they are able to truly see and hear others. Open and sensitive to what others are experiencing, these gifted listeners are real healers. Listening with a nonjudgmental and open heart is a way to bring bodhicitta and loving-kindness into your communication with others. The Dharma tells us that if we listen carefully, we will be able to hear the natural Buddha in everyone.

# DON'T GOSSIP OR TELL TALES

*We would have much peace if we would not busy ourselves with the saying and doings of others.*

—THOMAS À KEMPIS

The Buddha specifically instructed his followers to avoid bearing tales and indulging in idle gossip. As an awareness exercise, the pioneering insight meditation teacher Joseph Goldstein sometimes asks his students to refrain from saying *anything* about *anyone* who isn't present. No talking about people who annoy you as well as not talking about people who enthrall you. That means no conversations devoted to analyzing or dissecting anyone else's problems or behavior good or bad—unless the person you are talking about is there to hear what you say. This is not an endlessly ongoing behavioral restriction, but a temporary practice, an experiential experiment. Try it, and watch your reactions. When we stop talking about others, we discover how much time and energy we waste daily with conversations that not only serve no constructive purpose but also seduce and carry us away from the present moment.

Gossiping about others is another obvious way of feeding junk food to the ego. When we gossip, it's easy to feel part of the "in crowd"; for a moment we might feel superior. But telling tales or making unkind jokes only serves to objectify and distance others. The people or group about whom we are talking lose their humanity—just as we lose ours. Impeccable speech asks us to utilize awareness to start unraveling the cocoon of ego. Resist the urge to talk about others and begin to live in the present moment, with whoever is with you and no one else. This very moment is sufficient, perfect, and complete. Enjoy and appreciate what is before your very eyes, and all will be revealed—fresh and radiant as any dawn, as at the very dawn of creation.

## AVOID HARSH ABUSIVE LANGUAGE;
### SPEAK KINDLY

It's not just what you say, it's *how, when,* and *why* you say it.

*How:* Deidra is telling her husband Jacob that she hates finding his dirty socks and smelly sneakers on the bathroom floor. Her tone is harsh, accusatory, and sarcastic. Jacob uses much the same tone when he complains that Deidra always wastes energy by keeping the thermostat on high during winter days, even when no one is home. Do these complaints serve their purpose, or would not a clearer, more direct request or suggestion help alleviate these problems?

*When:* Sandi is feeling very pleased and enthusiastic about her new job interview. She's so very happy. Why has her friend Martha chosen this moment to tell Sandi all the things that could possibly go wrong? Why is Martha raining on Sandi's parade? Is this perhaps Martha's pattern? And why does Sandi inevitably find friends who undermine her and use speech to dampen her hopeful enthusiasm?

*Why:* Criticism can be helpful and constructive; it can also be destructive, abusive, undermining, and petty. When your car mechanic tells you about the rust on the underside of your car, he's trying to help you. But if your neighbor tells you that your old car has become the neighborhood eyesore, is that genuinely meant to help?

Abusive speech is most frequently associated with anger and hostility, even when the anger is expressed as annoyance, sarcasm, surreptitious verbal sniping, or barbed wit. We all know what anger feels like. When we feel angry, it can take a real effort to look at the other person and see a living spirit, just like yourself. Equally challenging is finding a way to let the Buddha speak through you with healing words of acceptance, love, and compassion.

Sometimes the greatest challenge of Right Speech is not sounding overly harsh and critical with our nearest and dearest—mates, children, parents, and colleagues. You love your mate, or your child, but he or she does things that make you furious and cause both your voice and your blood pressure to rise. Sometimes what we need to do is simply stop for a moment, breathe, and come into an awareness of precisely what is taking place; and then try to act more skillfully, more appropriately, with consideration for all parties to the situation.

People often ask me how they can find more constructive ways of dealing with anger and aggression. It's a difficult question. What do we do when someone is pushing all our buttons? In Buddhism, anger is considered the most problematic of the negative emotions, or kleshas. Yet anger is just an energy, a reaction; it is workable. Frequently we need to learn to say "no" clearly and firmly without aggression—before a situation escalates into an intense conflagration. Sometimes *no* is more positive and affirming than an indiscriminate and poorly thought out *yes*. Anger need not be suppressed, repressed, or bottled up. It actually has something to tell us, if we just listen.

Even such a gentle and well-trained spiritual leader as the Dalai Lama has to deal with these issues. He says that for decades he has been turning the other cheek and trying not to react precipitously against the Chinese, accepting the movements of karma as he seeks peaceful reconciliation and mutual understanding. But every time he has compromised, they didn't give anything in return. He told me that maybe he needs to do something different. These are not simple questions. After all, isn't there such a thing as righteous anger? Doesn't anger have its own intelligence and logic, useful in certain ways and at certain times?

The next time you feel so angry that you could scream, ask yourself: Who is making me angry? Perhaps the anger is subtly directed at yourself. When our expectations are not met, we tend to blame others and become angry. But is our discontent really their fault? Shantideva said that anger is the greatest evil because it is so destructive and can cause so much harm. The trained mind of a Bodhisattva, like a peaceful lake, is able to transcend anger. Even if people throw sparks into it, it doesn't explode because it's like water and not volatile. The untrained mind, on the other hand, can be likened to a big pool of gasoline. Every spark makes it explode. In life, there will always be sparks. But does there have to be an explosion? That's your responsibility. No one can make us angry if we have no seeds of anger left inside.

When we think about austerities, we usually imagine a yoga

practice like fasting, keeping all-night vigils, lying on beds of nails, or walking barefoot in the snow or on live coals. Shantideva taught that patience in the face of anger is the greatest austerity; patience and forbearance is the hardest inner-outer practice. Concerning right speech, Jesus said that it isn't what we put into our mouths that defiles us, but rather what comes out. Through awareness practice, we can develop a patient and tolerant inner fortitude; this is the way to transcend the ego reactivity that makes us lash out uncontrollably with words. Shantideva wrote:

> *Whenever I wish to move*
> *Or to speak,*
> *First I shall examine my state of mind,*
> *And firmly act in a suitable way.*

> *Whenever my mind becomes attached*
> *Or angry,*
> *I shall not react, nor shall I speak;*
> *I shall remain mum and unmoved like a tree.*

## THE LESS FULL OF OURSELVES WE ARE, THE MORE ROOM THERE IS FOR OTHERS

To talk about speech is also to talk about listening. When I first started teaching meditation, a colleague told me that the most important teaching skill to develop was the ability to be still and listen. It was great advice. In our conversations we can be so intent on getting our messages across that we're not really paying attention to what other people are trying to say. It's as if we're just waiting for them to stop speaking so we can say what we already have in mind; our preconceived agendas get in the way of any real dialogue. As you practice Right Speech, try to be open, still, and aware of what others are thinking and feeling. Can you hear when others are happy, sad, depressed, confused? As we become more conscious, more aware, we discover the joys of listening and we let go of our need to broadcast. I call this opening the third ear, the inner ear of genuine listening. If we are sufficiently sensitive and aware, we can listen through all the senses.

Haven't you ever known someone who seemingly could not listen, someone whose ego seemed so overpowering that he or she couldn't stop speaking—someone who used words to dominate and control, as if in a filibuster? Some loudmouth who seems to take up almost all the oxygen in any room he or she enters? Or someone whose rude, inappropriate, or provocative remarks constantly invade your space? This is simply "Station Ego" broadcasting, loud and unclear.

Mirror-like awareness clearly reflects things just as they are, without distortion, coloring, or expectation. True listening is a way of stopping and being present so that whatever is being said is immediately apparent, as are all movements in the entire inner and outer energy field. This is one aspect of developing awareness. It's a skill that good psychotherapists use to clearly reflect, without distortion or interference, whatever is brought up in a counseling session so that their clients can better see and know themselves, and in this way discover for themselves what they want and need. Freud called it hovering awareness, just being present without judgment or preconception.

Can you hear what's between the lines? Can you sense where the words are coming from, not just hear the words? Can you perceive and even feel what others are feeling as they speak? Good fences may make good neighbors, but good listeners make good friends. We can learn to hear with whatever is being said in the present moment. Simply tune in to a greater emotional bandwidth, and receive more channels and stations. Some people can hear the music of the celestial spheres along with the dakinis, the muses, angelic hosts, and other celestial songsters. Tune in to all that is. It's worth it.

# WORDS FROM THE HEART

When I was about six, one of our neighbors was a very elderly man who had a medical condition that made it impossible for him to speak. Instead of talking, he made a noise that sounded like "boop-boop." At the time it seemed as though the only people he talked to were the neighborhood children, whom he always greeted with his signature sound. He really seemed to enjoy communicating with us in this way. My sister and I called him Mr. Boop-boop or the Boop-boop Man. Every day we would run outside and wait for him to walk by at his regular hour. He was happy to see us, and we made him smile. We had a real relationship, and we loved him because we could feel that he loved us. In fact, I think we had more of a relationship with him than we did with any of the other adults who lived on our block at that time. I don't really remember much from the early fifties about the other adult neighbors—how they looked or what they said. But every now and then I still remember and think fondly about Mr. Boop-boop, with a smile on my adult face and a large burst of laughter from my inner child.

Often when we think we are communicating with sentences, we are really communicating as much or more through energy, emotions, and gestures, body language, eye contact, and facial expressions. Mr. Boop-boop radiated kindness and warmth. As children, that's what we responded to; that's why we felt as though we had a real relationship with someone who couldn't speak with words, yet spoke eloquently heart to heart.

Frequently in life, words are extraneous, although we depend on them so much. Think about the people with whom you have relationships that are built primarily on smiles, hand waves, and body language. The mailperson, the helpful dry cleaner, the kind woman who owns the bakery, the nice guy who butters your bagel and smiles when he hands it to you, the jolly person on the corner who sells you your newspaper, the cheerful supermarket cashier, the good-natured car mechanic, or the neighbor who sees you standing on a wintry street corner and offers to drive you home. Pets and other animals are extremely communicative, and we love to commune with them, don't we? We often seem to understand each other quite well, almost without words. I get a lot of teachings and inspiration, along with love, from my dog, Bodhi-dogma, and my friend's cat, Bodhicattva. These nonverbal relationships add joy and dimension to our lives. We could scarcely live without them.

# THE TREASURY OF SACRED SOUND

## PRAYER AS SACRED SPEECH

*My greatest weapon is mute prayer.*

—GANDHI

In theistic religions, prayers are addressed to a supreme being or higher power. In nontheistic Buddhism, as we pray, we are not petitioning for something so much as we are reaffirming our intentions and asserting our vows. The word we translate as prayer in Tibetan is Monlam. It roughly translates as aspiration-path or wishing-path. In the Dzogchen tradition, prayers are like the self-resound of Buddha-nature, Dharmata, a spontaneous display of innate wisdom mind—as prayers to the primordial Buddha in the Dzogchen tantras say.

The following, my own daily morning loving-kindness prayer, is based on an original Buddhist scripture called the Metta Sutra. It's an excellent example of how we can cultivate benevolent intentions and bring them forth through the speech door in the form of a prayer of affirmation that can be chanted, sung, or spoken. This kind of meditational prayer helps us develop more loving, kind, warm, constructive, and positive mental habits and external behavior.

### METTA PRAYER

*May all beings be happy, content, and fulfilled.*
*May all beings be healed and whole.*
*May all have whatever they want and need.*

*May all be protected from harm, and free from fear.*
*May all beings enjoy inner peace and ease.*
*May all be awakened, liberated, and free.*
*May there be peace in this world, and throughout the entire universe.*

The Buddha himself said that if you repeatedly practice this meditation and recitation—with a forgiving, loving heart, while relinquishing judgment, anger, and prejudice—great benefits will definitely ensue: You will sleep easily, wake easily, and have pleasant dreams; people will love you; celestial beings will love you and protect you; poisons, weapons, fire, and other external dangers will not harm you; your face will be radiant and your mind concentrated and serene; and you will die unconfused and be reborn in happy realms.

Through the karmic laws of cause and effect, praying for peace will certainly help bring peace about. We pray for peace for the sangha and the community of all beings, but we recognize that peace begins with oneself; thus we also pray for our own outer and inner peace as a member of that sangha. In this way we learn to better love, forgive, and accept ourselves; the prayerful phrase "for the benefit of all beings" should not exclude ourselves.

# USING A MANTRA TO FIND
# YOUR OWN VOICE

Mantras are sacred words of great power and blessings. In most Asian countries, including Tibet, mantras are still typically chanted in the original Sanskrit language, which is considered the language of the gods. The word mantra is literally translated as "something to lean the mind (manas) upon." And that's what a mantra can do. Mantra practice can be relied upon as a quick, effective, and powerful way of focusing, stabilizing, and freeing the mind. Mantra practice can help inculcate constructive states of mind; reinforcing mind-training, it enhances our basic intelligence, wakefulness, concentration, and present awareness.

There are different kinds of mantras: healing mantras; wisdom mantras; compassion mantras; awareness mantras; purification mantras; wrathful mantras (used to dispel obstacles); and peaceful mantras. We sometimes hear short one-syllable mantras such as "Om" or "Ah." These are known as seed syllable mantras. Like the seed of a beautiful plant, the single syllable carries within it all the teachings, mysteries, wisdom, and realizations of the final fruit or flower of awakened enlightenment.

Mantra practice, a highly effective centering skill, can legitimately be regarded as a tool of transcendence or a kind of technology of the sacred. We also combine mantra with other centering devices. For example, while we chant the mantra, we concentrate on breathing, hold a visualization in our head, and hold a rosary (mala) of beads for centering as well as a way to keep track of the number of recitations. Mantra meditation can alter the atmosphere and effect swift transformation, both externally in the world and within ourselves.

## OUTER, INNER, AND INNATE REASONS FOR CHANTING MANTRAS

On an outer level, we use mantra to consecrate or bless each activity. For example, as an exercise, chant or say to yourself the cosmic, all-sounds-in-one seed mantra, "Om," each time you enter a room to heighten your awareness of what you are doing in that very present moment. This is a very good mindfulness practice in daily life.

On an inner level, we use mantras as concentration devices when we meditate and as a way to transform our ordinary perceptions into purified perceptions. One day when we were discussing meditation practice, the enlightened Dzogchen master Dudjom Rinpoche told me that when he was distracted he would chant the one-hundred-syllable purification mantra to, as it were, return to himself. In Tibet, mantras such as Om Mani Pedmé Hung, the divine mantra of unconditional love and compassion, are often combined with radiant visualizations of geometric shapes like stars, lotuses, or the cosmic holograms known as mandalas, or the sacred hand and finger gestures known as mudras—facilitating an experience of this world as a Buddha Field, as nirvana.

On an innate or secret level, there is the ultimate centering device, the mystical, wordless, effortless mantra of indwelling wisdom. Here is a place that you can rely upon, a place where you can lean your mind. The innermost, most secret, mystic, nonverbal mantra is the intrinsic, ever-present reality of "isness" itself, indescribable and self-authenticating.

Although you can certainly translate mantras, they are chanted more for their nonconceptual energy vibrations than they are for literal meaning. If you listen to the sound of a deep gong, you might easily feel it rippling, vibrating, and penetrating through your diaphragm, abdomen, and other energy centers. Chanting mantras has a similar effect. The outer vibrations are sound vibrations; the inner vibrations are energy, consciousness, directed attention-cum-thought. In Avalokitesvara's Mantra of Great Compassion, "Om" is the universal sound. "Mani" means jewel, and "Pedmé" means lotus, so together they mean the jewel in the lotus. Then there's "Hung," but that's not there for its meaning; it's there for the completeness of the vibrational tone. "Hung" is the consort of "Om." It is the seed syllable of the five wisdoms of Buddha-mind. Om Mani Pedmé Hung.

## OPENING THE THROAT CHAKRA

*The temple bell stops*
*but the sound keeps coming*
*out of the flowers*

—ZEN HAIKU MASTER BASHO

I first learned about chanting as a child standing next to my parents in a synagogue. Although like most people there I had very little idea of what was being said, the rhythmic effect and sonorous soulful sound was delightful. After my bar mitzvah at age thirteen, I must admit I didn't try to chant again until I was in college and started chanting with some traveling Hindu yogis. Then I immediately felt the powerful healing and renewing effect of chanting, and suspected that there might very well be something more than mere senseless rites and rituals in such mysterious and foreign-seeming spiritual practices.

A renowned Dzogchen lama of old, the fearless Master Jigme Lingpa, spontaneously sang innumerable enlightened songs and lengthy poetical texts and treatises. Although he was not learned, by opening his throat chakra via chanting and meditative practices, lineage teachers tell us that he accessed the splendid dimensions of sacred sound. We too can give voice to all that is within us even if we don't have a lot of formal training or qualifications, simply by breathing deeply, overcoming inhibitions and hesitation, letting go, and singing our hearts out. It's a great way to lose our finite sense of self, at least momentarily, and encounter our greater Buddha-nature.

I myself could never really carry a tune and felt tone deaf. Having unsuccessfully attempted to master a few different musical instruments, I thought I had no musical abilities whatsoever. Then I learned to memorize and chant sacred devotional hymns and songs in India; later I ended up as one of the chant leaders of our retreat group in France.

From Gregorian chants to Native American rain chants to Hebrew davening, some form of chanting is common to just about every culture. When you give voice to the truth within you, the angels also sing. Just as angels can fly because they take themselves lightly, you can use your voice and breath to soar. Begin your chanting practice by relaxing, breathing deeply, and enjoying yourself. Open up, loosen up; no need to be embarrassed. Don't worry, no one's judging. Sometimes the best way to start is to think of it as exercise. You are exercising energy, vocal cords, throat chakra, and higher mind; and you are opening your heart. Stretch and relax your arms and shoulders, neck, and chest. Work your breathing in and out, just like a bellows. Spread your wings. Singing is believing.

As you begin to chant, just concentrate on the syllables without thinking about anything in particular or trying to suppress your thoughts and feelings. The power of spiritual practice and mantra combined with your devotion and purity of heart can carry you a long way—further than you might think. Just chant. Surf on the sound waves; catch an updraft of this delicious inner energy and soar effortlessly—beyond yourself.

Chant faster as you begin to ease into it. Feel the energy moving through your body, throat, lungs, diaphragm, navel chakra, mouth, tongue, and breath. Chanting is an engaging, totally involving, active form of meditation. It's also a constructive way to get your energy moving. If you're feeling depressed or sluggish, you can alter your mood and your inner emotional weather with mantra practice. In the car, instead of changing radio stations and driving your passengers nuts, carry your own chosen atmosphere with you by chanting, smiling, and entering the dimension of sacred sound. If you have trouble falling asleep at night, instead of counting sheep or popping pills, try counting your breaths or very gently chanting mantra to yourself as a relaxant and soporific. Count mantras instead of sheep. Join the sangha herd.

## CHANTING THE HEART SUTRA

The teachings of sunyata about the true nature of reality are at the heart of Mahayana Buddhism, the Great Middle Way. These teachings are explained in one hundred thousand verses known as the Prajna Paramita Sutras, which translates as the Scriptures of Transcendental Wisdom. These sutras are also condensed into shorter forms. The shortest is known as the Heart Sutra—the Heart Essence of Wisdom Scripture. Many people say it is their favorite sutra. The Heart Sutra is chanted daily and studied and taught in almost every monastery and Buddhist center, be it in the East or West. I fondly call it the Not Sutra; you will see why.

According to legend, the Buddha entrusted the one hundred thousand verses of these Sutras of Transcendental Wisdom to the hands of semidivine, dragonlike sea dwellers, known as Nagas, who kept them safe until they were rediscovered by an Indian philosopher sage named Nagarjuna who lived in about the first century A.D. Because he brought these highly treasured teachings about emptiness back from the Nagas, his name became Nagarjuna, literally translated as "charioteer of the Nagas." The original exponent of Madhyamika, the Great Middle Way doctrine of Buddhist logic and epistemology, Nagarjuna is considered the Buddhist philosopher of relativism: Madhyamika reveals how it is that nothing exists independently. Everything is conventionally, relatively real, arising through interdependent causes and effects. Thus it is said that nothing exists forever in any ultimate sense. This is true whether we are talking about a soul or a table. Things just appear to be real and substantial, without being exactly so. This is the mysterious, fertile intersection of the void of nothingness and everything we so vividly experience.

## The Heart Sutra

Here is the Heart Sutra, the condensed essence of the Prajna Paramita Sutras:

*Avalokitesvara Bodhisattva, practicing deep prajna*

    *paramita*

*Clearly saw that all five skandhas are empty, transforming all*

    *suffering and distress.*

*Form is no other than emptiness, emptiness no other than form;*

*Form is exactly emptiness, emptiness exactly form;*

    *sensation, thought, impulse, consciousness are also like this.*

*All things are marked by emptiness—not born,*

    *not destroyed;*

*not stained, not pure; without gain, without loss.*

*Therefore, in emptiness there is no form, no sensation,*

    *thought, impulse, consciousness;*

*no eye, ear, nose, tongue, body, mind;*

*no color, sound, smell, taste, touch, object of thought;*

*no realm of sight to no realm of thought;*

*no ignorance and also no ending of ignorance*

*to no old age and death and also no ending of old age and death;*

*no suffering, also no source of suffering, no annihilation, no*
> *path;*

*no wisdom, also no attainment. Having nothing to attain,*

*Bodhisattvas live prajna paramita*

*with no hindrance in the mind. No hindrance, thus no fear.*

*Far beyond delusive thinking, they attain complete Nirvana.*

*All Buddhas past, present, and future live prajna paramita*

*and thus attain perfect awakened enlightenment.*

*Therefore, know that prajna paramita is*

*the great mantra, the wisdom mantra,*

*the unsurpassed mantra, the supreme mantra,*

*which completely removes all suffering.*

*This is truth, not deception.*

*Therefore, set forth the prajna paramita mantra,*

*set forth this mantra and say:*

*Gaté, gaté, paragaté, parasamgaté, Bodhi Svaha.*

Buddhists believe that the sacred energy, blessings, and wisdom released through this chant, combined with focused attention, is of benefit in subtle ways to all beings seen and unseen. The efficacy of prayers depends as much or more on the concentration and intention of the practitioner as upon the prayer itself. Sometimes in Tibetan monasteries if someone is ill, monks will chant this sutra all day long; witnessing this, I perceived an almost palpable energy field around these chanting monks.

If you chant outside in nature, or in your backyard, remember that your Vajra (enlightened) speech is informing and spreading the Dharma to everything out there—people and pets as well as crickets, fireflies, beetles, mosquitos, wild animals, and even ticks and fleas. Dharma energy that blesses and edifies the land and everything on it is being generously shared. Lamas say that wherever this sutra is recited, chanted, studied, copied, or taught, the teachings of enlightenment will be established and eventually flourish. So we do our part daily by chanting the Heart Sutra.

# SILENCE RESOUNDS LIKE THUNDER

During the early days of Buddhism in India, there lived an enlightened layman, a family man named Vimalakirti. An ethical businessman and an impeccable member of the community, Vimalakirti was known as the wisest person in town.

One fine day all of the Bodhisattvas, enlightened arhants, monks, and nuns gathered to discuss transcendental wisdom. They congregated in Vimalakirti's small bedroom, which was only about six feet by six feet square. It is said that this august sangha gathering included all the most exalted Bodhisattvas, including Manjusri, Avalokitesvara, Vajrapani, and Tara; amazingly, through the magic of interpenetration and emptiness, all of these enlightened beings and human sangha members too were able to fit into this one room. Perhaps they all made themselves as small as those angels that reportedly dance on the head of a pin. However they managed it, the Mahayana sutra that tells this story recounts that they were all there—arhants, monks, nuns, and Bodhisattvas alike, with their robes and lotus thrones, in Vimalakirti's tiny bedchamber.

Once gathered, each member of the assembly expounded on transcendental wisdom; one by one each gave a brilliant verbal description of the absolute, the indescribable and ineffable. Each speaker was more eloquent than the last; each speaker in turn delved deeper and deeper into the true meaning. Finally Manjusri, the Maha Bodhisattva of Wisdom, began to speak. And his golden speech was extraordinarily marvelous; it was the ultimate exposition of non-dual truth, the highest and most profound transcendental wisdom. When he was finished, everybody bowed reverently to him. And if you ever read this Vimalakirti Nirdesa Sutra, I guarantee that you will feel like bowing also. What else can be said?

Finally they all turned to Vimalakirti and asked him to pronounce the final word on transcendental wisdom. And then the sutra says,

"HIS SILENCE RESOUNDED LIKE THUNDER."

Amen.

———

True inner silence puts you in touch with the deeper dimensions of being and knowing—gnostic awareness and innate wisdom. Because it is impossible to express the inexpressable, the spiritual sound or song of silence is beyond words and concepts. Mere words are weak translations of what we really mean to say. Inner silence and emptiness can help provide easier access to universal mystery and primordial being, for almost anyone, without relying on foreign forms and arcane concepts.

Silence is the threshold to the inner sanctum, the heart's sublime cave. Silence is the song of the heart, like love, a universal language, a natural melody open to anyone, even the tone deaf or religiously challenged. Try going out into the woods or sitting very near the ocean's waves. Look up at the bright stars at night; open your mind's inner ear and listen to the lovely song of silence. Here is the joy of contemplative sweetness. Follow this bliss.

# THE BEAUTIFUL SOUND OF SILENCE

When I participated in my first ten-day Vipassana retreat in India, what impressed me most was the Buddhist practice known as Noble Silence. No speech, no sign language, no radios, no television, no newspapers, no books, no notes, notebooks, or tape recorders. Even though we sat in the meditation hall and ate together, there were no interpersonal relationships or interactions—except for the most basic shared sense of being there together in the simplest, most stripped-down and exposed-to-one's-own-gaze sort of way. Quieting the heart, mind, energy, and mouth. Then, during the 1980s, when I did two back-to-back three-year, three-month, three-day Tibetan Buddhist retreats in Dordogne, France, we practiced Noble Silence for six months at a time, avoiding even eye contact, which would have been considered an interpersonal interaction and thus a lapse in the silence. This extended period of Noble Silence, which furthers the sense of spiritual solitude or existential aloneness, was the most intense and fulfilling part of that long, intensive meditation retreat.

In such an intensive practice period, at first the initial sense of relief and quietude is, naturally enough, combined with missing one's habitual talking and sharing of experiences with friends; one also misses study, poetry and journal writing, as well as sending letters and cards. But as the mirror of silence and solitude deepens, one starts to understand what scriptures mean when reminding us to see the Pure Land, or Buddha Field, nirvana—the radiant perfection—in everything, right here and now. "This land where we stand is the Pure Land, paradise; this body the body of Buddha," as Japanese Zen master Hakuin sang.

Ancient Tibetan teachings describe a creative imagination-cum-visualization practice, which consists of learning to hear all sounds as mantra, recognize all beings as Buddhas and dakinis, and perceive all thoughts as creative displays of innate wisdom. Noble Silence helps the practitioner transform his or her ordinary limited self-image and recognize the natural state of great perfection—no matter what the environment. This is why awakened masters, who have inwardly transformed their perception, seem to carry their own atmosphere with them wherever they go. Theirs is like another reality, another dimension, right here in this world, but not entirely of it.

Noble Silence, which does not necessarily have to be for extended periods of time, is an excellent way to quiet our habitual busy bodies and overactive rational minds while becoming more receptive, self-reflective, and sensitive. Think about what it means to take a vow of silence for a short period of time; like one day or even a half day, for example, your own personal time of rest. Consider an outer and inner silence that is not broken by the continual static of talk, mental chatter, and interpersonal dynamics. For that period of time, by design, commune only with yourself; for that time, stop asking of others, and ask only of yourself. During Noble Silence, we stop discussing and negotiating; instead we pray and attend only to the present; we chant and sing, opening ourselves to other dimensions of our being. We can just do nothing— just show up as it were—and see what happens.

Sublime solitude and genuine inner silence is far from lonely. Milarepa, the eleventh-century Tibetan poet and cave-dwelling hermit sage, found that this solitary life in the Himalayas was true completeness. He sang:

> *When I am alone meditating in the mountains,*
> *my guru is always present;*
> *All the Buddhas are always with me.*

# THE JOY OF SILENCE, SOLITUDE, AND VOLUNTARY SIMPLICITY

Inner solitude and Noble Silence is a way to empty, cleanse, heal, and renew the heart and mind. This is a voluntary way to start the process of simplification and personal downsizing. The peace will help you purify your perceptions and make presence of mind more acute, clear, spacious, and even luminous. Incredible satisfaction is available when you begin experiencing the timeless truth that less can actually be more; that the most elegant solution is often the simplest one. Gratitude and appreciation serve us better than attachment and grasping. Peace of mind is the inmost secret treasure.

⁂

## Try a Little Silence

Why not take a Sunday off, or half a day, to be by yourself, with yourself in voluntary simplicity, and experience for yourself the unspeakable joy and virtue in Noble Silence? Spend the time in your room, house, or garden without using any communication devices. Or spend your time alone in nature, communing with yourself. You'll love it.

> *Stop.*
>
> *Be still.*
>
> *Remain silent.*
>
> *Meditators should be seen,*
>
> *not heard.*
>
> *Ssshhh.*
>
> *Still*
>
> *All the senses.*
>
> *Let everything be.*
>
> *Let go, and let it all*
>
> *come to you.*
>
> *Relax.*
>
> *Being is in;*
>
> *doing is out.*
>
> *Do nothing.*
>
> *For a moment*

*Just be.*
*Silence*
*is*
*golden.*
*Enjoy it.*

# RIGHT ACTION

## *The Art of Living*

*In our era, the road to holiness necessarily passes through the world of action.*

—DAG HAMMARSKJÖLD

One day near the end of his life, when Gandhi was boarding a crowded third-class compartment on an Indian train, some reporters caught up to him and asked him what his message was. As he leaned out of the train door he said, "How I live my life, that is my teaching."

Right Action, the fourth touchstone on the Eight-Fold Path, asks all of us as spiritual seekers to focus on how we live our lives. Life is the ultimate art form, and we are the creators. Are we creating the lives that we want? Are we doing what we want to do—behaving as we want to behave? Do our actions demonstrate generosity, patience, awareness, wisdom, and discipline? In short, are we "walking our talk"? Or are we running away from our true selves?

A clear perspective on Right Action teaches us that our actions are like seeds—karmic seeds. The commonsense wisdom of the laws of causality helps us understand that apple seeds don't produce lemon trees. When we behave positively, we get positive results; when we cling to questionable values, we get questionable results. If we hurt others, we hurt ourselves; helping others, we serve ourselves as well. The practice of Right Action is about cultivating goodness and virtue in the way we treat others; it's about creating harmony in our world, our home, in this very life, right now.

## GOODNESS IN ACTION

> *Do not do anything harmful; do only what is*
> *good; purify and train your own mind: This is*
> *the teaching of the Buddha; this is the path to*
> *enlightenment.*
>
> —THE BUDDHA

Right Action often comes down to the age-old principle: Treat others as you would wish to be treated yourself. Can you and I do that with a generous spirit and an open heart? Or is it just Jesus, Buddha, Mother Teresa, the Dalai Lama, and a few other sages and saints who are able to live that sublime ideal? Buddha Dharma has been called the Lion's Roar because it is a challenge and a call to awakening. As the lion's roar awakens all the other animals in the forest, the Lion's Roar of Dharma awakens and challenges us to be as wise, sane, loving, and compassionate as we are able to be—to be all that we *are*. Not to be somebody else, not to live somebody else's life, but to awaken and be true to who and what we are, every day—not just in what we think and say, but also in what we do.

Goodness and virtue should be good for something. According to the Buddha, actions that are kind, unselfish, and virtuous serve three primary purposes: (1) They help others; (2) They help you, the doer, accumulate merit and stockpile good karma, which helps propel you along the practice path leading to enlightenment; (3) They are also an expression of wisdom, higher sanity, and enlightenment itself. This kind of manifold benefit is true of each of the steps on the Eight-Fold Path. Live impeccably and you will further happiness and reach enlightenment; live impeccably and you will be living an enlightened life. As Plato said, "Virtue is knowledge."

## MAKING RIGHT ACTION A PRIORITY

> *The Buddha's entire life was powered by a strong sense of mission. Immmediately after his enlightenment, he saw in his mind's eye the whole of humanity—people milling and lost, desperately in need of help and guidance.*
>
> —HUSTON SMITH

The Buddha said that he taught about one thing, and one thing only: "Suffering and the end of suffering." From the time he first became aware of life's difficulties and left his father's royal palace, he committed himself to helping others in both the temporary and ultimate sense. Having achieved enlightenment, he didn't just sit there in nirvanic peace—although he certainly could have. Instead, he selflessly devoted his life to going wherever he was asked and teaching whenever he was asked, while setting a standard for impeccable behavior. His own karma purified and fulfilled, he devoted his life to helping others liberate themselves through their own spiritual efforts. In Tibetan, the word for karma is "leh," literally defined as action. The Dalai Lama once wrote "The true religious person . . . accepts the truth that he or she is responsible for the pleasurable and unpleasurable feelings he experiences, these being the fruits of his own karma [actions]."

Without even considering the possibility of karma that you may have created centuries ago, think about the "past life" that you were leading five or ten years ago. Think about how your actions back then created the life you now have. Each of us is on a personal and unique journey, filled with its own complexity and wonder; on these journeys, we will consistently be presented with a wide range of opportunities, large and small, for Right Action. All of these represent different stages or seasons of spiritual evolution. Do you have the same issues, joys, and difficulties today that you did five years ago; or have you changed, and has your life changed accordingly?

For a few years now, I've had an "Ask the Lama" column on the Internet. Most of the questions I receive are from men and women and teens who are trying to bring the spirit of bodhicitta into their actions as they struggle with moral dilemmas and personal choices:

"I would like to leave my husband who belittles me and my interest in spiritual and psychological growth but I'm afraid that will hurt our child. What is the right thing to do?"

"My old dog is in a great deal of pain, can no longer walk, and won't live more than a few days. Is euthanasia, which will ease his misery, the right or wrong choice?"

"I have to make a choice and promote one of two equally qualified people. No matter what I do, someone will be hurt. I want to do what's right—but what's right?"

Questions like these remind us that right and wrong aren't always simple and clear cut. We live in a complex society filled with complex problems, and sometimes the right thing to do is not immediately apparent. One of the things that I most value about Buddha Dharma is that it is practical and path-oriented; the emphasis is on process. We learn to have trust in the process and in the virtuous life; thus we have little fear or anxiety about the future, trusting that if we are virtuous and do the right thing, the future will take care of itself.

Buddhist ethics inform us that what is "right" is behavior that is helpful rather than harmful, that is conducive to liberation and freedom. Although we may judge certain "deeds" as undesirable or unskillful, we don't judge the "doer" as negative or undesirable. The Dharma does not tell us what to do; instead it opens the way to understanding by revealing how things work. The traditional ideals for accumulating good karma and living an impeccable life through Right Action are expressed in simple concepts, but there is far more to them than meets the eye.

## CHERISH LIFE, DON'T KILL

Spiritual practice is a sane and humane way of life, a positive end in itself; it's not just the means to a nirvanic end. Conscious, mindful living calls us to be fully present—as if totally intimate with all and everything. While it's easier than you think, it's also harder than you think. During the sweltering rainy season, when bugs are rampant, some of the most conscientious and careful monks in India and Southeast Asia use a broom to sweep insects and worms from the path as they walk. They do this not just because they worry about being bitten, but because they are wholeheartedly trying to preserve, cherish, and respect life. All life. This saintly attitude is not essential to begin a Buddhist practice, but remains an ideal to consider. Well-developed practitioners who are able to consistently act on the belief that the smallest insect is a precious being remind us of the degree of effort, awareness, and love such behavior demands.

Not killing may seem to be a very simple instruction to follow, but in reality it's quite difficult. For example, if I say, "Of course I don't kill," I am conveniently forgetting that in a single hour of night driving in my speeding car, I am probably killing dozens or even hundreds of moths and insects who are attracted to the headlights. "But," I may assert, "I don't intentionally kill." I don't act out anger with violence; I don't fish; I don't hunt. However, sometimes I eat meat, wear leather shoes and belts, have an ivory bead on my mala beads. Did millions of tiny silkworms wish to give up their lives so I can wear my yellow Tibetan lama shirt? In truth, it's very, very difficult to never, ever kill. If you live in the country and have a driveway, each summer day you are running over insects. Think about all the tiny ants that are crushed when we picnic in the park or dig up a foundation for a house. What if you have cockroaches in your kitchen or parasites in your intestinal tract? To kill or not to kill, that is the question.

Even the indomitable Dharma can be touched by an infestation

of cockroaches. Karmapa's KTD Monastery in Woodstock, New
York, was established in 1976; two years later we faced a unique
moral dilemma. The gentle Buddhist monks in that old hotel on
top of the Catskill Mountains were being overrun by roaches.
Where, we joked, had they come from? From New York City, like
so many of the monastery's inhabitants? We laughed and laughed,
but it soon became a huge problem. Cockroaches were teeming in
the corners and between the floorboards. The cockroach community was growing much faster than the human sangha; they threat-
ened to take over the building as well as put us in jeopardy with
the health department. And new Dharma students were being put
off. It appeared that roaches were threatening the survival of the
monastery itself. A decision had to be made—to exterminate or
not to exterminate. The lamas, visibly distressed by this decision,
spent hours in debate and discussion. What to do? Leave the
monastery in threat of being closed down or violate the first Buddhist injunction against killing? It was not a small issue for us.

Finally after many phone calls between Woodstock, Nepal, and
the mother Rumtek Monastery in Sikkim, a difficult decision was
reached. Within days, an exterminator's van showed up at the
monastery gates. Mounted on the top was a large scuptured insect—it looked like a giant cockroach. Prayers were made, heads
were bowed, hearts were touched, and the deed was done. Sometimes in life we make decisions which appear to be as practically
necessary as they are painful.

Because I am a lama and teacher, people often approach me
looking for satisfactory ways to think about life and death matters:
What should they think about capital punishment? What should
they do about the termites chewing on their houses? What position should they take on assisted suicides? Abortion? Is war ever
justifiable? To pick our way through these thorny issues, we must
appreciate and examine all the details and consider each case individually on its own merits. Each of us has to reach into his or her
own heart and search for the wisest, most compassionate, caring,
and reverent attitudes. One of the few things the Dalai Lama
specifically requested of Western Dharma teachers is that we work
against capital punishment. Still many people wonder whether
capital punishment might be enough of a deterrent to violent

crime that it would ultimately save lives. These are questions with no simple answers.

If we manage gracefully to pass through life without killing even a single ant, spider, or slug, obviously we will avoid some of the negative consequences of bad karma. But is it enough only to be careful that none of our footsteps harm a single being, or do we also need to direct our energy and actions towards goodness and helping others? As we try to better access our own pure Buddha-nature, let's think about accumulating positive karma by cherishing life, respecting life, and saving life.

The Dalai Lama often reminds us that bodhicitta, the compassion and love which is the heart of enlightenment, is cultivated by considering not just our own welfare, but the welfare of all sentient beings. To do this requires a deep understanding of our connectedness with others and of what it means to cherish all life. This often means developing a different point of view about even the smallest details of living. Is it really necessary on summer evenings, for example, to get out the electrified bug zapper and even almost enjoy the sound of sizzling insects when you can just as easily use a less lethal natural repellent which might protect both you and the bugs? Mosquitos too, like ourselves, have parents and offspring, homes and lives. Issa, the haiku poet, wrote: "Look at the tiny gnat. See him wringing his hands, wringing his feet."

It is challenging to alter your perspective on the world to such a degree that you recognize all beings as having needs equal to your own. It becomes even more daunting when we try to put that belief into action by being consistently, impartially less selfish. We can learn to cherish and venerate each individual life and life-form by reflecting on how we are all equal, all like God's children—children of truth. All beings—insects and snakes, fish and fowl, as well as humans—have the right to live and pursue happiness; none of us is the rightful arbiter of another's fate. Life is a gift.

## Vowing to Gentle Our Spirit

We develop an attitude of cherishing life when we learn to yield, to give in, to let go and soften our hearts and souls. Yet statistics and newspaper headlines remind us that we live in a violent society. Emergency wards are filled with men, women, and children who have been the victims of violence—domestic as well as random. Some of us may have been very fortunate—our lives have not been directly touched by violence, but men and women sometimes attack loved ones, strangers, and ultimately even themselves. As far-fetched as it may seem to some, I feel that we all need to be on the lookout for any of these tendencies within our own psyches. We help keep our lives balanced and sane by being aware of the darkness within us as well as the light so that we are never taken unaware by unconscious negative impulses. We make a vow not to kill or harm so that we never forget to be gentle, caring, and kind, cherishing all forms of life on our fragile planet.

There is absolutely nothing in the gentle spiritual teachings of the Buddha that advocates or condones violence. It seems to me almost ludicrous that any spiritual seeker would need to be exhorted not to harm others, but not all people who "claim" to be on the spiritual path abhor and avoid violence. In 1995, the Japanese cult leader, Shoko Asahara, grossly distorted ancient spiritual teachings he learned in India; and by using classic mind control techniques such as fasting, drugs, isolation, and intimidation, he convinced a large group of men and women to believe in his distorted dogma and follow his diabolical plan to launch deadly sarin nerve gas attacks throughout Japan.

Afterward, I happened to counsel some of the followers of this cult and was stunned by the extent of their brainwashing. I think there are powerful lessons in this for anyone with spiritual inclinations—just as there were lessons for all of us in what happened at Jim Jones' Jonestown, David Koresh's compound in Waco, Texas, or the Heaven's Gate cult in San Diego.

The capacity to trust, to believe, and even to surrender to something greater than ourselves is a wonderful quality that we need to cherish. Yet naive, overly credulous seekers can be especially vulnerable to exploitation by charismatic leaders, sometimes even leaders who are unscrupulous charlatans and megalomaniacs advocating inverted values and actions difficult to reconcile with humane ideals. We must regularly remind ourselves that the shadow side is never as far away as we would like to think.

## DON'T TAKE WHAT ISN'T FREELY GIVEN; GIVE TO OTHERS

This teaching is frequently translated with only two words, "Don't Steal," thus interpreting the word "steal" in a very literal narrow sense. When we do this, we may fail to see the broader social and psychological implications. The Buddha recognized the many ways that we humans try to take more than is given, thus stealing from each other, day in and day out. Maybe you and I don't consciously or intentionally steal, but let's think about this together for a minute. Do we cheat on our taxes? Do we misinform our insurance companies in order to save money? Do we invest in companies that steal? Do we buy products made by companies that steal from the local population, destroy the environment, exploit workers, or violate human rights—robbing adults as well as children of their innocence and freedom, thus causing the world to be a more benighted, unhappy place?

The Buddha warned his followers of the danger of taking too much from the environment and told them not to pollute lakes and streams, not to hoard wealth and resources. Some 2,500 years ago, monks were encouraged to give something back to nature by planting a tree each month. The nobly born Buddha set an example of simplicity for his monastic disciples. He often wore a robe stitched together from different pieces of cast-off clothing, an example still symbolized today by the multipieced yellow monastic robe of the fully ordained monk and nun. He encouraged members of his sangha to have only one change of clothes so they wouldn't use up more than their share.

That's the point, isn't it? Whenever we use up more than our share, we are taking from somebody else. And it's not always material objects or goods; perhaps we are stealing the center of attention or using up more than our share of time, but the underlying issues, which are very similar, speak to the fundamental core of Buddhist teachings about the defects of clinging and grasping. Gandhi once said, "The world has enough for everyone's need, but not enough for everyone's greed."

To live simply and with purity of heart, without grasping, as the

Buddha and almost all spiritual sages have instructed us to do, seems to become more difficult every year. Our grandparents didn't deposit radioactive wastes underground or in our oceans; they used waxed paper on their sandwiches and brown paper bags in the garbage can rather than mountains of nonbiodegradable plastic and styrofoam. Now every load of wash has some potentially lethal chemical components. What happens to all that chlorinated water?

Think about all our CD players, cameras, TVs, computers, printers, and phones. That's a lot of excess, particularly when we know that millions of children die every year from malnutrition. Think about all the forests that are being wiped out throughout the world. These natural forests are like a gift, a miracle; they make it possible for us to breathe good air. If they are destroyed, what will happen to future generations—perhaps even this generation? Populous China used up its own vast forests; now it is deforesting previously unspoiled Tibet. The powerful often exploit the weak, with far-reaching results. Isn't this grasping akin to stealing? If lofty teachings that stress ethics and morality don't filter down from the highest sphere right into our daily lives, where it really counts, what use are they? I think that we must regularly ask ourselves how we can simplify—use less and share more.

We all need to consider how our often exploitive short-term gains and economic policies contribute to larger global issues; we need to find ways to help our communities and countries develop policies that protect global resources and work toward equitable distribution of wealth. When the Dalai Lama had a private meeting with the American president he said to him, "You are the most powerful man in the world. Every decision you make should be motivated by compassion." In our daily actions we all face a similar challenge.

Using up fewer natural resources and recycling more consistently may seem insignificant, but this attention to detail is how we start to make the world a safer place: safer for us, safer for all, now and in the times to come. When we can bring more of our spiritual beliefs into the way we live, then we will become responsible guardians and planetary stewards.

## Training Ourselves in Generosity

The Buddha didn't only deliver negative edicts such as "Don't steal." He also exhorted his friends and followers to let go, give, love, rejoice in everyday life, and share. He said, "Giving brings happiness at every stage of its expression. We experience joy in forming the intention to be generous; we experience joy in the actual act of giving something; and we experience joy in remembering the fact that we have given."

A classic teaching tale relates how the Buddha once counseled a wealthy householder. The man's problem was that he just could not give or even share any of his wealth or possessions. This was a clear-cut metaphor for his inability to "let go" in *any* area of his life. In this teaching tale, as the Buddha shows the stingy householder how to train himself from the outside in, the Buddha appears to be an early and intuitive expert in the benefits of constructive behavior modification.

Buddha instructed the rich householder to begin by thinking of his two hands—right and left—as being separate and disconnected; then he told him to practice generosity by taking a coin in his right hand and giving it to his left. Once the householder learned to part with a small coin, from one pocket to another, from one hand to another, the Buddha told him to experiment with larger sums of money. Eventually the man began to cultivate letting go, generosity, and nonattachment. As he became accustomed to parting with the money, the Buddha told him to soften his hardened heart and better use his riches by making gifts—first small, then larger—of his money and possessions to family members, then to friends, and finally to beggars and strangers. Through this practice of dana—giving—this man became much happier, freer, more content, and beloved by all.

Don't we all need some concrete form of retraining so we may learn to be more generous and let go more gracefully? We all— each of us without exception—have so much to give, if we only knew it! We can make gifts of kindness, prayers, support, time, and empathy; we can give to friends, family, strangers, and even to the earth itself. We can train ourselves to become more yielding, equanimous, and flexible, giving up our rigid stances and fixed ideas. Each act of giving is a good deed that will be carried with you as part of your good karma. We can't take our wealth, possessions, or friends with us beyond the grave, but we can ride good karma as far as we can imagine and even further. Give now; use your wealth, talent, and energy for the greater good, and it shall indeed follow you into the afterlife.

## Opening Up to the Heart-mind That Is Free from Craving

The instruction to "refrain from stealing," of course, reaches far deeper, and is ultimately connected to the desireless natural heart-mind and the utter peace of nirvana. It's a continuum: We begin by not taking more than our share, and eventually that can evolve into an attitude of profound letting go and letting be. "This is the heart's sure release," as Buddha said. The act of working with our life and our karma, learning to accept whatever comes our way—and even saying "thank you" for it, as some sages teach—is one of the most difficult challenges on the path to enlightenment. Are we able to be open to each experience and every moment just as it is? Or are we always looking for something else, something more, better, or different? Are we able to accept what our families and loved ones give or don't give? Can we accept what our nearest and dearest do, think, and even wear? Or do we squirm, demand, complain, resent, carp, and argue? The nongrasping heart is naturally open, accepting, and able to say thank you for whatever is. It is the threshold of an unconditional way of being, the supreme spiritual value.

## REFRAIN FROM UNWHOLESOME SEXUAL CONDUCT

Sexual energy pulses in almost everything we do. As one of my teachers once said to me long ago, "Sex is part of life." When I was a young man living like a monk in a monastery in the Himalayas, it was a big relief to hear this from a Tibetan master who was a celibate monk. While sex itself can bring joy, pleasure, intimacy, and even transcendence, sexual repression, sexual identity, sexual preference, and semiconscious sexual behavior often bring con-flicts. The Buddha recognized this by embracing and advocating celibacy as one extraordinary method for simplifying life. However he also realized that not everyone can be a monk or nun, nor would that be desirable for society as a whole. He instructed avowed monastics to be true to their chastity vows by sublimating the personal human longing for union and a home into a more transpersonal longing for a higher form of union and homecom-ing. For lay people, the Buddha advocated restraint through mod-eration, commitment, and responsibility, and he exhorted us to refrain from sexual misconduct. The question, of course, is how to define sexual misconduct.

The Buddha talked about several activities that he considered unwholesome and out of harmony with truth and reality: adultery, forced or violent sex, sex with a minor. We can be fairly certain that he would have also considered unwholesome any sexual ac-tivity that was addictive, exploitive, deceitful, unsafe, irresponsible, or downright harmful.

In these days of shifting sexual mores, there are many new is-sues: teen pregnancy, wide-scale sexual experimentation, serial monogamy, and life-threatening sexually transmitted diseases, to name just a few. In the past many religions founded in patriarchal societies—Buddhism included—have looked askance at certain forms of sexual behavior such as masturbation and homosexual sex. Yet most contemporary Dharma teachers feel these behaviors are within bounds and karmically workable. Without discarding the underlying values of sanity, love, or decency, I think today's world asks that we review all of our old positions from an honest, compassionate, nonjudgmental point of view, and take a fresh look at sexual relationships as well as sexual identity. This is one way we can help keep the Dharma alive for all of us.

Many of us still struggle with an inclination to treat sex as though it were separate and disconnected from who we are. Weren't the majority of us raised to believe that what goes on be-hind closed bedroom doors is disconnected from everyday reality, as though it should remain hidden in shadow? Don't we still tend to talk about unconscious sexual drives as though sex is governed by different rules of behavior than everything else we do? If we are going to experience our lives as sacred, we must be open to the possibility of considering sexuality as part of our spiritual evolution. It's important that we all learn to communicate about our sexual feelings in a wholesome nonjudgmental fashion in order to avoid hypocritical chasms between our words and our actions.

As with other activities, some personal scrutiny and self-inquiry regarding the nature of our sexual behavior, feelings, and relationships could be extremely rewarding. One might wonder: Do we have ego needs that are all wrapped up and mixed in with our sexual identity and sex appeal? Does sexuality sometimes dominate our life? When we find someone attractive, what is our real motivation and intent—will we be joyful and caring, or exploitive and harmful? Would we sometimes do almost anything for sexual gratification? Is the sex we are having mutual, or is it one-sided? Are we engaging in behavior that is addictive, deceptive, exploitive, or emotionally or physically abusive? Is it spontaneous, or did it "just happen—as if by accident"? Is it natural, is it appropriate, is it intimate, is it responsible, is it loving? Do our sexual needs cause us to tune out reality or sanity? Do we ever treat others as sexual objects, and in so doing fail to see that they are real people with real feelings? Do we find ourselves lying, telling half-truths, or concocting stories about our sex lives? Do we preach honesty and practice deception? These are important questions to reflect on.

## Channeling Sexual Energy

In classic Buddhism, not unlike other world religions, sexual energy has often been regarded as a volatile force that can create complications and prove antithetical to holiness, solitude, and inner silence. In the broader Mahayana Buddhist approach, it is recognized that personal love can be a heart-opening spiritual experience. Even the briefest experience of unconditional love can be transformative. Human love can give the serious practitioner a concrete, visceral glimpse into the meaning of universal love and unconditional compassion. Thus intimate relationships, family life, and sexual energy can be viewed not just as a hindrance to spiritual development, but also as a means of combining passion and compassion in such a skillful way that we will be able to be more engaged and intimate with others and the world.

In the later-developed remarkable tantric teachings which utilize all of our energies as part of the path, sexual energy is recognized as a very powerful and potent force that, like electricity, can be harnessed. Tantra talks about integrating and assimilating all our life experiences into the path rather than excluding any aspect of life as monastics choose to do. Tantric texts tell us to find the right partner, or consort, with whom one can practice tantric sexual exercises as a transformative consciousness-raising practice. The numerous specific tantric practices to accomplish such a goal include visualizing yourself and your partner as deities rather than as an ordinary lustful human couple. There are a variety of ancient traditional yogic practices such as seminal retention, withholding orgasm, touch and hand gestures, special internal muscular movements, rotating the breath and holding it in and out.

Other tantric practices are astrologically connected and reflect the complementary solar and lunar energies within our own being. One practice, for example, involves the visualization of multipetaled lotuses above the heads of you and your partner; this is to help raise your energy level in an upward rather than a downward movement by intentionally elevating your well-honed attention. In the ancient Hindu Tantras, there is a tradition that prescribes both total penetration and stillness. In this practice the yogic couple joins together sexually and then remains in a meditative way, without moving, for thirty minutes, four times a day, without orgasm. This helps develop mastery of breath, energy, inner psychic channels, and the mind and vastly opens the heart center as well as other chakras (energy centers). Tantric practice, if authentic, is a way to use the natural concentration of intense passionate desire to direct our minds further beyond ourselves.

I think it's important for all of us to remind ourselves that tantric sexual practices are spiritually risky and come with a huge *Warning* label. In truth, these practices are very advanced, and are rarely genuinely performed or accomplished today. Think of tantra as like the golden roof of the house or temple—before we can work on this beautiful roof, strong, deep foundations and walls must be settled firmly in place. Similarly our spiritual life needs to be mature and developed before we utilize these intense energies, which can easily become misdirected.

In Vajrayana Buddhism, the image of a masterful tantric practitioner is that of a peacock who loves to eat deadly snakes and poisonous plants, which only make his tail feathers blaze more brilliantly. In the Mahayana tradition, the image of the Bodhisattva practitioner is of the learned physician who knows how to use these poisonous plants medicinally. If you lack these master skills, poisonous plants can kill you; working with the poison-laced intense passions can kill the spiritual life too, if misdirected.

Too often, tantric sex has been used as a rationalization and justification for self-indulgent behavior, exploitation of power imbalances, and even sexual misconduct. Some yogis have fallen off the path and deviated into sensuality, rather than continuing to develop spiritually congruent with their original intent. This reminds us that for the sincere practitioner, tantric sex can become like a dangerous high-wire act. Tantric sexual practice was never intended as a way to justify sexual addiction or hypocrisy. Some notable modern teachers have slipped down this slope. Buddhism has not been immune to the same kinds of sexual scandal that have hit other religious institutions. Even those who have taken vows of celibacy have been known to rationalize their sexual relationships in the name of the higher spiritual practice of Tantric sex. If we are involved in this so-called Crazy Wisdom, an advanced tantric style of teaching and practice, we would do well to remember to ask ourselves whether our lives are thereby becoming more wise or more crazy.

The sexual act, if approached with utmost sincerity, can provide a way for men and women to be transported beyond our habitual sense of finite, separate selfhood and experience a rapture that is akin to divine mystic union—even if only momentarily. Buddhist tantras present a way to take that experience and use sexual energy as a propellant to the broader and more penetrating experience of spiritual development, liberation, and awakening.

# REFRAIN FROM INTOXICANTS
# THAT CAUSE HEEDLESSNESS

*The best mind-altering drug is truth.*

—LILY TOMLIN

The Tale of the Hapless Monk is a traditional teaching tale—
reminiscent of the wisdom of Aesop—that is often used to illus-
trate how intoxicants cause heedlessness. As you read, notice how
the training precepts are interlinked and dependent on each
other:

> One lovely spring day, a monk was out on his begging rounds
> when the beautiful wife of a wealthy businessman, recognizing
> the monk as susceptible to temptation, invited him into her
> home. There she engaged him in a spirited conversation. When
> the monk finally realized that too much time had passed, he went
> to the door only to discover that it was locked.
>
> "Please," he asked the woman, "would you open this door?"
>
> "Not just yet," the woman said, "I will let you out of the
> room only if you do one of the following: Kill the goat who is
> tied up outside the back door, have sex with me, or drink this jug
> of wine."
>
> The monk tried to think his way out of this dreadful situa-
> tion. As a peaceful Buddhist, he couldn't resort to violence
> against the imposing woman in order to fight his way out of
> the house. Killing a goat would mean breaking the pre-
> cept against killing; having sex would be breaking his monas-
> tic vows of chastity; here it would also mean adultery, which
> is sexual misconduct and stealing as well. The perturbed monk
> decided that the least offensive thing he could do would be to
> drink the wine, which would harm no one but himself. So
> he did.
>
> Not accustomed to strong spirits, the hapless monk got very
> drunk, which quickly weakened all of his resolve. By then he was
> so hungry and lacking in mindfulness that he killed the goat; and
> while it was cooking, he and the woman had sex. Thus all his
> pure vows were lost.

The moral of this story, of course, is that intoxicants, whether they be liquor or drugs, can fan passions and create a heedless state of mind, which in turn leads to other problems. The traditional teaching is that mind-altering substances can start the practitioner off on a long, slippery slope; although you may start out on the high ground, if you are not mindful and conscientious, before you know it you can find yourself sliding uncontrollably into deep and murky waters.

I'm frequently asked about drugs, particularly whether or not so-called consciousness-raising drugs can help raise one's mystical sights. This is a fair question and one that I once asked of my teachers. Like many of my generation, I myself cannot in all honesty say that I never inhaled. What I can say is that once I got to Nepal and afterward became gradually established in the spiritual life, drugs lost their appeal, and I no longer sought mystical or religious experiences through chemical substances or drugs. Meditation and other Dharma practices proved so much more fruitful, sane, healthy, and delightful—not to mention safe and legal.

Back in the early 1970s, I remember trying to discuss drugs with Lama Yeshe. I described to him in colorful detail my cosmic mystical experiences during a one-week solitary trek through Nepal. I spent two days meditating at a Himalayan hot spring, under the influence of hallucinogenic mushrooms. I had hoped and even expected Lama to explain these things and even help me understand. Instead, he laughed loudly and exclaimed, "Western boy's dream!" He would say no more. He just kept laughing.

I intensely longed to become one with the infinite awareness of luminous presence I had experienced on that trek in the mountains. I wanted to *be* that, not just visit that through a drug-induced state. I knew that my vision quest deserved further development. Lama Yeshe generously taught me how to be closer to these realities through the practice of Tibetan meditation and breathing exercises; he wanted to show me the difference between chimerical dreams and the realistically achievable, immanent reality of clear light within each of us.

Like me, during the late sixties and early seventies many of the men and women who were my fellow companions on the path were attracted to the writings of people like Carlos Castenada,

Timothy Leary, R. D. Laing, Gary Snyder, Aldous Huxley, Allen Ginsberg, Suzuki, Jack Kerouac, Watts, Krishnamurti, and Ram Dass. Some of this consciousness literature romanticized the psychedelic experience and touted the sacramental value of certain drugs. We were young; many threw caution to the winds and played with their heads. It was simply what was happening back then. In the intervening years, we've become more sophisticated and wise; we've seen too many examples of bright men and women who left too many brain cells behind in the name of mysticism. Now I personally don't use drugs, and I don't recommend drugs.

Buddhism is unswerving in its bottom-line respect for reality. Once Allen Ginsberg asked one of my own late teachers, Dudjom Rinpoche, for advice about the awesome visions he had experienced from taking psychedelics. The kindly old Tibetan sage sighed and simply said, "If you see anything horrible, don't cling to it; if you see anything beautiful, don't cling to it. Whatever the mind produces, it's the same teaching. Don't cling to it." Buddha himself never said it better.

## BETTER LATE THAN NEVER

When one aged Zen master was asked to relate his biography, he exclaimed, "Just one mistake after another!" As we think about Right Action, we also can't help but reflect on *our* mistakes. We've all done things we wish we could undo; we all have regrets. Recently a young man I never met wrote to me saying, "Am I doomed to bad karma because of the abortion my girlfriend and I decided to have performed three years before we married? Since then we have become Buddhists and discovered that traditional Dharma teachers consider that we killed a sentient being, which is the worst kind of sin, and that the karmic repercussions are said to be rebirth in hell. Is there any way to expiate our sins? I wonder if it is even worth pursuing the spiritual path if we are irrevocably doomed already."

I told him that first of all, I personally would wish to consider each situation individually on its own merits, rather than according to an ironclad rulebook interpretation of karmic cause and effect. The question of motivation is always relevant in Buddhism. Why was the decision to have an abortion made? Was it made carelessly and without much consideration, or were there substantial reasons, perhaps? Was the health and safety of the mother—either physically or emotionally—a realistic issue? When weighty life decisions are made with utmost care and conscientious deliberation, cherishing life in all its forms and considering the broader implications of the act, with genuine intention to accomplish the most compassionate, skillful, right and appropriate action—rather than just taking the easy way out—the karma is not so heavy to bear. Talk of hell need not enter the picture.

Buddhist tradition tells us that everything is impermanent; that no everlasting hell exists for anyone, although we can experience hellish states of mind and experiences. These are created through intensely violent, hateful, negative deeds, words, and thoughts— which are karmic actions.

Just about everyone has done something that he or she regrets. The Dalai Lama himself has written about how as an adolescent he aimed his slingshot at a bird that was flying by. Fortunately, he recounts, he didn't hit it, but he still remembers the impulse. Buddhist teachings reveal that negative karma does have one positive facet or aspect: It can be repaired. This makes everything workable. We can, in fact, expiate our negative actions through acknowledging and confessing to our conscience our misdeeds, with sincere repentence and regret. By vowing not to do such evil again, by saving lives, protecting creatures, and so forth, Buddhist practitioners learn to purify and transform bad karma, and actually exhaust its impact, eventually becoming free of it and liberated from such consequences.

As in Christianity, there are many Dharma stories about people whose lives and karma were purified and transformed. One of the most memorable is the story of Anguli Mala, an enraged jungle dwelling giant. His horrific, aggressive evokes his history of evil deeds, and his name, Anguli Mala, tells his story. Anguli means finger bone; mala means necklace or rosary. Around his neck Anguli Mala wore a necklace of 999 human finger bones—one from each of the people he had killed. So lacking pity or mercy was he that he was even planning to murder his own mother, whose finger bone could then also be strung around his neck.

Everybody has aspirations of some sort; Anguli Mala's was to add the thousandth bone to his prized collection. This was his single-minded desire. With that in mind, one day as he was walking down a jungle path, he spied a yellow-robed mendicant walking slowly alone. Another finger bone! Anguli Mala hurried forward, murder in his twisted mind and violence on his face. But when he reached his intended victim and gazed into the Buddha's peaceful shining countenance, he was unable to complete his plan of action.

"Who are you?" Anguli Mala asked. "Why do you shine like that, and what is it about you that immediately calms and pacifies my blazing inner fires?"

The Buddha replied, "I have calmed my own inner fires."

Anguli Mala was so awed that he knelt down and confessed, "I was coming to kill you, a saint, but now the bonfire raging inside has gone out. Why?"

"This," the Buddha told Anguli Mala, "is the effect of inner peace, enlightenment, nirvana."

When Anguli Mala confessed to all of his sinful, cruel, and evil deeds and stated his heartfelt intention to repent, the Buddha took pity on him. Buddha told Anguli Mala that his actions had created enormous bad karma which could result in rebirth in the lowest realms. But the Buddha also assured him that in the Dharma there is no eternal hell. Nothing is eternal; everything changes. When karma is expiated, it is exhausted, and then even the worst sinners can move onward and upward. Thus although our deeds are the seeds of our future destiny, even a killer like Anguli Mala could repent, atone, and make reparations by living his life differently.

Anguli Mala was so moved by the Buddha's words that on the spot, he became a disciple of the Buddha and through practice and perseverance in the three trainings of Wisdom, Ethics, and Meditation, he was eventually able to purify and expiate all of his sinful karma. Within that one lifetime, Anguli Mala was able to become an arhant, a liberated sage. If even a serial killer could purify and transform himself, and expiate his negative karma, why couldn't any one of us do the same? It is completely doable. This is the good news, the gospel of Dharma.

It is said that in order for the full effect of negative karma to take place, the negative action has to have four completed parts: (1) The act is done intentionally; (2) The act is accomplished and completed (for example, a theft is not only planned but actually takes place); (3) The act is not regretted and repented; (4) The act is not atoned for, with vows not to repeat such an act again. When all four of these conditions are present, contributing to the weight or impact of the karmic result, then the full effects will eventually be reaped. Without all four, bad karma can much more easily be transformed. In other words, if you feel regret and repentence for some past act, that alone helps lift the karmic burden.

## REBIRTH HERE AND NOW

Classic Buddhism explains that although good actions and good karma will lead to a better rebirth, it doesn't necessarily bring enlightenment, which is liberation from karma and conditioning. The good karma that stems from deeds alone can even bring rebirth in the angelic or divine realms, where all is beauty, pleasure, and abundance; but eventually that good karma will be spent, your flower garden adornments will wither and fade, and the wheel of samsara keeps turning, toward yet further rebirths. In order to reach enlightenment and nirvana, we must accumulate two different kinds of merit—accumulation of merits from virtuous actions, as well as the merits that come from wisdom, insight, understanding, and awareness.

Some people say they don't believe in rebirth and seek a more here-and-now philosophy. Right Action in this world in this present moment is a liberating practice that allows one to go through life free from guilt and self-doubt, secure in the knowledge that virtue brings its own just rewards. Even the murderous Anguli Mala could reach realization after he heard the Dharma teaching and put an end to his volcanic anger and malice. Purifying negativities—large and small—brings contentment and inner peace. Virtuous living is a boon to the entire world. When we transform our lives, we ourselves become transformed. It is a spiritual rebirth, in this very life. We don't have to wait for an afterlife of some kind. This is how we can usher in the kingdom of heaven, in this world, in our homes and community. We need not wait.

# CRAVING: A MAJOR CHALLENGE TO RIGHT ACTION

*The secret waits for eyes unclouded by longing.*

—*Tao Te Ching:*
*The Way and Its Power*

*Craving,* or lust, as it is sometimes called, is one of the primary five hindrances, or challenges, that Buddha warned seekers they would meet on the path to awakening. When Buddha Dharma speaks about craving, it implies psychological hunger and thirst, unhealthy desire, longing, attachment, and psychological fixation. Who among us is so completely fulfilled and content that he or she is above "wanting" of any kind? Is there nothing wanting in your life right now? As we try to purify and refine our actions, we need to be aware of the myriad ways by which our desires create pitfalls on the spiritual path.

It is said that a thief's vision is so distorted that even when he meets a saint, all he can see is the saint's pocketbook. Ask yourself: Is there anything or anyone you crave so much that it clouds your judgment and vision? What do you hunger for? Is there anything that engenders feelings so intense that your pursuit of it becomes a substitute for furthering your inner development? It has often been said that everyone has a price; what is yours? Don't sell yourself short, or you'll pay for it.

Meeting the challenge of desire is a very puzzling experience. It can be tempting to regard this particular hindrance and rationalize it away, saying that it isn't really desire we're feeling, that it's really something else. For example:

◉ John doesn't believe that he "lusts" for money and success; he thinks he is just trying to earn a living for his family. However, when John is making a sale, he completely loses track of the other person's humanity as well as right and wrong. All he can think about is closing the deal, which is his way of winning and asserting his dominance and superiority. Money means more to him than a livelihood. It is his way of keeping score.

◉ Mary is obsessed by the ups and downs in her relationship with her boyfriend. She doesn't know what she would do if he wasn't in her life so she tolerates a range of frustrating and emotionally abusive behavior. She doesn't think what she is experiencing is lust or craving because her feelings are so much more complicated than sex. She clings to whatever contact she can have with him and tells herself that since she is so completely absorbed in another human being, she doesn't desire enough for herself. Mary doesn't see this as an inner spiritual problem. She feels everything depends on him.

◉ Greg craves a more exciting, less domestic life. His need for excitement is so great that he doesn't realistically see how much his children want their father's attention. Instead of cherishing his family and the time he can spend with them, he shows his resentment in dozens of small ways.

## MOTHS R US

Purifying oneself of craving and desire is a complex and subtle process. The analogy of a misguided moth being consumed by the candle flame to which it is fatally attracted is a good one. Sometimes we want something so badly that we think we can't possibly let go of our goal. Clutching at such objects of our desire, we get carried away and completely lose our perspective. Our grip is so tight that our grasping mind's hands get rope burns from hanging on for dear life, when it is hardly a matter of life and death at all.

*Desire brings more desire.* Many of us lead lives in which we are always "wanting" something; that's how we think we are going to find happiness. However, in truth, incessantly going from one object of desire to another only perpetuates dissatisfying, addictive patterns in our lives. Whether it's a better relationship, better sex, a better job, better clothes, better real estate, a better car, or a better mood—desire can easily consume one's life. Like drinking salt water to alleviate thirst, trying to satisfy our momentary desires is not satisfying—at least not for very long.

On the spiritual path, be prepared to confront compulsive desires again and again. Watch what you desire; observe what attracts or repels you most. Notice what buttons are pushed in you by external stimuli, and how you respond to each of them. We have all invested emotional intensity and energy in wanting, achieving, accumulating, and grasping. How does it happen? What is it for you? Just round up the usual suspects and look them over—love, ego gratification, sex, sensual pleasures, money, possessions, fame, security, power. Are we making Faustian deals with the devil?

When the Buddha gave the Fire Sermon to a thousand disciples at Gaya, he told them that "All is burning . . . burning with the fire of lust, with the fire of hate, with the fire of delusion." Desire nothing, and you will be liberated and free. The third Zen patriarch sang, "The way is not difficult for those who have no preferences."

As you make the choices on which you will base your actions, watch to see what is motivating you. Desirelessness is nirvanic peace. Relinquishing attachment and clinging does ultimately pay off. Let go and let Buddha.

# BEING CREATIVE IN
# ACCOMPLISHING GOOD DEEDS

*To laugh often and much; to win the respect of
intelligent people and the affection of children;
to earn the appreciation of honest critics and
endure the betrayal of false friends; to appreciate beauty, to find the best in others; to leave the
world a bit better, whether by a healthy child, a
garden, or a redeemed social condition; to know
even one life has breathed easier because you
have lived. This is to have succeeded.*

—RALPH WALDO EMERSON

The Dharma consistently instructs us that it isn't enough to avoid
negative behavior; we must also encourage positive action. I find
this philosophy very appealing, perhaps because of my Jewish heritage that places so much emphasis on ethical behavior, social service, and caring for others. My grandfather used to tell me, "A
mensch [real person] does a mitzvah [good deed] every day."
Sometimes we want to help others, but we are so overwhelmed by
all that needs to be done in this world that we don't know where
to start. We hope that tomorrow or next week, when everything
calms down, we will be able to become the actively compassionate
human beings we know we can be. We put off "goodness" like we
put off going on a diet. We don't know what to do first, and we
lack appropriate frameworks for our good intentions.

For example, as much as you may love children, you may have
limited time and resources; you may care deeply about people who
are ill, but you lack medical skills. So what can you do? At one
time, entering a religious order was a realistic option for people
who wanted to devote themselves to good works. But today, if you
want to act on your compassionate intentions, you will probably
have to do it within the context of the life you are now living. I
think it helps if each of us stops for just a moment to consider the
many ways we can practice Right Action daily by being decent,
caring people.

When you are trying to reach out a helping hand, it's important to stay flexible and imaginative. It also helps if you focus on actions that are specific and doable. And remember: It's okay to have fun. After all, giving is an act of joy. Here are what some people I know have done recently:

◎ Barbara, my talented literary agent, is known for her sense of adventure, athleticism, and also her ability to raise money. This year, she signed up for a three-day, 400-mile bike ride to raise money for AIDS, and committed herself to raising ten thousand dollars in pledges for her ride. To do this, she gave up many of her usual summer activities as she focused on training for the long, arduous bike ride from Boston to New York City

◎ Dorothy loves children and reading; she volunteered to help her local literacy group. Last year she was assigned a shy twelve-year-old girl from central Europe who couldn't read or write in English. By the end of the year, her student had not only progressed academically, she had also gained self-assurance and skills that will last her a lifetime.

◎ David loves animals. When he sees stray dogs or cats, he wants to take them all home with him. But his apartment building does not allow animals. David volunteers at the local humane society, where he takes dogs waiting to be adopted out in the park for exercise.

◎ Once a week, writer Kate Wheeler takes her beautiful white dog Chandi to an Alzheimer clinic, eliciting warm smiles, pats, and even hugs from elderly patients who usually shy away from human contact and interaction.

◎ Diana, who loves the great outdoors, volunteers with a group that takes inner-city children on weekend excursions to camp and hike outside the big city.

Here are some other good deed ideas: Call your local blood bank to give much-needed blood or platelets; become a volunteer for an organization that delivers food and other services to shut-ins; visit retirement homes or places that care for sick children without families; try to find homes for stray animals; sign up for an organization that provides emotional support or teaches reading skills to needy children. Recycle, recycle, recycle. Many cities, for example, have people who will recondition old bicycles to give to children who can't afford them. Donate your used computers, clothes, books, and tapes, as well as your services and money, to worthwhile charities. Try to look into the eyes and heart of each person you meet; try to treat everyone with kindness, warmth, and acceptance. Maybe you can't save the whole world all at once, but if you can make even one other person's life a little happier, you are making a difference. One pair of warm gloves for one pair of cold hands can help. One less piece of litter along the highway helps. Every smile helps. Perform "random acts of kindness and senseless acts of beauty," as writer Anne Herbert tells us.

If you want to make Right Action a part of your everyday life, you might find it helpful to become a part of an active spiritual or social service community. The Buddha often told seekers, as I am going to remind you again: A group of like-minded friends and kindred spirits can do a great deal to keep you connected to your higher nature. Whether you find this group in a Buddhist sangha, a church, a temple, a Quaker meeting, an ecology or support group, it really doesn't matter. Start associating more often with other concerned men and women trying to incorporate good works and meaningful goals into their daily activities; it will help you find a focus and loving support for your positive intentions. No matter what your age, gender, or occupation, there are endless ways for you to act with wisdom, compassion, and altruism, which will bless you manifold. Remember the bumper sticker: *Think Globally, Act Locally.* Just do it.

## AVOIDING IDIOT COMPASSION

A friend addicted to alcohol, drugs, gambling, or shopping pleads with you to loan him money—"just one last time"—to feed his habit. Your child begs for permission to do something that you know is potentially self-destructive or dangerous. Your mate is consistently hurtful, abusive, and unkind, yet you consistently forgive him or her. Your troubled relative or friend does something that you know is wrong, and then convinces you to participate in a cover-up so that he or she will not have to face the consequences. If you give in to such demands, you are practicing "idiot compassion." Trungpa Rinpoche coined this apt phrase to name this false, inverted brand of compassion.

We are being foolish when we congratulate ourselves on our compassionate behavior when in reality we are simply giving in and giving up too easily. In all likelihood we are being lazy, fearful, frightened, or even codependent. This idiotic pseudo-compassion is counterproductive, and can enable others to hurt themselves further. Sometimes to say "no" is far more affirming and supportive than to just say "yes" without reflection.

Wisdom is an essential component of compassion. The enlightened mind is often defined as radiant wisdom endowed with warm love and compassion. Wisdom helps us develop a mirror-like awareness that responds appropriately to what is truly needed in any and every situation. Mirror-like wisdom requires the capacity to stand back and look at the reality of a situation before we jump in. Sometimes we give in because we are trying to manipulate a situation—perhaps we are afraid of rejection or we want to get something in return. We all need to be really clear about what it means to give with a pure and unselfish heart.

Often we do what we always do and give what is easiest for us to give instead of what is needed in each different situation. A friend of mine says that one of the hardest lessons she has had to learn as a parent is to be open to her children's real needs—beyond what she thinks they need. When her teenage daughter comes into the kitchen wanting to talk, my friend says her knee-jerk maternal response is to start busily rushing around the kitchen trying to give love through food. She seems to get stuck on a single channel, which in her case is the food channel. This mindless busy activity gets in the way of on-the-spot communication. It would be far better to sit down and have a conversation with her daughter. Compassion calls for empathy and listening to what is really being said. We must keep our channels open to the wide variety of possible responses that can appropriately address real needs. Then enlightened activity can spontaneously flow through us and into the world.

# DANCING WITH LIFE

*Activities are endless, like ripples on a stream.*
*They end only when you drop them.*
*Human moods are like the changing highlights*
    *and shadows*
*on a sunlit mountain range.*

*All activities are like the games children play,*
*like castles being made of sand.*
*View them with delight and equanimity,*
*like grandparents overseeing their grandchil-*
    *dren*
*or a shepherd resting on a grassy knoll*
*watching over his grazing flock.*

—NYOSHUL KHENPO RINPOCHE,
FROM A SPONTANEOUS VAJRA SONG

Right Action doesn't have to be a daunting and seemingly un-reachable prospect. As we go through life, it's as if we are playing with sand that sifts through our fingers. When we were children and built our castles in the sand, they were filled with fun. Our adult projects could be almost the same way: full of joy instead of fear, openness instead of defensiveness, equanimity instead of du-alism, anxiety, and doubt.

Like me, you are probably trying to fine-tune your actions so they reflect your deepest-held beliefs and values. Fine-tune is the operative term here: how to live and act more and more in a manner congruent with our inner beliefs and words. This is a constant, ongoing, and gradually unfolding process. Remember we are all works in progress, striving to refine our spirits and our lives. It's unrealistic to expect to instantly transform from seeds into healthy, fully blossomed shade trees. In this spiritual business, we are growing Bodhisattvas, not shade trees; we are growing up in a spiritual sense. We are refining our true nature; refining the ore and extracting the gold. A process-oriented philosophy, Bud-dhism doesn't believe in finality. It is about coming home, not about impossible, pie-in-the-sky promises. It can be as simple as we can be. Because we are quite complicated, our paths are complicated.

To take up our spiritual beliefs and concerns and apply them in everyday life, we have to learn to treat life like an intimate dancing partner. Why withdraw and turn into wallflowers—mere spectators? Feel the music of your own life; dance to the drumbeat of living spirit through your own being.

As you walk the path, remember to practice self-forgiveness and self-acceptance. Life is like an experiment, and everything we do is improvisational. Right Action essentially requires of us only that we be perfectly sincere, appreciate things as they are, understand causality and its ethical implications, and try to do our best. For doing our best is the very best any of us can do.

# YOU CAN'T TAKE IT WITH YOU, BUT . . .

Everyone says that when you die, you can't take wealth, family, or possessions with you. But there is something very important that you do take with you, that you can bank on, and that's your accumulated virtue and wisdom—your karma. The Tibetans say that when we die, so little remains with us from the life we are leaving that each of us is "like a hair pulled out of butter." Nothing comes with us. All is left behind. The only thing that remains is the karma that we have accumulated through our actions, words, and thoughts. Whether or not you believe in the traditional rebirth doctrine, consider that at that crucial stage of the journey, at death, each of us carries with us nothing more than our accumulated wisdom and virtue. This is an investment plan that can't go belly-up. You can place your faith in that.

# Meditations on Right Action

A Buddhist Meditation known as the Five Remembrances asks us to reflect on the nature of reality and our actions. This can help us to decide what our priorities are and how we should spend our days.

## THE FIVE REMEMBRANCES

1. There is no way to escape aging. I too will grow old.

2. There is no way to escape physical degeneration. My body too will weaken.

3. There is no way to escape death. I too will die.

4. Everything and everyone changes; we must part even from loved ones.

5. My deeds are always with me as propensities. Only my karma accompanies me when I die; my karma is the ground on which I stand.

## BEGINNING AND ENDING THE DAY

Kalu Rinpoche used to tell us to evaluate our own actions daily by making two little piles of stones each day—one for positive actions and one for negative actions. Each day you count up the positive and negatives, and then assess, evaluate, and consider what is happening in your life. I personally have found that this simple childlike teaching has brought me deeper into my own practice in the last few years. I will admit that here in the United States I am more likely to use a notebook than stones, and you may well feel the same way, but the point remains.

This little exercise can be combined with an analytical meditation that we can do while we are lying in bed at night before we fall asleep and also immediately after waking up. This practical way of examining our intentions and actions corresponds with one of Atisha's mind-training slogans *"Two Things to Do at the Start and Finish of Every Day."*

When you wake each morning, start the day by reaffirming your intention to practice loving-kindness and compassion. Remind yourself each day to work at letting go of ego clinging, selfishness, controlling behavior, negative thoughts, possessiveness, aggression, resentment, and confusion. Resolve each day to find one small way that you can change a frozen behavior pattern, and try to do so.

When you lie down at night, reflect on the day that was. Remember your accomplishments and your frustrations—things done as well as undone. Who or what pushed your buttons? Use clear discernment and discriminating awareness to genuinely examine your behavior and the quality of your life. Recognize your familiar repetitive patterns. Assess how fruitful they actually are.

Finally, examine your day for lingering resentments and self-destructive, harmful, egocentric, or narcissistic thoughts. Find joy in awakening the noble-hearted spirit of bodhicitta. Rejoice in all the good works of both others and yourself, and share in all that good karma. It will help you find rest.

Then rest. "Done is what had to be done," as the Buddha said.


"Wait, wait," a follower once cried after the Buddha as he disappeared into the forest.

"I stopped a long time ago," Buddha replied. "When will you stop?"

# RIGHT LIVELIHOOD

## *Work Is Love Made Visible*

*When you work you are a flute through whose heart the whispering of the hours turns to music. To love life through labor is to be intimate with life's inmost secret. All work is empty save when there is love, for work is love made visible.*

—KAHLIL GIBRAN

The Supreme Cambodian Patriarch, Venerable Monk Maha Goshananda, has spent a lifetime working for peace. When he led an international peace walk from Auschwitz to Cambodia and Hiroshima, thousands of men and women from around the world followed. Maha Goshananda's country, Cambodia, a major battlefield of the Vietnam War, is still littered with millions of live landmines left behind by the Khmer Rouge. Maha Goshananda, who spends much of his time searching these "Killing Fields," says that removing these mines is his Dharma practice. Recently when an interviewer asked him why he so determinedly continued to do this, he explained simply, "I am making peace with myself." Each day Maha Goshananda's love for all shows itself in his work—a beautifully concrete and exalted example of Right Livelihood.

For centuries Right Livelihood has asked us to love our world through our work, instructing us to avoid vocations that harm others. Anything that leads to harming or killing other beings, such as selling or making arms and ammunition, are obvious examples of livelihoods traditionally considered inappropriate for an enlightened life. There are some current occupations that might be included in this list: drug dealing or any other livelihood that is deceitful, unwholesome, corrupting, encourages heedlessness, or is exploitative (of beings or the environment). Junk bond trading is a new development in poor livelihood. In the past, as now, the preferred work is altruistic and furthers the spiritual life. According to the ancient scripture, the Dhammapada, Right Livelihood is said to be "in tune with increasing helpfulness for beings and decreasing harmfulness."

# BRINGING SPIRITUAL ENERGY
# INTO DAILY LIFE

*Those who see worldly life as an obstacle to Dharma see no Dharma in everyday actions; they have not yet discovered that there are no everyday actions outside of Dharma.*

—THIRTEENTH-CENTURY
ZEN MASTER DOGEN

Many of us have experienced waking up hours before sunrise in order to drive long distances. At 4:00 A.M., houses are dark and roads are empty, but as you continue along, you become aware of increasing activity. More trucks speed by as lights start illuminating the houses you can see from the road. It's easy to imagine parents waking up to take care of early-rising children, farmers walking to the barn to feed the animals, and commuters heading for highways, trains, buses, and subways. As the workday revs up, all over America people are eating toast, gulping tea and coffee, and looking for clean socks. Some of these men and women are approaching their work with passion and zeal; others are already beginning to feel tense and resentful; still others are rushing forward, as if to combat.

In one way or another, every Buddha (awake or asleep) needs to work. We all work: We go to jobs, we take care of children, we study, we drive cars, we prepare meals, we do laundry, and we empty cat litter. We all work at something. Right Livelihood is how Buddhas and Bodhisattvas work to make an enlightened life.

In our electronic world, several of the issues surrounding work have become more complex than those addressed by Gautama, the Buddha, 2,500 years ago. Yet the themes remain constant: Can we use our hands, our heads, and our hearts to help others? Can we transcend grasping and egocentric behavior, act with enlightened leadership, and embody the impeccable values of sila?

For seekers now, as then, work provides a major opportunity to put one's beliefs into action. This is the *real* work. This is something we can really invest ourselves in, which makes the work come alive. Tibetan lamas pray:

*May I practice Dharma from now until enlightenment is reached.*

*May I mingle the Dharma totally with everything I do until the moment of death.*

In this way, Bodhisattvas articulate their intention to remember Dharma values, practice good works, and integrate spirituality with even the most mundane day-to-day activities. Despite its mystical appeal, the Dharma and its masters reflect the Buddha's profoundly realistic view of life. At a Western Buddhist Teacher's Conference in India in 1993, for example, the Dalai Lama told us, "Learn all that you can. Anything may be helpful. Atisha [who introduced Mahayana mind-training to Tibet] could even mend shoes." The Dalai Lama himself knows how to fix clocks and watches.

Right Livelihood is a practical as well as spiritual concept, and reading ancient scriptures today, one notices just how much commonsense day-to-day advice the Buddha personally imparted dur-

ing his long lifetime and teaching career. When the monks asked
him how the monastic sangha could get along better, the Buddha's
advice was not otherworldly. He did *not* say, "Try to turn your
body into a rainbow," or "meditate on emptiness." What he *did* say
was, "Don't hide the vegetables on your plate under the rice," thus
reminding them that for the monk who wants more than his share
of vegetables, selfishness expresses itself in dozens of small acts.
This is spirituality made practical and real.

The Buddha once told the layman Dighajanu that there are
four things conducive to happiness in this world: to be skilled, efficient, energetic, earnest, and learned in whatever profession one
has; to conscientiously protect one's income and family's means of
support; to have virtuous, trustworthy, and faithful friends and spiritual aspirations; to be content and to live within one's means. This
advice aptly demonstrates the Buddha's commonsense approach as
well as his capacity to relate to laymen.

Nonetheless, students who ask me questions are sometimes less
than thrilled when I offer commonsense suggestions rather than a
mystical visualization technique or the name of a holy guru on a
Himalayan mountaintop. Finding wisdom in the most ordinary
matters of everyday life is a Buddhist tradition. When asked by a
student, "What is Buddha?" one Zen master replied, "Which side
of the door did you leave your sandals on?" Another Zen master
who was asked, "What is enlightenment?" answered, "Wash your
dinner bowl."

Chogyam Trungpa Rinpoche used to tell his students, "Pull
your socks up." To a student who joked, "I'm not wearing any
socks," Trungpa said, "So pull your pants up!" In other words, get
yourself straight. Reality, after all, is spiritual enough. Spirit is
meaningless without being grounded here and now in this plane
of existence.

# GOOD WORK IS HELPFUL TO
# YOURSELF AS WELL AS OTHERS

Margaret supports herself and her daughter by selling real estate. When she turned on the television last night, a story came on about surgeons who regularly donate their medical skills to help economically disadvantaged children in Central America. She was deeply moved. Margaret very much wants to make goodness part of her life; she envies people with skills that she thinks can really make a difference.

Frank, a stockbroker, feels the same way, yet he believes his good intentions are stymied by a career that calls for a competitive, even cutthroat, attitude rather than a caring and compassionate spirit. He thinks his coworkers care only about the economic bottom line and doubts that they place much value on compassion. Frank can't exactly add a list of good deeds to his résumé or can he?

For centuries, well-intentioned men and women have confronted difficulties in combining spiritually motivated behavior with secular lives. I too grapple with this conundrum.

Margaret needs to know that every time she lovingly makes lunch for her little girl, helps a client solve a housing problem without making the realty commission her main priority, or cheerfully drives the babysitter home in foul weather, she is practicing Right Livelihood or good work. Parenting itself is an example of the real work, calling for wholehearted, unselfish effort.

Of course it's challenging for Frank to let go of his competitive attitude and find ways to use the skills he already has to help a co-worker. That *is* Frank's challenge, and part of his unfolding path. Meditative awareness can help Frank see that a collaborative attitude combined with small considerate actions can make a difference in another person's life, even when those actions take place on Wall Street. Frank might discover that a change in his attitude could transform his own relations and life, even in the workplace; it might even transform his workplace. Wall Street is but one lane of the great way of awakening—or at least it can be.

## PAYING ATTENTION PAYS OFF

A friend of mine works in a law firm in a large city office building; one day she walked out of her office and saw a baby bird sitting in front of the revolving doors. She stopped, unsure of what to do. She could only imagine the worst for the bird's survival, but at the very least, she thought, she could keep the bird from being trampled. To her surprise, soon others congregated, eager to help the little creature. Finally a lawyer she recognized noticed the small tree that was planted in the sidewalk near the curb. There the mother bird waited. All they had to do was get the baby bird over to the tree, so they did that.

If Frank could become more aware of all that is needed in the world, he might be able to commit himself to a straightforward helping project at work—raising money for toys or clothing for needy children or organizing volunteers for a homeless shelter, for example—he might discover, as did my friend with the baby bird, that he is surrounded by men and women who want to do more for others, but don't know what to do or where to start.

I don't think it helps anyone to get too judgmental about different occupations. Some may say that a doctor or nurse is more helpful to humanity than a banker or mortgage broker, but who really knows? An impeccable businessperson can do a lot of good. Some say that the legal profession lacks an ethical center, but Ralph Nader is a lawyer and Gandhi was a lawyer. So was Lincoln. I think it helps if each of us stops for a moment and considers the many ways we can practice Right Livelihood—using our hands, our heads, and our hearts to help others—no matter what we do for a living. Right Livelihood helps us make a life, not just a living. It affords us spiritual renewal, right here and now, without going elsewhere. Buddha said: "Sustaining a loving heart, even for the duration of a finger snap, makes one a truly spiritual being."

# RIGHT LIVELIHOOD IN THE MARKETPLACE

*Few men have virtue to withstand the highest
bidder.*

—GEORGE WASHINGTON

*Virtue has never been as respectable in society
as money.*

—MARK TWAIN

Let's not be unduly naive. The workplace often seems confused,
agitated, weak in humane values, and all too eager to reward ego-
centricity and greed. Trying to practice enlightened living—
authentic spirituality—will create some interesting challenges. If,
for example, you discover the firm where you work is lying and
overcharging customers, what do you do? If the only job you can
find is as a minimum wage cashier for a retail company that is ex-
ploiting workers overseas, what do you do? If you're a Dharma
teacher, and you have a choice between a well-paying academic
position or what amounts to a nonpaying or subsistence job at a
small Buddhist center, what do you do? If your boss has a wickedly
caustic tongue and everybody in your office loves to gossip, does
Right Speech go out the window? It sounds wonderful to assume
a lofty position and pretend that none of us ever has to deal with
these issues, but it's not realistic.

In the late seventies, I left India and returned to the U.S. for
three years. I escorted a dozen Tibetan lamas and teachers from
Kalu Rinpoche's monastery to France and to this country, translat-
ing for them, driving them on tour, and working to establish retreat centers and monasteries in Wappinger's Falls and Woodstock,
New York. Working for Dharma, Inc. was not a paying position; I
did not have any savings or assets after living in India for six years.
I tried to think of a way to make a living that was moral, ethical,
constructive, and interesting and still be potentially lucrative
enough to help finance myself and colleagues in further spiritual

practice, while bringing more of our Asian teachers to this country. My friends and I very much wanted to establish Dharma centers here for Westerners to meditate and learn more about this ancient, yet for us, newly discovered wisdom work.

I had learned about ginseng in Korea, and after much discussion and some market research, a Zen photographer friend and I decided that an organic ginseng farm would provide a right form of livelihood. We got financing and bought an old 180-acre farm in the Catskills, where ginseng naturally grows wild, employing several other members of our Woodstock Tibetan monastery. We intended to work together as friends, encourage cooperation, reduce competitiveness, treat everyone fairly, bring out the best in our coworkers, rein in our egos, and adopt ethical business practices. It was my first and only clearly capitalist venture. I discovered that even in the context of a Buddhist sangha, it was a challenge to live according to the principles we espoused—to really practice what we preached. Why should I have been surprised?

Perfection is an ideal, difficult to find here on earth. Every work situation is a little flawed, a little fraught with hypocrisies, compromises, and egotism—sometimes even our own! In some job settings, anything other than "me first" logic and dualistic thinking can seem out of place or even strange. In these environments, our spiritual paths often appear to be littered with hindrances. The workplace provides a rich arena for us to become more aware of our actions and intentions, as well as help us take some concrete steps on the spiritual path. Working on ourselves as we work at our jobs can be self-transforming. In this way, we learn the wise principle of making lemonade from the lemons we unexpectedly find on our plates.

For a moment, think about what is known in Buddhism as the "poisons" or conflicting emotions (kleshas) that veil and cloud reality: Ignorance, Pride, Jealousy, Enmity, and Desire. On some level just about every work situation is going to provoke at least some of these kleshas. If the person at the next desk gets the promotion you wanted, you might well feel jealousy and the desire for your own promotion. If you receive a big raise, what's wrong with feeling good about yourself and your work?

Don't misinterpret the Dharma's message to mean that we should deny our feelings or be oblivious to the whole range of human experience. Strong emotions are not the primary issue; the primary issue is grasping and attachment. When we cling to and grasp at passionate emotions, losing ourselves by too strongly identifying with them, they take over the mind, possess our thoughts, and obscure our clear seeing—tarnishing our present awareness and clear vision.

I often have to remind myself not to hang on to my feelings— not to allow my emotions to impel me to crush things in my grasp but rather to enjoy experiences as they pass by, and then let go. It helps to recall a favorite William Blake poem:

> *He who binds to himself a joy*
> *does the winged life destroy;*
> *But he who kisses the joy as it flies*
> *Lives in eternity's sunrise.*

The Dharma shows us that understanding the *why* of our speech and behavior can be more important than the words and deeds themselves. No matter what is going on in your life, and no matter what you are doing, you would do well to regularly look into the mirror of your own mind and examine what is taking place, while checking out your motivation and intentions. Self-reflection and inquiry can help us turn every part of our work into part of our spiritual path, just more grist for the mill.

## DEALING WITH NEGATIVITY IN THE WORKPLACE

People sometimes complain to me about the level of negativity they experience at work where there can be so much competition, backbiting, dishonesty, and sniping. It's particularly difficult when you are on the receiving end of some of this negativity. This presents an immediate challenge to our benevolent bodhicitta intentions. For centuries Dharma students have found solace, guidance, and inspiration in some ancient words of the Buddha known as the Metta Sutra (The Scripture of Loving-Kindness), which says in part:

> *Let none deceive another, or despise any being in any state.*
> *Let none through anger or ill will wish harm upon another.*
> *Even as a mother protects with her life, her child, her only child,*
> *So with a boundless heart should one cherish all living beings,*
> *radiating kindness over the entire world.*

In this dog-eat-dog world and impersonal marketplace, consider these sterling thoughts. Hang this quote over your desk as a reminder and enjoy a practical application of taking refuge in the Dharma.

## HOW THE EIGHT WORLDLY WINDS BLOW US OFF COURSE

Buddhism teaches that most of us are too often motivated and driven by the Eight Worldly Winds or Influences. This ancient teaching, which can be applied to all of our interactions, is very appropriate to the turbulent ups and downs of the contemporary workplace.

More than twenty years ago, Kalu Rinpoche first taught me about the Eight Worldly Winds. He pointed out then how recognizing these influences or concerns could help me distinguish for myself whether my motivations in any given situation were spiritual or worldly. I believe that you can do the same thing. The Eight Worldly Winds are actually four pairs, each pair representing opposite poles on a desire-aversion axis—in other words, what we want and what we don't want, two different yet totally interrelated forms of desire.

◎ Pleasure and Pain

◎ Gain and Loss

◎ Praise and Blame

◎ Fame and Shame

Concern about and attachment to pleasure, gain, praise, and fame are powerful forces that can sometimes seize us with hurricane ferocity, blowing us about like leaves in the wind. We've all seen people jeopardize life, limb, ethical considerations, and contentment for the briefest of pleasures, the possibility of financial gain, the right kind of praise, or for fifteen minutes in the winner's circle of fame. It's easy to respond to these driving forces with knee-jerk reactions and lose sight of our inner goals. Sometimes we are distracted for only a second; nonetheless, we get blown off course. Regarding the consequences of reaching for instant gratification, a Weight Watchers slogan says, "A moment on the lips, a lifetime on the hips." This is Dharma wisdom, the practical ethics of conscious restraint.

To better understand the way you react to the Worldly Winds, imagine yourself driving down the road, heading for your goal of enlightenment or nirvana. Suddenly out of the corner of your eye, you see something that captures your attention. Perhaps it suggests something you want desperately—a winning lottery ticket, a prestigious job, an old love, or even an ice cream cone—your favorite flavor. Perhaps it's something you fear, something that personifies loneliness, depression, or terror. You respond almost without thinking and are so overcome that you veer off, ending up in a roadside rut. There your wheels, stuck in the mud or sand, spinning round and round. This is like being mired in samsara.

Look around the marketplace, and you will see the worldly forces that blow people every which way. To get a sense of how you might be blown about by one of these "Winds," stop long enough to check out your motivations on a regular basis. Are you caught up on the pleasure-pain axis? Do you find it difficult, or sometimes even impossible, to overcome your impulses and resistances in order to do what has to be done? Do thoughts of loss or gain (financial or otherwise) dominate your life? Are you so easily inflated or deflated that praise or blame can make or break your day? Do you simultaneously long for the fame of center stage and fear the shame of exposure? When one of the Worldly Winds gusts in your direction, do you find it difficult to just proceed straight ahead, while overcoming your fleeting impulses? Lama Yeshe always exhorted his students to "check up yourself." The words, "check up," were like his mantra. He transmitted that helpful and useful mantra to me, and I can still hear his words ringing in my ears today.

True spiritual masters are so centered and inner-directed that no matter what is happening in the outer world, they don't lose touch with their innate Buddha-nature; they are guided by their own principles instead of merely reacting according to momentary conditions and temporary circumstances. Going through life with their hands on the steering wheel of awareness, they are paying attention; they understand karmic causation, how things actually work. Many of the rest of us, of course, are still gripping the rearview mirror and wondering why we so often end up lost or in the ditch.

It's easy to become so enmeshed in our worldly goals that we lose sight of the bigger picture. Without more foresight and perspective, we cannot help but prioritize foolishly. The ups and downs of office politics and interpersonal dynamics, for example, will overly affect the untrained mind. One minute you can feel like a winner, elated and on top of your game; the next you're in a slump, defeated, hopeless, and depressed. Buddhism reminds us that nothing lasts, not even our successes or defeats. When gods in the celestial realms use up their accumulation of good karma, even they must come back to earth; even Superman can fall from the sky. The virtue of equanimity helps us not to become overly invested in success or unduly disrupted by disappointment. Commonsense wisdom reminds us that there is a difference between making a living and making a life. Our pursuit of worldly success in this thorny rosebush-like world can be no more satisfying than the pursuit of a mirage in the arid desert.

The Wisdom Sutras teach us to hear all sounds as echos. All the words we hear from the outside world, including the praise and blame, are empty and hollow. Genuine Buddhist training helps each of us develop our own autonomy and inner self-mastery. Rather than being overly influenced by and dependent on the opinions and reactions of others, we learn to recognize everything as impermanent, ephemeral, intangible, dreamlike, and unreal. We can grow away from dependence and codependence into healthy individuation; we can finally understand independence and inter-dependence.

If you are unduly attracted to pleasure, gain, fame, or praise, reflect on the hollow, fickle nature of the world's applause and the insubstantial nature of the flickering movielike projection of all that we see, feel, and think. Consider that in the end, everything you want to achieve will be washed away like sandcastles on the shore. Tomorrow, you may not even want the same things you want today. Everyone can remember at least one passionate emotional response that in retrospect seems humorous at best. As my teacher Nyoshul Khenpo always says, "The mind is fickle, don't rely on it."

Several of Atisha's mind-training slogans that further reinforce these teachings on the insubstantial nature of worldly success are:

## "Don't Be Best Friends with Pride and Vanity"

This slogan has everything to do with how you look at the world and can be a very helpful reminder to transcend ego. We tend to filter all our thoughts through our own complicated ego investment plans. Reflecting on this slogan reminds us not to tell ourselves stories about our own accomplishments and remarkable specialness. Instead appreciate the virtues of others, and the wonderful joy of loving-kindness and genuine friendliness.

## "Abandon All Hope for Rewards. Don't Expect Applause"

These two slogans address a certain unpleasant reality. A friend of mine says that her grandmother always told her, "Always do the right thing, but don't expect anyone to notice or thank you for it." In short, if you expect people to pat you on the back for walking a spiritual path, in all probability you will be disappointed. Regardless, it is in your own higher self-interest to do so, with or without accolades.

## "If We Let Go of Worldly Values, Will We Seem Foolish or 'Nuts'?"

When I talk about bodhicitta values, I recognize that as a Dharma teacher I'm doing so in a framework in which they are valued and appreciated. In a bottom-line business world, it's reasonable to be concerned that these values may seem out of place and even "foolish." This reminds me of a wonderful story about a Moravian Rabbi named Schmelke, who was well known for his generous spirit. Beggars for miles around knew that they would never go away from Schmelke's door empty-handed. One day, when a beggar knocked, Schmelke, who had no money in the house, gave the beggar a ring. "What are you doing?" his wife exclaimed. "That ring cost hundreds of ducats!" "Wait," Schmelke yelled out to the beggar. "That ring is worth hundreds of ducats. When you sell it, make sure you get what it's worth."

I like this story because it shows that Schmelke wasn't a simple fool who didn't understand the value of money. He recognized the values of this world. Yet, knowing this, he chose to put his trust in transcendental virtues. He wanted to give; he even gave business advice to a beggar. Schmelke had clearly made a decision to live by what he believed and accept the consequences of his actions, no matter what others thought.

There have always been those who laughed or made fun of men and women with genuine spiritual passion. Even in Tibet, some great spiritual masters have been known as "crazy yogis" or "divine madmen." For each of us, in every situation, it's always our own decision: Do we act on what we believe and know to be true, or do we go along with what others consider "normal"? In these situations, there is a mind-training slogan that can be helpful:

## *"Of the Two Witnesses, Listen to Your Conscience"*

When confronted with different points of view of what is right, use this slogan to remind yourself that your own conscience is the main judge of your actions. Of course we can always learn from others, but finally each of us can only trust our own intuitive heart.

The whole thrust of the bodhicitta mind-training and Bodhisattva path is to be able to become naturally more loving and compassionate without expecting or hoping for anything in return. Although your ego may want some form of positive reinforcement or reward for what you do or say, your innate Buddha-nature doesn't require that kind of acknowledgment. Whatever occurs is what occurs, and it is all positive. Even if a Bodhisattva is the last person on earth, he or she would continue on the way of awakening.

Gradually we learn to loosen our tightfisted grip on worldly values. We become more centered, balanced, straightforward, calm, and clear amid any temporary weather conditions—outer circumstances as well as internal emotional weather. We learn to both sit and stand erect, needing nothing to lean on. We stand up for ourselves and our beliefs and stand behind our words and deeds. We become masters of our own domain.

This is how we awaken our inner guru, our inner guide—the Buddha within, the secret master comfortably ensconced forever in our own heart cave. This inner guru is none other than truth itself—our own innate wisdom and heart center's noblest intuitive understanding and love. This is the inner meaning of the provocative, iconoclastic Zen saying: "If you meet the Buddha on the road, kill him!" (Because he must be an impostor, since the only real Buddha or divine being is within.) When you invoke the gods or angels, when you pray, you are awakening this sublime being within yourself. There is no one else to rely upon.

# EQUALITY IN THE WORKPLACE—AND THE SPIRITUAL COMMUNITY

As Buddhism emerges in the West, it is struggling, successfully I believe, to become more gender equal, with women sharing an equal role in both the practice and teaching of the Dharma. At the time of the Buddha's enlightenment in Asia, there were only men in holy orders and being educated in lay society. The Buddha's aunt, Queen Maha Prajapati, the woman who raised him after his own mother died in childbirth, was the first woman to ask to become a member of the Buddhist order. At first the idea seemed incomprehensible and risky to almost everyone, including the Buddha himself: How could a pampered noblewoman adjust to the disciplined, renounced, dangerous life of an unattached wandering mendicant?

To demonstrate that women were also capable of the holy life, Maha Prajapati gathered together several hundred women. Cutting their hair, donning saffron robes, and carrying alms bowls, they began to live like the monks. Even so, the Buddha was still adamantly opposed to the notion that women would be able to lead such arduous, insecure, and potentially dangerous lives. One day his gentle cousin and attendant Ananda interceded by asking the Buddha whether women were capable of enlightenment. "Yes," the Buddha replied, "women are no more or less capable of enlightenment than men." Then Ananda asked in logical fashion, typical of Buddhist reasoning, why they should not be ordained as well? Finally won over by Ananda's arguments and the women's sincere determination, the Buddha allowed women into the order. The Buddha thus became the first societal leader to flout the rigid Hindu caste system and openly educate and ordain women.

We can't pretend that Buddhism—like other world religions—doesn't have a troubling patriarchal streak. There have always been female lamas in Tibet—stretching back to Padma Sambhava's main disciple, the youthful queen, Yeshe Tsogyal, but these instances have been rare. For too long, women practitioners were treated more as tea makers than learned teachers. Sexism was eloquently addressed at the first Western Buddhist Teacher's Conference with the Dalai Lama in India when one female teacher asked the assembled male lamas, monks, and teachers to envision what it would mean to engage in a spiritual practice surrounded only by women. How, she asked, would these assembled men feel if all the religious statues and paintings were saintly women rather than men, as is customary, and if all the scriptures were written by women? How would they feel if no matter how long they had been attached to a specific monastery, the newest woman in the order would automatically have a higher status than any man, no matter how senior? For in traditional Buddhist monasteries, that is the bias women have found when taking ordination.

A British nun reinforced this position when she talked about the pain she had personally experienced trying to be part of the predominantly male Tibetan monastery where her teacher lived. She found it so overwhelmingly difficult that she felt forced to go meditate alone, living the life of a hermit for ten years in a cave in Ladakh. As the Dalai Lama listened, he was moved to tears by the problems some women have faced in traditional Buddhist settings; he seemed to be hearing this candidly for the first time. Recently he said that there are no theoretical obstacles against a female Dalai Lama.

Buddhism has always had a strong feminist spokesperson in the form of Tara, the liberated female principle of enlightenment. Many people refer to this female Buddha as Green Tara. In fact, however, like all mothers, Tara has so much to do, so much to give, and is so responsive to the needs of beings that she has many forms and is imaged in twenty-one different colors symbolizing twenty-one aspects and modes of activity. As White Tara, she is a peaceful presence who heals disease and pacifies discord; as Red Tara, she is a passionate presence who devotes her inexhaustible energy to others' needs. As Green Tara, she personifies the qualities of the protective nurturing earth. It is taught that Tara helps us help ourselves. Tara has special meaning in Tibet where she is known as its protectress and is called Mother Tara. Children are taught to invoke Tara's aid through prayer whenever they feel fearful or anxious. Every monastery chants her beautiful "Twenty-one Praises of Tara" liturgy every morning as a group in the meditation hall. As a fully enlightened Buddha, Tara personifies the sacred feminine side of all of us—male and female.

Legend has it that one day many centuries ago, Tara was meditating and chanting her mantra in her Lotus Buddha Field, when some monks happened by. They felt her powerful vibrations and profound meditational energy, and they said, "Oh Yogini [female practitioner], you are such an excellent spiritual practitioner. In the future may you be reborn as a man and become a Buddha." And Tara replied to those arrogant macho monks, "May I throughout all my lifetimes always take female form. Until all beings realize the nirvanic peace, bliss, and freedom of full enlightenment, may I always embody the sacred feminine and be a female Buddha."

In images of Tara, she's not sitting in the full lotus position. She has one leg and one hand down because she is reaching out. She is putting legs on her prayer. She is actually enacting enlightenment, bringing it forth and manifesting it to the world. She sometimes wears a hat as if to go out, she is dressed up, she is wearing jewelry. She is dancing and playing with reality. She's not afraid of it. She's not running away from life or trying to hide in the corner.

So yes, there are innumerable female Buddhas. And you might meet, or—for a brief, but incandescent moment—even be one. Dzogchen masters say that if a woman gives birth to the Bodhisattva Vow and practices bodhicitta, she will develop on the path of awakening faster than a man.

# MAKING MONEY: TOWARD A
# BUDDHIST THEORY OF ECONOMICS

Many of the people I know spend a great deal of time thinking about money—how to keep it, spend it, invest it, donate it, as well as make it. Of course, there are innumerable ways of making money. Decades ago, when I was in North Africa, my genial host told me a story about how some native people in the far south of that continent did it: "The men of the tribe go off into the bush at dawn," he said. "When they return at dusk, their hands are laden with lucre, coins cut out of the metal and beaten into shape with primitive tools. The women, who stayed at home to separate grains and care for the children, welcome these money-making males home with drums and chanting. Each family then buries their share of the coins beneath the dirt floor of their hut." I've always remembered that story for its literal straightforward interpretation of "making money."

Like most religions, classical Buddhism has a certain amount of disdain for money and views it as a potentially corrupting influence. To reinforce this attitude, Buddhist monks in the Southern school vow never to touch money. For centuries, monks in Asia survived because of the generosity of patrons who provided their daily food and supported their monasteries. Within these monasteries, there is the ever-present idea of giving back to society. In Tibet, for example, it is taught that the genuine religious practitioner and the generous patron are inextricably yoked together, with the practitioner pulling the patron along toward nirvana. When you support a practitioner, it's almost like practicing meditation yourself. Because generous giving, known as *dana,* is a spiritual practice and a Bodhisattva virtue, the lay person as donor and yogi as practitioner travel the path together.

In Thailand, monks make a point of going with their begging bowls to every door every morning to give everyone—man, woman, and child—the chance to have a relationship with the noble Dharma and a spiritual person. That way even the smallest child, who is typically encouraged to carry the food to the door, is considered an integral part of the spiritual community and its user-friendly, lovingly interconnected life.

Zen communities traditionally tend to be more self-sufficient, stressing the cause and effect connection between labor and its rewards. When the great Zen master Hyaku-jo of ancient China was in his eightieth year, his monk disciples hid his hoe and rake so he would get some rest. Hyaku-jo responded by refusing to eat, saying, "One day no work, one day no eat." This practical dictum has come down to us today.

Although Buddhism distinguished itself by grappling with the spiritual aspects of work and livelihood at a very early stage of human history, a Buddhist theory of economics has yet to evolve fully. We often hear statements about economics that are in tune with Buddhist principles. For example, E. F. Schumacher's fine book *Small Is Beautiful,* like Buddhism, advocates the richness of simplicity—streamlining and downsizing our lives can help us find peace and happiness. Duane Elgin's *Voluntary Simplicity* is also a mine of inspiration. So is *Simple Abundance* by Sarah Ban Breathnach.

Simplicity is certainly central to Dharma values. Meditators intimately come to understand how simplifying and quieting the mind helps simplify and clarify one's life. But today, it seems like a great challenge to try to live simply. When I was living in a monastery, for years at a time I walked around in the same pair of rubber flip-flops. Here in America I'm constantly amazed by the amount of extra possessions I accumulate. I am hardly Imelda Marcos, yet I find that I have at least a couple of dozen pairs of shoes cluttering up every inch of my extra closet space—jogging shoes, dress shoes, sneakers, walking shoes, summer sandals, rafting sandals, snow boots, work boots, climbing shoes, ski boots, as well as shoes given to me by my father and uncle. Each pair has its own history and its own reason for being there—but are they all really necessary? Can I honestly say that I need to keep them all—or that they make my life easier and more comfortable, rather than more unwieldy and messy? When is enough enough?

A theory of Buddhist economics would be based on and well grounded in an understanding of interdependent origination: Wealth like energy cannot be created or destroyed; it just moves around, according to karmic causality. Dharma compassion would pray that it move around more fairly. Too many members of our human family—from the homeless in our own cities to starving children throughout the world—go to bed hungry every night. Buckminster Fuller often told us that there were enough resources on this earth to support each and every adult individual, allowing each person to pursue his or her true heart's direction, if these resources were equitably distributed. Marx was also not far from the heart of the matter with his slogan "From each according to his ability to each according to his need." But Marxism as an experiment has yet to be worked out as a viable way of living together in this world.

Some say, "Money is the root of all evil." Buddhists would disagree; they say ignorance is the underlying problem. How we relate to money can either further good or further evil; it is helpful or harmful depending upon whether we use it or abuse it, and whether we possess it or it possesses us.

However even within Buddhism there are different views about the possible corrupting influences of wealth and possessions. For example, the Burmese teacher S. N. Goenka advised against taking donations from people with wrong livelihoods, saying it was tainted money with unwholesome karma attached to it that would impede your spiritual progress. Kalu Rinpoche, with whom I discussed this, said that he accepted these donations on behalf of his monastery partly to help purify and transform the bad karma connected with it into meritorious good karma.

No matter what the view of money, however, in reality, religious and spiritual institutions need money as much as the rest of us. There is an old Arab saying, "The Koran itself is free, but the binding costs a little something." This saying is as true now in our air-conditioned temples and meditation halls as when it was first coined in a nomad tent or around a desert campfire.

It is easy to say we should be in the world, but not totally of it. But how do we do this and, among other things, find a sane and appropriate approach to money and economic reality? Without the gold standard, money seems to become whatever we believe it to be. We make it up as we go along. The family pet isn't scheming to get into your purse to get his share of the money in your pocket; he's trying to figure out a way to get those pungent chicken bones out of the garbage pail. The value of anything is always the value we vest in it. Both money and chicken bones are essentially neutral; their value, or lack of it, is dependent on each being's desire system.

We get into difficulty when we imagine that we need more than we really do—when enough never seems to be enough. Think of the millionaire who strives for billions or the dissatisfied computer user who fiddles with his system long into the night, adding more and more bells and whistles. In Buddhist cosmology, there is the concept of "the hungry ghost." The image is of a being with a huge swollen body, a needlelike neck, and a tiny open mouth. Suffering from insatiable hunger, the hungry ghost is continuously trying to accomplish an impossible task—getting enough food into its small mouth and down its thin neck to satisfy its huge gut. Doesn't this symbol graphically represent certain familiar mental states of longing, neediness, and insatiable desire?

A workable Buddhist theory of money has to get down to essential Dharma principles. We know that some of the things we value most have no monetary worth. How much is happiness, health, a garden, or a child's smile worth? As we attempt to make our lives more sacred by integrating issues of money into the awakened, mindful lifestyle, don't we need to discover new ways of striking the proper balance between legitimate need and overweening greed?

## THE HAPPINESS QUOTIENT

In life there is a phenomenon that I call the "Happiness Quotient," or "HQ." To me the HQ is found in establishing a balance between what we have and what we want. If we want ten things and have eight, we are more or less happy and content. If we want twenty things and have eight, then the balance is too far out of whack. When there is this kind of ratio strain, dissatisfaction and frustration may fester within us. This HQ demonstrates why Buddhists equate desire with dissatisfaction, as in the reality principle called dukkha. This is one of the ways that greater desire delivers more dukkha.

Remember the Buddha's example when he pointed to a middle way, balanced between the extremes of hedonistic self-indulgence and ascetic self-denial. He stressed sanity, moderation, and a broad and inclusive well-balanced golden mean. Reflecting on Buddhist wisdom, sooner or later, we each should be able to come up with our own personally satisfying balance between need and greed. It is eminently achievable.

Many masters have said that the less we need, the richer we can be. Living contentedly in the high Himalayan wilderness, Milarepa survived by gathering wild nettles and eating nettle soup, which gave his skin a greenish hue. More recently the erudite Tibetan teacher and hermit Patrul Rinpoche was known for his simple mendicant lifestyle and unconditional generosity. When queried about why he immediately distributed whatever alms were given to him, he replied, "One brick of tea is one brick of extra baggage. Who needs more burdens to take on my way?" The famous Buddhist philosopher Nagarjuna said that contentment is true wealth. Success will not be found through the gratification of desire, but in the end of desire—which is contentment. Wealthy is he who enjoys what he has.

# FINDING YOUR OWN VOCATION

*Most people die with their music still locked up*
*inside them.*

—BENJAMIN DISRAELI

Until recently in Tibet, people consulted the lama about everything from travel plans to entering a monastery to starting a carpet
factory. It's the old way. Certain lamas in particular have shown an
uncanny ability to give prescient advice based on astrological or
other methods of predicting the future. As a normally cynical
Westerner, it's not something I think about or study too much.
Nonetheless people ask me all kinds of questions, for which a crystal ball would come in handy.

Last week, when Dan came in for a private interview, he asked
if I performed ritual divinations like the lamas in Tibet. I said,
"Not really," and inquired as to what he was thinking about. He
said he was having a midlife crisis and couldn't decide whether he
should stay with work he hated until retirement or if he should
try to reinvent a career and a life. Many men and women ask for
advice on how to find authentic vocations; they want to put more
meaning and purpose in their lives. Typically they recognize that
work is a spiritual issue and they want spiritual advice. Often, like
Dan, however, they have some very practical nitty-gritty considerations.

Someone asked me recently to define the concept of "authentic vocation." I had to think about this, but finally the definition I
came up with was work that helps us live here and now while
keeping us connected to a higher, more timeless, reality. Right
Livelihood is work that genuinely develops us as we develop it. In
an interview, the wonderful poet Maya Angelou defined work as
"something made greater by ourselves and in turn that makes us
greater."

Finding meaning and purpose through work is a major part of
finding out who you are and what you are here to do. It's very important not to miss out on this element of truth in your life. When
we're dissatisfied, sometimes we find that truth by changing direc-

tion and looking for work that is more satisfying. I remember reading how Joseph Campbell at the age of thirty retired to the Catskill Mountains and spent three years reading and reflecting on the history of the cultures and religions of this world. Could he have become the great sage and teacher he did without that solitary inner time for study and reflection?

Other times in our lives the only thing we can reasonably do is try to find more satisfaction in the work that we already have. I've certainly had this kind of experience. I love my work; I like to say that I've found peace, freedom, and joy through Buddhism and I'm finding it more and more every day. However, when I was in lama training, there were certainly things—like calligraphy and religious handicrafts—that didn't motivate me.

When I was still a relatively new Dharma student in Nepal, I ran out of money and possessions to sell. I decided that I would go to Japan for a year. Friends had told me that I would be able to study and practice Zen Buddhism while I made a living as a teacher. In the meantime I would be saving money to return to Nepal.

I was studying with Uchiyama Roshi at Antaiji Temple in Kyoto and working at Seika College some forty-five minutes away by subway train. I taught English to college students during the day and to Komatsu Company executives at night. At first I really struggled against this way of life. I had been living and meditating for a few years in the Himalayan mountains; what was I doing riding during rush hour every day on a crowded Japanese subway train? In my mind, at first, this all seemed like a terrible waste of time. What did this have to do with the spiritual life, I wondered? Was I wasting my life? My girlfriend, Suil, meanwhile was happily studying Zen painting, tea ceremony, and flower arranging.

In order to fill time on the subway I started reading junk books—fast-paced thrillers like *The Godfather* and *Shogun*. I liked these books; I could reread them on vacation even now, but then I worried that my mind was turning to mush so I started to read better books—*The Brothers Karamazov* and *War and Peace*. This made me feel better about the train rides because I felt as if I were getting more out of them—improving my mind and writing skills and so on. But I still hadn't solved this particular koan, the conundrum of daily life. The conflict I experienced was between the pleasure and delight I had in reading the great novels and the ordinariness of teaching vocabulary and grammar. The stretch was too great. This gnawed at me as I dreamed of going back to what I thought of as my real life with my lama teachers, in Kalu Rinpoche's monastery in Darjeeling.

Finally I talked to my elderly Zen master about this. He pointed out, reasonably enough, that my problem was "the koan of everyday life." We all have to solve it in our own way; how we live our lives and what we do depends ultimately on ourselves. Then he said something very important. "You have forty-five minutes each way on the train; that's like a meditation hour twice a day. Why complain that you are wasting your time? Time doesn't go to waste. . . . it doesn't go anywhere. If time is wasting, you're wasting it."

As I reflected on what he said, I realized that by killing time and treating anything as though it were a tedious chore to be endured, to get through and put behind me, I was only deadening myself. From that day on I started trying to meditate on the train. Of course there were certain practical hassles. Do you close your eyes or do you sit with a rigid stare and risk having people think you're some kind of zombie? How do you keep track of time and get off at your stop? But it wasn't that hard. You don't always have to sit in the same seat; you don't even have to have a seat. And, yes, you can meditate with your legs down, instead of cross-legged, even in Japan. I just relaxed and meditated, and nobody noticed. In some ways, you are never more alone than in a subway during rush hour. There was a certain perfection to the whole experience.

Amazingly enough—and this is the magic of Dharma wisdom—I began to enjoy what I was doing. I started to love getting off the train and walking through the college campus, which was like a garden. I began to get pleasure from seeing the fresh-faced teenagers with sparkling eyes and welcoming, laughing spirits. They were always so happy to see their English teacher from New York. My heart leaped with joy. I had a lot to give and receive, and my work took on a whole new energy and meaning. Meditation works!

For each of us, the koan, or riddle, of existence is the work of puzzling out the meaning of our individual lives. The gift of Dharma helps us find joy in working at this puzzle. I firmly believe that your true vocation or calling is knowing yourself and being yourself. The word Dharma—like the Jewish word Torah and the Chinese word Tao—means our way of life as well as truth, the universal law, and the spiritual teaching. We each have to find our own Dharma, our own truth—our true nature, lifestyle, and vocation— and stand firm in that truth if we would reap the promise of the miraculous gift of life.

## RIGHT LIVELIHOOD IS DOING WHAT NEEDS TO BE DONE

*There should be less talk; a preaching point is not a meeting point. What do you do then? Take a broom and clean someone's house. That says enough.*

— MOTHER TERESA

Not that long ago, I was in a Manhattan restaurant having dinner with a friend. We were sitting at a table next to a series of floor-to-ceiling windows that looked out on a busy avenue. On the street, we could see an unkempt homeless man pushing a large shopping cart filled with boxes and trash bags. Pieces of clothing and odds and ends stuck out of the cart every which way. Suddenly a New York City bus swerved and almost hit a small passenger car, which grazed the front end of the man's shopping cart, knocking it over on its side. Dozens, perhaps hundreds, of empty soda cans rolled to the ground, spilling absolutely everything along the street. Seeing this sad sight, I felt helpless at the totality of this man's predicament—homeless, collecting soda cans in order to gather together a few dollars. I barely had time to register these emotions when I noticed that another diner, a well-dressed man wearing a business suit and tie, had stepped out to the sidewalk. Quickly and efficiently he set to work chasing down the cans rolling along the gutter and placing them back in the cart. With the two men working together, it was only a matter of minutes before the man was again rattling down the street with his shopping cart, and the diner was slipping back into his restaurant seat.

All "good work" means is finding a way to act upon your bodhicitta intentions and doing what has to be done. This isn't complex; it simply means taking care of business—in the present moment. I remember once when I stumbled into the doorway of Kalu Rinpoche's room. He was sitting on the floor with two young monks, surrounded by cut-up pieces of maroon cloth. One of the boys was measuring thread, and Kalu Rinpoche had a large old-fashioned pair of scissors in his hand. Kalu Rinpoche was an expert tailor and was very involved with making robes for members of his monastery. Spirituality does not contradict practicality; the two might even complement each other.

The present head of my own Nyingmapa school, Penor Rinpoche, is known as the best plumber in his refugee village in southern India. When no one else could fix the broken septic system, we've seen him go down waist deep into the reeking pool of sewage and unstop the pipes with hand tools while his monks looked on with awe saying, "Rinpoche is a true master."

A lovely example of Right Livelihood that every schoolchild knows is found in the work of John Chapman, known as Johnny Appleseed, who during the early nineteenth century traveled throughout the Midwest sowing apple seeds and caring for the young trees. When Chapman planted those seeds he knew that someday there would be apples, even if he never saw them. What a wonderful gift he left behind. In Tibet, everybody knows the story of Thang-Tong Gyalpo, a wandering fifteenth-century yogi and master who wasn't allowed to cross a river on a ferryboat because he seemed insane to the ferryman. After this incident, Thang-Tong experienced visions in which the Buddhas and Bodhisattvas themselves gave him a work assignment: Help others by constructing bridges—strong iron bridges—the first in the Himalayas! And with the help of disciples and students, that's what he did, developing techniques for finding and refining iron ore in the process. Some of the nearly sixty chain-link bridges he built are still in use.

Right Livelihood is about "earning your keep" on this fragile planet. But as millions of female homemakers have always known, money is not always part of the exchange. A pedestrian stumbles, a passerby reaches out a steadying hand; a baby cries in the night, a parent sings an off-key lullaby; a student finds geometry confusing, a teacher uses after-school hours for extra coaching; a shopper vacillates between the coleslaw or the potato salad, a smiling counterperson understands the indecision; an elderly man needs to hang a heavy mirror, a neighbor arrives with a drill, the right hardware, and a pair of willing hands; a woman comes home from work tired, hungry, and cranky, an understanding mate prepares a simple meal. All of this is "Good Work." All of these helping situations revolve around "doing what needs to be done," partnership, and good intentions. As such, they are all examples of authentic vocation and following the principles of Right Livelihood on the path of awakening.

## Contemplating the Possibility of Right Livelihood

Sit down for a moment. Stop doing whatever you were doing. Relax. Settle down. Still the hands, head, and heart. Arrive fully in the immediacy and richness of the present moment.

Now let's consider how we spend our time and our lives. Let's examine our choices, our current condition, and where we are now. Tune in and listen; open the third ear, the inner ear of true listening—and see if we can hear, feel, sense, and know for ourselves, with certainty, what compels and calls us. Let's see if we can find and accomplish our genuine vocation, our own true calling—not just making a living, but making a life.

Ask yourself: How do I spend my days? For the most part am I doing what I love or just "doing time"? Is my work life mostly composed of chores and compromises, responsibilities, duties, and

obligations? Or am I passionately engaged in following my own
star? What would I do differently if I could? (For I can.) What is
the most direct route to our highest, deepest happiness and well-
being?

Is my field of endeavor basically honest, meaningful, and helpful to myself and others—or at the very least, harmless? Is it emotionally fulfilling: financially, psychologically, and socially
rewarding; engaging, creatively satisfying, and bringing the best
out of me through utilizing and further developing my own
unique combination of special gifts, talents, experiences, and interests? Or am I hiding the truth from myself in order to get by
or get away with something? (The implications of my acts, perhaps?)

Does my work sufficiently support my loved ones and myself,
while contributing to a brighter, happier, safer world and a better
society? Or does it work against that positive end?

Is there anything I am putting off until later that might best be
undertaken now? How often am I waiting to get through something and on to the next thing? For killing time is just deadening
ourselves.

If I could do anything that I could possibly want to do in the
world—if I held the Cosmic Credit Card—what would I choose
to do?

What is keeping me from doing that, right now?

# MEDITATION TRAINING

## Awareness, Attention, and Focus

*The Noble Eight-Fold Path is the path of living in awareness. Mindfulness is the foundation. By practicing mindfulness, you can develop concentration, which enables you to attain understanding. Thanks to right concentration, you realize right awareness, thoughts, speech, action, livelihood, and effort. The understanding which develops can liberate you from every shackle of suffering and give birth to true peace and joy.*

— THICH NHAT HANH,
OLD PATH WHITE CLOUDS

Westerners who are attracted to Buddhism because of meditation often make the mistake of seeing meditation in the most narrow sense of going into a quiet room, crossing your legs, and closing your eyes. What the Buddha actually intended by this part of the path was mental discipline, an effort to train the mind through the cultivation of mindful awareness and attention to the present moment. If all the difficulties of life are the result of ignorance, deluded thinking, and conflicting emotions, then the obvious solution is to get wiser, more aware, balanced, and loving. We do this through the practice of meditation training or samadhi, which is the ancient word for mental discipline or contemplation. Meditation training includes Right Effort, Right Mindfulness, and Right Concentration.

Awareness is the common denominator of all sentient beings. Meditation is the most direct and effective way to cultivate that innate awareness; it is the essential ingredient on the path to awakening the Buddha within. We meditate in order to purify and discipline our minds. We meditate in order to become enlightened—in order to understand and directly perceive reality or truth—defined by the Buddha as "clear seeing," or "seeing things as they are." We meditate in order to wake up to what is, and thus arrive at the total immediacy and authenticity of life in this very present moment. That's the goal, and it is also the practice. Cultivating present, moment-by-moment awareness helps you come home to who you are and always have been.

Demystified and divested of religious and cultural trappings, meditation basically means the intentional cultivation of mindful awareness and pure attention—an alert, wakeful presence of mind. This development of awareness eradicates ignorance—about ourselves and others as well as reality. Meditation awakens and frees the mind, and opens the heart, helping us develop inner wisdom, clarity, joy, and compassion, thus bringing spirituality and a larger perspective into every aspect of daily life. Meditation training helps us to concentrate as well as to see and think more clearly. In this way we develop spiritually into wiser, more selfless, and caring men and women.

Meditation is not just something to do; it's a method of being and seeing—an unconditional way of living moment by moment. Through meditation we perceive and know things as they actually are. This directly connects and brings us to truth according to its simplest definition—things just as they are. Meditation is how Buddhas pray.

The Dharma teaches that everything, good and bad, originates within our minds—minds that have been conditioned by years (and lifetimes) of deluded and delusional thinking. Don't our minds buzz with anxieties, with regrets for the past as well as plots and plans for the future? Doesn't it sometimes seem as though our minds are awash with conflicting feelings, thoughts, and fantasies? Every second of every day, the mind and senses are being flooded by external stimuli—sounds, smells, sights. So much is going on—so much extraneous information is going in and out of the mind that it seems impossible to "see straight"—to see with clarity.

The mind is capable of so much: It has given birth to all the marvels as well as all the horrors of the modern world. How we use our unique gift of consciousness makes all the difference. Thought and intellect are good servants—great tools, but poor masters. We so often fall prey to the tyranny of thought and are controlled by our own motor minds and surrounded by the static and empty echoes of our own motor mouths. Our restless imaginings, obsessions, and incessant anxieties, uncertainties, and worries run amok, leaving us not a moment's peace. At these times, it's good to take stock and renew our heart's soulful search for happiness and fulfillment, to begin afresh our journey and exploration toward finding what really matters in life, and staying with it. What really matters—to us? How to learn to love and live better. How to make a life, not just a living. How to make life into something worth living. How to find ourselves—our true selves—not just our persona or image. How to use the special talents and gifts we have.

If we want to simplify and deepen our lives, we must simplify and deepen our minds. When we become more centered, clear, spacious, caring and open, there is suddenly much more room in our frenetic lives for both others and ourselves. Marshall McLuhan said, "Our mind is a magazine with a new edition every four seconds." In the Dhammapada, the Buddha said, "The mind is restless, unsteady, hard to guard, hard to control. The wise one makes it straight, like a fletcher straightens an arrow. The mind is mercurial, hard to restrain, alighting where it wishes. It is good to tame and master this mind, for a disciplined mind brings happiness."

There are actually two kinds of Buddhist meditation:

### 1. Concentration Meditation

A yogic practice that existed before the Buddha's birth, concentration meditation can help the practitioner reach the highest mystic states. Although the Buddha attained states of inconceivable bliss, he did not believe this type of meditation alone would guarantee enlightenment. Right Concentration is based on relaxation and centering exercises, in which we learn to collect ourselves, focus our energy and attention, and quiet the heart-mind. It has also been shown to be extremely helpful for stress reduction, tension management, and other health-related problems.

### 2. Insight Meditation

Developed and taught by the Buddha, this type of meditation is often called Vipassana. It is how the practitioner develops deeper wisdom and insight into the nature of reality. Insight meditation cultivates mindfulness and awareness, bringing about spiritual realization while uprooting negative karmic conditioning and kleshas—thus bringing purity and peace of heart along with freedom of mind. Insight meditation is the path to enlightenment, and has been called the heart of Buddhist meditation.

The ideal, of course, is to unify the sharply honed edge of concentration with insight meditation in a larger, more panoramic way. In the non-dual teachings of Mahamudra and Dzogchen, it is often called the higher Vipassana or higher vision of panoramic awareness. This combination of concentration and penetrating insight is the method the Buddha was practicing when he realized ultimate truth and attained perfect liberation beneath the bodhi tree at dawn in the wilderness of northern India.

These two types of meditation show up in the different practicing schools and traditions. For example, there are two kinds of Zen sitting practice, "just sitting" and koan (conundrum-inquiry) practice. Tibetan Buddhist meditation practice includes resting the mind as well as investigating or analyzing. The common principle of understanding the distinction between concentration and insight underlies all the various schools' practices and styles of meditation.

Meditation requires so little. All you have to do is stop doing whatever else you are doing, and just be there. You must be present to win. Just show up! Once you are accustomed to meditating, you can do it while standing, walking, lying, or even arranging flowers. The Buddha once said that there are four positions for meditation: standing, sitting, walking, and lying down. In other words, all the time.

In the beginning, meditation is a matter of focusing and calming the mind. Later it develops much more into panoramic awareness. For these many centuries, meditators have been taught to use breathing as a tool. I was taught, and I now teach others, to begin by breathing in through the nose, concentrating on the feeling sensation of air coming in through the nostrils; then breathing out through the nostrils—again while concentrating on the feeling sensation of air going out of the nostrils. Simply observe breathing, and focus on nothing else. Whatever happens—people moving, mosquitos buzzing, radios blaring, focus on nothing else. If you have a physical sensation—a cramped foot, an itch on your shoulder—just try to let it go and focus on the breathing. If you have a thought, a memory, a yearning, use your breath to give your mind a gentle tug back, and continue to focus on your breathing.

It sounds so simple, but as we try to do this, we begin to notice how unruly our minds are and how difficult it is to focus on only one thing. Adults understand that children have short attention spans. Meditation masters understand that ordinary adults have similar difficulties with concentration. However, with effort, mindfulness, and concentration, meditation will work for even the most unruly mind. What are the contents of meditation? You, your life, and your world. You don't have to go to Tibet or Nepal to find something to meditate on.

As the Zen master Dogen once wrote:

> To study the Buddha's way is to study the self;
> To study the self is to transcend the self.
> To transcend the self is to be enlightened by all things.
> To be enlightened by all things is to remove the barrier
>      between self and others.

# RIGHT EFFORT

## *A Passion for Enlightenment*

*With sustained effort and sincerity
Discipline and self-control
The wise become like islands
Which no flood can overwhelm.*

—FROM THE DHAMMAPADA
(SAYINGS OF THE BUDDHA)

There is no word for Buddhist in the Tibetan language. The word used is *nangba,* which means insider. This term is not about exclusion. It's a way of describing those who look inward for what they are seeking. "Insiders" are not seeking refuge in anything that can be found externally; they are looking for the kind of existential meaning that can only be found within. Through this sixth step on the Noble Eight-Fold Path, we become "insiders," committed to doing the genuine inner work—with energy, discernment, and love.

It's interesting that Right Effort is considered part of meditation training (samadhi). It reminds us that meditation is dynamic, not passive. It tells us that Right Effort really means spiritual effort. We are working to elevate ourselves, trying to develop more wholesome mind states, while gently striving to go deeper and live more fully. Through this effort we are opening and awakening our hearts and minds, body and soul.

When Socrates said, "The unexamined life is not worth living," the sentence struck such a profound chord of truth that even now, more than two thousand years after Socrates' death, these words continue to resound. It takes sincere spiritual effort to examine our lives and work at cultivating ourselves. Through introspection, prayer, and contemplation—mindfulness and awareness practices— we utilize the timeless, tried and true, effective inner science of spiritual awakening and transformation. This is how Bodhisattvas—past, present, and future—do their productive Dharma farming, bringing forth the beautiful flowers for the entire world to enjoy.

# EFFORT AND INSPIRATION
# DRIVE THE SPIRITUAL PATH

Effort is defined and expressed in so many different ways: exertion, perseverance, courage, self-discipline, diligence, consistency, patience—the words seem almost endless. Because we all have different spiritual paths, we are each going to be called upon to exert different kinds and degrees of effort. What looks easy for one person is difficult for another. And since we have all been conditioned in different ways, our senses, propensities, and personal histories pull us each into different spiritual arenas. It is a karmic principle that we usually go with what we know; it takes effort to change our patterns. For example, every day, Doug, a recovering alcoholic, exerts enormous spiritual effort not only in avoiding liquor, but also in trying to undo the mistakes that his heedless behavior caused in the past. He is struggling to rebuild relationships with his children, parents, and siblings; he is also trying to develop satisfying friendships and relationships that don't resemble the ones from his past.

Every morning, Maggie starts her day with an hour of meditation and quiet reflection. She is also making a prodigious effort to read and learn more about Buddhism. In the evening after work, she takes classes in yoga and tai-chi. She does this because she wants to change. Like Doug, she also hopes to make new friends and would like to find a romantic partner who shares her spiritual interests. People joke about meditation nights at the local meditation center as being the "singles bar-do." Maggie has begun to truly love the meditation group she meets with once a week, and she has made several new friends.

Although she has an exhausting career in sales, Jane volunteers for two overnights a month in a homeless shelter in addition to numerous hours trying to gather money, food, and clothing for the homeless. Several years ago Jane was totally despondent over the breakup of an important relationship; she says all she could think about during that period was herself. Sitting in a church, praying to get her boyfriend back, she noticed a poster asking for volunteers at the shelter. She couldn't sleep anyway, so she figured why not? At first Jane saw this simply as a means of getting out of herself. Now she says she has reaped great rewards in many ways, including self-understanding and feeling more connected to others.

All of these people have made right-on efforts at self-understanding and inner development. Doug, Maggie, and Jane have different lives, different interests, different paths. What they share is some understanding of what it means to make heroic efforts to stay on the spiritual path, even when it's inconvenient or uncomfortable. Certainly there are days when Doug might like to call up his old drinking buddy Charlie to hang out and have a couple of beers; he doesn't do it because he has learned enough about himself to not want to backslide. There are rainy mornings when Maggie would rather skip her meditation practice and sleep late or watch the news, but meditation and yoga are helping Maggie make sense of her life, and she doesn't want to lose touch with that. Many evenings Jane would rather drive to the shopping mall than head for the shelter to help a woman deal with her rebellious teenage daughter, but Jane wants to keep reaching out rather than shutting down. These people continue to make the effort needed to walk away from the old patterns of the past and toward new possibilities in the future. This requires commitment, consistency, patience, courage, determination, and enthusiasm. This is Right Effort.

## EFFORT AND MEDITATION

We can develop an awareness of ourselves and the world in an infinite variety of ways. All of them take effort. Who can deny that it takes courage to examine our thoughts and behavior? It's not easy to admit when we act from pride, jealousy, or ill will instead of honoring our Buddha-nature. Who has the courage and the spiritual zeal to face all the facts about ourselves?

There are numerous ways of making spiritual effort and developing a more soulful life. What Buddhism offers seekers are the tried and true techniques of meditation, passed down by centuries of experienced practitioners and illumined masters who understood how our inner lives determine our life experiences. Meditation has been used by millions of people over thousands of years to transcend human limitations, gain self-realization, and experience the divine. In practical terms, this means developing intellectually and emotionally to the point where we are balanced and in harmony with ourselves, capable of grappling with life's deepest issues.

In Buddhist practice, the effort to transform and awaken is connected to meditation, which often begins with watching the breath. This frequently confuses people. What, they want to know, does inner growth and change have to do with breathing? What does the mind have to do with breath? What does watching the breath have to do with spiritual transformation?

We start with breathing because it is a basic physical process that we all share. Etymologically, the roots of the word breath and spirit are the same. Breathing is our common connection to life itself. This is fundamental and tangible. We can all experience this. Watching the breath is the most basic centering and grounding exercise, one that we can practice no matter where we are. Inhale. Exhale. It's calming. It's quieting. It helps us to concentrate and to focus. Putting effort into observing the breath causes us to slow down, to become more reflective, more contemplative. Take a deep breath. Exhale. Relax. Release. Let go. Smile to yourself. At ease.

Meditation is essentially a way of life. That's why it is so intrinsically connected to spiritual effort. It requires effort to cultivate awareness through attention training. The meditative *way* doesn't require that we join or reject any particular faith, sect, or religion. The sole incentive to continue meditation is the confidence and inner conviction that develops through one's own authentic experience. Meditation is not merely a program of mental gymnastics. In the art of meditation, simplicity is the key: the simple necessity of unburdening oneself of all excess baggage, and turning the searchlight inward. For everything is available within our own intangible spiritual core.

We are conditioned to think about effort as goal-oriented striving, filled with hard work and sweat. I think it's important to remember that when we talk about Right or Spiritual Effort in the context of Dharma, we are describing a perfectly skillful balance of endurance, energy, enthusiasm, grace, and dignity. Images of Right Effort include the majestic eagle effortlessly soaring above his mountain aerie or the stately swan gliding among the lily pads without making a ripple to disturb the pond's tranquility.

We all have instant-coffee mind today: What we want, we want now. Just add hot water, and it's ready. But in the spiritual dimension, however urgently you may feel the need to progress—hasten slowly, and you will soon arrive. Pulling upon the flowers with your hands every day does not help them grow more, and may even harm their natural blossoming process. On the other hand, skillful nurturing with the right combination of water, air, sunlight, and fertilizer can maximize their innate growth potential. This wise gardening method is not unlike the appropriate effort that is just right for individual spiritual growth and personal development.

The Buddha himself outlined what he described as Four Great Efforts that, together, form the most effective way of undertaking the wisdom work.

## FOUR GREAT EFFORTS

1. *The Effort to Avoid* any new unwholesome, negative thoughts or actions.

This First Great Effort in many ways is the easiest because it doesn't require giving up an established way of being. However, it does ask that we be aware, alert to the ways that new negative patterns might establish themselves. In meditation, we closely observe our senses to see what attracts and repels us. As we go through the day, we do the same thing. This effort helps us gain mastery over our reactions and better manage moods and emotions.

In 1984 at the conclusion of my first three-year retreat, our group had a joyous feast and celebration. Then our teacher took us down the road to visit the old man of the monastery, Lama Gendun Rinpoche, a lovely elderly retreat master who had spent most of his life meditating alone in the wilderness in Tibet.

For three-and-a-half years our group of twenty-two had spent most of the time meditating indoors; we had not been farther than the courtyard of our cloistered monastery. Suddenly the monastery doors were open; as we walked down the road, everything seemed so bright, vivid, and colorful. In some ways, it was like coming out of a sensory deprivation tank. We went into Gendun Rinpoche's cell-like room, and sat down in front of him, all bright-eyed and bushy-tailed. Gendun Rinpoche reminded us that our three-year experience had purified us; we were like new slates on which anything could be drawn or written. "Watch yourselves," he said. "Don't let your minds be sucked out of you by your senses. Don't lose your mind every time you smell, see, or touch something. Maintain present awareness, rest centered in essential natural mind, and appreciate everything equally."

As we practice this first Great Effort, I think it helps if we can imagine ourselves as children, scrubbed clean, open to new experiences, new actions, and new karma. At every moment, we are creating our future. What will it be? Can we make the effort to avoid the destructive, the harmful, the self-indulgent, and the foolish? Can we see through and avoid the sights, sounds, smells, sensory experiences, and thoughts that might pull us in a direction of creating new negative karma?

2. *The Effort to Overcome* any existing unwholesome thoughts or actions.

Anyone who has ever gone on a diet knows how much effort is required to change entrenched behavior patterns. Let's say you have gained some weight and decided to give up the cake and cookies you crave. Suddenly you have new cravings—frozen yogurt, sweet fruit juice, and baked potatoes. You don't lose weight; in fact you may even gain weight. So you give up the yogurt and potatoes, and you start stuffing yourself with bagels, popcorn, dried fruit, and bananas. No matter what you give up, you still manage to find things that you want to eat in excess. Working on your food desires has made your eating pattern a little healthier, but cravings and the impulse to overeat are still there. The same principle applies to a wide range of negative thoughts and patterns. For there are deeper hungers causing us to overeat; inner hungers waiting to be addressed.

Each of us has a past and a past life that has conditioned our behavior. We all carry around negative habits, old angers and resentments, worn-out obsessions, weary vendettas, and counterproductive ways of being. Diane nags and screams at her family; Bob's work-related anxiety reveals itself as tyrannical behavior toward his employees; Gigi is jealous of her sister; Donald resents his parents; Pamela lies to her husband; Carrie is flirting with her best friend's husband; Marion can't stop criticizing others. It costs us a great deal to carry all this negativity around. Yet we can change; we can choose to use spiritual effort to chip away at unproductive behavior; we can choose to let go of what isn't helpful, either to us or those around us. What's past is past. We create new karma by what we do from this point forward. Here and now is the turning point upon which our present and future existence revolves. Now is the border between samsara and nirvana.

Take a breath, and think about your existing thought-behavior patterns. What would you like to get rid of? What would you like to change? Use the practice of meditation and deep introspection to gain greater self-awareness and insight. We can use Right Effort to transform ourselves while making room for more satisfying thoughts and fulfilling mind-moments.

3. *The Effort to Develop* only good and wholesome thoughts and lead an enlightened life.

Consider how you would like to be and to live. Reflect on what it means to be a Bodhisattva, a spiritual warrior; reflect on what it means to lead an enlightened life. Bodhisattvas practice the Six Paramitas or Perfections—six transcendental virtues which I like to call the Six Principles of Enlightened Living. We make an effort to lead an enlightened life by striving to embody these Six Perfections:

> *Generosity*—Giving, yielding, boundless, unconditional love—open hands, open mind, open heart.
> *Virtue*—Ethics, honesty, morality, integrity, helping others.
> *Patience*—Tolerance, forebearance, acceptance, forgiveness.
> *Effort*—Energy, diligence, courage, enthusiasm, endurance.
> *Meditation*—Concentration, focus, self-inquiry, and reflection, presence of mind, mindfulness.
> *Wisdom*—Discernment, sagacity, sanity, centeredness, understanding.

A friend has a problem. You show generosity of spirit by listening and supporting. Who is doing whom a favor? As an example of our interconnectedness, the Dalai Lama points out that when anyone presents you with the opportunity to embody one of these Six Perfections, you are the one who is actually receiving help on the path to Buddhahood. Remember this the next time someone tries your patience to the limit. Perhaps then even an adversary can become your best teacher.

4. *The Effort to Maintain* the goodness that already exists.

We all have purity of heart. Effort is necessary to find the Buddha within. Realize the Buddha-nature in every moment, the clear light shining in every moment. Reflect on a time when you felt pure joy and unconditional love—even if only for a few seconds. Can you return to this feeling and carry it with you? As Chogyam Trungpa once said, "We are far more Buddha-like than we know."

## MAKING THE EFFORT TO MEDITATE DAILY: "JUST DO IT!"

Milarepa lived in the eleventh century, and yet even today Tibetans talk about the thin, white, and often torn cotton robes that he wore year-round in the snowy Himalayan wilderness. Everyone refers to Milarepa as the greatest yogi; it is said that his effort was so great that the Dharma Wheel he put into motion is still rolling, and the blessings of his practice lineage continue to spread out even today.

My favorite Milarepa story involves his main student, the devoted physician-monk Gampopa, who loved his teacher dearly. When after many years Gampopa had to part from Milarepa, he asked for one final teaching, one instruction that he could carry away with him. At first Milarepa seemed reluctant, saying that what was required after all these years was more effort, not more instructions.

Then, as Gampopa started on his way, crossing the narrow stream that parted him from his master, Milarepa shouted out. "Hey, Doctor-Monk, I have one very profound secret instruction. It is too precious to give away to just anyone." As Gampopa joyfully looked back to receive this last teaching from his beloved guru, Milarepa turned around and bent over, pulling up his flimsy cotton robe. Milarepa's buttocks were as callused and pockmarked as a horse's hoof, toughened from all those hours and years spent in seated meditation on hard rock. Then Milarepa shouted, "That is my final teaching, my heart-son. Just do it!"

I often remember Milarepa's intense instruction to "just do it." When I was on a pilgrimage to Bodh Gaya more than twenty-five years ago, I attended a meditation course given by S. N. Goenka, and he asked us to take a vow to meditate for an hour daily for a year. I did, and I've been doing so ever since. A daily meditation session is part of my routine, and I would like to suggest that it become part of yours. You can meditate anytime, anywhere; it doesn't have to be for an entire hour. Practically speaking, most people find that first thing in the morning and last thing at night are generally most conducive to spiritual practice. Dawn and dusk are also good times to use inner work—just being, not doing—to gracefully bracket a busy day.

For centuries, millions have made the effort to undertake inner wisdom work through meditation practice. The mind precedes the body. "As goes the horse, so goes the cart." While we reflect upon the issues we face in life, we also make an effort to be attentive and mindful. This helps us to proceed with integrity, grace, and clarity. This dynamic inner life naturally overflows into our outer life, and the two eventually become interwoven as one.

In 1930, Mohandas Gandhi struggled to find an appropriate and effective way for his country to react politically to the high taxes the British government placed on salt. Hardest hit by this tax were the poorest among his countrymen. "What shall we do?" his followers asked. "The British have a stranglehold on our econ-omy." Unable immediately to come up with a suitable plan, Gandhi went home to meditate and pray for more than a month. It was out of this spiritual retreat that Gandhi came up with his now-famous plan to gather natural salt by hand. He set out with his followers on foot, on the ceremonial "salt march" to the sea as an act of civil disobedience. This simple act enlisted millions of Indians along the route, and broke the back of British colonial rule in India.

Faced with difficult decisions, Gandhi went on a retreat to meditate and pray. Gandhi, one of the greatest nonviolent political activists of the twentieth century, is a stellar example of someone who understood how a dynamic inner life provides the foundation for a skillful and effective external existence.

## GENTLE ANANDA'S AWAKENING

A Buddhist story about spiritual effort involves Buddha's devoted disciple, Ananda. By the time Buddha became ill and died, he had been teaching for forty-five years and many of his disciples had become enlightened. One who had not was Buddha's ever-present attendant, Ananda. This might be considered peculiar because of all the disciples, Ananda had heard every word that the Buddha taught and memorized them all. But Ananda, who had the kind of demanding daily schedule many of us can identify with, had been so busy accompanying the Buddha wherever he went and assisting the sangha members that there had been little time for his own solitary meditation practice.

Several months after the Buddha's death, there was a reason why it suddenly became imperative for Ananda to become enlightened. The First Council of Buddhist Arhants was to take place in order to recite and codify all the teachings spoken by the Buddha. Ananda was essential to this meeting because he more than anyone else would be able to speak and verify the sutras. However, because he wasn't enlightened, he wasn't qualified to attend.

Ananda did the only thing he could do under the circumstances: Almost as if he were cramming for exams, he went into retreat—a meditation marathon—striving round the clock for enlightenment. Finally it was the morning of the day before the First Council meeting, and Ananda was still meditating. Then midnight, 2:00 A.M., 3:00 A.M. on the day of the meeting, and Ananda was still striving for enlightenment, sitting in his small monastic cell. At 3:45 A.M., fifteen minutes before the 4:00 A.M. wake-up call on the very day of the meeting, Ananda finally just gave up and thought, "Well, that's that. I am not an arhant." Exhausted, he began to tip over from meditation into a sleeping position. Ananda stopped trying to be something he wasn't; and then, before his head hit the pillow, in an instant he was a liberated arhant—totally awake. Ananda became enlightened finally by letting go, simply stopping and seeing things just as they are. It was the end of the struggle. No more trying to become an arhant, and Ananda became an arhant. In surrendering and giving up, Ananda got what he was looking for. By being just who he was, Ananda woke up.

Ananda had behind him a lifetime of pure effort and virtuous dedication, personally assisting the Buddha. His selfless personal service, in itself, didn't bring him to enlightenment; neither did round-the-clock meditation. Without his service or the meditation, he would not have accomplished his goal. Yet it was in letting go and surrendering to effortlessness that he finally reached enlightenment.

As a Japanese Zen master recently said during an intensive meditation retreat known as a sesshin, "The perfect way is without difficulty. Strive hard. We are all perfect, and yet we can perfect ourselves endlessly."

## THE DZOGCHEN VIEW OF EFFORT

The balance between effort and effortlessness is the essence of Impeccable Effort and self-mastery. This is true whether we are striving to cultivate a spiritual life, a relationship, a work project, or the most indispensable art form of all: the art of living.

Jazz saxophone great Charlie Parker once said: "First perfect your instrument. Then just play." This practical wisdom combines both the age-old adage that practice makes perfect and the Dzogchen-style playfulness that tells us that practice *is* perfect. The practice of Dzogchen is often described as beyond effort—not something to do, but a way of being. The emphasis in Dzogchen is on "what is," the natural mind, a state that is beyond concepts such as effort or non-effort.

This can be confusing to new students. It's too simplistic just to assume that if everything is perfect, then anything goes. If everything is perfect "as it is," they ask, why bother oneself with ethical conduct, mind-training, or any of the transformational meditational practices? But this nihilistic misconception is not what Dzogchen, the practice and art of freedom itself, implies.

Padma Sambhava, one of the earliest Dzogchen practitioners, once said regarding enlightened view and action, "Although my view is higher than the sky, my conduct regarding cause and effect is as meticulous and finely sifted as barley flour."

This means that we cannot live with our heads in the clouds without keeping our feet firmly here on earth. No matter how deep our philosophy, our view, our understanding is, we still have to walk our talk and practice what we preach. There is no excuse for glossing over daily behavior while using ultimate reality or emptiness as a rationalization. And we can't say that meditation and awareness practice doesn't matter when we know that it does.

Dzogchen practitioners come to recognize that it is not enough to just meditate a little each day; they learn to integrate meditation with every moment of every day. Infusing whatever we do and all our relationships with a sense of meaning and sacredness is the goal—it is also the practice. Applying our view into action every minute is our meditation practice, which reaches far beyond the confines of the meditation seat or the explicitly religious setting.

One of my favorite American Buddhist teaching tales about the value of regular daily practice concerns the peerless basketball great, Michael Jordan. Air Jordan was not born a protégé, like Mozart. In fact, while growing up Jordan was cut from his junior high school team; he was just not good enough. It was only through practicing basketball every morning before school with the kind coach who had cut him from the squad that he became good enough to play high school ball. The rest is history. This is a wonderful example of mastery through perseverance and practice. This is why yogis and meditators practice their disciplines every day, just like athletes and musicians.

The pianist expends hours of effort memorizing a difficult sonata, and only then plays it effortlessly. The potter learns to center the wet clay perfectly on the wheel so that it's stable and can hold its place by itself. The same is true with meditation: First one gets the mind unified through quiet and calm practice; then it's free, stable, and unbound yet centered at any speed, maintaining itself effortlessly.

Working out the contradiction between effort and effortlessness—hard work and simple surrender—helps us become more energetic, steadfast, patient, and persevering; it also helps us soften up through the graceful complementary virtues of yielding acceptance and heartfelt gratitude for whatever comes our way. In short, because Right Effort is spiritual effort, it implies being able to just let go, at the right time and in the right way, and simply do what must be done.

# RENUNCIATION:
# GIVING THINGS UP AND AWAY

*Leaving one's homeland is accomplishing half
the Dharma.*

— MILAREPA

Renunciation is a time-honored way of working on oneself. The Buddha himself is probably the best-known example of renunciation. The Buddha, like other seekers of his time, left his homeland in order to meditate in dense jungles and blazing deserts. But what does the word renunciation realistically mean today in the modern context of Buddhism? We today are far more socially mobile. Phones, faxes, beepers, and the Internet have made almost everyone reachable, no matter where we are. How can we leave our homeland, now that our homeland has become the planet itself? Do we really have to turn our backs on family, friends, and work in order to practice Dharma? I don't think so. Renunciation doesn't mean walking away from our responsibilities and loved ones; it does mean abandoning our intense emotional attachments and compulsive preoccupations.

Trungpa Rinpoche said, "Usually we think of renunciation as celibacy, poverty, obedience, shaving your head, going off somewhere and leaving everything behind." He then gave a wider tantric interpretation of renunciation: "Renunciation means to let go of holding back."

In Tibet, the term renunciation did not imply a sacrifice, or any notion of penance. Instead it meant the relief of finally dropping and getting rid of excess baggage through an arising of inner certainty about the illusory nature of created things. If we get even the smallest glimpse of liberation and what it means to experience freedom from want, we see where our happiness truly lies. This is the arising of inner certainty. When that occurs we begin to renounce and give up the unfulfilling thoughts and behaviors that create negative karma.

Renunciation refers to opening the tight fist of grasping and relinquishing our weighty burden of accumulated excess baggage.

The heart of renunciation implies allowing rather than controlling. It requires letting go of that which is negative and harmful while opening up to sanity and wholeness. The question is: Can we let go of holding back? Can we relinquish our fears and defenses? Can we forgive? Can we surrender and learn to better accept things as they are? Typically, this is accomplished in small gradual steps. We grow up, and we adopt a more mature attitude. When we do this, we leave the homeland of our childhood. We give up our childish ways. We depart from the nest of our family of origin and free ourselves from frozen behaviors. We stop telling ourselves stories; we stop spinning fantasies. We're all carting heavy baggage that is not helping us get where we want to go or do what we want to do. Once we realize that we no longer need this baggage, we can relinquish it; once we have inner certainty, we can leave our old habits and negativities behind.

# MAKING AN EFFORT TO RELINQUISH GRASPING AND CLINGING

> *If there is clinging, the practitioner's view is not*
> *the vast view.*
> *If there is resistance, the meditation is weak.*
> *If there is partiality, the activity is not enlight-*
> *ened action.*
> *Free from these three is the way of the Natural*
> *Great Perfection.*

—DZOGCHEN VERSE

The Buddha points out that resistance and clinging is a conditioned, learned response. Clinging is superficial, not essential. Can we come to understand this and relearn and retool our inner machinery? This is truly working on oneself. There are antidotes to suffering, stress, and anxiety: We find them by resisting less, grasping less, and identifying with things less. Nothing is half as important as we usually think it is.

Here are some forms of clinging to renounce:

◎ *Clinging to the ego*

I think one of the reasons people love being out in nature is because there is so much less ego conflict. It's a respite from the bumper-car effect of colliding egos. That's also a reason why people love spiritual retreats. On retreat, we are less demanding and less demanded of; we find that we need to prove less. Too often in our lives we think mostly in terms of "my space," "my time," "my work," "my goals," "my people." When we let go and stop cherishing me and mine, we are able to open up and allow others in. Letting go of a dualistic view of the world allows us to see who we truly are; it can help us recognize our own Buddha-nature.

◎ *Clinging to narrow-minded opinions*

Although some behaviors are consistently considered wrong—harming others for example—it is always understood that our different perceptions of reality are open to interpretation. Clinging strongly to opinions obscures the mind and distorts clear vision. In this way we become attached to unworkable conceptions. This plays out in all the arenas of our life. Think about the mother who has an idea that her athletic daughter should study ballet rather than learn to throw a softball, or the friend who always insists on the last word. Let's use nonjudgmental, meditative awareness to help us open up our minds and dance with ideas—instead of fixating upon them.

◎ *Clinging to the pleasure/pain principle*

Will a bag of M&M's bring happiness? How about a beer and some peanuts? What about romance and a sexual partner? Let's face it, nobody is ever going to find lasting peace and contentment through enchantment, addiction, sensuality, or even romantic attachment. Sometimes we even become attached not only to pleasure but also to pain. We get so stuck in the familiar ruts of hurtful relationships that we don't know how to let go and move on, although it is so obviously in our interest to do so.

◎ *Clinging to empty rites and rituals*

Nothing in pure Buddhism encourages blind faith or cultlike environments. People cling to tired dogma all the time, but that is not Dharma. The Buddha wisely challenged his followers to open their minds and think for themselves, rather than believing in anything just because it had been said by authorities, including himself, or written down in books.

◉ *Clinging to the limited, short-sighted view that sees only this world and this life*
To some people it is no more amazing that we are reborn again and again through many lifetimes than that we are born here on this earth at all, even once. To think only of today and invest only in what we can see, touch, and weigh has certain very definite limitations, even in the scientific materialist's view of reality.

When we open our inner eye, listen with our inner ear, sense divine fragrance, or intuit an impalpable yet authentic invisible presence—does that not strongly suggest to us that there is more to life than meets the eye? If we feel deeply compelled to learn and to love, we must peer more deeply into the intricacies of our experience with all its boundless interlocking levels, numerous dimensions, and myriad forms of existence.

# MEETING THE CHALLENGE OF SPIRITUAL LAZINESS

*Nothing great was ever achieved without enthusiasm.*

—RALPH WALDO EMERSON

The Buddha warned about five primary hindrances on the path to awakening. One of them, spiritual laziness, is a direct challenge to the vigor and energy necessary for Right Effort. The words that have been used for centuries in Asia to define this challenge to enlightenment are sloth and torpor, two old-fashioned terms that include apathy, lethargy, indolence, spiritual laziness, complacency, and even depression.

Consider the Buddha's intense passion for enlightenment: He meditated for six years in the wilderness before he realized perfect awakening under the bodhi tree just as the morning star rose over the horizon. Milarepa achieved enlightenment in a lifetime spent above the Himalayan tree line, living in snowbound caves, warmed only by the heat of his inner light. Remember the courageous effort of the Buddha's aunt and the other women who joined her in breaking out of the strict social order of caste-bound ancient India in order to pursue a spiritual life.

All of this doesn't mean that even the most committed Dharmacists and Dharma farmers like myself don't have days when we detest jumping out of bed in the predawn hours to sit in meditation. When I was in a monastery, I found waking up at 4:00 A.M. every day, year round extremely difficult. When the gong sounded, my tendency was to roll over and incorporate the resonant sound into my dreams. Finally I asked the diligent doctor-monk who rang the gong if he would kindly open the door to my room and do something to get my attention. Monastic tradition prevented him from entering my cell, but at 4:30 A.M. he would crack open the door to my room and if I was still asleep, he would toss my sandals at me.

I was never fully able to become accustomed to arising so early for meditation. However, as a night owl who doesn't wake easily, I was elated that I could do it at all. The French monk in the next room, on the other hand, was getting up at 3:30 each morning to begin his prayers and meditation routine. At sixty-two, he was older than most of our intrepid band; he felt that he had to do as much as he possibly could because he had less time to reach enlightenment than the rest of us. He was a wonderful example and inspiration, and I admired his energy as much as his kindness and genuine savoir faire.

With the hindrance of torpor, we also have to discuss the spiritual crisis known as depression and the lethargy that accompanies it. During the Buddha's lifetime, the word depression didn't really exist, yet there is nothing new about the age-old emotion known as despair. Today I speak to many men and women who express their despair; often they feel as though the fatigue of depression is robbing them of the energy to walk the spiritual path or even to keep living. Depression seems to overwhelm them with negativity and lethargy. They say it is hard to do anything when you feel as though you have lost your way and nothing you do can possibly matter.

Depression typically carries an overwhelming sense of feeling abandoned, alone, exhausted, and disconnected— profoundly weary from the difficult business of living. If this ever happens to you—and it happens to many of us at one time or another—self-inquiry needs to be directed at ways in which you have abandoned or lost touch with yourself. When you're working on depression and other difficult life situations, it's important to summon your faith, fall back on soulful inner practices, and go for refuge where you can find spiritual solace. Try to remember to have faith in your own Buddha-nature, your own inner light, and seek guidance from a reliable teacher or Bodhisattva-like mentor who inspires spiritual wisdom and energy. Go for refuge to the Dharma by staying true to yourself and your sense that you are on the right path. And look to your friends and your sangha, or spiritual group of any denomination, for support.

When you're feeling low or lethargic, place some trust in physical activity to mobilize your energy. Practice yoga, tai-chi, breathing exercises, and self-inquiry. Dynamic meditation gives back far more energy than it takes. It's very common for someone to arrive at a meditation center exhausted and enervated. Yet if this person continues through the entire session, almost inevitably he or she will leave feeling energized. Even when we are heartbroken, a meditation retreat can help us to take heart.

In my experience, however, I've also seen that people who are in the depths of despair may not benefit from the quieting effects of simple sitting meditation. Frequently what they need most is to get their energy moving and be less turned in upon themselves. So if you're in the middle of a depression, you may want to try more active spiritual activities like chanting, breathing, singing, praying, or yoga. Meditative arts like gardening, calligraphy, tea ceremony, or martial arts are often very helpful activities. Even vigorous walking, jogging, or dancing can be beneficial. Also, remember that there is nothing in Buddhism that is incompatible with psychotherapy, and I often recommend it. We have to remember not to use meditation as a spiritual bypass, to avoid our psychological and daily life issues.

And don't forget to find spiritual strength by reaching out to a spiritual community or some kind of support group.

A meditation weekend always leaves me raring to go. Although meditation seems to take time and energy, it gives us back even more time, as well as a sense of spacious ease and clarity. The same can be said for the spiritual life. You truly do get back much more than you give. This is something you can see for yourself.

## MY GREATEST DHARMA EFFORT
## AND CHALLENGE

Often when we see photographs of lamas and monks in Tibet, they are pictured in their maroon robes prostrating themselves on the ground. What they are doing is a foundational practice of Tibetan Buddhism called Nöndro. Westerners who are drawn to study with Tibetan lamas quickly discover the level of effort and energy required for meditational practice in the Tibetan tradition. Monks, nuns, and lay yogis all complete these foundational practices, sometimes several or even many times. Consider the discipline these preliminary practices require. The Nöndro includes: 111,000 full bodily bows or prostrations, performed while chanting the three-fold Refuge Prayer; 111,000 Bodhicitta and compassion prayers; 111,000 of Vajrasattva's hundred-syllable purification mantras; 111,000 offerings of the universe in the form of a mandala to the enlightened ones, to accumulate good karma and cultivate generosity and nonattachment; 111,000 guru yoga practices, which merge one's dualistic, limited mind with the infinite Buddha-mind embodied in the form of the Buddha-lama. In Tibet, the word "boom" is used to refer to this 100,000+ number of meritorious practices. Any time someone does more than a 100,000+ prayers or mantras, it is called a boom.

My own elderly teachers, like the Dzogchen masters Dudjom Rinpoche, Tulku Urgyen Rinpoche, and others performed these foundation practices every morning, even into their seventies and eighties, typically including at least a few physical bows to the floor.

Almost all Tibetans practice the Nöndro regularly. The Nöndro is referred to as preliminary or foundational practice because these practices provide a firm foundation for undertaking the higher Vajrayana (tantric) practices, which then culminate in Mahamudra and Dzogchen. It is said that the learned Lama Patrul Rinpoche practiced daily prostrations outside in a meadow with such zeal that eventually an imprint of his body was left in the ground.

For me, accomplishing these preliminary foundational practices of Vajrayana and completing a boom of full-length prostrations while chanting the Refuge Prayer was the hardest thing I've ever had to do in Dharma practice—and probably in anything else as well. When I first started studying with lamas, all the students were encouraged to practice the Nöndro. It was a wonderful experience to be with the sangha, going for refuge, chanting and praying together, while visualizing all the Buddhas and Bodhisattvas. Since Mahayana Buddhism and the Nöndro emphasizes the ideal of all beings—friends, relatives, animals, insects—entering into the joy of Dharma, all becoming enlightened together, it's a very joyous, boundless, all-inclusive, spiritual practice.

However, from the outset I found the physical prostrations incredibly difficult. It was hot in India; I was skinny. There was little protein, no vitamins, and no hot showers. We Westerners were typically pretty uncomfortable, afflicted by various intestinal "bugs" and often feeling unhealthy. Yet we were supposed to bow as many as three thousand times a day, not to mention the prayers and visualizations that went with the practice.

And then there were the obvious Western-type questions. Bow? To whom? Why? Most of us had been taught not to bow to idols or graven images. We just wanted to get enlightened; what was all this bowing and scraping about?

I would accost Kalu Rinpoche with these questions. Again and again he would patiently explain that the physical bows purify the mind and the body's energy. Again and again he would say that the practice developed devotion, focus, attention, and a contemplative state of awareness—that it was like being in the presence of the Buddhas themselves, as though you were bowing right in front of them. It would sound good when Rinpoche said it, and I would toddle off to do a few more thousand. Feeling inspired for a few days, all would go well; and then once again I would start wondering exactly what it was we were all doing.

Eventually the practice became much more deeply joyful; and after two thousand or three thousand prostrations during the day, the meditation when you sat down at night would be fantastic. Pushing yourself beyond where you would normally let yourself go does develop aspiration, will, and concentrated focus. I remember one early dawn at Karmapa's monastery in Sikkim trying to do a few thousand prostrations in the temple before the midday sun made it too hot. I was counting the bows and prayers with my beads in hand. The Karmapa was walking around in his informal clothes, carrying his rosary. He smiled, came near, and sprinkled white rice over me, and whispered prayers and blessings. It was really inspiring; it felt like flowers and blessings raining down upon my head, reaching right into my heart.

In 1974, at Lama Norla's hermitage high on the mountain above Kalu Rinpoche's monastery in Darjeeling I stayed in retreat to practice Nöndro during a rainy season that lasted eighty-nine days straight. With the generous assistance and coaching of the energetic young Lama Norla, and his kind stepmother's cooking, I completed the boom of 100,000+ prostrations. I assure you when I completed that huge number, it felt like a sonic boom. But just to make sure I didn't get too proud of my accomplishment, Lama Norla said, "Don't forget the other four booms." He then told me about a woman practitioner in Sikkim who had accomplished these five booms no less than seventeen times. Of course, I asked why. Lama Norla laughed and said, "Great merit, very good practice." What more could I say? Eventually I completed the five-boom Nöndro practice along with our group in each of our three-year retreats, and each time it was a deeper and richer experience.

In actual fact—this is news to no one but it needs to be said— quality counts more than quantity. One refuge and bodhicitta prayer and one internal bow done genuinely is better than any number of mere physical calisthenics.

In Kalu Rinpoche's monastery, we Westerners would do whatever we could to lessen the physical difficulties involved in

Nöndro. We used knee-pads, washcloths, talcum powder, gloves—anything to make it easier. We must have been a ludicrous sight, but Kalu Rinpoche was tolerant. Years later, another teacher, Dudjom Rinpoche—who was the most kindly lama imaginable—took a different view. No pads or sliders were to be used to ease the prostrations. "In this tradition," he said, "we just throw ourselves down, like a wall collapsing." It was a quote that some of us will never forget. My scarred knees recall that tale.

# THE YOGA OF RELATIONSHIP: INTIMACY AS A PATH TO TRANSCENDENCE

*Love is the pursuit of the whole.*

—PLATO

The yoga of relationship is, I think, very appropriate and even indispensible for our time. This is not a time when most men and women will develop through monasticism, but rather through relationships and other forms of interpersonal engagement. Our relationships with friends, family, and the earth itself provide amazing opportunities to work on ourselves in an effort to get things right.

In Asia for centuries, monastics were often viewed as the first team, and everybody else like second-stringers. That's not the tantric outlook. In tantra, since one assimilates everything into the path, all aspects of our experience, including sensuality, can become like firewood in the bonfire of awareness. Many of us can understand this from firsthand experience. Think about the intensity of some of your most intimate relationships. Frequently even if you can fool yourself, a friend or partner will see through you, reflecting your foibles and failings, like a clear mirror.

An authentic spiritual teacher can function in much the same way. What is important is seeing yourself and recognizing your intrinsic nature, not worshiping the mirror. Like a spiritual teacher, a relationship can help you evolve and transform more quickly. The inevitable irritations and disappointments in your relationships can produce jewels of deeper understanding, just as the grain of sand irritating the interior of an oyster can produce a luminous pearl. I like to call this the Pearl Principle.

Thinking this way about your relationships can keep them vibrantly alive as well as spiritually challenging. The yoga of relationships isn't just for couples. It is about seeing God, Buddha, or the Light in everything. One of my teachers, Neem Karoli Baba, said, "It's better to see God in everything than to try to figure it out." In the light of pure perception, we learn to see everyone as spiritual beings, rather than seeing others as mere objects who may or may not momentarily be pleasing or displeasing. This is how we develop loving hearts.

Perhaps you and your partner disagree one evening on which movie to see. This too can be a growth experience. Can you let go of control? Can you let go of preconceived notions about what you find entertaining? Can you see the light in your partner even as you bicker about movie reviews? Can you recognize that it doesn't really matter so very much which movie you see, since you are going out to have a relaxed time together and that fighting about how to relax together may be starting off the evening on the wrong foot? This is a contemporary challenge. Nor is this challenge so very different from the challenges faced by people anywhere who are living together, including in monasteries and meditation centers. People are still people. When we encounter a can of worms in our midst, as likely as not we have brought it ourselves.

One Tibetan lama I know was getting divorced from his wife. A student asked him, "Rinpoche, why are you two getting divorced?" The lama replied, "Because we are not generating bodhicitta together. It is important to have the right life-companion on the Path." For some people and some relationships, the primary effort needs to be in learning to let go and move on when things can not be worked out.

On the other hand, marriage vows can, just like monastic ordination vows, help us develop, maintain, and further deepen our profound commitments. Commitments, resolutions, agreements, and vows help us persevere when the going gets rough. Almost every relationship must meet crises; how well we can deal with them together often defines the character and longevity of the relationship. I always find it interesting that the Chinese word for crisis is composed of two characters: danger and opportunity. Two people who are in accord about wanting to be together would do well to focus on the opportunities that an interpersonal crisis can present. Remember the pearl principle.

We all have many relationships, not just with people, but with all forms of life, the inanimate world, and our planet. We enjoy kinship to everything and everyone. One challenge is acknowledging that kinship and acting accordingly. What is our true relationship to things other than people and animals? There was a book published years ago called *The Secret Life of Plants*, which explained the ways in which plants have sensations or feelings. All of this is fairly uncharted territory.

We don't have to withdraw from relationships in order to be good Buddhists, or good anything. Let's just try to be good-hearted people. In one sense, of course we are all alone, existentially speaking. In another sense, it's very hard to try to make this journey alone. We talk about Milarepa, meditating alone for many years, but even Milarepa had a disciple, Gampopa, and a sister. We all need friends. Relationships are essential.

Can we take what we know and what we learn from Buddhism and apply it in our relationships? Can we see the Buddha in those to whom we feel close, even when they annoy us? Can we stop clinging to others, trying to shape and control them, and instead allow them more space, freedom, and time? From possessiveness comes conflict; letting go delivers satisfaction. Can we create relationships that are warm, trusting, and kind? Can we take our bodhicitta intentions and use them with friends, family, coworkers, as well as strangers? Can we be consistently supportive, friendly, and well-intentioned? This is an effort we must make.

It takes trust to be present, to be able to let go, to just be— open, unconditional, unguarded, without maintaining any armor or false persona as a means of self-protection. Fear keeps our guard up; love, relaxation, self-confidence, assurance, honesty, and trust lets us open up more, paving the way for love, unconditional openness, and fearless acceptance of whatever comes to us. Faith and devotion help us develop such trust, such inner conviction, such certainty that we can open up and let go, without all the balls we have up in the air crashing down around us. Mindful awareness and attention helps us realize we actually can live like that. This is the natural state. We can return to it; we don't have to buy it or acquire it elsewhere or from someone else. We reinforce our constricted hearts when we cower in the corners of life. Step up and step out.

## BALANCED EFFORT

I think it's important that we not overlook the joy of the journey due to an excess of goal orientation. One story about the Buddha concerns a young neophyte who was struggling to meditate. It seems when this young monk sat in morning meditation, he couldn't stop his thoughts from rushing in. Finally he went to the Lord Buddha to confess his frustration and ask him what to do.

"Do you remember," the Buddha asked, "how you used to tune the sitar strings as a young lay person?"

"Yes," the young man replied.

"Was the music sweetest when the strings were taut or slack?" the Buddha gently inquired.

"Neither too tight, nor too loose, Lord; the middle way of moderation and balance always proved best," said the monk.

"Thus it is with meditation, young monk," said the Buddha. "In meditation and spiritual efforts, as in all things, balance is always best."

In 1990, I went to Tibet with some of my teachers and a group of Westerners. There at Gyangze, I was delighted to find two huge old copper prayer wheels. They were filled with mantras and prayers, and with huge calligraphed Sanskrit syllables engraved on their exteriors. Gigantic prayer wheels such as these are sometimes found at pilgrimage sites and near the entrances to monasteries. One walks around them in a clockwise direction, turning them like spinning tops or huge mantra-embossed, blessing-filled merry-go-rounds. Practitioners circumambulate them, setting these prayers in motion through the turning of the wheel while they quietly chant and pray in the contemplative mood of a walking meditation.

These huge, heavy prayer wheels at Gyangze were slick with oil from the millions of pilgrims' hands that had touched and turned them over the centuries. If one of these large prayer wheels were still, it would be almost impossible to get it started. And if it was already going, and you pushed too hard, it would get out of synch, jerk, and rattle off its axis. But if the prayer wheel was moving at an easy regular speed, you could keep it in motion almost without touch; all that was required was walking along and giving it a gentle turn every now and then with a light hand on the handles of the wooden rim.

Right Effort is not always goal- and achievement-oriented; it also includes the subtler virtues of nondoing, of yielding, and going with the greater flow. When Paul McCartney sang "Let It Be," we all responded to his words. Through Right Effort we learn how to do the best we can in life, living fully and with all our heart— and then let go, knowing that whatever happens, happens. The universe is beyond our control, anyway. Trying to control things creates more stress, struggle, and irritating friction in the greater system.

This balanced combination of effort, inner detachment, and genuine equanimity helps us to come home within ourselves, and arrive at a feeling of inner peace and oneness. We can live in the total fullness of being, just as we are, rather than always striving for the illusory pot of gold at the end of some vivid yet intangible rainbow. This great letting go and letting be brings forth the soulful wisdom of allowing, of being precisely where you are, who you are, and what you are—beyond running toward or away from anything. All this running to-and-fro is a symptom of attachment and aversion, and is unfulfilling in the ultimate analysis.

The Buddha said, "There is no way to happiness and peace. Happiness and peace *is* the way."

# INSPIRED EFFORT: A MEDITATION ON THE FOUR DIVINE ABODES

Bodhisattvas are impelled by the motivation to bring about enlightenment and ease suffering on a universal scale. This ambitious task may seem daunting, but Bodhisattvas—moved by the travails of the world, and of their loved ones too—are powerfully motivated to accomplish it. This kind of transcendent undertaking requires Perfection of Effort—one of the Six Principles of Enlightened Living, the Six Paramitas, which we discussed earlier. These six virtues propel us, like a warm updraft, on to the heights of enlightenment.

## *The Best Place to Live: A Meditation on the Four Divine Abodes*

Some of us grew up with a fantasy about someday living in a sublime mansionlike setting. The Dharma says that this is not just a fantasy: It is possible to live in a divine abode by making an effort to cultivate sublime states of being, known as the Brahma Viharas or Four Noblest Qualities of Mind. These delightful states of being are:

1. *Loving-kindness* and *friendliness* (known as metta)

2. *Compassion* and *empathy*

3. *Joy* and *rejoicing*

4. *Equanimity* and *peace of mind*

Meditation practice can help us live in such a state—all the time. That's why the Brahma Viharas are called divine abodes. They are places to be and places to live. These abodes describe an atmosphere that we can create and carry with us always. No matter what the circumstances, your house can always be filled with love, compassion, joy, and equanimity. Think about all that these four qualities encompass—acceptance, forgiveness, hope, celebration, affirmation, delight, reconciliation, peacemaking. We could go on indefinitely finding synonyms that describe these boundless qualities, which are so important today. That is why, in Tibetan, these four divine abodes are called the Four Immeasurables.

But these are not just qualities of the mind; they are also attitudes of the heart. That's why I call them the Four Heartitudes. These Four Heartitudes, which are like spiritual beatitudes, can totally transform our lives, and particularly our relationships with others. I have found them profoundly effective in taming my own unruly, egotistical nature, and in transforming my experience of the world as well as my relationships with others; I heartily recommend them for others.

Thanks to teachers like Sharon Salzberg and her deservedly acclaimed book, *LovingKindness: The Revolutionary Art of Happiness,* more Westerners have become aware of these meditations, which can be practiced by beginners, advanced practitioners, Buddhist and non-Buddhist alike. These teachings on love and compassion reverberate deeply with the Christian, Jewish, and humanistic values and sentiments to which we Westerners remain connected.

The concept of loving-kindness, or metta, is so important that we find it constantly stressed. In Right Speech, we talked about the metta prayer. Here we take the same compassionate aspirations and make them the focus of our meditation.

Although many meditators do metta meditation on loving-kindness, I think it's important to remember that there are *four* of these heartitudes. They can be likened to four pillars of the temple of divine abode.

To enter this divine home, and experience these qualities for yourself, sit down and center yourself. Collect yourself, and let your energy and mind arrive in this place, here and now. Begin to breathe gently through your nostrils. Ease into an awareness of breathing. Let awareness and experience feel itself. You are just breathing. Awareness is there. Close your eyes. Place your hands on your knees or in your lap. Turn your attention inward. Let go a little. Relax, and begin chanting:

May all beings have happiness and the cause of happiness.

May all beings remain free from suffering and the cause of suffering.

May all beings remain unseparated from the sacred joy and happiness that is totally free from sorrow.

May all beings come to rest in the boundless and all-inclusive equanimity that is beyond attachment and aversion.

If you look at these four lines, you will notice that each of them refers to one of the Four Heartitudes: The first is loving-kindness; the second, compassion and empathy; the third is joy and rejoicing; and the fourth is equanimity and peace of mind.

You can meditate on these four lines by chanting or saying them silently to yourself, again and again. As you do so, reflect on each of the lines. We are cultivating attitudes of the heart, so put all your heart into your chanting—your prayer. Focus on one at a time, and reflect on that single line's meaning. Make a noble wish from deep in your heart. Think of your heart as a brilliant sun that is radiating in all directions. It is warming your heart, your body, and your mind. Feel your overflowing heart flowering and blossoming like a sunflower. Visualize this golden, glowing, warming sun in your heart, radiating outward in all directions at once. Love unconditionally, loving yourself as well. Forgive yourself, accept yourself, embrace yourself. Open yourself up to give love and receive love. Soften up. Share the blessings and merits with all.

Sometimes in retreat we chant these four lines 3,000 times a day, which takes about ten hours. You can resolve to cultivate these Four Heartitudes for the next half hour. Let this divine state of mind settle and take root in your inner being, like a powerful affirmation. This is like a New Year's resolution for your heart, which can make every moment a fresh new year.

Here are some more wishes, prayers, and affirmations for the good of all: May all beings be happy, content, and fulfilled. May all be peaceful, harmonious, and at ease; may all be protected from harm and fear; may all have whatever they want, need, and aspire to. May all be healed and whole. May this planet be healed and whole. May all beings awaken from the sleep of illusion. May all beings be awakened, delivered, liberated, and free. May all realize their true nature and awaken to the Buddha within. May all equally enjoy, actualize, and embody the innate Great Perfection.

We can recite these, or simply contemplate them in a profound and soulful way; you are radiating unconditional love and acceptance to all beings equally, praying that all be awake and free. Radiate loving-kindness to the world; compassion to the world; joy to the world; equanimity and peace of mind to the entire planet. As you do this, start to bring the light back to yourself. Embrace, love, and forgive yourself. Open yourself to receiving the same kind of love and blessings you are sending out. Outside and inside become merged, without separation. This is the natural state, oneness and wholeness.

We rejoice in the good fortune of all. We rejoice in the virtuous good deeds and accomplishments of others. We put an end to covetousness and jealousy. We forgive and accept others, and put an end to feelings of ill will and enmity. Blessings to the world. Blessings to ourselves.

Repeat these words too. Then rest in the afterglow of this meditation for a few minutes. Just sit in the light. Be peaceful in the light. Be light. Enjoy this divine abode, this heavenly home. Rest in the sublime awareness of these Four Heartitudes.

# RIGHT MINDFULNESS

## Keeping Your Eyes Open

*The whole thrust of Buddha's teaching is to
master the mind. If you master the mind, you
will have mastery over body and speech. . . .
Mastery of the mind is achieved through constant awareness of all your thoughts and
actions. . . . Maintaining this constant mindfulness in the practice of tranquility and insight, you will eventually be able to sustain the
recognition of wisdom even in the midst of ordinary activities and distractions. Mindfulness
is thus the very basis, the cure for all samsaric
afflictions.*

—DILGO KHYENTSE RINPOCHE,
*JOURNEY TO ENLIGHTENMENT*

One day in 1982 when I was in France, temporarily serving as
an attendant to the Dalai Lama, His Holiness was dining with another grand lama, Pawo Rinpoche. The pair were recounting stories and anticipating the rebirth of the recently deceased Sixteenth
Gyalwa Karmapa, when the elderly Pawo Rinpoche spied an ant
struggling across the polished floor, wending its way toward the
sunlit doorway.

The aged Pawo Rinpoche, who no longer had the use of his

legs, asked the Dalai Lama if he would be so kind as to rescue the little creature and help it on its way. His Holiness did so with alacrity, gently carrying the insect across the regal chamber, setting it down safely outside in the warm sun, and sending it on its way with a whispered blessing. Chuckling with delight, he rejoined his venerable colleague.

"Now I have done a service for you, Rinpoche. Your old eyes are better than mine! People talk so much about emptiness and high Mahayana philosophy, but loving regard for the equality of all that lives is the true sign of a Bodhisattva."

His Holiness himself later recounted the story, during a teaching in France about the necessity of selfless service and universal responsibility.

This is a wonderful story about sensitivity and loving-kindness, but it also reflects the impeccable awareness and alert mindfulness of Pawo Rinpoche. He was elderly; he had less than perfect eyesight; he was engaged in animated conversation with the Dalai Lama, in a foreign place in a foreign land. Yet he was conscious of the movement of an ant. Pawo Rinpoche was awake to what he was experiencing, so the little ant became part of his awareness. This is true presence of mind. His mindfulness opened the way for a spontaneous act of compassion.

Right Mindfulness, the seventh step on the Noble Eight-Fold Path, might even be called the escalator to enlightenment. Fortuitously, the timeless teachings of mindfulness also seem tailor-made for today's fast-paced world. Many Westerners, in fact, have already benefitted from the truths contained within Right Mindfulness even if they haven't recognized their roots in Buddha Dharma. To get a sense of how mindfulness teachings have become part of our culture and are at the root of a significant part of New Age philosophy. Consider all the books, articles, and personal-growth techniques reminding us to "let go and live in the moment," to "be present," to "live a conscious life," to "slow down," and to be "in touch with our feelings." Conscious presence, here and now, is the lesson of mindfulness. It's one we all need.

# WHAT ARE YOU DOING, AND WHY ARE YOU DOING IT?

Once years ago in China, a young monk asked his Zen master, "What is enlightenment? What is it like for you?" The master replied, "When I eat, I eat. When I sleep, I sleep."

Most of us are not usually paying attention to what we actually do and say. We are not really eating when we eat; we are not really sleeping when we sleep. Our minds are distracted and our thoughts are scattered. Too often we are either lamenting about and clutching at the past, or anticipating and fearing the future. Instead of fully inhabiting our bodies and experiencing our experience, we're semiconscious at best—not fully present, barely aware. This sad state is reflected by the foolish and mindless things we do as we whizz along life's fast lanes as if driving on autopilot.

We become so busy and we scurry about so quickly that we forget to stay in touch with who we are, what we are, and what we are doing. In this way, we miss the beauty; we miss the sadness; we miss the actuality, the full texture of our lives. We miss the truth of our experiences, moment to moment. Our lack of mindfulness makes us careless: Often we hurt others without thinking or sometimes even without noticing we've done so. And we hurt ourselves. We keep falling asleep at the switch of our lives, leaving ourselves vulnerable to all kinds of accidents, both physical and emotional.

Not fully aware, we step on the ant—or worse. Not paying attention to our lives in the immediacy of the present moment, we look up only to find ourselves embroiled in disastrous personal relationships. Not present for our loved ones, we find ourselves with alienated children and angry mates. The direct human repercussions caused by a lack of mindfulness and awareness are omnipresent—from misplaced keys to misdirected lives. Present awareness and mindfulness implies an understanding of what we are doing and saying. This sounds simple enough. But it isn't easy to live fully in the present moment; it isn't easy to sustain clear awareness and mindfulness.

One day, on three-year retreat, our teacher Nyoshul Khenpo,

writing in the Tibetan language, used a Magic Marker to scrawl the following spontaneous words on a large paper towel. He tacked the paper towel on the inside of the wooden gate separating our enclosed forest cloister from the dirt road leading to the outside world. We were so inspired by it that we wrapped the paper in Saran Wrap to protect it from the elements and left it hanging there as a constant reminder to stay awake.

## THE MIRROR OF MINDFULNESS

*Mindfulness is the root of the Dharma.*
*Mindfulness is the body of practice.*
*Mindfulness is the fortress of the mind.*
*Lack of mindfulness will allow the negative forces to overcome you.*
*Without mindfulness you will be swept away by laziness.*
*Lack of mindfulness is the creator of evil deeds.*
*Without mindfulness and presence of mind,*
*Nothing can be accomplished.*
*Lack of mindfulness piles up shit.*
*Without mindfulness you sleep in an ocean of piss.*
*Without mindfulness you are like a heartless zombie, a walking*
  *corpse.*

Our teacher wished to remind us that without the vital heart of awareness practice, mere form and ritual is meaningless. Without mindfulness, staying in monastic retreat would accumulate few spiritual rewards. All we would have to show for our time would be piles of excrement. All the hours of meditating would lose much of its deeper value unless we were mindful while doing it. Practicing mindful awareness is how we develop insight and self-realization. The same thing is true outside of monastery walls, whether we are meditating or washing our laundry. The more fully engaged in simply doing what we are doing, and the more awareness and insight we bring to bear upon it, the more we get done, spiritually speaking.

# MEDITATION IS HOW WE TRAIN IN MINDFULNESS AND AWARENESS

*Only that day dawns to which we are fully awake.*

—HENRY DAVID THOREAU

The pioneering Japanese master Dr. D. T. Suzuki was unofficially the first patriarch of American Zen. When Dr. Suzuki, who had taught at Columbia University during the fifties, was approaching ninety years of age, he was present at a meeting of scholars, seated at a long conference table. It seemed to everyone as if he were asleep or in deep meditation. "How to tell the difference?" some of his younger colleagues wondered, perhaps with a little private laugh. Then, one of the lecture papers in front of the speaker seated at the head of the polished mahogany table flew down the table, carried by a gust of wind. It traveled past half the Buddhist scholars and professors seated along the table before the thin hand of the seemingly hibernating elder Zen master snaked out and snatched it without moving the rest of his body or raising his half-closed eyelids. Everyone was awestruck at the realization that the old tiger's presence of mind and quick reflexes were still sharper than those of anyone else present. After that, no one imagined he might be sleeping . . . even when he was.

Pure mindfulness is relaxed, open, lucid, moment-to-moment, present awareness. It is like a bright mirror: nonclinging, non-grasping, nonaversive, nonreactive, undistorting. Fortunately, mindfulness is a skill that can be learned like any other. Classical Buddhists in the Vipassana practice lineages always emphasize mindfulness. This is the primary practice of Dharma teachers like Jon Kabat-Zinn, Jack Kornfield, Sharon Salzberg, and Sylvia Boorstein. Pioneer teacher Joseph Goldstein calls mindfulness the central practice of the Dharma, the first ingredient in Buddha's recipe for awakening.

Meditation is the method we use to train in mindfulness. Meditation is unique in its ability to wake us up; it opens what is constricted, closed, and fixated in us. Sylvia Boorstein says: "At the beginning of meditation practice you need to remember to be mindful. After a while, you can't forget."

Meditation explores, investigates, unveils, and illumines what is hidden within and all around us. This contemplative, introspective experience helps us to awaken from our dreams and illusions about how things are and go beyond our subjective view of the world to the actual reality. Through meditation we can enter directly into more intimate, immediate engagement with our experiences in a way that reflects simplicity and a deeper, more authentic connection to life. This is not just about being more consciously alive. It's about *being* itself.

# WAKE UP! BUDDHA'S LESSONS IN MINDFULNESS

Some 2,500 years ago when the Buddha was first giving his disciples instructions on what it means to live with Right Mindfulness, he said, "The disciple acts with clear comprehension in going and coming . . . acts with clear comprehension in looking forward and backward . . . acts with clear comprehension in eating, drinking, chewing, and tasting . . . acts with clear comprehension in walking, standing, sitting, falling asleep, awakening . . . acts with clear comprehension in speaking and keeping silent."

The Buddha was asking his disciples to be fully conscious, wide awake to all that they do. Let's never forget that the practice of awareness and mindfulness is directly related to reality. It *is* clear seeing. The Buddha was telling his followers not to live in the past or the future, but to be conscious and wake up to the present moment and the truth of what is. And that's what we cultivate when we meditate: awareness of what is. For Dharma students, this directly brings us to truth and reality according to its simplest definition: *Things just as they are.*

In the original Mindfulness Sutra, the Buddha described what he called the Four Foundations of Mindfulness. These teachings remind us to be aware of our bodies; aware of our feelings and emotions; aware of our thoughts; and aware of events, as they occur, moment by moment. In his essential meditation instructions passed down until today, the Buddha told his disciples how to begin their training in present awareness and mindfulness, saying: "The disciple retires to the forest, to the foot of a tree, or to a solitary place, seats himself . . . and with mindfulness fixed before him, mindfully he breathes in, mindfully he breathes out. When making a long inhalation, he knows: 'I make a long inhalation'; when making a long exhalation, he knows: 'I make a long exhalation.' . . . thus he trains himself."

"Is this really meditation?" people often ask. "Is it really that easy?" If these meditation instructions sound almost too simple to believe, there is another oft-told story about the Buddha: Once an elderly grandmother came to him, telling him that she too would like to reach enlightenment; she too would like to learn how to meditate. But, as she explained, she was very old, infirm, illiterate, and busy with family obligations and household chores. She couldn't renounce her family and enter a monastic order. However, she was already open and conscious enough to perceive the beaming countenances of the enlightened Buddha and many of his followers. It was her heart's desire to learn to meditate in order to join them in developing spiritually.

The Buddha told her, "Respected grandmother, every time you draw water from the well for you and your family, remain aware of every single act, movement, and motion of your hands. As you are carrying home the water jug atop your head, be aware of every step of your feet; as you do your chores, maintain continuous mindfulness and awareness every single instant, moment after moment, and you too will become a master of meditation."

These instructions, which reflect the essence of simplicity, are not always so easy to follow. Have you ever had the experience of having to pick up a brimming bowl of hot soup in your hands while you were wearing dress clothes? Do you remember the alertly vigilant state of mind you maintained until you were able to put the bowl down? In mindfulness meditation, we cradle the present moment in the very same way. We do this with the intention of carrying this vigilance with us into every moment of our lives.

In his book, *Peace Is Every Step,* meditation master Thich Nhat

Hanh wrote, "I must confess it takes me a little longer to do the dishes in mindfulness, but I live fully in every moment, and I am happy. Each second of life is a miracle; the dishes themselves and the fact that I am here washing them are miracles! Every conscious step we make, a flower blooms under our feet. We can do this only if we linger not in the past or future, but know that life can be found only in the present moment."

In meditation training, we learn to approach everything we do with attention and mindfulness. Mindfulness is also the end product of meditation as in total wakefulness, unified attention, focused awareness, and even enlightenment. After the Buddha realized enlightenment under the bodhi tree, he lived for several decades—teaching and enjoying the enlightened life—but he no longer had to formally sit down to meditate. Since everything was natural, meditationlike wakefulness for him, it was no longer something to be cultivated, developed, and achieved.

Living the mindful life is a sacred way of being in this world, with or without the safe container traditionally provided by more elaborate religious forms. Knowing things as they are, knowing how they function, is enlightened wakefulness. Beyond that, there is nowhere to go. Nothing to do. Nothing wanting.

## THE LESSON OF "NOWNESS"

> *Too often, people think that solving the world's problems is based on conquering the earth, rather than touching the earth, touching ground.*

> —CHOGYAM TRUNGPA

Hidden between the lines of mindfulness teaching is one of the most important Dharma lessons: Meditation is a simple direct way of coming home to "now." As we begin to be mindful, living in the "now" and directing our attention to the smallest fraction of the present instant, something extraordinary takes place. We begin to relinquish our fascination with both the past and the future. We stop living in fantasies, fears, and anticipation of the future, and we learn to let go of time-consuming preoccupations with what was or what might have been. As we learn to let go, we see that our energy is returned to us. All that wonderful energy that was being expended and leaked out in fantasy, bitterness, and regret is, once again, ours! We are returned to our natural state of pure nowness. This is authentic being. The joy of now. Holy now.

Some of us have spent entire lifetimes fixated on our attachment to either what was or what will be. Because we're not accustomed to present-moment awareness, we need retraining to stay in this immediate nanosecond. To more fully develop the power of mindfulness, we begin by becoming more completely and lucidly conscious of individual bodily activities like breathing and walking. In walking, for example, we take a step, and then another step, totally consciously. Piece by piece, we break each step into further microcomponents like lifting the foot, moving it forward, and placing it down. If I say this so often that it sounds repetitive, that's because it is repetitive. That's the point. It's a training, and like all trainings we need to keep reminding ourselves of the basics, going over it again and again. We learn to be aware step by step, breath by breath, thought by thought, feeling by feeling.

One day Lord Buddha gathered his most realized disciples, as if to address them. Instead of saying anything with words, he simply held up and slightly turned a yellow flower. At that moment, one arhant, Kasyapa, broke into a great smile. The enlightened Buddha said, "Today only the venerable monk Kasyapa has understood my teaching." Kasyapa became the first patriarch of what has come down to us through history as the Zen Buddhist lineage. That brief wordless sermon is called the Flower Sutra.

Without an opened wisdom-eye, who can understand such ineffable, naked teaching? Therefore Zen meditation instruction is often articulated in concise yet not entirely incomprehensible teachings and instructions, like "Just sit when sitting," and "Just breathe when breathing," and "Just walk when walking." What could be more simple?

In meditation training, we use our own rich natural resources—like breathing, bodily sensations, thoughts, and feel-ings—as objects of meditation. In this way, we are able to readily access our object or method of meditation whenever we need it—in any circumstance, any place, and any time of day. Mindful-ness means attention and lucid awareness. Paying attention and the ability to really be present pays off in so many ways, giving us en-hanced satisfaction, broader vision, greater mastery and effective-ness in everything we do.

By simply being right there, on the spot, you can make your life become workable and wonderful. A Zen master says, "Awakening to this present instant, we realize the infinite is in the finite of each instant." American poet Emily Dickinson wrote, "Forever is com-posed of nows."

## AWARENESS CURES

On the most practical level, if you feel confused, tangled, or bent out of shape, meditation is a way to straighten it all out. As a snake untangles its own knotted, coiled-up body, the meditator's heart and mind gradually, gently, releases and untangles itself.

I frequently hear people say they don't have time to meditate. I also often feel the same way. However, like most meditators I know that meditation gives back so much mental clarity and spaciousness that it actually adds time to the day. We feel less overwhelmed be-cause we are more centered. We become more effective, and more relaxed.

Mindfulness practice is also an effective way of helping us deal with our feelings and develop our "emotional intelligence." We become aware of our feelings as they arise in the moment; we ex-perience them without suppressing or denying them. In this way, we have the space and perspective to choose how we can best re-late to them. Meditation allows us to be more in touch with our feelings without being driven or controlled by them.

Many people say that meditation practice is what keeps them feeling balanced and sane. That's because meditation helps us watch the mind, without clinging, beyond the bounds of desire and aversion. It is an exercise in, and an expression of, integration and centering. *This* is basic sanity. This is a natural remedy for the frustration and anxiety that is inherent in the scattered, fragmented lives so many of us lead. Tension, fear, and stress don't come from outside. These are internal weather conditions we ourselves produce. Try to let go of everything for a moment. Take a deep breath. Relax. Become more receptive, permissive, aware. Soften up. Give yourself a break.

I travel a lot, and I find that meditation is a great way to get where I'm going. Let's say the plane is winging at six hundred miles an hour high over the Atlantic. I stop, take a breath; smile, breathe out, and let go. Anybody can do this anywhere, for any amount of time, without believing in anything. The passenger next to me doesn't even notice. No one knows what I am doing, and no one cares. But the Buddhas know, and I know, and we are in agreement. This is enough.

I find it quite natural to do instant One-Minute Meditations—which I amuse myself by calling quickies—twenty-five to one hundred times a day. My Dzogchen masters said, "Many quickies rather than few longies." In this way we can keep our awareness fresh and vivid.

Meditation is not about duration, but about quality time. If it's just for a brief moment, it's almost like lighting a candle on an altar or seeing a shooting star. If it's for half an hour, it can become a deep contemplative practice. If we're distracted or harried, it helps us relax, calm down, and focus. If we're overheated or speedy, it feels like a cool fresh breeze on a sweltering hike, helping us center and return to the present moment. If we're bored, restless, full of doubt or uncertainty, it helps heighten and sharpen our awareness, clarify and stabilize the mind.

## DO-IT-YOURSELF MEDITATION

People often ask me for specific guidelines on how to meditate. They sometimes want to know if they can teach themselves how to meditate. Since meditation is a fluid and open process, there are very few absolutes. However, there are some techniques and helpful hints that centuries of meditators have found useful.

## SETTING UP CONDITIONS CONDUCIVE TO MEDITATION

Accomplished meditation masters can meditate in the middle of a traffic island in Times Square, New York City, but even they usually prefer quiet and solitude. When you are first learning to meditate, and your mind still has a tremendous tendency to wander, it's best to follow some general guidelines:

◎ Find a peaceful place to meditate, where there are few external distractions, preferably a place without television, radios, children, or phones. As much as possible choose a spot where you feel emotionally comfortable and safe, far removed from stress and pressure. If you can't look at your desk without feeling work-related anxieties, don't try to meditate in your office. Make an effort to keep your environment as simple as possible. Zen students learn to meditate in rooms or gardens remarkable in their stark simplicity. Nature can often provide a suitable site. The Buddha meditated both by a river and under a tree. You might prefer a hilltop, a rooftop, or the shoreline on a sandy beach.

◎ Try to keep the temperature comfortable and not overly warm. You want to stay cool, calm, and alert. A master once said, "Practice with eyes like ice and heart on fire."

◎ Decide ahead of time how long you plan to meditate, and try to keep that commitment. At the beginning, keep the meditation under thirty minutes. Don't push yourself.

◎ Wear clothing that is comfortable and loose. You don't want a tight belt to become the focus of your meditation.

◎ As you prepare to meditate, bring a sense of moderation, restraint, and self-discipline with you. Approach the meditation session (and the world outside) with reverence and respect.

◉ Prepare yourself mentally for meditation by trying to let go of images or things that bring to mind what you crave or desire. This isn't always easy to do, so don't be discouraged if it doesn't happen right away. Even trained masters have lamented some of the images that come uninvited to mind while meditating.

◉ During your meditation sessions, practice contentment. We are very fortunate in being able to meditate; it is a gift we give ourselves. We try to cultivate gratitude for what we have been given.

◉ Make the effort to let go of discursive thinking and compulsive, obsessive thoughts. Notice repetitive, compulsive thoughts and the familiar stories we tell ourselves. Label them as "that old tape again" and return to the object of your concentration.

◉ Cherish the simplicity and quiet of meditation. Nothing is missing. Enjoy the richness of the present moment.

## BODY AND BREATH

Traditionally we learn to meditate while sitting. Meditators are often seen cross-legged in a lotus or half-lotus position, often using a cushion beneath their backsides. However, a cross-legged position isn't necessary. You can also sit in a straight-backed, comfortable chair. Here are some basic instructions:

◉ Straighten your body and sit erect. Don't lean to either side, and try not to bend forward or backward. Let your shoulders drop naturally.

◉ Try to keep your nose in line with your navel and keep your head placed so that your ears are over your shoulders. Keep your head on straight.

◉ Let your tongue rest lightly on the roof of your mouth, with lips and teeth gently closed.

◉ Place your hands in your lap or on your knees.

◉ Keep your eyes closed or half closed.

◎ Allow yourself to experience some spaciousness, ease, and clarity, letting the mind settle naturally into its own natural state.

◎ Begin by breathing in through the nostrils, then out through the nostrils. Concentrate on the physical sensation of air going in and out the nostrils. Simply observe your breathing at that very sensation point, and focus on nothing else. Connect to your present experience by maintaining contact between your mind's concentrated attention and that sensation of breathing.

◎ Whatever occurs while you are meditating—noises, an itchy foot, a memory, be it pleasant or unpleasant—let it go and return your focus to the breathing.

◎ Keep your body still and your breathing free and easy.

◎ Stay loose, open, and accepting.

◎ Enjoy the moment.

## WHAT WE MEAN BY "LET GO OF YOUR THOUGHTS"

"But what do I do with my thoughts?" is a question I often hear. Some people think meditation is about suppressing thoughts, trying not to think, or even seeking oblivion. This is a major misconception. Meditation is about bringing awareness to whatever is, in the present moment. It is about knowing reality. In meditation we bring awareness to everything, including our thoughts and feelings. We are cultivating present moment-to-moment awareness. We want to be conscious, awake, and aware—not oblivious. Because of our meditation training, we will be better able to notice and appreciate the flowers coming through the cracks in the sidewalk. We will be better able to find joy in the children playing at the beach with their tiny shovels and plastic pails.

Of course you will have thoughts in meditation. Thoughts arise all the time, like waves on an ocean. You don't have to iron out the ocean. Just notice the waves as they arise and disappear on the ocean's surface. In meditation, we maintain that same attitude regarding our thoughts. We observe the process of thinking. We notice that there is a thought; we watch it arise, and we let it go and pass by as we continue breathing. As we get deeper in meditation, we notice that the breath gets more still, the body gets quieter, and the thoughts become calmer. This isn't the primary goal of meditation, but it is a beneficial side effect and sign of progress along the way.

Through meditation, we come to know that we are not our thoughts. As we develop what is often referred to as "a steady mind," our thoughts lose the power to upset us or throw us topsy-turvy. We learn that we have a life apart from our thoughts. *We are not what we think.* We create our thoughts and we are responsible for our thoughts, but we are not limited by them or enslaved by the thinking process.

In meditation, we simply watch and become aware of our thoughts as they arise. We label them as "thinking." But we are not controlled by them. And we don't judge them. If, for example, you have an angry, mean thought about another person, you don't have to tell yourself, "I'm an angry, mean person." We all have all kinds of wild thoughts, but that doesn't mean we must be defined by them.

In meditation, we also make a point of not building upon our thoughts or feelings. Let's say your mean thought was, "I wish so-and-so would get fired." There is no need to follow up the thought with scenarios on how this firing might take place. If you think, "Gee, I was a nice person for giving Dolores a ride," why follow that up with further back-pats? Just be aware of the thought, and then let it go. In meditation we mind our mind, so we can better know ourselves, so we can be true to ourselves. We don't hang on to our thoughts, or use our thoughts to manipulate what is taking place.

Think of each of your thoughts as a wave on the ocean of awareness. No matter how large or outlandish your waves, the boundless ocean retains its essential quality. The ocean of awareness never leaves its bed, no matter what kind of waves are moving along the surface. That's why in Dzogchen we say thoughts are the mind's adornments, or creative displays. In meditation, as thought waves ripple on the surface, we keep returning to the deeper ocean, which some people would call God or inner light. Meditation is a soulful exercise that helps bring us home to that light that we call Buddha-nature, the natural mind, or the Buddha within.

Sometimes when we first start meditation practice, we seem to be swamped with even more thoughts and feelings than usual. The fact is that they are always there. Meditation helps us be more aware of what is always there. Daniel Goleman writes, "Self-awareness—recognizing a feeling as it happens—is the keystone of emotional intelligence." In Buddhist psychology, thoughts are considered one of the six sensory fields. Thoughts are objects of the mind, just as sights are objects of the eyes, and sounds are objects of the ear or auditory system. In meditation, we observe all these phenomena in the same way. We notice, we label, we let them go, as we keep going back to our deeper nature, the natural mind. We let everything slide without sticking, off of our Teflon brain pan.

Let's take the following simple example.

## MEDITATION WITH MOSQUITO

You are meditating. Breathing in. Breathing out. Minding your own business. Suddenly there is a buzzing near your right ear. You think, "Oh no, mosquito on right ear."

Meditation is being aware of whatever is. So at that moment, your meditation could simply become awareness of buzzing. The buzzing is not an interruption, unless you allow it to become one by becoming overly involved in it. Distraction would be carrying you away if you turned to see what the buzzing is all about. But if you are meditating, you know that it's just buzzing. It's simply a vibration in your eardrum. Buzzzz . . .

Should you do anything about the buzzing? What *can* you do about the buzzing? Mindful awareness provides you with more space to choose your response or lack of response. In that moment, in that space where you are simply aware of nothing but pure and simple buzzing, you find pristine awareness. Freedom lies in that moment, where awareness saves you from responding to the mosquito, or anything else, with a knee-jerk reaction. In every situation in life, there are many options. In this case, there are many ways to deal with the mind-mosquito.

The same principle applies when someone says a harsh word,

or even a flattering word. Awareness gives us the vivid presence of mind to notice the words and count to ten before reacting and responding. That's freedom. The point is that mindful awareness slows things down enough so that you can see how things work before being swept along by old patterns. You have a choice between blind reaction and a creative, considered response. We all do regrettable things and make mistakes because we are semiconscious at the wheel of our life. By giving us time and awareness, mindfulness can help us live our lives in a far more fulfilling way.

Let's go back to the mosquito. A Buddhist saint might wish that the mosquito finds a tender juicy spot, has a decent meal, and a safe flight home. A novice meditator might try to scare the mosquito away with a twitch. But if you are a meditator who has committed yourself to a period of time without moving, all you do is notice the buzzing and label it "buzzing."

## The Three-Stage Meditation

In my own meditation practice and when I teach, I think of each meditation session as having three stages.

### STAGE ONE:
### ARRIVING AND CENTERING

We stop doing what we were doing, and thinking what we were thinking. We relax. We arrive. We sit. We get comfortable. If we are sitting cross-legged on the floor, we adjust our cushion and our legs. If we are sitting on a chair, we place both our feet on the floor, relaxed with an erect spine, while leaving our hands at rest in a comfortable position. We simply stop and drop everything.

Start by letting the breath settle naturally. Let everything settle naturally. Let the body settle naturally on its seat in its own way, in its own time. Let the breath and the energy settle naturally in the body. Let the thoughts settle. Simply collect yourself. Simply arrive, relax, and come home to the present moment.

Tibetan yogis and meditation masters teach us how to totally relax and let go of our body, speech, and mind.

*Leave the body at rest, like an unmovable mountain.*
*Leave the speech at rest, like an unstrung guitar.*
*Leave the mind at rest like a shepherd after dusk who has brought his flock*
*    home and sits content by the warm fire.*

Once you have arrived, done is what had to be done. Heart and soul are one. The body, the speech, and the mind have let go. You are there.

## STAGE TWO:
### INTENSIFYING AND FOCUSING

Now awareness of the present moment is rising. We are heightening our sensitivity and intensity. We are making a conscious effort to pay attention. We focus on the out-breath going out; we focus on the in-breath coming in.

Simply observe breathing. Inhale. Exhale. Let go of everything else. As you breathe, become aware of what you are feeling at each moment: the physical sensations in your body, your belly, your diaphragm, your nostrils. This is cultivating mindfulness and alert presence of mind. Direct your attention to the process of breathing, and stay on that and that alone.

Be vigilant and watchful. Each time the mind wanders, bring it back again to the breath. Bring it back by tugging gently on the leash of mindfulness. Watch the breath. Inhale. Exhale.

Pay attention. Observe clearly; see things just as they are. Clarify. Penetrate with insight. Stay with the breath, unifying and stabilizing your wandering mind. Concentrate all your energies on the breathing.

S T A G E   T H R E E :

R E L E A S I N G   A N D   A L L O W I N G

This third stage is the main part of the meditation. There is nothing left to do. Opening to effortlessness, you have arrived fully in the present moment. You are there, in nonjudgmental, mirrorlike awareness—choiceless awareness. You're not trying to get anywhere or do anything. You have arrived. You are present. You win.

This is the time to enjoy being there, totally, one with yourself and the world, in harmony with your surroundings—in harmony with everything. Just being. Enjoying the joy and peace of meditation. Yes!

> *The meditative mind is silent. It is beyond thought. . . . The meditative mind is the religious mind—the mind that is not touched by the church, the temples or by chants. . . .*
> *Meditation is not a means to an end. It is both the means and the end.*
>
> —J. KRISHNAMURTI, *MEDITATIONS*

# ENLIGHTENMENT IS THE GOAL; MEDITATION IS THE WAY

> *You are the Buddha. You are the truth. Then why do you not feel it? Why don't you know it through and through? Because there is a veil in the way, which is attachment to appearances, such as the belief that you are not Buddha, that you are a separate individual, an ego. If*

*you cannot remove this veil all at once, then it
must be dissolved gradually.*

*If you have seen through it totally, even
one glimpse, then you can see through it at
any time. Wherever you are, whatever presents
itself, however things seem to be; simply refer
to that ever-present, spacious openness and
clarity.*

— KALU RINPOCHE

As we practice meditation, we are peeling layers off our persona. Peeling and peeling toward the center, letting go and unmasking layer after layer of the many faces we present to the world and ourselves. We are not our thoughts, but then who are we? Who is the person who is trying to meditate? Who is the experiencer, experiencing our experience? Is it our mind, our body, our soul, our spirit? This is the big question: the question of identity.

Most meditators bring with them a shared aspiration: to directly experience things as they are, in the present moment. *Now* is the only place we can ever be. Both memories and plans take place in the now. In meditation, we come home again and again to this exquisite present, waking up to the truth of who and what we are. We know that we can't cop out, so we just have to keep showing up again and again. We breathe; we practice mindfulness; and we unpeel layer after layer. Going deeper and deeper. Seeing through our mental states, continuously letting go, unmasking and unmasking; peeling after peeling until ultimately we arrive at our original, unprocessed, natural state, our genuine being. That is Buddha-nature, our true nature—the natural mind. Awakened is the Buddha within.

To just be—to *be*—amidst all doings, achieving, and becomings. This is the natural state of mind, our original, most fundamental state of being. This is unadulterated Buddha-nature. This is like finding our balance.

# BIG MIND/SMALL MIND

To help us understand that we are not what we are thinking, Buddhist teachings make a distinction between what is called Big Mind, or Natural Mind, and "small mind," or ordinary, deluded mind. Small mind, or deluded mind, is the buzzing, unpredictable, frequently out-of-control ordinary mind. This is our finite mind, our limited conceptual mind; our ordinary, rational, discursive, thinking mind. The deluded mind has so many impulses and needs; it wants so many things. It's frequently confused; it's subject to mood swings; it's restless. It gets angry; it gets depressed; it becomes hyper. Some ancient traditional texts refer to this small mind as "monkey mind," where it is pictured as an untamed mustang or an adorable but chaotic little monkey jumping from tree to tree, looking for satisfaction in all the wrong places.

What is meant by Big Mind is the essential nature of mind itself. This is what we call Buddha-nature, or natural mind. This is our true nature—the pure boundless awareness that is at the heart, and part, of us all. The Buddha described it as still, clear, lucid, empty, profound, simple (uncomplicated), and at peace. It's not really what we usually think of as our mind at all. It is the luminous, most fundamental clear light nature of our ground of being. This is Rigpa, the heart of enlightenment. This is our share of nirvana here on earth.

Dzogchen teaches that all we have to do to become enlightened is to recognize and rest in this natural state of mind. In Zen they call this original mind. This is raw, naked awareness, not something we've learned or fabricated. This is the Buddha within—the perfect presence that we can all rely on. Waking up to this natural mind, this Buddha-nature, is what meditation is all about.

# MAINTAINING THE VIEW: REMEMBERING THE BIGGER PICTURE

> *The Innate Great Perfection combines enlightened view, meditation, and action.*
>     *With view as vast and open as the infinite luminous sky;*
>     *Meditation as unshakable as a stately mountain;*
>     *Action as spontaneously free and unhindered as the ocean's waves;*
>     *The result is realizing the Natural Mind—the Innate Great Perfection.*

> —A SONG OF YOGIC JOY, FROM THE
> DZOGCHEN ORAL TRADITION

When Dzogchen masters talk about staying in the view, what they mean is recognizing the natural state of mind—Buddha-nature—and resting in that lucid awareness. This implies spontaneous immediacy and choiceless awareness. This vast view or outlook means being able to see things as they are, with total clarity. This view or higher vision is beyond distortion. It is totally open and without judgment. When we remain in the view, we don't try to manipulate or change the truth of what is. A mirror doesn't pick and choose what it wants to reflect. Similarly, as things arise in our minds, they simply appear, without distortion or editing, in clear mirror-like awareness.

With this kind of view, we keep sight of the bigger picture—Dzogchen, the natural perfection of things just as they are. In basic meditation we practice mindfulness of breathing. Dzogchen training is more advanced; it teaches us how to be vividly wakeful and one with *what is.* In Dzogchen practice, we carry this choiceless awareness with us wherever we go, so that every moment becomes a moment of mindfulness, a moment of reality, and hence a moment of freedom and enlightenment. As a Zen master said, "Eternity is one instant, and this instant is right now. Wake up to it!"

Although this may sound esoteric, it's actually a very practi-

cal, here-and-now teaching. My younger students sometimes describe it in slang: "Stay in the view, Lou." "Keep your head, Fred."
"Go with the flow, Jo." All you have to do is remain in the view.

This teaching introduces a way to keep the bigger perspective
in mind and go with the greater current in the river of reality,
without becoming caught up in life's little whirlpools. Whether
you are practicing formal meditation or shampooing the family
dog, preserve your natural mind; remain mindful and awake rather
than being carried away by thoughts and projections. They are all
mere illusory appearances. If you can maintain this view, then
meditation in action develops spontaneously, and there is less distinction between formal religious practice and the mundane acts of
daily life.

> *We live in illusion*
> *And the appearance of things.*
> *There is a reality.*
> *We are that reality.*
> *When you understand this,*
> *You see that you are nothing.*
> *And being nothing,*
> *You are everything.*
> *That is all.*
>
> —KALU RINPOCHE

# Finding the Natural Mini-meditations in Your Own Life

Each day we all have dozens of opportunities for short, homegrown, natural meditations to help bring us in closer contact with
reality and insight into the truth of what is. This is one such sim-

ple, natural meditation. You don't really need a beach chair for the following mini-meditation. You can do it anywhere.

### BEACH CHAIR MEDITATION

*Lean back in a comfy beach chair*
*or chaise longue, with legs outstretched,*
*and totally relax.*
*Let go of body and mind;*
*let go, and let goodness*
*do it.*

*At poolside, or on your patio or porch;*
*in a garden*
*or on the beach;*
*raise your gaze,*
*open your eyes and heart and mind.*
*Elevate the scope of global,*
*three-hundred-and-sixty-degree panoramic awareness.*

*Simply relax*
*and watch the rolling waves*
*of sea or river,*
*or the clouds pass by*
*while the mind unfurls,*
*as the soul unfolds*
*and the infinite sky opens up*
*revealing the joy of meditation.*

In your own life, try to find more of these organic little meditations that you already know how to do, but have not yet thought of as meditation per se. Enjoy them daily.

# MAINTAINING THE VIEW
# IN TIMES OF CRISIS

For all of us, there are times when it becomes particularly difficult to maintain the view. We can get caught up in our own patterns and lose sight of reality. Sometimes life is hard. We have financial problems, family problems, personal problems. It's easy to say that everything is an illusion, but when it's your child who is crying, your parent who is ill, or your lover who is leaving, this can be almost too much to handle. Maintaining one's perspective, one's overarching view of reality, under difficult conditions can be a challenge even for meditation masters.

In Tibet, there are ancient tantric training practices specifically designed to help practitioners keep their perspective and stay in the view. Some of the ancient practices may seem fairly outlandish to our Western way of thinking. For example, in Asia of old, people would meditate in terrifying graveyards, which were often filled with pieces of bone or even bodies being eaten by wild animals. In Tibet, we still find the custom of sky burial. When I visited a mountaintop sky burial site there, I expected to find windswept bones among an ancient circle of stones, perhaps watched over by a half-crazed old caretaker. What I found instead was an eighteen-year-old kid with a hatchet, whose job it was to cut up the corpses. He was proud to show me one of his treasured possessions, a postcard some tourist had given him of the Empire State Building.

I don't mean to suggest that anyone seeking enlightenment

ought to take up the practice of graveyard meditation. However, let's understand that graveyard practice and others like it are simply trainings in facing one's fears while maintaining mindfulness, balance, and overview. Often in the process of facing our fears, we discover that what we fear often isn't really so very frightening. Each day we all have our own demons to face. These demons can take many forms—demands from a tyrannical employer; rejection from a hurtful mate; unconscious wounds and compulsions; stress caused by a pressing deadline. Learning to maintain mindfulness and perspective when we are facing personal upheaval is extraordinarily relevant to these modern times.

The more we can train ourselves and learn how to maintain mindfulness and "hang in there" even for the briefest of moments, the more we mature and grow in breadth and depth. We don't need to hang out in ghostly cemeteries at night to find things that frighten us. We face such situations every day. Sometimes it is a particularly disturbing person whom we are afraid to touch or reach out to. Sometimes it's something as simple as not wanting to make an unpleasant phone call because we fear what we will hear. At other times it's facing the challenge of a genuine life-and-death problem.

We train in maintaining the view in times of crisis so we learn not to shut our eyes and avoid reality or responsibility. It's too easy to rely on fears, denial, and other defense mechanisms to shield us from life's painful moments. Maintaining the view helps us open our constricted minds and tender hearts, allowing the world in rather than walling it out.

We can train ourselves by intentionally facing some of the things we fear. We can duplicate some of the benefits of tantric graveyard meditations by visiting or volunteering in places that make us nervous—such as hospitals, emergency wards, nursing homes, homeless shelters—and maintaining meditative mindfulness and self-awareness as we face what we fear. This is another application of the tonglen practice of breathing in unwanted circumstances and difficulties, rather than always pushing them away. Facing our fears and anxieties is a way of using painful emotions to work any and all situations. In this meditation training, we use passions, illness, crisis, and conflict to cultivate wisdom, compassion, understanding, and fearless courage. In this way we can actually purify our habitual, unsatisfying cravings and aversions (I like, I don't like; I want, I don't want). Thus we loosen the grip of our negative patterns and karmic propensities, opening the way for a more open, accepting, and joyful love of life.

There are three principles, or methods, for maintaining the view in difficult circumstances:

1. Simply be present, fully there, without judgment or prejudice, with whatever occurs. Again and again, use mindfulness to see whatever it is, just as it is. Just see what's there.

2. Try to see difficult circumstances and happenings as bad-tasting medicine or learning experiences. Look at the reality of the situation without resistance, struggle, aversion, or avoidance. Try the tonglen practice of breathing in and willingly assuming the burden. Remember that everything is grist for the mill of awareness. The particular difficulty can transform your awareness, right now.

3. Recognize whatever arises as pure energy, like a magical display or projection of awareness and wisdom itself. It is part of the entire mandala of wholeness and integral being. Enjoy the spectacle; watch the show; observe the parade with its dramatic and colorful floats. Observe the play of light and shadow. Here before you is the natural great perfection of things just as they are.

# CONSCIOUS LIVING, CONSCIOUS DYING

*Now when the bardo of dying dawns upon
    me,
I will abandon all grasping, yearning and
    attachment,
Enter undistracted into clear awareness of the
    teaching,
And eject my consciousness into the space of
    unborn
Awareness.
As I leave this compound body of flesh and
    blood
I will know it to be a transitory illusion.*

—PADMA SAMBHAVA,
IN *THE TIBETAN BOOK OF THE DEAD*

In Tibetan teachings, death is but another moment during which
to practice mindfulness. Remembering the inevitability of our
own death—addressing the unavoidable fact of our own mortality
and the impermanence of all things—can be the most liberating of
meditations. It introduces the reality of how things actually are,
helps loosen gross egotism, attachment, and short-sightedness—
and places our lives in proper perspective.

Death is a mirror, which reflects and illumines both the vanity
and the meaning of our lives. Death is the moment of truth, when
we come face to face with reality. For all of us, it is also a moment
of opportunity when we can realize our true original self-nature.
Death is more certain than love and more surely in store for each
of us than either ill health or old age. Perennial wisdom tells us that
we would do well to prepare for our demise, and thus be better
prepared to live, as well as die, in an enlightened manner.

It is said that at death, two things count: whatever we have
done in our lives, and the state of mind we are in at the moment
of death. These two factors determine what ensues. Buddha
taught that the actual experience at the time of death is crucial
regarding the next rebirth, and that at the actual moment of

death, extraordinarily profound spiritual experiences occur, providing a gateway to great liberation. Therefore, the physical atmosphere and states of mind of those surrounding someone who is dying are extremely important; peace, comfort, gentleness, love, acceptance, and harmony help usher the deceased onward in the best possible manner.

Traditionally in Tibet, the *Bardo Thodol,* which we know as *The Tibetan Book of the Dead,* is read at the bedside while someone is dying, and for several days thereafter. It is a guided meditation read aloud, usually by a lama, to help direct the dead and dying through the various transitional bardo states. This marvelous ancient work is a wisdom scripture that helps lead us to freedom and enlightenment through recognition of the clear light of reality at the time of death and afterward. It also reveals how to recognize and realize the clear light (the luminous innate quality of natural mind) within each of us, in this very life. Although ostensibly written to provide comfort, guidance, and liberation-through-hearing to the dead and dying, the *Bardo Thodol* shows us how to live, for each and every moment is both a birth and a death.

Bardo is a Tibetan word that means "in between" or "in transition." It is taught that there are six bardo states in all, each one of which provides unique opportunities. Three of these bardos occur while we are still alive: *the bardo of this life* covers the entire period from our birth up to our death; *the bardo of meditation* refers to the meditative state when we are able to recognize our Buddha-nature; and *the bardo of dreaming,* which occurs while we are sleeping and which can also be used to train the mind.

The other three bardo states, covering the time between death and rebirth, are the primary focus of *The Tibetan Book of the Dead.*

## The Bardo of Dying

This bardo refers to the process of dying itself. In Tibet, dying is seen as a process of purification, for we are returning to the clear light, to our intrinsic natural state of ground luminosity—dissolving in it. At the moment of death, this clear light of reality dawns for everyone. This is your own radiant nature, sometimes known as Rigpa—enlightened wakefulness. However, to take advantage of this "moment of truth," to gain liberation, you must be prepared. Otherwise it will too swiftly pass by. Because most of us are still so connected to the habits and behavior patterns we have established in life, we don't recognize ground luminosity for what it is. We react inappropriately and unconsciously. Instead of making a leap of faith and surrendering to this luminosity, we hold back. Thus the moment passes. Kalu Rinpoche's instructions for that moment of ground luminosity were: "Let go of body and mind, and dissolve in the clear light of inner luminosity. Recognize the dawn of clear light and be liberated in that very instant. Go beyond the snares of dualism, life and death."

My teachers say that when we miss that moment of liberation-through-recognition, we enter into a state that is similar to being totally oblivious, unconscious—a deep dreamless sleep that lasts for several days. Then the karmic winds assert themselves, and the next bardo begins.

## The Bardo of Dharmata (Reality)

In this second bardo state after death, we have another opportunity to gain liberation. Kalu Rinpoche used to teach that the important thing to remember is that, much like a dream, everything you see is the creation of your own mind and can be changed just as we can awaken within our dreams and alter them. In this state, it is as if we are dreaming, and nothing can really harm us. Liberation can occur if we are able to erase resistance and doubts, let go, and surrender to the innate luminosity of the natural mind. If we cannot do that, then the next bardo stage inexorably begins.

## The Bardo of Becoming

In this third bardo state after death, our perceptions are returning. We again have likes and dislikes, and we are drawn to the kinds of places and people that are familiar. As our attachments, passions, and karmic propensities begin to assert themselves, we are moving closer to rebirth. At this point, we would do well to turn our minds toward the unique intentions of the Bodhisattva to benefit and serve all beings without exception. Free from the snares of attraction and repulsion, we must seek an opportune environment to fulfill the Bodhisattva Vow. When you are in this bardo state, through fearless courage and pure vision, go beyond and abandon your attraction and desire to the male and female coming together in sexual union. Rather, perceive this loving couple, who will be your new parents, as a Buddha couple—Mr. and Mrs. Wisdom and Compassion. Gracefully enter that human temple and find your new life.

## Living Up to Death: A Meditation

We all have to face issues of life and death. Whether we face them in the aging of an elder or in the birth of a child, birth and death are part of life. Philosophy, science, religion, the arts—all address the issues of birth and death, death or rebirth. Don't we all wonder what happens when we die? Is death simply our end? What does that mean for us? How can we make our own lives more meaningful?

There are many religions and cultures, yet in many ways they all share at least one common principle: All have rites, rituals, and specialists for dealing with death and dying. These rites give us solace and security in the face of the tenuousness and insecurity of existence. Do we go on? Do we just come to an abrupt end? Is there nothing more? What about heaven? Hell? Is there an afterlife? Will we face God or karma? Truth or consequences? How can we know any of this for certain? Can it be verified, or is it just myth and imagination that we are asked to believe in and trust? Are we to believe the people who say they have returned from near-death experiences? Are we to believe Edgar Cayce and the other psychics? Are we to believe the incarnate lamas, many of whom say they remember their past lives and seem to have some kind of conscious control over the process—as if evolving, by choice, through the different grades of life's spiritual school? How can we know? Who knows?

Buddhists have long realized that contemplating one's own mortality helps us focus and prioritize. The spiritual life, the journey of awakening and making sense out of our lives while learning to love, is actually as much a matter of life as it is of death. The tenuousness of life itself helps us be totally awake in the present moment.

What Tibetan Buddhism offers, along with its pragmatic, ethical, here-and-now life teachings, is a way of dealing with the death experience itself—a way of facing death in the present moment. This training can vastly help us deal with the reality of the moment of death. In so doing, we become far more appreciative, tender, and mindful of the richness and fullness of each moment of life, made all the more poignant because of its impermanence.

By learning to let go in this life, we learn to live each moment without regrets. We learn to make each decision without regret. Each decision becomes the right decision. By learning to let go in this life, we relinquish our grudges, gain forgiveness, and unburden ourselves of resentment, bitterness, and hostility. In this way, we find closure and are able to let our old hang-ups, hurts, and frozen patterns die. This is how we die without regrets, while learning to live anew. In this moment. Breath by breath. Here is a meditation that helps us do that:


Take a deep breath and completely relax. Let everything settle. Be totally present, naturally present, effortlessly present. You are just sitting for one moment, one eternal instant at a time. Don't miss it. This is the only moment, right now.

Just sense everything, as it is. Be present, aware, wakeful, and relaxed.

Open to effortless presence, pure awareness. Total presence. Aware of awareness itself, a luminous, centerless awareness here and now. Let everything proceed effortlessly, transparently. Let go of control, manipulation, and judgment.

With each breath, let go just a little more. With each exhalation, let go, relax, open, and center a little more deeply. Each exhalation is like a little minideath. Simply attend to the exhalation. Inhale and exhale and with each out-breath, let go a little more. Let go of someone or something you may be holding onto. With each exhalation, let go a little more. Release a little more . . . loosen the knots in your psyche. Let go. Drop everything. Release that little tension in the shoulders, breathe it out. Breathe out that thought bubble, that memory, and let it go, go, go, go . . .

Let go of the out-breath. Die a little with each exhalation. Die into the present moment. Whatever sensations you may feel, let go of them. Drop your body; let go of your mind; let go of your thoughts and personality. Drop it all. Let go. Let go of your self-image, your house, possessions, plans, and career. Let it go. Everything is perfectly resolved in the unborn and undying natural mind.

Let go of any attempts to control the mind. With each exhalation, let it go. Push the clutch of spiritual detachment and disengage your habitual gears. With each exhalation, let go of one more thing—whatever comes to mind: a sensation, an emotion, a feeling, a relationship, a person, a fear, a possession. Breath by breath, fleeting moment by fleeting moment—simply let go. Get used to evolving, transforming, passing on without resistance, without clinging and attachment. Breath by breath, let go. Let all this illusory, dreamlike phenomena pass by.

Breath by breath, forgive others. Forgive those from the past—those with whom you no longer have contact, as well as those who are still around you. Forgive yourself. Accept others for what they are. Accept yourself totally. Let go and let be. This is wisdom working.

Breath by breath, let go of fear, expectation, anger, regret, cravings, frustration, fatigue. Let go of the need for approval. Let go of old judgments and opinions. Die to all that, and fly free. Soar in the freedom of desirelessness.

Let go. Let be. See through everything and be free, complete, luminous, at home—at ease.

With this kind of meditation, the subtle layers of who we are start to sort themselves out, and we go more deeply into the natural state—the naked state of authentic being. This is here-and-now transformation. Spiritual rebirth.

# DREAM YOGA:
# WAKING UP FROM LIFE'S DELUSION

*We practice illusory practice in an illusory way, in order to reach illusory enlightenment and deliver all illusory beings from illusory suffering.*

—TWELFTH-CENTURY TIBETAN
MASTER KHYUNGPO NALJYOR

*I dreamt that I was a butterfly, flitting around in the sky; then I awoke. Now I wonder: Am I a man who dreamt of being a butterfly, or am I butterfly dreaming that I am a man?*

—CHUANG TSU

Although all Buddhist teachers stress the transitory, dreamlike, and ephemeral nature of this world, the practice of dream yoga is unique to Tibetan Buddhism. This is a marvelous way to bring awareness training into our sleeping as well as our waking hours. Dream yoga is somewhat similar to what Western psychology has recently begun to call lucid dreaming.

Lucid dreaming refers to the ability to "wake up"—make conscious choices—within a dream while remaining asleep. Within the dream we can transform the circumstances and ourselves into anything we can imagine. This can be an extraordinarily meaningful and profound real-life experience. The dream state is one of the bardos. Remember that what we perceive in a dream might be as real as the things we see reflected in a mirror. Many psychic powers, including clairvoyance and recall of past lives, can be developed through these sort of esoteric practices on the border between reality and illusion.

Let's say for example, that Nancy is dreaming that she and her mother are having one of their recurrent arguments in a fast-moving car. If Nancy were experienced in lucid dreaming, she might be able to change her dream. For example, Nancy might say to her mother, "We are driving too quickly. Let's stop arguing; let's stop and get some ice cream and then go fly over the rainbow. We can eat our ice cream on a beach in Hawaii." Although Nancy would be aware that she is asleep and dreaming, she would still be able to make the choice to change a little nightmare into a loving, seaside picnic.

Tibetans call this "seizing the dream." By seizing our dreams, we can learn to play with and change the outcome of our dreams in ways that help us to realize the insubstantial and dreamlike nature of all of our experiences. We take hold of the dream, rather than the dream having a hold over us.

Tibetan dream yoga exercises can vastly help us to achieve certain benefits for both self and others. By seizing a dream we can perform spiritual activities, multiply our bodies, as well as go to pure realms of existence to receive teachings and blessings from Buddhas, transcendent Bodhisattvas, and saintly sages. In this way we train to master altered states and different ways of being, including astral travel and other out-of-body experiences; for in dreams we are less encumbered by our corporeal form, moving through the lighter, more subtle "mental body" or "illusory light-body."

Lucid dreaming has another significant purpose: The lessons we learn from dreams often carry over into our waking life. Since our psyche in dreams is so much more light and sensitive and free from the sheath of gross corporeality, it is more profoundly open to out-of-this-world experiences, blessings, teachings, and transformative transmissions, healings, initiations, and revelations. Dream yoga provides valuable lessons in facing fear, staying awake, and making conscious choices that will serve us in the bardo states that take place after death and before rebirth. We learn how to die more consciously and to awaken in the bardo state after death; thus, we can more intentionally and consciously choose and direct our re-birth.

Everyone has lucid dreams, but we don't always recognize them or remember them. You can start trying to become more conscious about your dreams with the simple act of keeping a dream journal by the side of your bed and recalling your dreams as soon as you wake each morning. When I first did this, I discovered that the more I wrote down, the more dream-material kept pouring out of my subconscious mind.

In the traditional Tibetan lama-training retreat, we would sleep sitting up all night in a meditation box, which is like a seat, instead of sleeping in a bed. With repeatedly chanted Tibetan prayers and affirmations, we would resolve to awaken within the dream and know it as a dream. With guidance from my teachers, even I was able to remember more and more dreams every night and to learn from them. In some instances I was even able to get some indication of future events and to understand certain signs, portents, and omens. I was able to better see for myself how similar are all the various bardos, including living, dreaming, and dying.

The important thing to remember is that lucid dreaming is a spiritual practice. It is not meant to be a parlor trick or a way to psychically predict whether certain stocks are going up or down. Dream yoga is a spiritual training and a powerful, experiential way of pointing out the insubstantial, malleable, dreamlike nature of reality. By learning to be aware in our dreams, we prepare ourselves for more moment-to-moment awareness in daily life. By transforming our dreams, we train in spiritual transformation. Let's put on our natural night-lights. Merrily, merrily, merrily, merrily—we can find out for ourselves exactly to what extent—"life is but a dream."

# *Dream Yoga: A Meditation*

Before retiring at night, assume a meditative, prayerful posture
and affirm your intentions by chanting:

> For the welfare and well-being of the world
> And the sake of spiritual awakening
> May I seize my dreams and awaken within them
> And realize the true nature of mind and all things.

This can be repeated three or more times to plant the seed
and intentionally set up the conditions to awaken within your
dreams, without waking from sleep.

After reciting this chant, lie down. Relax; breathe. Stay calm
and tranquil. Place your head as if in the peaceful Buddha's
warm, soft, accepting, welcoming lap. Visualize yourself actually
lying down with your head in the lap of the orange-robed,
seated, cross-legged Buddha.

> Then close your eyes. Take a rest.
> Drop all the day's tensions, activities, and memories.
> Relax.
> Rest peacefully.
> Rest in light.
> Rest your weary heart and mind, body and soul.
> Gaze into the shimmering dark light behind your eye-
> lids.
> To illumine your mind, visualize a shining white letter
> A, there before your eyes,
> glowing like a luminous full moon.
> Concentrate on that white light. Focus on it.
> Dissolve gradually into that light.
> Enter into the inner light, and spontaneously awaken
> in the perfectly luminous, clear, dream light.
> Know everything is like a dream.

Let it go as it goes
and be as it is,
in the natural Great Perfection,
the radiant light
of the natural mind.

# RIGHT CONCENTRATION

## *The Joy of Meditation*

*O let us live in joy, in love amongst those who hate! Among men who hate, let us live in love.*

*O let us live in joy, in health amongst those who are ill! Among men who are ill, let us live in health.*

*O let us live in joy, in peace amongst those who struggle! Among men who struggle, let us live in peace.*

*O let us live in joy, although having nothing! In joy let us live like spirits of light!*

—FROM THE DHAMMAPADA
(SAYINGS OF THE BUDDHA),
TRANSLATED BY JUAN MASCARO

The Buddha said that he experienced indescribable bliss, rapture, peace, and transcendence through concentration and that you can too. Right Concentration, the final step on the Noble Eight-Fold Path, involves more than the simple act of focusing. After all, a cat is able to focus unwaveringly on a mouse hole for hours. Right Concentration implies a unification of spiritual intentionality, focus, mental discipline, energy, and attention. In Right Concentration we skillfully collect and harness all of our energy so that every part of our being is integrated and focused, working together toward our goal of enlightenment. Once you have arrived at this point, concentration in this sense is not forced, restricted, or fixated, but instead rests naturally where it is placed.

Learning how to practice Right Concentration is a little like finding your balance. Remember when you were a child and someone taught you how to ride a bicycle. At first it seemed impossible, and all you could do was wobble and hope for the best. Then eventually you caught on, and the balance became an integral part of you. The same thing is true of concentration.

Buddha taught that in order to concentrate we need a combination of Right Effort and Right Mindfulness. Concentration thus integrates all of the factors and aspects of mindful awareness into a coherent and vividly present, functioning whole. Right Concentration involves recollection, remindfulness, vigilance, alertness, and perseverance; it thus brings us full circle back to the wisdom of Right View and authentic understanding.

## ATTENTION, ATTENTION, ATTENTION

Many years ago, a Zen master was on her deathbed. All the monks, nuns, and disciples respectfully came to ask for her final word. "What," they questioned, "is your final instruction to us? What did you learn in your life? What is the secret of Zen?" She just said one word, "Attention."

The disciples weren't satisfied. They wanted a death poem, a meaningful story, or a wisdom sutra. So they asked again, "What is the most essential secret? What's the main practice? What's Buddha?"

And again, she answered, "Attention."

The disciples became confused. It still wasn't enough. They wanted her to say more, like "pay attention to your teacher," or "pay attention to the Buddha and the Dharma." So they asked again.

"Before you breathe your last, tell us what to do with attention. Tell us what is the essence, how to meet the Buddha?"

You know what she said. "Attention."

Simone Weil defined prayer as "absolutely unmixed attention." This definition works for concentration and meditation as well. It means being totally in the moment and aware of it, at one with everything and at peace with yourself. These are precious moments. We've all had momentary glimpses of what this sense of "oneness" can be. Perhaps when we are playing with a child or grandchild. Perhaps when we are playing with a dog or cat. Many of us have had the experience of listening to music and suddenly feeling a sense of everything coming together. Instead of listening to the music for a brief moment, we are the music. Some people feel that same degree of concentrated oneness during orgasm. These moments feel perfect because we are perfectly, unself-consciously present, focused, and aware—with all the parts in agreement. Suddenly everything feels just right. The right person in the right place at the right time.

When natural concentration unites with the heart of non-dual awareness it achieves a oneness and completeness in which everything fits together. We don't feel scattered; we are not caught up in many disjointed activities and thoughts. We are *there*. There is no separation between self and other, between man and God, between heaven and earth. This is what mystics describe as the joining of heaven and earth, the union of the sacred and mundane. Concentration and meditative awareness implies coming home to that and getting used to being there, naturally. One has arrived at last. Whew!

# MAKING A COMMITMENT TO CONCENTRATION

*Continuity is the secret of success.*

—S. N. GOENKA

Early on in my training in India, our teacher would have us take a vow to sit in meditation, *without moving,* for an hour, or two, or even three. It was hard to do this—not only because of the normal itches, pains, and sensations that arise—but because there were so many flies in the area. They had the annoying habit of landing on our faces, poking around, and having a bite to eat. Resisting movement certainly called for unprecedented self-discipline and concentration on my part.

In Goenka's ten- and twenty-day silent Vipassana meditation courses, we had twelve one-hour sitting periods every day. Three of them were "vow hours," one each in the morning, afternoon, and evening. The sangha atmosphere was very supportive. You knew that if you moved, it would ripple through almost everyone. No one wanted to be the one who disturbed the calm surface of concentration with even a tiny wave of motion.

Sometimes one hour would progress to two. The *real* fanatics, including my girlfriend, Suil, would go at midnight beneath the bodhi tree with Goenka where they would sit, motionless, for up to three hours at a time. By that time, I had almost concluded, "I'm not so sure this is good for me. It's starting to feel weird. Soon we'll just die; we won't move at all, and then we will have accomplished the goal!"

Some teachings say that when meditating, "Be like a stick of wood." There's a Tibetan teaching that says, "Sit like a tent peg driven into the earth." I find it more poetic to say, "Sit like a mountain." Ideally in meditation we are centered and well balanced while remaining flexible and relaxed too.

A refinement of our group vow hour—a variation on the theme of nonmovement and nondistraction—had us sitting in rows facing each other with eyes half open and slightly lowered. It was not to look into each other's eyes, nor to check on one another. This practice helped us sit still longer and concentrate more intensely. The synergy of our group mind kept us going, individually and collectively. In that Buddhist boot camp this was one way to train Olympic meditators and spiritual athletes.

Concentration can be developed to such a high degree that we achieve advanced states where the mind is so one-pointedly absorbed that we are for a time beyond thought, feelings, pain, external stimuli, or sensory perception of any kind. This is like a profound mystic trance. One reaches these states—traditionally called infinite consciousness, infinite light, boundless bliss, and beyond existence—through long and intensive training. There are yogis whose concentrative absorptions are so intense that they are absolutely impervious to external stimuli—yet this alone is not enlightenment.

In order to attain enlightenment, this laser beam–like concentrated attention must be directed toward insight and wisdom practices. Although concentration alone does not guarantee enlightenment, the practice of Right Concentration can put wings on the practice of insight meditation. Some spiritual virtuosos are able to reach such intense levels of concentration that when they apply it to their insight practice, the attention is focused like a blowtorch or laser beam instead of simple lamplight.

## THE FIVE T'S OF CONCENTRATION

During meditation, if we want to settle down and concentrate, we must work with our thoughts and feelings. It becomes easier if we give our discursive mind something to do. To do this, we assign the restless small mind the concrete task of focusing on an object of concentration. We do this so that the holy person of innate awareness that is within each of us can rest at ease in the broader view or natural mind.

The ability to focus and intentionally bring back our wandering attention over and over again is at the root of mental discipline, willpower, and even character development. Any meditation training can be understood according to what I like to call the Five T's.

## 1. Taming
For a moment, think of your restless, discursive mind as a beautiful wild mustang. First it must be tame enough to get it into the corral. Your mind must be willing to at least enter the arena of meditation.

## 2. Training
We teach the mustang to lose its fear of the unfamiliar. It will learn to give up bucking and thrashing in return for the safety of a warm, safe haven. Eventually it will be able to gallop freely at full speed, and its movements will have purpose and meaning. But for now it is learning to walk on a tight rein. In meditation we train the restless mind to slow down and relax.

## 3. Testing
We must work with the mustang; we have to take it out and ride it. What happens when it's exposed to outside influences, distractions, noises, temptation? Will it be able to maintain its poise and disciplined attention? In developing our awareness practice, we test whether we can maintain our mindfulness and concentration when we move away from the meditation room into the outside world.

## 4. Transforming
The mustang has been transformed. It is now able to carry its owner long distances at any speed. In meditation we are no longer controlled by our thoughts; instead we can use the mind's unique abilities for our own higher purposes. We have tapped into the inexhaustible power of mind.

## 5. Transcendence
In transcendence the rider and the horse become as one. There is no longer a separate "you" who has to tame, train, or test "it." We realize oneness, completeness, and harmony with the universe. Concentration practice helps bring us back to that unified wholeness at our source. We can go with the flow of things just as they

are, without resistance or clinging, knowing that we are part of the infinite flow . . . And that wherever we may go, it goes with us.

# Concentration Exercises

We can use just about anything as an object of concentration. Traditional centering devices include mantras, candles, prayers, or visualizations. We could also choose to concentrate on a vase, a flower, or any other object near at hand. Over the years many Christians have read *The Way of the Pilgrim,* a charming old book that tells of a wandering Russian seeker who is searching the countryside trying to learn how to pray without ceasing. Extended prayer is but another example of concentration leading to transcendence.

For our purposes, I have found that the easiest, most tried and true concentration object is the breath. The breath, which often accurately reflects our mood and our physical being, can hold our interest, while allowing for some flexibility. When we are excited, we breath rapidly; as we relax, our breathing becomes slower and more relaxed. When the mind becomes quiet, the breath becomes quiet.

The first thing we need to do with our concentration device or object is to locate it. If we were to use a mantra, for example, we would need to remember the mantra, to call it to mind. With the breath, we find it and focus on it by locating the exact spot above the lip where the breath hits the base of the nostrils. Finding the physical sensation of our breath at that spot helps us find ourselves in the present moment. This is an experience of reality right now. Returning to reality and *what is* time and time again helps us *stay* in the present moment. This is a way to genuinely connect to the real, tangible world. Such a connection cultivates a sane and balanced response to life.

The following series of six meditations are exercises for increasing your concentration and mental focus.

## 1. Breath Counting

We begin with breath counting. Remember that we expect the mind to wander. By numbering each breath one through ten, we keep bringing the mind back to the task at hand—focusing and staying in the moment.

Begin as always by taking your seat. Relax and let go of anxieties, preoccupations, and ordinary concerns. Breathe. Let everything settle. Breathe. Let your body and mind become quiet.

When you are ready; when you feel as though you have fully arrived; when you feel centered and have collected yourself in this place—in this moment—on your seat, on the spot, on the dot, start:

Inhaling, count one to yourself. Exhaling, count two.

Inhaling, count three. Exhaling, count four.

Inhaling, count five. Exhaling, count six.

Continue this up to ten. Then start again: Inhaling, count one. Exhaling, count two. Inhaling, count three. Exhaling, count four. Let everything else go. Let it go as it goes, let it be as it is. Let go. Let be. *Relax.*

Keep counting. Watch the breath. Concentrate only on one thing: counting the inhalations and exhalations. Try to get to ten without losing the count. How far did you get this time?

When you lose it, start again: Inhaling, count one; exhaling, count two. It is so simple, yet staying with it is not so easy. When your attention wanders, simply notice this habitual tendency of your attention to forget what you are doing and be carried away by distractions—and bring it back to breath counting.

Don't count out loud. Count with your mind, but say it to yourself. Note the number. Take notice of each breath. Label it with a number: one, with inhalation; two, with exhalation; and so on. Counting will help. Concentrate. Focus. Stay with the breath. Let everything else go. Calm the heart and mind, settle the energy, the breath, the body. Let the breath be more naturally quiet. As the mind gets quiet, the breath gets quiet, energy harmonizes and the heart decontracts, unfurls, and opens up.

Keep counting: One, two, three, four, five, six, seven, eight, nine, ten. Very good.

Start again. Simple is beautiful. One, two, three, four, five, six, seven, eight, nine, ten.

Let everything else go as it goes, just like a river flowing by with you on the riverbank counting the waves—large clear repetitive waves of breath, easy to count.

Inhalation, one. Exhalation, two.

Focus one-pointedly, sharpening the attention by observing nothing else but the counting, the counted number. Paying intense attention, count the breath. Each breath counts.

Here there is nothing more to understand, to figure out, to achieve, to do or undo. Just counting. Just sitting. Just being. One through ten and back again. A complete circle. One through ten and back again. Excellent. Perfect.

---

*Remember, we are building the concentration muscle, exercising our powers of concentration.*

An editor who was working on this book tried this breath counting exercise, and reported back, with some surprise, that within five breaths, everything had really slowed down for her. That's a good example of how quickly these exercises begin to have an effect. Slugger Hank Aaron said he could count the individual laces on a fast-pitched ball coming toward him because intense concentration slowed everything down and brought it into sharp focus.

The important thing to remember is that this is a training. We are honing and developing our capacity to concentrate. Think of it like muscle-building. Right concentration is serene concentration. We build our concentration until it is enough to allow us to penetrate further into the practice of wisdom and insight. In this case, it doesn't mean how long you can control your mind without having a thought. That's mere mind control, not Buddhist meditation. Concentration is being fully present with what is, whatever is. It means being right there, not scattered; able to keep your total attention on your task. When your concentration abilities are fully developed to their farthest reach, you can achieve super focus, a complete absorption, total *oneness*.

---

## 2. AWARENESS OF BREATHING

Awareness is an interesting thing. When we first learned how to drive a car, many of us were worried that we would never be able to simultaneously coordinate and be aware of all the many things that driving entails—watching the road in front, watching the rearview mirror, being conscious of the movement of traffic on the left and right. Eventually we learned how to do all those things at once. That's because although your mind can have only one thought at a time, awareness can take in much more. Focusing your mind through concentrative exercise can really access and free up more and more of your intrinsic awareness. By placing your mind on breathing, awareness becomes heightened and brighter. It's like using a magnifying glass to focus the sun's rays to start a fire.

Once we are accustomed to Breath Counting, we are ready to move on to a more natural meditation. This is called Awareness or Mindfulness of Breathing. Because we have trained in breath counting, we can now keep track of each individual breath. Now the training becomes more subtle, and we begin to broaden slightly our concentration. In this exercise we see whether we can keep our mind on the breath without the crutch of mental counting. We watch and feel our breaths until we seem to become our breaths, and nothing else.

This is natural meditation. We are already breathing. Now, let's simply become aware of it—aware of what is already going on—right here and now. Just breathing, natural breathing, not forced or manipulated in any way.

Arrive, collect yourself. Let the breath settle.

Let the body settle, let the mind settle, let the energy settle.

Let everything settle in its own place, in its own way, in its own time—naturally at home and at ease. Settle down. Settle in. Yield. Soften, relax, enjoy. Simplify things by simplifying the mind. Arrive.

Gather your attention. Without counting, focus on breathing. Merely be aware of breathing. Mindful of the entire breathing process. Inhaling and exhaling. Closely observe each breath.

Direct your attention to your nostrils. Breathing through your nose, feel the air going in and out at the nostrils. Feel the sensation of the flowing air. Concentrate at the base of the nostrils, on the upper lip right where the air comes in and out. Exaggerate your breathing a little if you're trying for the first time to perceive that tactile sensation.

Arrest your attention at that very spot. Feel the actual sensation right now, and rest your mind there. Place your attention there. Focus on that sensation, on that spot in the nostrils as the breath moves in and out.

Focus. Pay attention. Concentrate. Unmoving, stabilize the mind. Place it right there, one-pointedly.

Sharpen your attention. Keep the point of attention on that very spot like a sharpened pencil point on a simple small spot on a piece of paper. The breath is almost like a saw moving in and out. The saw moves, but the place where the saw meets the wood is stable. Be like the good carpenter, concentrating on that very spot where the teeth of the saw are cutting the wood. Keep the mind on that in-and-out motion of the breath as it contacts the upper lip and base of the nostrils.

Inevitably the mind wanders. Rather than letting it mindlessly drift away into distraction, bring it back. With total presence of mind, rather than absentmindedly, be aware of the times when attention wanders and keep bringing it back.

Breathing centers us. It calms the mind and body, brings clarity and joy, and simplifies everything. When the attention wanders, just gently tug on the leash of attention as you would with a straying pet. Stay alert. Remind yourself to stay in place. Remindfulness is everything. Don't forget. Remain collected.

Gather your energy one-pointedly on this spot to hone your awareness, sharpen your focus, heighten your concentration. Stay with it. Rest right there, right here . . . now.

The breath, which is always present, helps connect us to present reality. We are not creating fantasies. While we are concentrating, we're learning to pay attention to how things actually are. Remember: Things as they are is the Buddhist definition of reality.

Don't be deceived by momentary feelings of failure when the mind wanders. The mind *will* wander; thought bubbles *will* arise and distract us. Simply remember to bring the attention back.

We are exercising and strengthening the muscle of mindfulness through this gentle tugging on the leash of attention and reminding ourselves to keep doing what we are doing. We recollect precisely what we are doing, and bring the attention back again and again to the object of concentration, the single point at the base of the nostrils. This is our meditation practice: We continually bring the attention back and keep it there, bring it back, and keep it there. We restrict the scope of activity to just that place. This is concentrative meditation.

Later we will use the sharpened tool of refined awareness to cut through illusion, to penetrate reality, while our view becomes more panoramic and less restricted. This is mind-training. We're gaining more discernment, penetration, and insight. Wisdom.

## 3. WALKING MEDITATION

In the previous two exercises, we found that we can be aware of our breathing and stay with that awareness while we are sitting. We see that we can sustain and hone our attention. Now we learn to bring that awareness with us into movement. In this walking exercise, we start to bring awareness more broadly into everyday life. Instead of sitting quietly and watching the breath, we are beginning to get more in touch with our body, our energy, and the earth; we are directly experiencing our connection to it. This kind of meditation further helps ground us in reality. It also helps us get our energy moving. This is called meditation in action.

Stand at ease. Erect, balanced on both feet, relaxed; head up, eyes open and slightly lowered. Start walking very slowly. Step by step, treading the path of awakening by mindful walking.

Lift your right foot, move it forward slowly, place it down. Feel the weight shift in the center of your body onto that foot. Feel the floor.

Then lift the heel of the left foot, pick the foot up, move it forward slowly, place it down. Feel the floor; feel the center of gravity shift again in your hips onto the other foot. Lift the right foot, with heel first, and then the rest.

Break each step down into parts: lifting a foot, moving it forward, placing it down, feeling the shift of the center of gravity onto the next foot. Not walking automatically like a sleepwalker or automaton, but very consciously attending to every single movement. Feel the sensations, feel the floor, feel the step, feel the feet—each step a complete step on the path of wakefulness. It has been said that beneath each step on the path a flower grows.

Breathe naturally. Just walking, step by step. Just breathing, one breath at a time, attending to each step, paying attention with full attention; focusing on each step, while letting everything else go. Just walking. Just doing what one is doing, for once—totally involved, one hundred percent; really being there. One step at a time, treading the delightful path of enlightenment.

## 4. WALKING-BREATHING-SYNCHRONIZATION MEDITATION

Now we've learned Walking Meditation and Awareness of Breathing. Let's combine them. In this way we are beginning to challenge and test our training.

As you breathe in, raise your right foot and move forward; and as you place your right foot down, breathe out. Moving slowly, synchronize each step with the breath.

Breathe in, lifting your left foot; breathe out placing your left foot down.

Inhale lifting your right foot, exhale placing it down. Inhale lifting your left foot, exhale placing it down. Use the cadence of the natural breath—not trying to breathe faster or slower—with each of your steps synchronized with your breath. Place your full attention on walking. Just walking. Just breathing. Just being. This is enough, and more than enough. To just do what we're doing, and be what we are—this is the fullness of meditation, of essential being. Let the thoughts, feelings, and sounds go. Don't be distracted by the scenery. Just let the sights and sounds go by, let them wash over and pass through. Just walking—just right.

## 5. STANDING AND WALKING BACKWARD MEDITATION

Practicing this meditation heightens your presence of mind and brings you another step closer to razor-sharp awareness. As you project awareness backward, you are enhancing your wider, multidimensional, global awareness.

We begin this meditation by standing, solidly grounded and erect. As you will see now, even with your eyes closed, in this case, walking backward is really going forward on the path.

Stand, stand like a tree.
Relax, breathe, let everything go.
Erect, relaxed, feet planted firmly on earth.
Stand like a mountain.
Can you stand it?
Standing meditation. Not doing anything else. Just standing.
Just doing what you're doing, one hundred percent.
Just being. Standing firm in your truth.
What more could you ask for?
Natural breath, natural posture;
At ease and at home on earth.
Standing your ground. Just stand.

Now, take a small step backward. And another. And another. Inching backward. Turn on your taillights. Open your fourth eye in the back of your head, in your spine, behind your knees, in your heels. Project your awareness backward, but don't turn your head. Project your awareness backward until it's like a luminous sphere of awareness all around you. Walk very slowly backward. Follow a line if it helps, like a line on a tennis court, or a driveway, or a carpet, or the water's edge on a beach or lake shore. Walking backward in a straight line, step by step, traveling the path to enlightenment. Undoing the habit of rushing forward. Undoing the habit of getting anywhere. Reversing. Walk backward slowly, mindfully, with total attention. One step after another. Walking Backward Meditation.

Now to further heighten your concentration and vigilant attentiveness, close your eyes, and keep inching backward as slowly as you need to. One step after another. Use intuitive awareness to feel your way backward. Notice how much more vigilant and attentive we instantly become when there is a little danger or fear involved. Pay attention. Keep walking backward. Slowly. Just walking. Just breathing. Notice what comes up for you, while treading the path of awakening. This is also a trust exercise.

Now, slowly come to a stop. Finish the last step. Keep your eyes closed. Stand still. Just standing. Stand your ground. Stand firm. Stand in truth. You can stand it. It's easy to take. Take your stand. Stand up for yourself. Be outstanding in the field. Stand up and shout. Stand out from the crowd. Stand up for what you believe. Stand up for this very moment. This is it. When you are ready, open your eyes. Orient yourself slowly. Gently move your body, shake it out, relax. You deserve it. Stand up and smile.

By the way, this meditation is a great way to include children in your practice. See if they don't enjoy it.

## 6. CHEWING MEDITATION/
## CHEW THIS OVER.

Eating meditation is a marvelous way of putting ourselves in touch with nowness. This simple meditation with raisins can also be used with individual nuts or even tangerine sections. Later you can practice with all kinds of food, from a bowl of cereal to a plate of lasagna.

The first time I did this eating meditation, it tried my patience to the limit. I was accustomed to eating raisins by the handful, not one at a time. But I discovered that the chewing meditation can really slow us down and make us more aware of compulsive behavior. It helps you notice how your mind and body works. It helps us cultivate mindfulness and awareness in more varied situations. We start with individual raisins, but we can treat each forkful of food with the same care and reverence.

Start by taking three raisins in your right hand; one raisin for the Buddha, one for the Dharma, and one for the Sangha. Sit down, make yourself comfortable. Look at the raisins. Look at them as if you have never seen a raisin before. Turn them over. It's said that infinite Buddhas reside in each pore of your body. How many Buddhas can fit within one raisin? We're going to direct our total attention to these three raisins.

Pick up one raisin with your left hand. Examine it closely. Feel its texture. Notice its colors and whether it's dry or moist. Notice any old associations you may have with raisins, such as like or dislike, or indifference. Smell it. Bring it to your lips. Notice any feelings of anticipation you may have about eating it.

Are you in a hurry? Do you wish perhaps that you could pop all these raisins in your mouth? Just notice whatever comes up in relation to this tiny little dried grape. Take the raisin in your mouth and chew it as slowly, as meticulously, as carefully and as conscientiously as possible. Taste the actual taste of the raisin, but don't swallow it. Keep chewing. Notice how much you feel like swallowing. There is an impulse to swallow and get another one, but just keep chewing. Chew on that raisin until it becomes raisin juice. Chew and pay attention.

If your mind wanders, if you hear a sound, bring your mind back to the raisin. Don't look around. Place your attention back on chewing the raisin. Point your mind, direct your attention, focus your awareness intently, intensely—like a light beam, like a laser. One-pointedly, focus on the raisin, on the place where your teeth make contact with the raisin; feel it directly. No need to understand why or how or what is the meaning of raisins, of meditation or life for that matter. Just chew the raisin twenty or even one hundred times if possible, concentrating totally. Relax and enjoy the experience. Get the most out of it, as if this is the only food you're going to have all day. Chew it totally, appreciating and absorbing everything about it. Through total attention, extract the essence of every aspect of it—the taste, texture and so on. Just

keep chewing the raisin. Swallow it, and then just rest in the afterglow of this delicious experience.

Now slowly take the second raisin from your right hand with
your left and bring it up toward your mouth. Look at it. Smell it.
Feel it. Examine it. Resist the impulse to rush it into your mouth.
Simply notice those impulses. Then put it in your mouth and start
chewing it. If it were a *mouthful* of macrobiotic brown rice, we
would chew it a hundred times. We see how long we can make it
last. Simply pay attention to chewing the raisin while letting go of
everything else. This stabilizes and unifies our mind. Just doing
what we are doing, for a change. One hundred percent. Just sitting,
and just eating. How delightful! How delicious.

Now you take the third raisin and do your own meditation on
it. A new raisin, a new experience. How is it different from the
other two? Does it look the same? Does it taste the same? Maybe
it's sweeter. Maybe less startling. Where did your attention go?
Bring it back. Concentrate.

This is a pragmatic example of meditation practice. We master
meditative awareness by doing it again and again. It's always different, it's always fresh, it always develops and reveals new discoveries. We are exercising the muscles of awareness, directing our
attention to precisely what we are doing.

When we chew our raisin, we are learning to thoroughly and
meticulously chew over whatever task we happen to have at hand.
In this way we learn to mingle mindfulness and concentrated
awareness with daily life.

# INTEGRATING THESE EXERCISES
# INTO YOUR PRACTICE

The dictionary defines *practice* as "doing or performing something repeatedly in order to acquire or polish a skill." I think it's really important that we remind ourselves regularly that meditation practice is just that—something that we repeatedly do in order to perfect our meditational skills. The more we practice, the more we cultivate our innate powers. As we continue to hone our natural capacity to concentrate, the deeper and stronger our powers of concentration become.

In your own practice, you may find as I have that you can use these six concentration exercises to round out your meditation sessions. For example, perhaps you plan to meditate for an hour. For the first ten minutes, you simply relax and practice breath counting; then you move on to the awareness of breathing. But after half an hour, you feel too stiff and dull to continue; perhaps you are even dozing. Instead of giving up on meditation, you can incorporate some minutes of standing meditation or walking meditation into your practice at this point. This can refresh you, so you can then return to sitting meditation. When we undertake silent intensive meditation retreats, the day is typically broken up into forty five minute periods of sitting, walking, sitting—with a little chanting, and then a break—plus instruction once or twice a day. In this way we try to carry mindfulness with us as we make the various transitions from sitting to walking, from solitude to group activity.

I use concentration exercises daily. No matter how experienced we become as meditators, we continue to go back to the same mindful breathing and walking exercises time and time again. Athletes start their training every day with the same simple stretching exercises and warm-ups. Even a great sprinter doesn't walk out the door and start sprinting. Sprinters know they need to return time and time again to their warm-ups and build to peak performance level.

The same thing is true with spiritual practice. As meditators, we start with the simplest awareness exercises and then move on from there. We are getting our minds into shape. In the beginning, these exercises may seem somewhat restrictive and controlled. And they are. Yet these exercises help us evolve toward greater freedom and panoramic awareness through the use of self-discipline. We are building up our own concentration muscle. The beautiful wild mustang of mind is being tamed and reined in before it can be totally let loose to run free. This principle of a little control followed by a little release is another example of the Buddha's middle way of moderation. With the right measure of control balanced with release, the natural mind finds its natural place, and so do we.

# BEING CHALLENGED ONCE AGAIN
# BY THE HINDRANCES

A discussion of concentration would not be complete without mentioning again the five classical hindrances that can impede our progress: craving, ill will, torpor, restlessness, and doubt. They will all try to interfere with your meditations. Your thoughts may be filled with cravings and desires; you may remember old arguments; you may feel too tired to continue; you may doubt whether meditation is working for you.

One challenge to meditation that just about everyone faces is *restlessness,* which sometimes masks itself as boredom. It may show up in a meditation session when we wonder when the hour is going to end—or even if it will ever end. Or sometimes a thought bubble appears, and even though we are meditating we still respond with knee-jerk impulses.

Restlessness also presents itself outside of the meditation hall. Many men and women are drawn to the spiritual path at times of life crisis. Meditation can be a real emotional life preserver. But when their lives improve and they are again on an even keel, they may become distracted by new interests and lose interest in their practice. Some people wander on and off the path for years depending on what else in happening in their lives. When we become restless in this fashion it may indicate that we are still placing too much emphasis on outer events and people; we are still looking for solutions outside ourselves. Meeting the challenge of restlessness requires focus and a real commitment to do more inner work. Continuity and repetition are the secrets of success.

Some of us have deep streaks of restlessness that prevent us from leading settled, well-balanced lives. Aren't we all a little guilty of this? We complain that we don't have time to accomplish what we want, and yet the moment one chaotic life episode ends, we create new chaos. We take on projects, love affairs, and financial obligations we can't manage. We keep stirring up our outer world as a way to deal with inner dissatisfaction. This restless motion will never end until we simply lay it down.

When we see someone who can't stop creating more complications for themselves, we may say he or she is making waves, looking for trouble, going around in circles, or playing games. The underlying impulse driving an out-of-control life isn't so different from the impulse that makes a meditating monk start fidgeting. A good meditation session is simply a microcosm of a well-lived life.

Restless impulses can be handled through meditation. An old Buddhist technical term that meditators use is called "the interest factor." Here's how it works: Let's say Debra is sitting in meditation, and it's going really well. Suddenly out of the blue, she remembers a project she wants to complete, and she hangs on to the thought for an instant too long. Like Velcro pressed together, she is suddenly enmeshed. At this moment, she is feeling so good, she is ready to handle anything. But the meditation session isn't over. Now Debra is bored with the meditation and wants to get out of there, and immediately take up that project where she left off.

What Debra could do is raise "the interest factor" in the meditation, by turning it into an investigation into her boredom and restlessness. She could ask, "Why am I bored? I'm in the perfect place doing the perfect thing; why am I feeling restless? Why am I never satisfied?"

Investigation is known as one of the principal factors of enlightenment—or agents as transformation. Investigation into the roots of our boredom and restlessness can help keep us present, awake, alert, interested, and developing. If your boredom or restlessness immediately translates itself into sleepiness, you might want to engage in self-inquiry about why you are sleepy. What provoked your fatigue? Are you using it perhaps as a way to avoid or deny something that is bothering you?

If that fails, see if some deep breaths can energize your mind and awaken your spirit. Then begin the meditation again. Some teachers frown on physical movement in the meditation period, but instead of nodding off and dozing on the cushion, I think it's better to stand and continue meditating while standing up, if that's going to help. Or even leave the room, get some air, splash cold water on your face, and then come back. If you are meditating by yourself, this is not an issue. But if you are sitting with a group, this might be something you want to discuss with the teacher or leader before you start.

# THE MULTILEVEL BENEFITS OF CONCENTRATION

Concentration and focus are indispensable in ordinary affairs as well as spiritual pursuits. Talking to Oprah Winfrey, Tom Hanks said that he felt so harried and frenetic during his successive Oscar-winning years that he made himself sit down alone to write every day "just to find relief from everything and concentrate on one thing in order to calm down and relax my mind." Champion athletes around the world speak with awe of "the zone," an almost mystical state of being entirely in the groove: a state of totally alert, perfectly focused balance and at-one-ness, an inexplicable state of total presence and alignment which Arnold Palmer called "rightness."

All-star quarterback John Brodie says, "A player's effectiveness is directly related to his ability to be right there, doing that thing totally, in the moment. When you are in the zone, it is as if you can't miss." Yogi Berra, famous for his folk wisdom as well as his big baseball bat, said, "How can you think and hit at the same time?" Nadia Comaneci said that for her to accomplish her feats as the perfect gymnast in the 1976 Olympics, intense concentration was the key.

There is no question that concentration helps make people more powerful, one-pointed on a goal, successful, and productive rather than hesitant, wishy-washy, or distracted. Some people, for example, suffer from attention deficit disorders. Meditation can often help improve attention span without chemical drug treatments or other invasive therapies.

Concentration techniques help us experience more clarity and spaciousness. If we are more concentrated, our energy is grounded and channeled; it can be wielded like a spotlight, a laser beam, or blowtorch instead of splashing out as if from a firehose. Throughout history, intentional mind-training, self-mastery techniques, and skillful methods of inner discipline have been proven to greatly reduce stress and help people better cope with chronic pain and disease as well as compulsions and addictive behavior problems.

Concentration meditation also provides an invaluable calming technique for coping with the emotional ups and downs we experience in the course of everyday life. Let's say for example that we have just had a very unpleasant and anxiety-provoking conversation. It could have been with a colleague, an employer, a child, a romantic partner. Whatever was said in that conversation left us feeling rattled and filled with a sense that we didn't say what we wanted to say. We didn't get our point across; we weren't understood. These thoughts swirl around in our head, filling us with anger, resentment, and a sense that we have been mistreated. We tell ourselves, "Let it go. It's over. Forget it." But the words alone don't do the trick. We need something more. This is one of the times that meditation can be most effective. Instead of trying to lash back at the person who upset us; instead of trying to have the last word or allowing our troubling thoughts to take hold and ruin our perspective as well as our day, we sit; we settle; we breathe. Spiritual space and perspective begin to return.

Metaphysical fitness is as important as physical fitness. I occasionally think of daily meditation as mental hygiene, a form of mental floss that retards truth decay. I meditate because it keeps me sane and sound of both body and mind, calm and clear, light-hearted and open-minded, and at ·peace with myself and the world. I never leave home without it.

Concentration training seems to increase our specific gravity, as it were, which in Buddhist language we might call authentic presence. Through heightened attention, increased presence of mind and alert, and moment-to-moment awareness, we can begin to more fully experience and appreciate every moment in our lives, just as it is, without changing anything.

This is the miracle of meditation, the magic of mindfulness, the joy of concentration. It is a secret known to skill trainers, competitive coaches in various disciplines, and sages throughout the ages.

## ABOUT DZOGCHEN MEDITATION

*In the beginning, meditative awareness is like a small flame, which can easily be extinguished and needs to be protected and nurtured. Later, it is more like a huge bonfire, which consumes whatever falls into it. . . . Then the more thoughts that arise, the more awareness blazes up, like adding logs to a bonfire! Emaho! Everything is food for naked enlightened awareness!*

—DZOGCHEN MASTER JIGME LINGPA

Emaho is the shortest Dzogchen teaching. It means wondrous. Amazing! Dzogchen masters always say it. The word expresses a tremendous sense of joy and wonder. Love of life in all its forms is a by-product of spiritual development. Let's not forget that joy is an important ingredient in a meditation practice. The aspiration for enlightenment can be happily balanced with appreciation of just where we are.

People often ask how Dzogchen differs from concentration or insight meditation. As we learn to meditate, we typically go

through three distinct stages. The first stage of concentration meditation initially implies real effort as we learn to hold our attention
on an object of meditation.

In the second stage, we have trained the mind; we are able to
hold a concentrated state for longer periods of time. Our directed
attention stays wherever we place it.

In the third and final stage, we have really mastered the art of
focused attention. In this stage we are able to relax, yet we remain
almost effortlessly concentrated and undistracted. The weighty
gravity of our heightened awareness keeps us centered. Our attention remains naturally in place, like a calm and reflective clear lake
when no winds or undercurrents move it.

Concentration practice is extremely helpful as a foundation for
the more advanced, deeper, broader, and more inclusive awareness
and discriminating insight practices such as the advanced forms of
Vipasssana, Zen, and Dzogchen. Concentration techniques help us
to get where we are going.

However, concentrated states of mind are put together, fabricated, built-up through intensive, continuous, one-pointed focusing practices. Whatever is put together inevitably falls apart. Like
muscle tone, concentration disappears when it isn't used. However,
the insight, wisdom, and understanding we can realize through
meditation training does stay with us. This greater perspective becomes part of us.

# Four Dzogchen Meditations

## A RUSHEN MEDITATION: DISCERNING DIFFERENCES

Part of the unique preliminary practice for Dzogchen is called rushen. It includes analytical contemplations that employ the rational powers of the mind; in these contemplations we use the well-honed, focused mind like a sharp tool to penetrate further into reality. This special self-inquiry helps us recognize the essential nature of mind.

The word rushen literally means "discerning the difference between"—traditional images are separating the wheat from the chaff or a kernel from its husk. We use the practice of rushen to distinguish between the dualisms that confront and confuse us: between samsara and nirvana; between bondage and freedom; between small mind and Big Mind, or Buddha-mind; between finite conceptual mind and infinite awareness; between finite self and our true Buddha-nature.

Now let's use the self-inquiry part of rushen practice. Let's penetrate further into heart and soul, and perceive the essential nature of mind. We can use investigative self-inquiry to unmask ourselves and deconstruct the illusory prison that ego built, thus gaining insight and the wisdom of awareness.

Exploring the age-old question "Who am I?" is an open-ended inquiry that takes us beyond thoughts and mere concepts. This is one of the very best practices to help you get to know your true nature, beyond your illusory conventional self. Recognizing our natural mind, Buddha-nature, helps us live freely in the present moment, without preconceptions about what we'll get out of it. Let's discern the difference between the ego, which strategizes and manipulates, and the spontaneous natural heart-mind. The heart and mind are beautiful in their natural state. We can afford to leave them alone. The better we come to know and accept ourselves, the more at home and profoundly at peace we can be, wherever we are. Whoever we may be.

Who or what is experiencing your present experience? Rushen meditation helps us to discern the difference betwen what we seem to be and think ourselves to be, and our original nature— who we really *are*. We identify ourselves with our body, but are we really our body? We identify with our thoughts, but are we really our thoughts and states of mind? This analytical meditation brings to bear the microscope of discriminating awareness.

Practice self-inquiry now by asking yourself:

Who or what is experiencing my present experience? Is it my body? Do the eyes and ears hear? (Remember a corpse has eyes and ears, but it doesn't see and hear.) Where is the experiencer, the perceiver? Is it in my head? my torso? my heart? Perhaps within the body and also all around it, like a nimbus, an astral body or a luminous sphere?

Mind is the knower. Consciousness animates the sense doors, perceiving all that transpires through the gates of the senses. What is the essence or nature of this mind? Peer into the nature of your own mind in this very present moment. Know the knower. See through the seer, and be free.

Does the mind have a particular shape or form? A color? A size or weight? Is it always the same or simply a stream of consciousness, a collection of various mind-moments and mental events—like the ever-changing weather, dependent on fluctuating circumstances and conditions? Do I have one mind, several, or many? Is it separate from the mind of another being and of all others—or is it connected? Is it perhaps part of universal cosmic consciousness?

In a moment of no thought, how is it, and what is it? When one dies, where does it go? Can you tell me? Can you say? Where do your thoughts come from? Where do they go when they pass on? Where does thinking stem from? Try to say *something* about this. The effort could be extremely revealing. You could have a close encounter with yourself.

Who is thinking, hearing, seeing, wondering? Who am I? What am I? What is happening right now, this immediate instant?

Turn the mind back upon itself with this laserlike question: Who is experiencing your experience right now? And then let go of thinking. See what comes up. Sense directly.

## DZOGCHEN FIVE-ELEMENT
## MEDITATION

Dzogchen meditations often emphasize nature—the awesome mystery and splendor of it all. Mother Nature is like a great goddess. In the Diamond Skydancer Tantra, the Great Dakini says, "The whole universe is my body, all sentient beings my soul, my heart-mind." The salient principle in this meditation is merging into five elements of nature—water, earth, fire, air, and space. This helps us return to our natural, innate Buddha-mind.

Let's meditate, let's contemplate; let's unify ourselves with these elements. The element of water with its cooling nature and natural flow is a good way to begin.

We can practice this meditation by the ocean, a lake, a river, or a pond. We can even practice this meditation while washing the dishes. The sound of water could be the tranquil lapping of waves against a dock, the dripping of a faucet in a kitchen sink, the melodic flowing of the water in an aquarium, a waterfall, or the thundering surf. The vision of water may range from a shimmering puddle to the Pacific Ocean. Water is water. The natural element is the same.

Merging and dissolving into the natural elements helps us to go beyond ourselves. We enter into the dimension of that element, unifying ourselves and the universe. In this way we transcend our separate selves and realize our primordial nature.

----

Listen to the "white sound" of water. Enter into the contemplative space, the flow, the reflectiveness of water. Concentrate on the sound of water. Let it wash everything else away. Just focus on listening to the sound. Dzogchen meditation calls for the senses to be left in their natural state. And that state is Natural Great Perfection, Dzogchen. Let the sound of the water wash over you, wash through you. Leave your senses open, sensitive, and receptive. Enter the resonant spiritual dimension of pure sound.

Open your eyes. Look at the water. Let all thoughts fall into the water and dissolve into the lake of your mind, like snowflakes settling and dissolving in the ocean. All waves of thought and feeling, and emotion and energy, gradually slow down and dissolve, like gentle ripples in a stream or in the placid sea of natural awareness. The ocean's waves come and go; watch them until you forget yourself and become one with the waves.

Contemplating the waves—just listening—let everything else be washed away. Enter into the non-dual dimension of just being. Be that sound, flow with the water. Relax into the natural state of the water element as if worshipping the spirit of nature or the deity of water. All of the elements are like embodied deities. Attend to them. Rest in their shrines. Be one with them. Enter into that sacred dimension right now.

———————

Being at one with water is not unlike being at one with all the other elements. With the element of fire, we meditate before a fireplace, a campfire, or a candle, and we let our thoughts mingle with the flame as the inner flame warms our hearts, melts us down, and dissolves the separation between us and the world.

With the air element, we can meditate on the wind. We feel it, and listen to it sigh. We can watch the wind blowing through the long grass on a hilltop or in the swaying treetops, or we can sit near the window of a city apartment, feeling the cooling breeze. The wind of breath constantly blows through us, blowing away our cares and purifying our mind—if we let it.

For earth, we can concentrate on the supportive, solid, and powerful earth element in a garden, in the woods, or looking at a far-off mountain. Whether we are meditating with a view of the Grand Canyon or next to a rock in a city park—it's all matter. All part of the earth element, the Earth Goddess . . . all one, single, divine element of our daily experience.

The principle in the Five-Element Meditation is directing our attention to nature in a way that leads us beyond ourselves and back home to the natural state of oneness. When we sit by the edge of the ocean, the incessant sound of the waves seems to wash our cares, thoughts, and worries away. This is like a natural meditation. In this way nature—which we all love, enjoy, and can easily relate to—helps us moving toward the wholeness and completeness of non-dual awareness.

## SKY-GAZING MEDITATION

This is another example of a natural, elemental Dzogchen meditation. The sky, which represents the element of space, is without shape or color. No one can say exactly where it begins or where it ends. It just *is*.

Meditation leads us into a way of being that is in perfect harmony, attunement, and oneness with nature, including everything and everyone around us—and with our true nature too. In this sky-gazing meditation, we dissolve into the infinite by becoming one with the open sky.

> Close your eyes. Still your hands. Have a seat. Take a deep breath, and let it out. And another. Relax. Let go. Drop everything. Rest naturally, and at ease.
>
> Just for a moment, let everything pass by like waves in the sea, like clouds in the infinite sky.
>
> Simply observe. Be still. And know. Everything is right here.
>
> Let it be.
>
> Let go and let be.
>
> At ease. Nothing more to do. Nothing to figure out, understand or achieve.
>
> Simply present.
>
> Natural. At home and at ease.
>
> Know yourself.
>
> See things just as they are in the present moment.
>
> Breathe in and out. Deeply and slowly. Letting it in, letting it out. Letting go a little more with each breath.

Let everything quiet down naturally, by itself.

Let the body settle naturally in its own place, in its own time. Let the mind settle naturally, in its own way, in its own time. Let everything go naturally for a few moments.

Moment by moment, one moment at a time.

Breathe, Smile, Be Aware

Breathe, Smile, Be Aware

Breathe, Smile, Be Aware

Now.

Open your eyes.

Raise your gaze.

Elevate the scope of the 360-degree sphere of total awareness.

Look at the sky.

Gaze evenly into space, with a soft focus.

(No eye strain necessary.)

Space, like mind, has no beginning and no end.

No inside and no outside. No actual form, no color, no size, no shape.

Mingle the gaze with space; merge mind with infinite, empty space.

Dissolve into space—spacious awareness.

Cast the breath into space, following the out-breath— out, out, out, out. Allow all thoughts, feelings, sensations, and emotions to come and go freely, casting everything off into vast space.

Gaze freely in vast space, into the open sky, in the crystal clear sphere of pristine awareness.

And let go, let go, let go.

Breathe out.

Breathe the sky in and out, and breathe and dissolve into the sky with your out-breath. Follow the out-breath— out, out, out . . .

Breathe out.

Open up.

Unfurl your infinite Buddha-mind.

Let it all go.

Let be.

Drop everything, past and future.
Drop off body and mind.
Mingle with the sky and slowly
　　dissolve totally
　　　　into the spacious
　　　　　　luminous
　　　　　　　　joy of meditation.

After this melting into the sky you can just sit. Sit and enjoy the infinite luminous emptiness. Maybe a thought will arise, but now you know how to watch it come and watch it go. A feeling may present itself. It, too, passes away. Perhaps your concentration begins to flag. You know how to bring attention back, refreshing yourself, by observing anew the in-and-out motion of the natural breath, with more attention on following the out-breath, while letting go.

## AHHH MEDITATION

To further enhance the sky-gazing meditation, we chant the user-friendly Dzogchen mantra *Ah.*

Take a deep breath, and with the exhalation, open your eyes and mouth wide, raise your gaze and chant a resounding, relieving
*Ahhhh . . .*

Again, breathe in deeply, and again exhale like a great, orgasmic release,
*Ahhhhhhh . . .*
As far as you can go.
Watch the breath.
In, out;
in, out.
Now chant *Ah; Ahhh; Ahhhhhh*
following the out-breath, dissolving into space.
Chant *Ah* again; then *Ahhh;* then *Ahhhhhh,*
with a huge exhalation, a cosmic out-breath.
Chant *Ah, Ahhh,* and *Ahhhhhh* at different volumes in different tones,

emptying yourself totally while dissolving
outward with each out-breath.
*Ah, Ahhh, Ahhhhhh.*

---

What a relief.
　What a release!
　*Ah . . . Ahhh . . . Ahhhhhh.*
　Mingle mind with space, space with awareness.
　Let everything dissolve in vast, open space.
　Simply rest in the view, at ease and precisely as is.
　Let the sound of the seed mantra *Ah* resound itself
away
　　into nothingness,
　　both within and without.
　　Rest
　　in the utter silence and simplicity
　　of the natural state
　　of just being.
　If thoughts arise, chant a few lengthy *Ahs,* following the out-
breath. Dissolve a little more each time.
　Then again rest in spacious openness and clarity.
　Alternate this dissolving and resting, at your own pace, in your
own natural way.
　Dissolving. Resting,
　Dissolving. Resting,
　*Ahhhhhhhhhhhhhhhh. Aha! Ahhhhhhhhhhhhhhhh . . .*

# VISUALIZATION AND
# CONCENTRATION

Many people are drawn to Tibetan Buddhism by its colorful esoteric iconography and the creative visualization practices associated
with it. Visualization is a powerful and profound way to use the
mind and its brilliant beacon light of awareness. These practices
help us transcend our limited self-concepts and identity. We learn
to transform ourselves into Buddhas and Bodhisattvas living in the
most splendid Buddha world mandala that we could ever imagine.
We thereby loosen up the hold our own karmically conditioned,
present-lifetime world has over us.

Through visualization practice we see how we continuously
project—every single day—the current visualization or self-
concepts we maintain of ourselves and our experiences. This practice helps us develop a greater perspective on how we could just as
easily reshape our perceptions and our entire life in any number of
fulfilling and meaningful ways. Visualization helps us learn that we
are not necessarily stuck with who or what we think we are; we
could be almost anyone or anything. Therefore, why not exercise
our power of choice and the intrinsic wisdom of awareness by
manifesting oneself as a radiant, empowering, and protective female Buddha Tara, or as a gentle forgiving Avalokitesvara, the
Buddha of love and compassion? Wouldn't this prove far more satisfying than any negative self-images we may currently hold?

These visualizations are primarily meditations on identity and
its transformation—how we create ourselves and our self-image;
how we create and recreate our karma and our world. In this way
we see how we can achieve mastery over forms and experience instead of feeling like victims subject to circumstances and conditions beyond our control.

Tantric practices involving visualized meditation deities and
primordial archetypes remain one of the least-understood aspects
of the rich world of Himalayan spiritual practice. They also represent one of the most recondite facets of the Buddhist culture of
awakening. Many Westerners have found it difficult, if not impossible, to understand and master these complex techniques that in-

volve constructing and holding an image in one's mind with one-pointed attention. Sometimes practitioners spend long hours studying these techniques only to find that the inner principles and deeper meaning elude them; then they return to simpler, more basic, and fundamentally conprehensible practices such as breathing, mindfulness meditation, and various forms of self-inquiry.

Actually, it is less important to be able to visualize or graphically imagine the forms and attributes of the deity than it is to viscerally "feel" the presence of the invoked meditational deity, embodying the universal qualities we are learning to cultivate. There are no deities per se in Buddhism. Instead these numinous forms are archetypes embodying the most noble and sublime qualities we can aspire to achieve—mere personifications of spiritual principles like wisdom, compassion, healing power, and so on. People often ask me if these deities exist outside and independent of our own minds. One might just as well wonder whether we too exist in such a way. As I often reply, they are as real, or unreal, as we are.

## Two Meditations

### CANDLE-FLAME CONCENTRATION / VISUALIZATION MEDITATION

This candle-flame meditation helps us look beyond the separation between inside and outside. While doing it we see how easy it is to retain the image of the candle flame long after it has been snuffed out. It prepares us for other, more detailed, creative imagination and visualization practices, as well as for entering into the clear light as we fall asleep each night.

Light a candle.

Turn off the lights and sit down one or two feet away.

Stare at the candle flame for several minutes;

just watch the flame.

When the mind wanders and is carried away by
thought, notice

that distraction and gently bring it back to totally paying

attention to the flame.

Watch the flame.

See the flame.

See fire burn.

Watch the flame;

go into the flame.

become the flame.

Suddenly, snuff or blow out the candle.

And close your eyes.

Watch the afterimage of the flame

forming on the inside of your eyelids.

Watch the flame.

See the flame.

Go into the flame.

Be flame.

Let go

and dissolve

into the clear light within

the natural mind—

and just like that

without further effort

meditate.

## BUDDHA LIGHT VISUALIZATION
## MEDITATION

In this meditation, we get a deeper sense of what it feels like to connect with all that is sacred and holy. During this visualization, we imagine ourselves in a space filled with formless, spiritual light. The visualization is called Buddha light, but if you are more comfortable visualizing angels, Jesus, a goddess, or Mary, don't hesitate to do so. We are dissolving into celestial light, entering into that sacred space. It doesn't matter which door we open to get there. We are trying to find our own light, our own innate luminosity.

Start by imagining that you have entered a sacred circle of light. You step into that magic protection circle, full of all blessings and love.

Bow gently toward the gold, glowing Buddha in Bodh Gaya.

Take your seat. Make yourself comfortable.

Imagine the radiant Buddha, garbed

in warm yellow robes, sitting under the spreading bodhi tree

right before you.

Visualize him surrounded by saintly yellow-garbed monks and nuns, seated in meditation,

all radiating rainbow light and blessings, peace and joy.

You dissolve into that light, and into them

and they into you.

And then you rest contemplatively in the view

With nothing more to do

In the natural great perfection of all things just as they are.

# FINDING THE HEART OF
# ENLIGHTENMENT

*Neither giving nor taking*
*Neither for nor against*
*Leave your mind at rest*
*With perceptions remain unconcerned*
*The great Way is a mind open to everything*
*which clings to nothing*
*which fixates nowhere*
*Radiant and stainless*
*Rest in the unmoved, uncreated and sponta-*
*    neous*
*and you will soon reach Buddhahood.*

— MEDITATION INSTRUCTION FROM
TILOPA, A TENTH-CENTURY YOGI

All meditative techniques, including concentration and visualization, are simply ways to connect to the source and to awaken gradually to the Buddha within—your original nature, your natural
mind. This is what people in the theistic traditions sometimes call
the Godhead, or Self with a capital *S*: the true Self, the natural
state. We come to our true state only by the practice of purifying
and mastering the heart and mind. If we master the mind by training it and bringing it back to the source, we arrive at and reconnect with our true state, which was there all the time. Yet we
hardly experience it.

As we walk the spiritual path and get closer to the innate luminous awareness that is the Buddha within, we discover that
there are many degrees and depths of enlightenment, just as there
are many different degrees and depths of love. Levels of enlightenment range from the momentary "Aha" experience or
epiphany all the way to the highest, full and complete, perfectly
blossomed enlightenment—Buddhahood. Mahayana Buddhists
and Bodhisattvas say that there can be no real enlightenment until all are enlightened.

The wonderful, yet more common, "Aha" experiences are temporary, however transcendent they may seem to be. I often say that

these days it seems easier to get enlightened than to stay enlightened. People have described a wide variety of these fleeting experiences as enlightenment—everything from meeting the Buddha in clear light dreams to awakenings during meditation to having visions of angels, saints, Mary, or Jesus.

In Buddhism it is accepted that there are many different degrees of enlightenment. Someone who has experienced the first level is traditionally known as a stream enterer. Stream enterers are those men and women who have directly experienced ultimate reality, however temporarily. Regarding the transcendent experience, my teachers always said, "One glimpse is not enough." By this they mean that someone who had seen reality would not be satisfied until he or she had realized far more. These glimpses of enlightenment can be likened to the moment when the clouds that have been obscuring the sun part for the briefest of moments and the sun shines through. When the clouds return, we no longer see the sun, but now we know for ourselves that there is a sun. We understand why there is daylight.

Because seeing is knowing, enlightenment experiences can be very important while traveling the spiritual path. These experiences uproot doubt and skepticism. They convince us that reality is there behind the mist and clouds of illusion—even if it is temporarily obscured. We know what we are looking for. As the great mystic poet of India, Kabir, sang, "I glimpsed it for fifteen seconds and I became a servant for life."

However, sometimes to our surprise we discover that we are almost as frightened by the idea of enlightenment as we are drawn to it. Sometimes we want enlightenment, but not until after we've achieved all our worldly ambitions. Sometimes we worry that enlightenment means we will no longer be able to have relationships with the people we love. Sometimes we fear that once enlightened we will become flat-liners, as if lobotomized, with no passion and verve. We might not like it. We might be disappointed.

We might fear that we will lose our reference points and not know who we are or why we are doing things. We experience tremendous fear of the unknown. We worry that by going beyond ourselves we will go over the edge and lose ourselves. This fear is a response we can anticipate as the ego begins to lose its grip, and

we start moving away from our habitual ruts and patterns of thinking. A spiritual path does not mean walking over the edge. If anything it is propelling us back to the center, the Golden
Mean—back to health, sanity, and authenticity. All we are doing is
opening up to truth and reality—the bigger picture.

I think it helps if we look to the example of the Buddha and
other enlightened masters. By these examples, we see that enlightened men and women who have walked among us continued to
lead rich, sane, healthy lives filled with loving relationships and passionate ideals and original ideas.

Another issue that deeply concerns many people is that they
will never be able to achieve enlightenment. They feel they can't
devote as many hours as they might like to meditation. They can't
follow all the traditional customs and rules. They may feel they are
too busy and already have far too many demands on their time and
energy. I think it's really important for people who are walking the
spiritual path to understand that the genius of Buddha Dharma is
that it really can provide anybody with a suitably appropriate path
to work through. Anybody can do it. Even if you can't memorize
or believe in anything.

One of my favorite stories is about the arhant Chunda. When
it came to brainpower, Chunda wasn't very swift. When Chunda's
elder brother became a monk, Chunda wanted to do exactly what
his brother did. He went to Ananda, Buddha's attendant, and
Ananda said, "Sorry, you could never make it as a monk." Ananda
thought this young guy was just too stupid to become a monk because he couldn't even remember the rules. So Chunda and his
monk brother appealed to the Buddha, who was known to be kind
and compassionate.

The Buddha scanned the past lives of this dull young boy
Chunda. He saw that, like most people, Chunda had at least one
seed or root of merit in his karmic accumulation that could help
him get enlightened. It didn't matter that he had limited intellectual powers; nor did it matter whether or not Chunda could memorize even one rule. Buddha told Ananda, "Ananda, you're not a
Buddha. You couldn't see that this youth can get enlightened. But
I am the Buddha, and I'm going to ordain him as a monk. Why
shouldn't he too become liberated?"

So the Buddha ordained Chunda. But Chunda couldn't remember anything, not even how to wear his robes. Sometimes it can be complicated to be a monk, at least at first. There are a lot of teachings, and since in those days there were no books, there was a great deal to memorize. Chunda couldn't keep up, so they gave him the job of cleaning the sandals left outside the door while the monks were receiving teachings.

But Chunda wanted to practice like the other monks, and get this enlightenment thing he heard about every day. He went straight to the Buddha to ask him what he could do to achieve enlightenment. The Buddha said, "When you're scraping and sweeping, just think, 'Now I am purifying all the obscurations of the mind.'" Then the Buddha gave Chunda a two-line verse to recite: "With each cleaning of the sandals, I am cleaning off the obscurations of the shining, perfect natural mind." The Buddha asked him to repeat it. He repeated it. The Buddha said, "Can you remember that?" Chunda said, "Yes."

Chunda went off to repeat the verse "With each scraping of the dirt, I am cleaning . . ." And he couldn't remember the rest. But he had good karma and he had gentle Ananda around to remind him of the verse. Still, he kept forgetting. So Chunda went to his monk brother at regular intervals to be reminded.

One day the compassionate Buddha came back and said to Chunda, "Are you cleaning the sandals?" Chunda said, "Yes." Buddha asked, "Are you cleaning the dust off the floor?" Chunda said, "Yes." And Buddha asked, "Have you cleaned the obscurations off the shining, perfect, natural mind?" And Chunda was suddenly enlightened! His heart leapt for joy. He realized that the sandals with the dirt were still the sandals. The floor, even with the dust, was still the floor. He became an arhant.

All the local people who knew Chunda could not believe he was an enlightened, saintly arhant. But wherever the radiant Buddha went, he saved a seat for Chunda, because he said he was the purest-minded, least proud arhant among all. He was the most pure-minded because he didn't know anything. And least proud because he acknowledged his limitations. Sincere intentions and purity of heart are what counts.

## FREE AND EASY: A SPONTANEOUS SONG
### *by Venerable Lama Gendun Rinpoche*

*Happiness cannot be found*

*through great effort and willpower,*

*but is already present, in open relaxation and letting go.*


*Don't strain yourself,*

*there is nothing to do or undo.*

*Whatever momentarily arises in the body-mind*

*has no real importance at all,*

*has little reality whatsoever.*

*Why identify with, and become attached to it,*

*passing judgment upon it and ourselves?*


*Far better to simply*

*let the entire game happen on its own,*

*springing up and falling back like waves—*

*without changing or manipulating anything—*

*and notice how everything vanishes and*

*reappears, magically, again and again,*

*time without end.*


*Only our searching for happiness*

*prevents us from seeing it,*

*It's like a vivid rainbow which you pursue without ever catching,*

*or a dog chasing its own tail.*

*Although peace and happiness do not exist*

*as an actual thing or place,*

*it is always available*

*and accompanies you every instant.*

*Don't believe in the reality*

*of good and bad experiences;*

*they are like today's ephemeral weather,*

*like rainbows in the sky.*

*Wanting to grasp the ungraspable,*

*you exhaust yourself in vain.*

*As soon as you open and relax this tight fist of grasping,*

*infinite space is there—open, inviting, and comfortable.*

*Make use of this spaciousness, this freedom and natural ease.*

*Don't search any further.*

*Don't go into the tangled jungle*

*looking for the great awakened elephant,*

*who is already resting quietly at home*

*in front of your own hearth.*

*Nothing to do or undo.*

*nothing to force,*

*nothing to want,*

*and nothing missing—*

*Emaho! Marvelous!*

*Everything happens by itself.*

—TRANSLATED AT DAKPO KAGYU
LING IN DORDOGNE, FRANCE

# EPILOGUE: TOWARD A WESTERN BUDDHISM AND CONTEMPORARY DHARMA

*What is important? The past is past; the future is important. We are the creators. The future is in our hands. Even if we fail, no regrets. We have to make the effort . . . to contribute to others rather than to convert others. Motivated always by the altruistic bodhicitta, you in the West should be creative in adapting the timeless essence of the Dharma to your own cultural times and circumstances.*

—HIS HOLINESS, THE DALAI LAMA

In the 1970s, I went to Asia, learned the Tibetan language, and haunted monasteries in the Himalayas for ten years, accosting innumerable lamas with questions and requests for teachings. When I returned to this country, I only came as far as helping to establish a Tibetan monastery in Woodstock, New York, and then turned right around and lived for nine more years in a cloistered Tibetan retreat center in the forests of southern France.

When I first left the United States, I could not have imagined that by the time I returned twenty years later, the Dharma would have fully arrived in the West. My first inkling of this occurred during a short visit back to America in the late seventies. At a family gathering, I had a conversation with my great uncle Max, who was born "in the old country," as he put it. At the advice of his physician, he had taken up meditation—twenty minutes every morning and night. He had learned how to meditate at a local "Y" in Brooklyn.

"I can't live without it, Jeffrey," he said to me in his middle European accent. "Now I understand what you have been doing for all these years." My great uncle Max was an unlikely harbinger of the future.

One of the best examples of the spread of Buddhist philosophy in the West is found in the work of Jon Kabat-Zinn who has taken the meditative practice of mindfulness out of the religious setting into the health and healing field, where it has proven effective in dealing with chronic pain and stress. Who but the enlightened Buddha could have imagined a time when mainstream medical doctors would regularly prescribe meditation as a treatment for a wide range of medical problems including stress, asthma, hypertension, and migraines? Who could have imagined the extensive, meaningful work being done in conscious dying at Western hospices and hospitals? Who could have imagined that yoga, tai chi, and meditation would be taught at the local "Y," synagogue, church, senior facility, and adult-ed class? Who could have imagined flourishing spiritual bookstores and bookclubs, graduate programs in Buddhist studies, and more than two thousand Buddhist centers in the United States alone?

# THREE GREAT TRADITIONS, ONE CONTEMPORARY WESTERN DHARMA

It has often been pointed out that historically whenever Buddhism has entered a culture, it has not only changed the culture, it has also been changed by it. This is the nature of Dharma translation and transmission. The Dharma is always able to retain its essence while reinventing itself anew in order to remain applicable, accessible, and relevant.

At the first Western Buddhist Teacher's Conference a group of Buddhist meditation teachers met in Dharamsala, India, to discuss the transmission of Dharma in the modern world. At one point during this conference, about thirty of us were sitting on chairs and couches in a circle in a room in the Dalai Lama's one-story house. Outside the windows we could see the towering white snow-clad Himalayan peaks.

At first glance, we probably appeared to be a fairly disparate group of men and women. Some of us were in sweaters and jeans, some in sports jackets and ties, some in dresses, some in Kashmiri shawls, some in traditional yellow, orange, maroon, gray, and black monastic robes. Coming from twelve Western countries, the group included senior teachers from most of the major Buddhist traditions. We came from different cultures; we had been trained in different traditions; we utilized different styles of teaching. Yet we shared much common ground.

The Dalai Lama teased us about the way we Westerners had taken up old-fashioned Asian ritual instruments, clothing, furniture, and decor. He pointed out that this was not the heart of Dharma, but mere culture that had changed in each country throughout the centuries as Buddhism moved from its homeland of India to the Himalayas, Southeast Asia, China, and Japan. He was reminding us once again that the Dharma is timeless and not culture bound. The essential truth of the Dharma, the heart of enlightenment, is not limited by the trappings of culture, language, or time.

Today, Buddhism is at a critical juncture as it encounters the West. It is no surprise that there have been formidable cultural, linguistic, political, and material barriers to overcome in the transmission of Buddha Dharma from East to West and from the past on to the present and the future. This is a transition through time as well as through space, spanning continents and oceans, from a traditional Oriental world to a scientific postmodern Western culture.

We have inherited from Asia the three major Buddhist traditions and their various offshoots. They have been translated, synthesized, and distilled into user-friendly forms here in the West, especially by teachers of the Zen, Vipassana, and Dzogchen practice lineages. Now this wisdom is undergoing the rich and fascinating phase of transformation and adaptation while we facilitate and midwife its rebirth into liberating and viable contemporary forms. At the same time, ethnic Buddhist groups have formed pockets where the Buddhist traditions of their Asian homelands are being transplanted almost intact.

Strong bridges have been built from East to West, and the Dharma has arrived in the New World. This inevitably raises all sorts of interesting questions and challenges and even a certain degree of confusion, contradiction, and paradox. This is the first time all of the extant schools of Buddhism have existed together, closely rubbing shoulders, in one place at one time.

Many of us study and practice with more than one teacher, each of whom may represent different traditions. It is conceivable that someone could attend a silent sitting group on Tuesday and a chanting or visualization group on Friday. This need not necessarily be considered superficial, dilettantish, or pop Buddhism. We in the West have the opportunity to sample various teachings and practices to see what best fits our own aspirations and interests. In the initial spiritual "shopping phase," we can try any number of paths and techniques before settling down and committing ourselves to one practice. The social mobility in our culture can be a wonderful catalyst to the spiritual search. We each have the opportunity to choose for ourselves, to find something that resonates and connects with our experience.

# WE ALL COME TO BUDDHISM FROM DIFFERENT DIRECTIONS

A few years ago, a sincere guy from the southern part of the United States came to be in a long-term practitioner program at a large meditation center in Massachusetts. After several months, he came for a private meeting with an instructor, and in the course of the meeting, she realized that every morning when the group chanted the three-fold refuge prayer, he had been chanting, "I take refuge in the Buddha, the Dharma, and the Sun God." But his mistake didn't seem to matter. It hadn't interfered with his meditation practice, which was coming along fine. If he was having a few problems with a mere matter of translation it was simply par for the course.

As Westerners we are all coming to the Three Jewels—Buddha, Dharma, and Sangha—from different directions. I think it's fair to say that few of us learned about Buddha Dharma or meditation from our parents. As children, some of us went to Sunday school, some sang in church choirs, some studied Catholic catechism, some learned Hebrew prayers and lit Shabos candles, some were brought up in the religion of science, and some were raised in families where God seemed to be persona non grata.

We didn't come from a monolithic culture where everybody used the same chants and knew the same prayers. We weren't born and raised in countries where everyone had the same images, ancestors, icons, and holy days. Small wonder that occasionally we get confused. We are part of the encounter between East and West and although the essential truth, the kernel of the Dharma, retains its integrity, the husk continues to evolve and change.

Although there are different views on this, one of the most interesting things about Buddhist spirituality is that it does not necessarily require that you immediately abandon your current faith or the faith of your ancestors. Kalu Rinpoche said that you could take refuge in the Three Jewels, practice Buddhism, and get results without necessarily renouncing an earlier faith or belief system. And, in fact, today many people have a Buddhist meditation practice such as mindfulness or zazen without identifying themselves as Buddhists.

I personally had to sift through many forms and varieties of the teachings before I could really appreciate the essence of Dharma within myself and in our own culture. I had to learn foreign languages, take ordination, shave my head, wear monastic robes, live abroad in monasteries, and learn to practice all the many rites and rituals of Tibetan Buddhism until finally finding the distilled heart-essence of the Dharma in the Dzogchen teachings. However, within that framework I discovered that finding my own practice actually required that I synthesize and streamline what I found most useful and applicable from different traditions, including my intellectual roots here in the West. My own makeup actually required this synthesis; I could not do otherwise. I am an American, and I am a Buddhist. This is our Western karma.

## LOOKING FORWARD

*I believe deeply that we must find, all of us together, a new spirituality. This new concept ought to be elaborated alongside the religions in such a way that all people of good will could adhere to it.*

—HIS HOLINESS, THE DALAI LAMA

Today I see a great need for us to be very forward rather than backward-looking in our approach to spirituality. To be torchbearers in a benighted and violent world we need to collaborate harmoniously, effectively, and with a spirit of mutual respect, genuine understanding, and openness. We need to keep to the high ground and remain honest, ethical, humane, and even lighthearted—not taking ourselves too seriously. We need to be willing to go beyond routine thinking.

There have been three waves of Buddhist transmission in the West represented by three generations of Dharma teachers. The first group were the Asian-born teachers, who were mainly traditional in their approach. They introduced meditation and related practices as well as personally instructing Western disciples, both in the West and in Asia. The second wave was the generation of Western Buddhist teachers who trained under these teachers. Their task was to further translate the Buddhist words, concepts, and forms of practice for transmission to Western students in their own countries. Now beginning to emerge are the first generation of Dharma teachers who have trained solely in the West under the guidance of Western teachers.

Some people from other cultures are proud that they have maintained much of their cultural identity; others have eagerly adapted and assimilated. We are bringing about a synthesized or an amalgamated Dharma distilled from the best of what has been

transmitted to us from the past and from Asia. Added into this
Dharma mix is what is most useful from our own modern experience. This is a present day version of what the Buddha himself
termed "Ekayana"—the single great way of awakening—when he
referred to all of his teachings as a whole. It is one Dharma, one
coherent liberating path to enlightenment.

To be contemporary, we can't ignore that our modern landscape is much influenced by democratic principles, ecology, feminist thought, civil rights, psychotherapy, entrepreneurship, and
reformist religious movements. Protestantism altered Christianity
without abandoning it; Reform Judaism loosened many of the re-
strictions of Orthodox Judaism while retaining the core of the
Jewish tradition. Something similar is happening to the Buddha
Dharma. I think these are mainly positive developments, revitaliz-
ing Dharma with a fitting new Western design. It's like good Cal-
ifornia wines made from transplanted European grapevines.

One of the main tasks of contemporary Western teachers is to
stabilize both the study and practice of Buddhist Dharma and to
provide leadership in further integrating wholesome Dharma values, Buddhist lifestyles, and contemplative practices into the mainstream of our postmodern society.

We owe it to ourselves to carry on the Dharma in a sane way.
We must keep the spirit, the very heart of the Dharma alive while
not being afraid to let outmoded forms die and be reborn in ac-
cordance with current conditions. Each of us can give birth to a
Buddha! This is Do-It-Yourself-Dharma, as the Buddha indicated.

## TEN EMERGING TRENDS

For a number of years now, I have been observing religious trends
and the transplantation of Asian Buddhism into the fertile fields of
the Western world. From my particular vantage point, I observe
what I call ten trends in Western Buddhism or American Dharma.

Speaking of the emerging Western Buddhism, there are many
colorful, smaller threads woven into the larger tapestry. There seem
to be groups variously emphasizing monastic Buddhism, lay Buddhism, ethnic Buddhism, meditation Buddhism, chanting Bud-

dhism, ritualistic Buddhism and bare bones Buddhism; there is mystical Buddhism and practical Buddhism, academic Buddhism, therapeutic Buddhism, intellectual Buddhism, as well as anti-intellectual, no-mind Buddhism. Some people are attracted to hermitage and retreat Buddhism, congregational Buddhism, socially engaged Buddhism, missionary Buddhism, health and healing oriented Buddhism, upper-middle path Buddhism, Jewish Buddhism, Christian Zen Buddhism, vegetarian Buddhism, pacificist Buddhism, tantric Crazy Wisdom Buddhism, Beat Buddhism, eclectic, New Age, and roll-your-own Buddhism, to name a few.

The Vietnamese Zen Master Thich Nhat Hanh said, "The forms of Buddhism must change so that the essence of Buddhism remains unchanged. This essence consists of living principles that cannot bear any specific formulation."

In *The Awakening of the West: The Encounter of Buddhism and Western Culture*, Stephen Batchelor writes, "Buddhism cannot be said to be any of the following: a system of ethics, philosophy, or psychology; a religion, a faith, or a mystical experience; a devotional practice, a discipline of meditation, or a psychotherapy. Yet it can involve all these things."

Like him I know there is really no such thing as Buddhism; there are only Buddhists. When I speak of the ten trends in Western Buddhism, I therefore do so with certain reservations, not the least among them that I am primarily emphasizing meditation practice groups. Remember, these are emerging trends, and there is still a way to go to fulfill this vision.

## *Trend #1. Meditation-based and Experientially Oriented*

As Westerners, we typically come to Buddhism for meditation and contemplation in an attempt to improve our quality of life. We want to bring more mindfulness to what we do. We are usually attracted to Buddhism not through academia but because we want personal transformation, direct religious experience, and we want to integrate wisdom, goodness, and compassion into our daily lives. The Dharma is not just something we believe in, but something we do.

## Trend #2. Lay-oriented

Although there is certainly room for traditional monasticism—both short- and long-term—Buddhism in the West is obviously much more lay-oriented than it has been historically. Practitioners are now bringing personal issues of relationships, family, and work to the Dharma center in an effort to make more sense out of life.

## Trend #3. Gender Equal

In an effort to go beyond traditional patriarchal structures and cultures, we have already made great strides in supporting women as well as men in teaching and leadership roles. There are more and more women teachers, and they are providing some of the finest teaching. Gender equality remains an ideal, but one that seems reachable. We all—male and female—have an opportunity to refine our more feminine aspects and practice a Buddhism in which we keep the heart and mind balanced, respectful of both body and soul. We are trying to learn from the past so as not to unwittingly repeat the mistakes of others.

## Trend # 4. Democratic and Egalitarian

Western Buddhism needs to become Western wisdom. As might be anticipated, it is evolving in a much less institutionalized, less hierarchichal, and more democratic fashion. Almost by definition, personal growth and the interests of the individual are going to be stressed more than institutional preservation and growth.

## Trend #5. Essentialized, Simplified, and Demystified

For the most part, noticeably absent from Western Buddhism are the complex, esoteric rites and arcane rituals designed for initiates only. Western teachers stress essence more than form, as well as teachings that are relevant for daily life. It is thus practical and this-world oriented, rather than otherworldly and hermetic, with great emphasis on integrating Dharma practice via mindfulness and compassion into daily life.

## Trend #6. Nonsectarian

Most Westerners seem to have a true appreciation for many different meditation techniques and traditions. We have seen how politics, the quest for power, and sectarian bias have created chaos within various religious communities. We understand it is essential that we strive diligently not to fall into those same traps. As practitioners, we are generally interested in broadening and deepening our experience of the various different Buddhist spiritual practices. I think it is safe to say that there is a true appreciation of the benefits of nonsectarianism, ecumenicism, and cross-fertilization. In fact, many teachers are already synthesizing the best of the various traditions into the one amalgamated Western Dharma that seems inevitable. American karma is our great melting pot. We have to live with that and make the most of it.

## Trend #7. Psychologically Astute

There is a growing appreciation for explaining Buddhist principles within the idiom of transformational psychology. Faith and devotion are important and useful for some, but the larger appeal is to the individual's spiritual development and psychological and emotional well-being. Dharma students are encouraged to bring spirituality into their lives as opposed to using spirituality as a way of avoiding personal issues. We are working on ourselves, and there are any number of interdisciplinary tools and methods. Psychotherapy and Buddhism are most often taken as complementary.

## Trend # 8. Exploratory

In line with our scientific and skeptical upbringing, questioning and inquiry are encouraged. We are striving to be dynamic and forward-looking instead of mere preservationists. I see contemporary Dharma as basically a Buddhism without beliefs, a Dharma that's less doctrinaire, dogmatic, and belief-based while being much more inquiring, skeptical, rational, and devoted to testing and finding out for ourselves. Western Dharma is trying to stretch beyond dogma, insularity, and fundamentalist thinking.

## Trend # 9. Community Oriented

Through our shared spiritual, ethical, and educational interests, we are strengthening and building our spiritual community as well as our connections to each other. There is a great emphasis on the needs of the sangha in the sense of the larger community instead of individual priests and leaders. One day Ananda asked the Buddha, "Is it true that the Sangha, the community of spiritual friends, is half of the holy life?"

Buddha answered, "No, Ananda, the Sangha community is the whole of holy life."

Spiritual friends, spiritual friendships, and simple friendliness—this is the holy life. Here in the West where more and more people are expressing their personal needs for spiritual growth, it is the the challenge of the sangha today to provide spiritual encouragement and a loving, supportive, nourishing environment for generations to come.

## Trend # 10. Socially and Ecologically Conscious

Gandhi once said, "Those who say that religion has nothing to do with politics do not understand religion." Increasingly as Buddhists we are attempting to extend our sense of social and moral responsibility to include others, particularly those who are suffering from various injustices and deprivations. We are also searching for ways to express our deep concern for the natural world. The contemporary lay sangha is like an interdisciplinary "Lobby for Wisdom and Compassion." This differs dramatically from the image of the traditional reclusive monk, who is often isolated and out of touch with the problems of the world.

The Dharma is very suited to a Western way of life. It need not be complicated, mysterious, or fancy. Buddha Dharma is ordinary life including everything from meditation to relationship yoga and parenting practice. Among other things, it involves itself with the body-mind connection, which might well include suggestions like eating right, exercising right, and having a sense of humor. One of my teachers, the late Dudjom Rinpoche, once said, "The Dharma is not fancy. It's like blue jeans: good for every occasion, every day. It's good for work. It's good for school. You can wear blue jeans to a wedding, to ride horses, anytime."

# VIRTUOUS REALITY: FINDING YOUR OWN PRACTICE PATH

*When the Buddha is gone, look to the Dharma as your teacher. Make the practice your teacher. The Dharma and the Sangha will be your teacher.*

— THE BUDDHA SPEAKING TO HIS DISCIPLES

Many of the issues in contemporary Dharma concern the student-teacher relationship. I regularly hear the same kinds of questions from people who are trying to establish a meditation practice and a more spiritually fulfilling lifestyle. Do I need a teacher? What kind of teacher do I need? Should I become part of a group? Where should I look for spiritual guidance? What is the appropriate role of the teacher?

Practical questions such as these are very relevant. When you choose a teacher or join a spiritual group you have a unique opportunity. These people with whom you will chant, meditate, and study will become part of your spiritual family. What kind of family will you choose? We need to be very aware of these issues in developing a sane Western Dharma, which I like to think of as a virtuous reality.

At one time seekers walked the path to enlightenment. Today we seem to be running. This is all the more reason why we need to keep our eyes peeled. We must conscientiously cultivate self-awareness, and we need to be very conscious of possible pitfalls, potholes, and problems that might deter us along the way. Otherwise we could easily be blindsided by the shadow of our own unconscious behavior, setting ourselves up for disappointment and even disillusionment. Searching for a teacher, a group and a practice requires both discernment and common sense. There is a quote from the Buddha that I have often relied on:

> *Do not believe in anything simply because you have heard it.*
> *Do not believe in traditions because they have*
>  *been handed down for many generations.*
> *Do not believe in anything because it is spoken*
>  *and rumored by many.*
> *Do not believe in anything simply because it is*
>  *found written in your religious books.*
> *Do not believe in anything merely on the*
>  *authority of your teachers and elders.*
> *But after observation and analysis, when you find*
>  *that anything agrees with reason, and is*
>  *conducive to the good and benefit of one and*
>  *all, then accept it and live up to it.*
>
> — THE BUDDHA

This is a very powerful teaching that has come to us. Those of us who have been involved with the Dharma over a period of time have seen these words written so many times that we tend to take them for granted. I think it's important that we pay careful attention to the Buddha's advice; we need not only to remember his guidelines but also to respect others when they are being cautious and skeptical in making steps toward finding their own authentic spirituality.

## CHOOSING A SPIRITUAL GROUP OR TEACHER

Students often ask me what they should look for or avoid. In general, I think everyone should be wary of joining groups that control behavior, thinking, emotions, or the right of individuals to question the leadership, the teachings, or the organizational policies. If information is tightly controlled, new students may be in for some unhappy surprises. Let's not forget that destructive cults sometimes masquerade as religious groups—like wolves in sheep's clothing.

More specifically, here are some things to consider:

1. If you're becoming a part of a spiritual group, don't give your power away too quickly to authority figures, thus disempowering and perhaps even infantilizing yourself. Don't become overly dependent on leaders; be aware and wary of projection, over-idealization, transference, and placing charismatic teachers and masters on too high a pedestal. We should not naively imagine that leaders are all-knowing, infallible, and omnipotent parent figures. Once again, the Buddha himself said:

*Rely not on the teacher [person], but on the teaching.*
*Rely not on the words of the teaching, but on the spirit of the words.*
*Rely not on theory, but on experience.*

2. Be wary of exotic gurus and leaders who make fantastic promises, claim fabulous powers, or expect blind obedience.

3. Take a long hard look at any teacher or group leader where there is even the slightest scent of self-serving conflicts of interest and misuses of power, sex, money, or intoxicants. Instead seek out teachers who practice what they preach.

4. When you are considering joining a sangha or being part of a spiritual group, be alert to prejudice or bigotry, self-righteousness, "group think," double standards, and an atmosphere that encourages inner circles, secrets, and white lies.

5. Walk away from any group that tries to separate you from your family or friends or exhibits cultlike behavior. Danger signs of spiritual blight include demands of unquestioning adherence to the party line; any indication that you will be asked to harm yourself or others; use of threats, curses, excommunication, and hellfire to

people who consider leaving the group; attempts to control your behavior and your finances.

In order to discover your own path, you may find it very helpful to read spiritual books, to cruise the bookstores, libraries, and friends' bookshelves. You can look at reading lists compiled by teachers, and access Buddhist Websites for recommended reading lists and discussion groups. Find what resonates with your personal needs. Go to lectures; sample introductory meditation classes and events at different spiritual centers. Let's appreciate the banquet of Dharma now available to us all. Often it helps to attend some weekend meditation workshops or residential retreats. Use your own discriminating mind, and trust your heart and your intuition. In short, follow your nose.

When choosing a teacher, don't be overly attracted to grandiose titles, church titles, past-life résumés, or any form of hyperbolic advertising. Even if these highly advertised masters or teachings are the greatest, perhaps someone more like yourself would be most helpful to you during the initial stages. You don't need a Nobel Prize–winning physicist to teach you arithmetic; such a person may even teach over your head instead of providing the basics you need. Keep in mind that the teachers' main purpose is not to be brilliant, entertaining, or fascinating. A teacher should be judged by different standards than a performer who plays to an audience.

Buddhism's purpose is to provide us with tools and techniques that we need, which is perhaps not always what we think we want. Whatever group or teacher you may become involved with, check them out for a good while before irrevocably committing yourself to anything. The Dalai Lama has said, "Why not learn from everyone as much as you can, wherever you can? Go and listen to ordinary instructors, taking what you find useful and leaving the rest. But if you're considering taking on a certain teacher as a guru, check them out meticulously for many years before signing your life away. Spy on them!" I have found this to be very good advice.

As Dharma students, let's not forget that Truth itself—Reality-Dharma—is our teacher. If and when we find it well-embodied in anyone, let's not overlook the opportunity to learn. In fact, we can learn from just about anyone. Chuang Tsu said that we can learn as much from the fools as the wise. From the fools we learn what not to do; from the wise we learn what to do and how to be.

Traditionally there are various kinds of teachers: the guru, the elder, the instructor, the spiritual friend. In the West, other kinds are emerging as well, like the coach, the mentor, the workshop leader, and the facilitator, who often acts as a role model for us instead of as an all-powerful, all-knowing guru. Devotional practice has its value, and I myself have benefited from a devotional relationship to my Tibetan gurus, but what Western students often need today is simply someone to midwife their spiritual transformation, rather than to make them into disciples and followers. We don't have to subscribe to a teacher forever. With the practice itself as our teacher, we spiritual seekers can retain our autonomy and responsibility and discover for ourselves a path of infinite possibility.

## EXAMINING YOUR OWN MOTIVATIONS

I also think it's reasonable for us to spend a certain amount of time in self-examination, checking out our own motivations and impulses. Some questions to keep in mind:

1. Are we genuinely trying to follow the Buddha's example of the Middle Way—balancing wisdom with compassion as we walk the spiritual path?

2. Are we in any way overindulging a fascination with extraordinary experiences and special, spiritual states of mind? In this way, are we running the risk of becoming an experience junkie or bliss addict?

3. Do we sometimes fall prey to bouts of superficiality, dilettantism, diluted Dharma Lite, instant-coffee mind—seeking instant enlightenment without sacrifice, training, sincere efforts, or relinquishing anything?

4. When we choose a teacher or a group, are we unconsciously trying to fit in by reproducing the situation in our family of origin? Are we acting like the child, trying to be the favorite daughter or son? Are we trying to manipulate ourselves into some kind of special relationship?

5. Is there any unhealthy way in which we are using spiritual practice to withdraw from the world? Are we engaged in excessive quietism, avoidance, hiding out, self-denial, and self-suppression?

6. Are we stunting personal growth and a genuinely significant life in an attempt to attain exalted spiritual states? Again, let's never forget that the Dharma is about clear vision—and a love of life in all its infinite forms.

7. Are we sometimes overly motivated by ambition to rise in the religious hierarchy—instead of truly trying to loosen the grip of ego and its selfish dominion?

8. Are we guilty of the Shangri-La Syndrome: naively idealizing foreign cultures as magically perfect and far superior to ours in every way? (No, the grass is not greener on the other side of the fence, and enlightenment is not shinier on the other side of the world.)

9. Are we using too much head at the expense of heart? Are we merely thinking about and studying Buddhism rather than fully feeling, experiencing, integrating, and assimilating the soulful healing message of Dharma?

10. Are we ourselves sometimes given to spiritual pride, hypocrisy, and arrogance? Are we truly softening up our hardened, recalcitrant nature, or just paying lip service while reinforcing our own ego needs?

## EXPECT TO HAVE QUESTIONS

As students of truth, we shouldn't be afraid to question anything—from the teachers to the teachings. The Dharma isn't fragile; it can withstand scrutiny. I am very grateful to my teachers.

They were very kind to me, like second parents. And I have a lot of faith in both my teachers and the teachings. However, I asked them a lot of questions. Kalu Rinpoche used to call me "The Ocean of Questions." When I lived in his Sonada Monastery in Darjeeling in the mid-seventies, when he said after a Dharma talk, "Are there any questions?" he knew where to look first in the crowd. One day I asked, "Rinpoche, is it okay to ask so many questions?" He replied, "Ask all your questions. Then one day you will know."

## ANTICIPATE ROAD BUMPS

Be aware of the tendency to give up too early because you have problems getting comfortable with meditation. Eventually you can get used to it or find a better sitting position. Perhaps you'll find that meditating in a chair instead of a cross-legged position is better for you in the long run.

I think it's important that new students don't give in to the "comparing mind syndrome" of looking around and thinking everyone else is "getting it" while you are not. In group meditation, it sometimes seems to the beginner as though everyone else looks like a Buddha while you're sitting there feeling distracted out of your mind. In fact, they may very well be distracted too; even the leader in front may be struggling with distraction or sleepiness. Why compare? Each of us is like a flower in God's garden, blossoming in our own time and in our own way, each in different seasons of our physical and spiritual life. Each of us has been given a special gift—just for entering. So remember, you are already a winner.

When we start to practice Buddhism, it may not be exactly what we expected. Try not to be easily swayed if it doesn't always go exactly as planned. The spiritual path is not just a straight ascending road to happiness; there are many bumps and rises and dips on the road. Things may get more difficult before they become more coherent and tranquil. A great deal depends on what you've been ignoring in yourself. Some things inevitably must come up in order for you to know yourself and free yourself.

The spiritual path isn't always a joyride; it can be like a roller coaster. Don't stop with the cheap thrills—go for long lasting fulfillment. Stick to it through the rainy days and the barren deserts and the feeling of being stuck on a plateau of development. It's often said that the brighter the light glows, the deeper and darker the shadow becomes. The shadows are always inseparable from the light. They come from light; they are light. Constancy and perseverance pay off. Furthermore, life is much like photography: You use the negative to develop.

On the spiritual path, we are unraveling the tight straitjacket that is the cocoon of ego. We are threatening ego's dominion over us. It's like when we squeeze a wet bar of soap and it suddenly squirts out of our hands. Ego is a slippery fellow, intent on survival at all costs. If we don't squeeze it, it's glad to just sit there as ruler of our domain. When practice heats up, the ego can become like the squeezed soap bar, and things can become a little confusing. That's when we really need to maintain the bigger perspective that is such an important part of the process. It is during these times that sangha practice, spiritual friends, and experienced teachers can be most helpful.

## USHERING IN THE FUTURE

*Whatever you can do or imagine, begin it;*
*boldness has beauty, magic, and power in it.*

—GOETHE

Each of us is like a jeweled star in the universal constellation called the greater Sangha, the complete circle of all beings. We are modern mystics—living in monasteries without walls. The entire planet is our heaven on earth. Instead of being overly dependent on anyone else, we must be the leaders and seers. We must take the lead and see for ourselves. We must pick up our meditation cushions and walk.

Here in the West, as we renew ourselves through the Dharma, the Dharma is also being renewed. We are the elders now. Let's remember that we are the ancestors of generations to come. This is no small responsibility. Yet we can manage to wear it lightly.

The Dharma is a gift, a present we can give ourselves. As a sage of old said, "If not you, who? And if not now, when?"

The summit of Mt. Everest is made of marine limestone; once upon a time it was part of the ocean floor. Awakening is simply a matter of spiritual evolution. Practice is perfect. What we seek we are. As the Buddha said, "Help yourself."

# RECOMMENDED READING

*Dzogchen, the Self-Perfected State*. Chogyal Namkhai Norbu (edited by Adriano Clemente, translated by John Shane). Ithaca, NY: Snow Lion Publications, 1996.

*Repeating the Words of the Buddha*. Tulku Urgyen Rinpoche. Hong Kong: Rangjung Yeshe Publications, 1992.

*Peace Is Every Step: The Path of Mindfulness in Everyday Life*. Thich Nhat Hanh (edited by Arnold Kotler). New York: Bantam Books, 1991.

*It's Easier than You Think: The Buddhist Way to Happiness.* Sylvia Boorstein. San Francisco: HarperSan Francisco, 1995.

*Insight Meditation: The Practice of Freedom.* Joseph Goldstein. Boston: Shambhala Publications, 1993.

*Lovingkindness: The Revolutionary Art of Happiness.* Sharon Salzberg. Boston: Shambhala Publications, 1995.

*The Tibetan Book of Living and Dying.* Sogyal Rinpoche. San Francisco: HarperSan Francisco, 1992.

*Zen Mind, Beginner's Mind.* Shunryu Suzuki. New York: Weatherhill, 1994.

*The Snow Lion's Turquiose Mane: Wisdom Tales from Tibet.* Surya Das. San Francisco: HarperSan Francisco, 1992.

*Thoughts Without a Thinker: Psychotherapy from a Buddhist Perspective.* Mark Epstein, M.D. New York: BasicBooks, 1995.

*A Path with Heart: A Guide Through the Perils and Promises of Spiritual Life.* Jack Kornfield. New York: Bantam Books, 1993.

*Shambhala: The Sacred Path of the Warrior.* Chogyam Trungpa (edited by Carolyn Rose Gimian). Boston: Shambhala Publications, 1988.

*Everyday Zen: Love and Work.* Charlotte Joko Beck (edited by Steve Smith). San Francisco: HarperSan Francisco, 1989.

*The Heart Treasure of the Enlightened Ones.* Patrul Rinpoche, explained by Dilgo Khyentse (translated by Matthieu Ricard). Boston: Shambhala Publications, 1992.

*Buddhism Without Beliefs: A Contemporary Guide to Awakening.* Stephen Batchelor. New York: Riverhead Books, 1997.

*When Things Fall Apart: Heart Advice for Difficult Times.* Pema Chodron. Boston: Shambhala Pulications, 1997.

*Natural Great Perfection.* Nyoshul Khenpo Rinpoche and Surya Das. Ithaca, NY: Snow Lion Publications, 1995.

*The World of Tibetan Buddhism: An Overview of Its Philosophy and Practice.* His Holiness the Dalai Lama (translated, edited, and annotated by Geshe Thupten Jinpa). Boston: Wisdom Publications, 1995.

*Freedom In Exile: The Autobiography of the Dalai Lama.* His Holiness the Dalai Lama. New York: HarperPerennial, 1990.

*Wherever You Go, There You Are: Mindfulness Meditation in Everyday Life.* Jon Kabat-Zinn. New York: Hyperion, 1994.

# INDEX

# ABOUT THE DZOGCHEN
# FOUNDATION

The Dzogchen Foundation is an institution whose mission is the transmission of Buddhist contemplative practices and ethical teachings to Western audiences and the transformation of these teachings into forms that help alleviate suffering and create a civilization based on wisdom and compassion.

The foundation conducts annual retreats in the U.S. and Europe, publishes a newsletter, sponsors a variety of conferences on the interface of Buddhism and Western culture, and maintains a cyber-Dharma outreach project on the Internet.

The foundation also offers books, videotapes, and annual monographs.

If you would like additional information about Lama Surya Das and the work of the Dzogchen Foundation, please send your name and address to:

Lama Surya Das
c/o Dzogchen Foundation
P.O. Box 734
Cambridge, MA 02140

E-mail:foundation@dzogchen.org

Or visit us on the World Wide Web at: ·
http://www.dzogchen.org

DZOGCHEN
FOUNDATION

# ABOUT THE AUTHOR

For almost thirty years, **Lama Surya Das** has studied and lived with the great spiritual masters of Asia. He has twice completed the traditional three-year Vajrayana meditation retreat in a Tibetan monastery in southern France. A leading spokesperson for the emerging Western Buddhism, he is a Dzogchen lineage holder and the founder of the Dzogchen Foundation. A poet, translator, storyteller, activist, and full-time spiritual teacher, Surya Das lectures and leads meditation retreats and workshops worldwide, brings Tibetan lamas to the West to teach, regularly organizes the annual week-long Western Buddist Teachers Conference with the Dalai Lama in Dharmasala, India, and is active in interfaith dialogue. He is the author of *The Snow Lion's Mane: Wisdom Tales from Tibet* and *Natural Great Perfection* (with Nyoshul Khenpo Rinpoche). Surya Das lives outside of Boston, Massachusetts.